I0810658

PRAISE FOR GAEL CHANDLER

"Once again, Gael Chandler has pulled together a useful book for both the seasoned and beginning director to make the process of realizing a vision easier. From getting it right in the field through ample coverage and detailed documentation, to choosing and developing a relationship with an editor early in the production process, Gael's knowledge, experience, and practical caveats provide a roadmap that ensures the director will reach their destination. Some points are fundamental, but in the hot traffic of production, missing the right turn can add hours, even days to the journey. Gael's smart review of the traditional workflow process, as well as how things have changed due to technology, is invaluable to every auteur."
Ken Roth, Producer-Director, *What We Didn't Know*
Producer, *The Fred Snowden Show*

"Chandler takes the director by the hand and leads them through the process of postproduction both fiction and non-fiction, answering the questions you were afraid to ask and many you didn't think of, illuminating the joys and pitfalls of editing from preproduction through delivery."
Paris Poirier, Director, *Last Call at Maud's*
Associate Professor of Film Studies & Entertainment Technology, Santa Monica College

"Never has such a clear and considerate handbook for editors been produced. It has become the go-to manual here at the busy Raindance Film Festival. Whenever we have a workflow question, we find the answer with the easy to navigate index. Indispensable."
Elliot Grove, Founder, Raindance Film Festival

EDITING FOR DIRECTORS

A GUIDE FOR CREATIVE COLLABORATION

GAEL CHANDLER

MICHAEL WIESE PRODUCTIONS

Published by Michael Wiese Productions
12400 Ventura Blvd. #1111
Studio City, CA 91604
(818) 379-8799, (818) 986-3408 (Fax)
mw@mwp.com
www.mwp.com
Manufactured in the
United States of America

This book was set in Arno Pro, Gotham and DIN

Cover design by Johnny Ink. johnnyink.com
Interior design by Debbie Berne
Copyediting by Doreen Alexander

Library of Congress Cataloging-in-Publication Data
Names: Chandler, Gael, author.
Title: Editing for Directors : a guide for creative collaboration / Gael Chandler.
Identifiers: LCCN 2020047530 | ISBN 9781615933280 (trade paperback)
Subjects: LCSH: Motion pictures—Editing. | Motion picture editors. | Motion pictures—Production and direction.
Classification: LCC TR899 .C455 2021 | DDC 777/.55—dc23
LC record available at https://lccn.loc.gov/2020047530

FSC www.fsc.org MIX Paper from responsible sources FSC® C011935

To Dave Chandler, my brother (1952-2018),
who lives forever in a medium wide shot in *Woodstock.*
A life cut short is the unkindest cut of all.

What do Editors do?

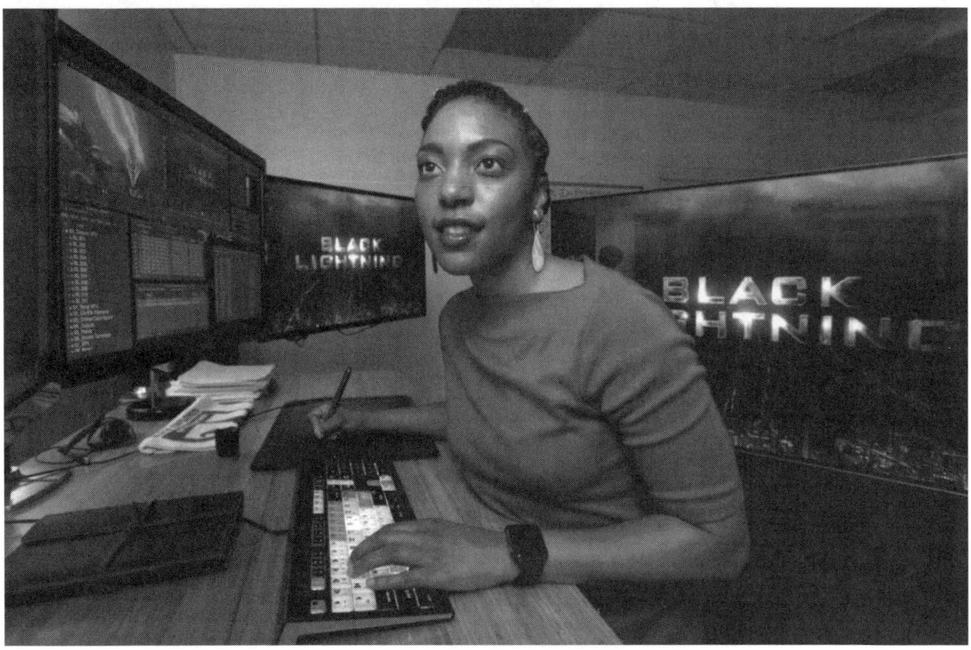

CONTENTS

FOREWORD

I love film, movies and the process of making the writers' vision come to life. I started my directing career on a show Gael was editor on. We had many discussions about the best way to approach the various problems I would have to deal with, and boy was there a lot of stuff to learn. From the information in her book, you will have enough knowledge to feel comfortable tackling anything thrown at you.

I believe the premise for this book is two-fold. 1) To act as a re-fresher course for seasoned directors and 2) To give enough information so a new director can step in, not with all the answers, but with enough confidence to manage a movie, television, or documentary set. You will appreciate the sections explaining what to expect when you walk into an unfamiliar environment.

STORY . . . STORY . . . STORY . . . Some directors approach the job from a writing standpoint, others from working with actors in the theater, and still others from technical experiences. But if the story is paramount in your decision-making, as the book makes clear, you'll be moving in the right direction.

I've spent over 60 years in the business, the last 18 as a director, and gosh do I wish this book had been around when I started directing. It has is a ton of information, but the most interesting part to me has to do with the teamwork and relationships necessary to squeeze all there is out of a sometimes not so great script. Egos are the enemy of filmmaking. Anybody who is any good at their craft has an ego, including you, but it must be kept in check if a working relationship is to survive. The success of a project is dependent on the connection you as the director form with those at your side willing to help, be it the writer, DP, production designer, actors, producers, editor, or many others.

A television series is the only place where you are limited in your decision making. The style of the show and the actors' characters are well defined and post pretty much runs on a schedule. On other projects, the director's input is essential in all areas from re-writes, to casting, to the final mix. You will be working with many different people with varied personalities; all, well, most all, are there to help you. They have years of experience for you to take advantage of if the working relationships you form are strong. I don't believe another book has been written that gives so much practical and technical information that really gets to the heart of the matter; how to approach relationships, so everyone can perform at the top of their game.

Tony Dow
Director-actor

PREFACE

Writing a book is a lot like making a film: You begin with a concept of a golden narrative that reaches people and makes a difference. You research, ponder and plan—preproduction. You start production, writing, and find yourself slogging through doubts, blocks, and turn downs, along with new discoveries, joys, connections, and the satisfaction of completing another section. Then you edit—move sections around, delete sentences, expand others. At all times, the project is never far from your mind. Finally, you send it in and let it go, accepting what it has become and hoping your intentions for your audience or readers will be realized.

And so it is with this book. Its chapter lengths are like scenes; some longer, some shorter, each saying what needs to be said, then moving on. While books are silent, they are not without pictures, and I enjoyed pulling frames and finding photos for this book, especially for the history chapter. Be you a director, an aspiring director, a producer, client, manager—the person who will be interacting with the editor and overseeing the show to the final cut—I sincerely hope this book helps you.

INTRODUCTION

It's been a long haul. Weeks, months, maybe years through preproduction and production. You've trusted the writer, the DP, the crew, the actors, and your documentary interviewees. Now all that hard earned footage is in the hands of someone you may not know, this editor person. Why should you trust them with your baby? How do you talk to an editor? Finesse cuts? Shore up a weak performance or interview? Compensate for bad audio?

For a so-called collaborative art, we filmmakers all too often become compartmentalized. We think we know about other parts of the process, but we don't fully. Writing and shooting seem straightforward, but editing? It's an alchemy of sound and image and arguably the most mystifying part of filmmaking.

This book helps you make your way through postproduction and tells you what to expect from an editor. Whether you're directing your first show or have a few or many shows under your belt, you'll discover how editing, like the rest of filmmaking, is both mundane and magical. Specifically, the book covers:

- How to plan for editing before you shoot a frame and during filming.
- The skills an editor brings to a film.
- The history of editing and cutting tools and how they have affected the language of cinema.
- What to look for when hiring an editor and the best ways to work with an editor.
- How to communicate with editorial: cutting room terms, practices, and workflows.
- Editing: How exactly an editor approaches the footage and puts a show together.
- The postproduction process, from dailies to director's cut to locked cut.
- Creating and overseeing VFX (video effects).
- Spotting your show with the sound and music crew and creating, editing, and mixing sound and music.
- Titling, color grading, the DI (digital intermediate) process, and producing your show's final deliverables.
- Archiving your show and why it matters.

1

SHOOT RIGHT FOR EDITING

When you're working on the set, your antennae are out and waving in a million directions. You're focusing on the actors, crew, weather, location, and countless other details. As time and light run out each day, your goal—to get the footage you want in the can—can be overrun by the daily compromises and challenges of running the set. So you worry: "Am I getting the right shots?" You fight: "Why do I need coverage?" You panic: "Do I have a film?"

These are all good signs.

You *want* to be thinking about the next phase—editing. This is where you're headed and is the finish line: Crossing it means you hand off your film to its audience. The best way to prepare for editing during production is to shoot the critical images in the format that best tells the story, and to capture the sounds you and your editor will need to create the show you envision. Shooting smartly also saves time, stress, and money in postproduction. Let's get rolling!

MAINTAIN AN ORGANIZED SHOOT

When you keep a well-organized shoot on location or set, you contribute to a well-organized editing room. Here's how and why:

Communicate clearly with your crew and the cutting room

Good interactions, particularly between you and your script supervisor, DP, camera operator, and sound recordist, translate into getting the shots you need and maybe even snagging extra ones you think up. Clear communicating also means that editorial is on top of the footage that is coming and does not have to chase down the crew to locate shots.

Editor on the set

Commonly, editors never visit the set; they are fully occupied with the myriad tasks that go along with cutting the show. Many editors have no desire to drop by; they want to keep aloof, so they can best put the picture together without being influenced by the challenges of obtaining the footage. Others want to visit the set to help you or to observe shots and performances and start mentally editing the footage. They like to escape the cutting room for a stretch, and meet the people on the other side, most if not all of whom will not recognize them. Editors know actors intimately—their gestures, reactions, characters—yet ordinarily remain the invisible people working behind the scenes.

You may summon an editor to help with the shoot, a re-shoot, continuity, or for other reasons of your own. Ordinarily, you'll contact the editor in the cutting room about issues. Also, your script supervisor will be in touch regularly with the editor about script notes and pages, and occasionally regarding continuity issues. Assuming you and the editor develop a simpatico relationship, there will be occasions when the editor will alert you to problems with scenes or tell you a shot is missing. Sometimes you swear you've shot something, but it never washes up in the cutting room. Better to know you missed a shot before you leave a location and arrive in the cutting room.

Stick to the shooting schedule as much as possible

This makes it easier to coordinate and schedule work in the cutting room.

Ensure your crew keeps accurate records

Script notes, camera logs, and sound logs are vital guidelines in the cutting room. If your production crew fails to keep these records or does a shoddy job, your editorial crew wastes time tracking down footage. Save time and money in the cutting room: Hire a crew that keeps clear, consistent logs and notes.

Frame and shoot every take with a slate clearly marked with:

- Scene and take
- Director and production name
- Date and location
- Camera designation (A, B, C, etc.)
- Camera roll and sound roll
- MOS (if shot has no recorded sound)

Voice slate every take

This is essential for dialogue editors who don't view slates and locate takes by sound. Properly slating takes consumes nanoseconds in the field and saves valuable time and tempers in the cutting room.

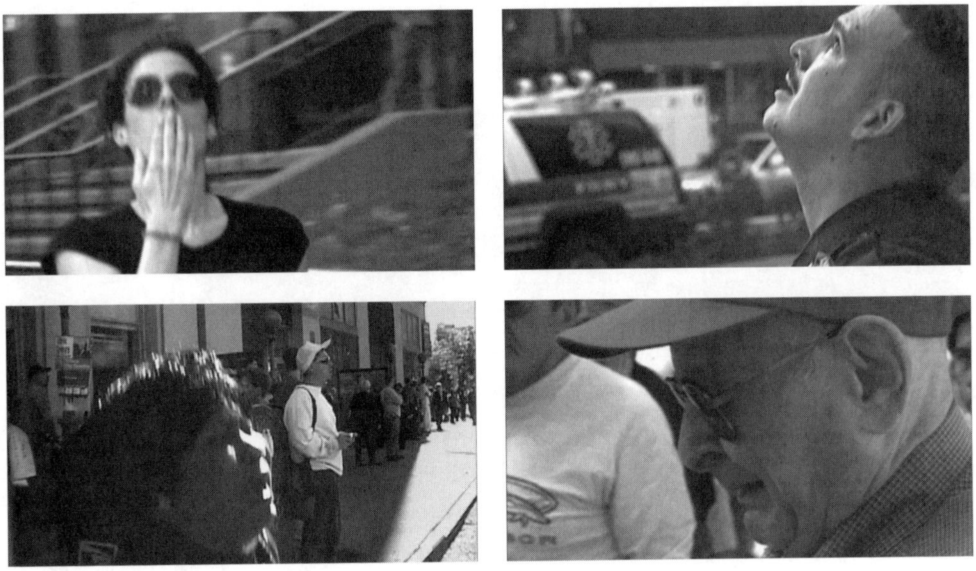

In *Fahrenheit 911* (2004), instead of showing the towers collapsing, Michael Moore told the story through shots of New Yorkers reacting.

CUT IN THE CAMERA

NOT! You don't know how long you may need a shot to run. Refrain from prejudging where the cut points will be by ending a shot or pointing the camera away from the action too early. Keep in mind: The actor and camera set the pace of the shots, while editing sets the pace of the show. An inexperienced camera operator, believing static shots are boring, may push the zoom button as if playing a trombone. This can irritate the audience and make the editor work overtime to find usable frames. The editor can set a fine rhythm with a lovely series of static shots and should not be limited by a hyperactive camera that zooms and pans without purpose and gathers little or no usable footage.

GET COVERAGE

Be kind to your show! Shoot angles in addition to the master. Coverage—reverses, close-ups, two-shots, overhead or Dutch angles, etc.—give you and your editor options in the cutting room. You can drop in a close-up to make your audience feel what a character is experiencing, insert a cutaway to a key detail such as a letter or a treasure map, milk a laugh in a comedic scene, or intensify a documentary or dramatic scene by sprinkling in reaction shots. Coverage provides punch, pace, and points-of-view to scenes, plus adds depth and information. Sometimes it can even substitute for revealing the main action, as the frames above demonstrate.

Pragmatically, coverage acts like the cavalry, routinely racing to the rescue to cover mistakes such as camera bobbles, interviewee fumbles, and continuity issues. Think of coverage as insurance. For example, as you screen your show, you may realize that part of a master shot drags or is repetitive—in some way it doesn't work to carry all the action in a scene or isn't engaging. By cutting to coverage, your editor can skip over the slow spot, and cut back at a more vital point. Directors who don't cover themselves usually regret it. Plan for it!

B-roll

Primarily perceived as establishing or transition shots, approach B-roll shots cinematically, as you would A-roll, by asking: "How can B-roll enhance my project and tell its story?" Don't just grab static background shots. Snag a variety of shots with different angles and focal lengths, as well as moving shots and rack shots. Try some experimental ideas that have been simmering. You never know what might end up being a memorable interlude or montage. In his self-deprecating acceptance speech for the Academy award for Cinematography in 1986, for *Out of Africa,* David Watkin remarked about how people complimented him repeatedly on the gorgeous shots of Kenya and its animals. He bestowed the credit where it was due; on the second unit—B roll—cinematographers.

This predominantly B-roll montage fortified the main character's romance as well as her love of Kenya in *Out of Africa* (1985).

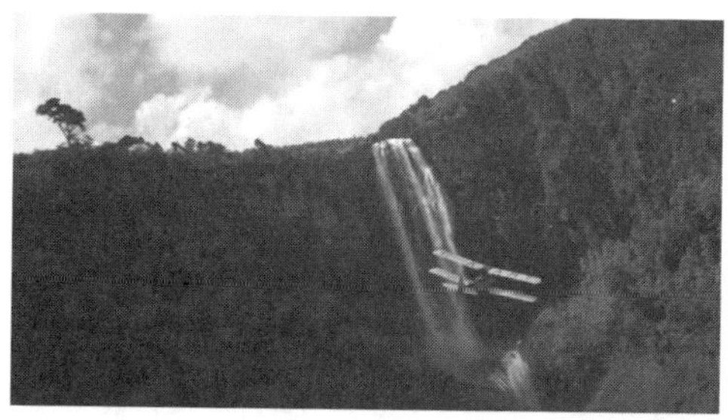

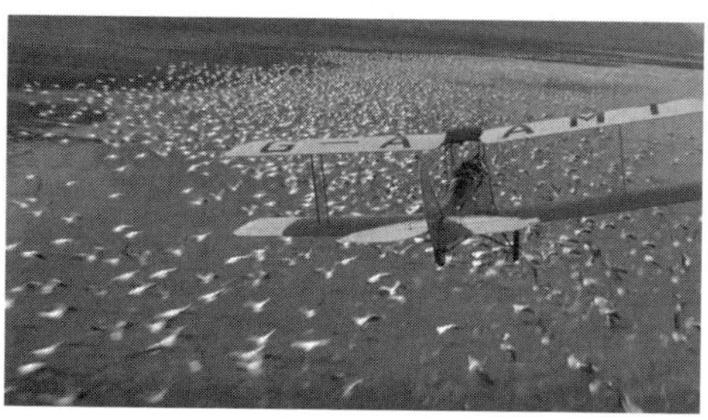

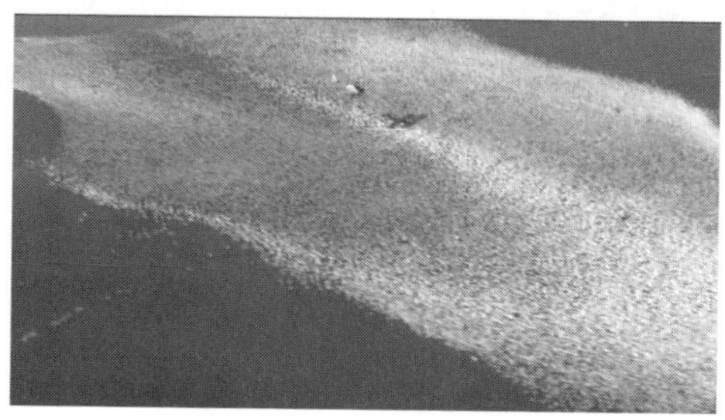

Consider transition shots

Along with anticipating and shooting coverage, consider how scenes start, end, and segue from one to another. The editor will likely be able to make something work from your planned masters and coverage, but you may want to shoot some specific shots to bridge scenes. Especially in documentaries, these transitions or interstitial shots can give your viewers time to breathe and absorb what you've just shown and told them.

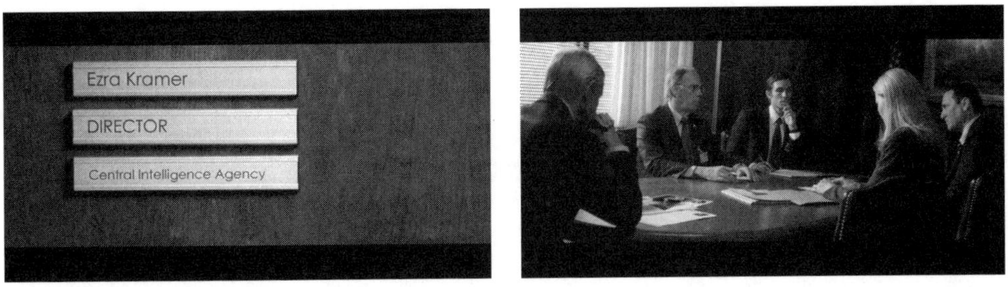

An insert shot of a name and title on a door succinctly informs your audience about a character's name, job, and workplace and transitions the story inside. *The Bourne Ultimatum* (2007).

Plan montage shots

You can pull a montage out of the best takes, out-takes, or stock shots, however, most outstanding montages (think of your favorites) the director planned and shot for. Consider a montage not just an interlude in your film, but a story (a short one) unto itself. What facts do you want to re-cap or information do you want to convey? What feelings do you want your images to evoke? Anticipate sound. Normally a montage is covered with music and possibly some narration or ambient sound, and usually doesn't contain dialogue or sound effects: Envision what might work for yours.

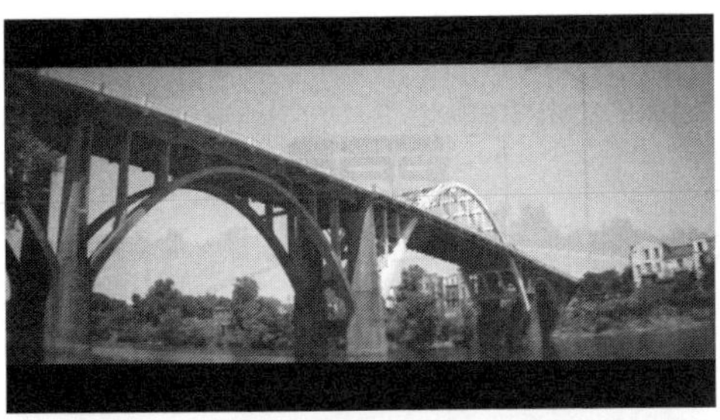

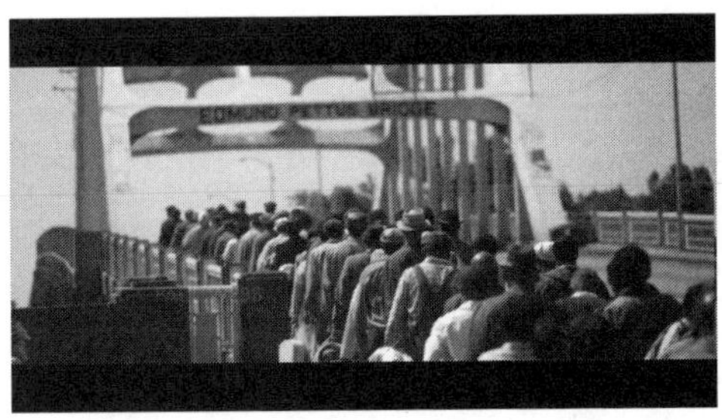

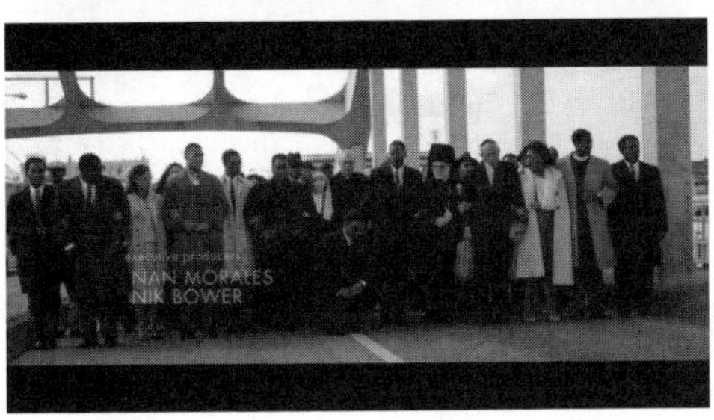

Selma (2004) ends with a searing montage under the credits, evoking the pain of history followed by the hope and determination of the future, underscored by the music, which starts with a Spiritual and shifts to hip hop.

HOLD AND REPEAT ACTION AT THE START AND END OF TAKES

When shooting a new angle, don't just continue from where the last angle left off; repeat dialogue and actions from shot to shot. As with getting coverage, this gives you choices in editing and can help tell your story more smoothly and efficiently. Here's an example:

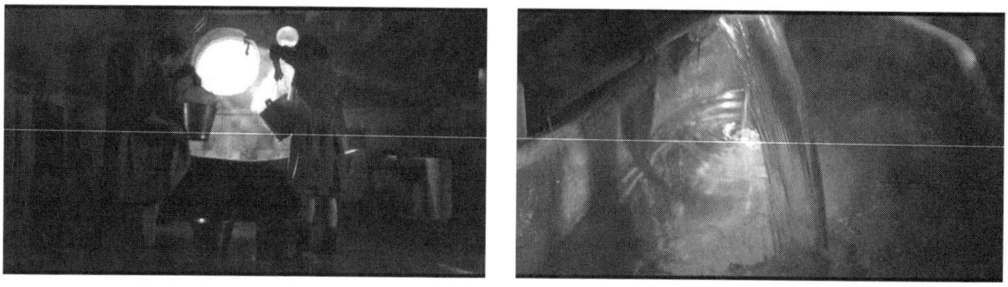

The repeated action of the cascading water advances the story in *Pan's Labyrinth* (2006).

You've filmed a master shot of a dining room scene where wacky Aunt Jackie sits down and tells a weird joke. When you film the medium shot of Aunt Jackie, don't start with her joking. Rather, begin with her sitting down, repeating the action of the master. Now, if desired, your editor can cut from the master to the medium shot, during the mundane action of sitting. This speeds your story along to the weird joke and the family responses that follow. When you repeat action at the tail of one angle, and the head of the next angle, you have the latitude to cut to an action at the best moment.

Hold the camera

Before starting and after ending every shot, be it a static shot, a zoom, pan, or dolly, direct camera to hold still for five seconds. As with repeating the action, these stationary seconds give your editor more elbow room in choosing cut points. In addition, these action handles provide the frames you'll need, should you want to dissolve or wipe to the next shot. Occasionally, holding the camera even solves an editing problem, as editors sometimes use the footage from when the camera was rolling before you yelled, "Action!" or after you said, "Cut!"

SHOOT GOOD CONTINUITY

We've all noticed the mismatch of a car traveling with different scenery in each shot. Mismatches underscore why continuity is critical. Mismatches can take viewers out of your film, risking their distrust, disengagement, and negative word-of-mouth.

Listen to your script supervisor. A good script supervisor who keeps an eagle eye on continuity is an MVP on a film set. Make every effort to match actions, lighting, wardrobe, position of props and people, hair, makeup, etc., from take to take. It's a shame to force your editor to cut earlier or later than optimal, due to a lack of continuity. Here are the five major components of achieving good continuity:

1) Shoot cuttable angles

Shots that are similar in angle and focal length jar the audience when cut together. If jarring jump cuts are what you want, shoot for them. Otherwise, stick to the 30-degree rule: Vary the new camera angle at least 30 degrees from the last, and your angles should cut together "like butter." (For more on cuttable angles, see the sections on smooth cutting angles and mismatches in Chapter 5.)

2) Match eyelines

Eyes convey emotion and vital reactions. When a scene calls for cutting back and forth between shots of interacting characters, they need to be looking at each other, which means their eyelines—lines of vision—must match. If you ignore this, their eyelines won't match and the characters will not be looking in the right direction. This may confuse the audience and cause them to take an unintended meaning from the characters' interaction. The example below illustrates what matching and non-matching eyelines show about characters.

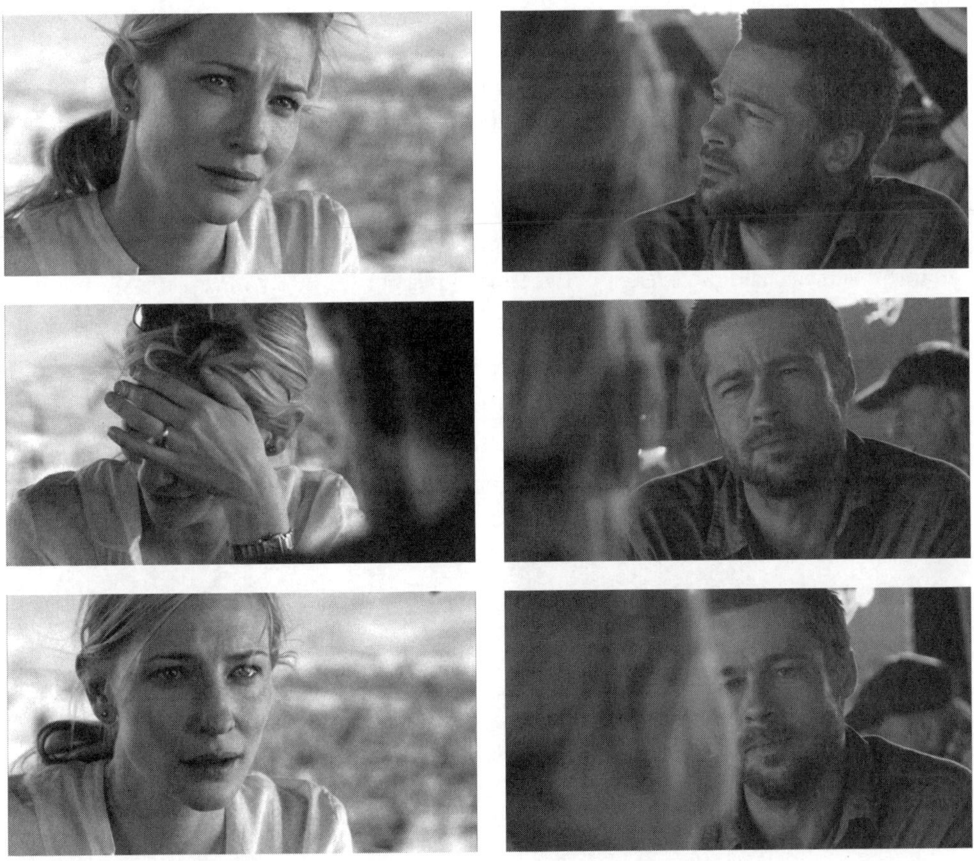

In *Babel* (2006), a married couple (played by Cate Blanchett and Brad Pitt) deals with the death of their baby. In Cuts 1 and 2, their nonmatching eyelines demonstrate their disconnection from each other. Their matching eyelines in Cut 3, show them beginning to grapple with their pain and each other.

POV and eyeline

A common eyeline error can occur when you shoot a Point of View (POV) shot. Regularly, you'll shoot a close-up of someone whose head and/or eyes move left to right as they look at something, let's say a mountain. When you film the mountain—what they're seeing—you're filming their POV. To match their eye and head movement, the POV shot must move in the same direction as the character's head or eyes, from left to right in this instance.

If filmed incorrectly, you might be able to reverse the POV shot, but this can be problematic if there are birds, cars, people, etc., in the shot as they will move backwards. And yes, a video effects (VFX) editor could likely paint them out, but oh the time and expense! Better to get it right from the start.

Phone conversation

You can fudge a little here, but normally when two people are talking to each other, screen reality requires that they face each other or at least look in the same basic direction, unless turning their back on or looking down or away from each other is part of the drama.

3) Match camera angle, framing, and pacing

Angle

You'll often be creating pairs of shots to work together during editing, such as a master and reverse. Dialogue scenes between two people routinely have pairs of medium shots, over-the-shoulders, raking shots, and close-ups. When you shoot pairs of shots for intercutting*, make certain that their angles match.

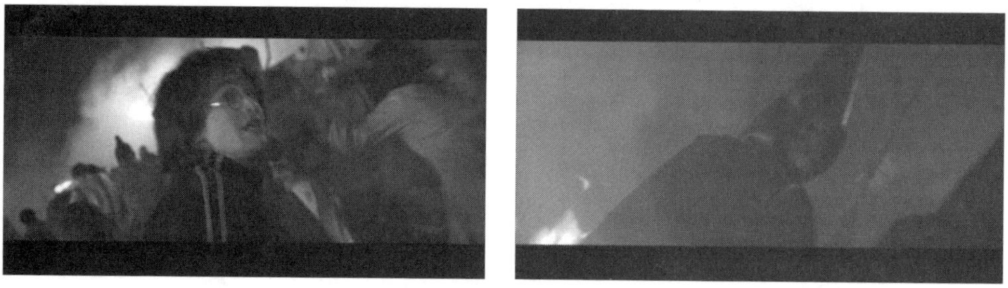

A matched pair of Dutch angles accentuates danger and chaos, as Lord Voldemort's followers menace Harry in *Harry Potter and the Goblet of Fire* (2005).

* When you cut between two sequential scenes so that they advance and complete together, you are intercutting.

Framing

Match the space around characters or objects—how they are positioned and framed—from take to take.

Pacing

When the camera pans, tracks, tilts, dollies, or follows, keep the speed of the movement consistent so it isn't slower in one take or faster in another.

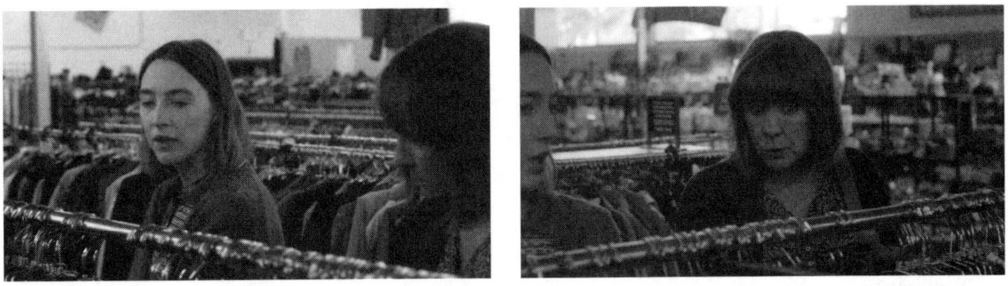

A pair of daughter-mother raking shots from *Lady Bird* (2017), matches angles as well as framing and lighting.

4) Match Screen Direction

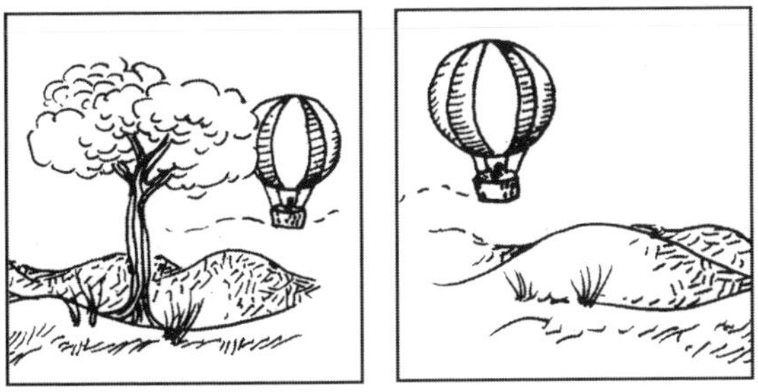

Follow the floating balloon as it matches screen direction.

If a character(s) or object(s) moves left out of the frame, shoot them entering the next shot from the right of the frame. This way, they look like they're moving normally, from left to right. If exits and entrances don't match, your viewers waste time keeping up with the action instead of immersing themselves in your movie.

5) Don't cross the line: Observe the 180 degree rule

Crossing the line (a.k.a. crossing the axis), is an extension of screen direction and can be avoided by following the 180 Degree Rule. It's important to understand the rule, then if you decide to deviate from it or to devise a new method you will understand the ramifications.

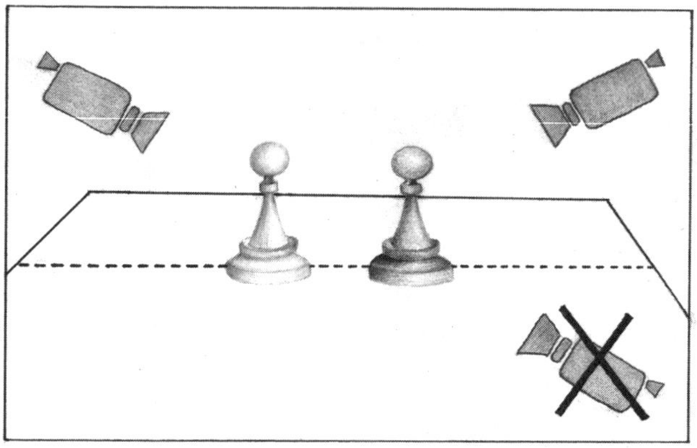

Crossing the line: Shoot the pawns from the correct cameras or they will appear to jump sides.

The 180° Rule: How to observe it

There is an invisible line in every camera set up that bisects the scene horizontally at 180 degrees.

Scenario. If two people face each other, the 180° line runs across their heads. During editing, if you cut to the angle behind them, the person on the left appears to jump to the right, disorienting your audience. Add another person, and you add another 180° line.

The rule. When shooting, keep Person A on the left and Person B on the right by not moving the camera across the 180° line.

Example. Sports crews observe this rule daily as they shoot football games from one side of the field only. This way there is no chance to cut to the other side of the field and make the players appear to be running toward their opponent's goal.

Get the angles you need without crossing the line

Of course, there are many times when you want to shoot a lot of angles that cover both sides of the action. Here are several methods:

Establish a new 180° line

Direct your characters to move or move the camera within the shot to break the line and create a new one as the frames below illustrate.

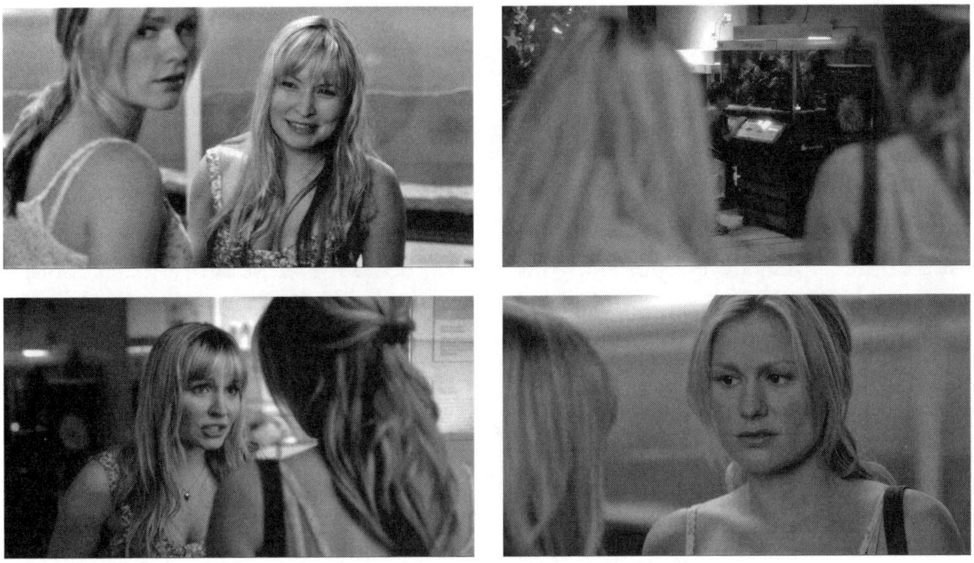

In this episode from *True Blood*, Frame 1 shows Hadley on the right in front of an aquarium. Motivated by her desire to introduce her son to Sookie, in Frame 2 she moves and establishes a new 180° line, completing the action in Frame 3. The scene then cuts to Sookie in Frame 4, who now has the aquarium behind her.

Shoot cutaways

Robert Wise would always plan his axis change . . . there was always one key shot. When you don't get those shots . . . then you have a scene where nobody relates to anyone. Nobody is looking anybody else in the eye and it's totally disorienting. The audience might get thrown out of the scene because it's non-connective. Film is connective; that's what film is.
—**EDITOR DEDE ALLEN,** *The Breakfast Club, Dog Day Afternoon, Reds*

Cutaways diminish the disorientation and allow your editor to cut away before cutting to the line-breaking angle. For instance, shooting an overhead angle keeps your audience oriented and frees you to cut to any angle. Jumping the line disturbs the audience, especially in 3D movies, which, by their nature, immerse viewers more deeply than 2D movies.

Break the 180° rule deliberately
If you're shooting a riot or battle scene, directors often strive for chaos and knowingly ignore the rule. If you break the rule in any scene, do yourself a favor: Shoot some cutaways, just in case things don't work out as you've planned in editing. Finally, of course there are some situations where you won't have a choice about observing the rule: If you're shooting a herd of wild stallions, you won't have any hope of the action matching on either side of the line.

CARRYING THE IMAGE THROUGH: CHOOSING YOUR SHOW'S FINISHING FORMAT AND LOOK

Part of putting your project on a proper path toward postproduction entails determining its finishing format and look. Base your decisions on what images will best suit your story and on how—on what venues and devices—your audience will watch your show. Your producer may have input and your DP will be your collaborator on all shooting decisions.

Format

The format you will shoot your show on will be digital or possibly film. Today it's not uncommon for a show to shoot with multiple camera types in multiple standards and aspect ratios: *Sense8* (2015-2018) shot its final season in nearly a dozen different countries. Even if you're shooting on film, you will edit digitally. However, you may finish on a different format(s), depending on how you answer this question: Where will the audience view my show? The table below outlines the four viewing venues and their formats. Study them to pinpoint which one fits your project and note its finishing format(s). You may pick more than one venue; for instance, your audience may see your show in a movie theatre and on TV.

Where audience will view show	Finishing Format(s)	Behind the scenes: How your show will be screened
Movie Theatre	File Film	Your show will screen from 1) A digital file on a digital projector or 2) On film reels run through a film projector (abroad and in a few U.S. theatres).
TV	File	Your show will be broadcast from a file uploaded from the network's server.
Home or Business Entertainment System	File Disk	Viewers will pop a disk (DVD or Blu-ray) into a drive, to see your show or stream it from YouTube or an internet entertainment service such as Netflix.
Computer (includes devices such as an iPad or cellphone).	File Disk	Viewers will watch your show on a file streamed or downloaded from their corporate intranet (example: a QuickTime file) or from the internet (examples: a YouTube video, webisode, or Hulu show). Alternatively, they may insert a disk to see it.

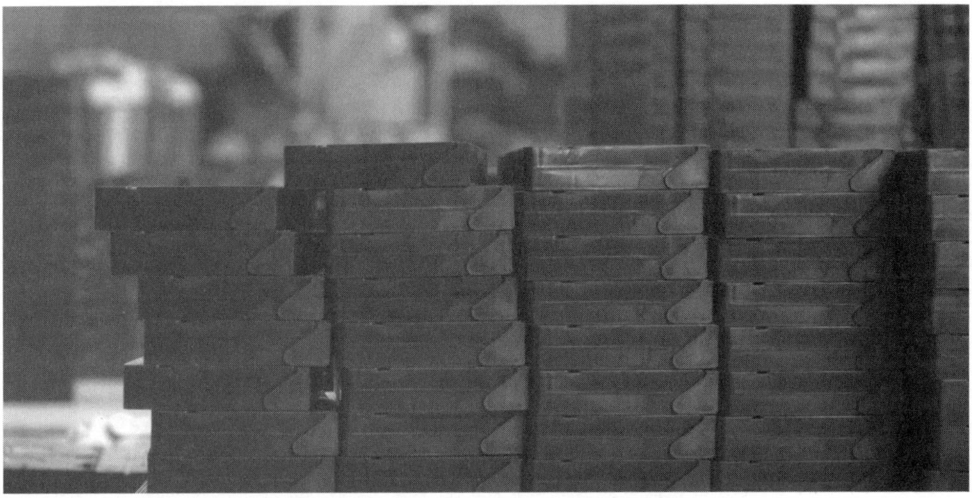

The 2019 documentary, *Recorder: The Marion Stokes Project*, depended on the 70,000 VHS tapes Stokes recorded 24/7 of news stations in a room of her home, for 30 years.

Shooting formats — picture

The format you shoot on may not always be the format you finish on. For example, you may shoot digitally to a file on a memory card or hard drive but deliver on film and disk. Usually, your finishing format is specified by your show's delivery requirements, which you'll find in the film festival submission guidelines, the TV network's contract, or your agreement with the distribution company. No matter what you shoot on, your editor may receive footage from on all different formats: film, file, disk, and tape. For instance, documentary projects often call for digging up footage from past decades on legacy formats such as 8mm film or ¾" tape. Luckily, all formats can meet up and be converted to digital files for editing on the editor's digital system.

Shooting formats — sound

Sound can be recorded by the camera with a high-grade audio input to the memory card along with picture, which is referred to as *single system*. This is preferable for shooting news or other shows with quick turnarounds as well as those with low budgets and little time for layered sound editing. For a higher audio sampling rate (better sound), you'll choose *double system* where the sound recordist records the sound to another format such as DAT (digital audio tape), memory card or stick, or hard drive. The post house will sync up the audio or the editorial crew will do it on the digital editing system.

Color

> I'm very aware of how color affects the way an audience experiences a character. With my DP, costume, and production designers we carefully choose a specific color palette for every character. —**RYAN PIERS WILLIAMS**, director, *X/Y* and *Dryland*

With the revolution from photo chemical film to digital images, directors and DPs are not making final color decisions in production, but instead at the back end of postproduction with a colorist during the color grading phase. However, it's still important for you to confer with your DP to establish a visual style or look for your film as well as to discuss lighting and your color palette. You want to shoot to set yourselves up for color grading, so you can spend the bulk of your time with the colorist creating, correcting, and tweaking the images and your visual style, not just saving poor shots. (More on color grading in Chapter 10: Finish and Deliver.) This does not mean that color grading can save everything; your DP must properly expose shots and set the white balance* correctly among other settings.

It's all in the data

You may engage a DIT (digital image technician), who will create a software chart called a LUT (look up table) containing the color and other image values for each frame. The DIT can also keep track of other data including files, drives, and camera info, such as exposure values and slates. During color grading (and if you're shooting film and doing telecine), you, the DP, and the colorist (who can also create a LUT), will depend on the LUT along with your artistic sense to perfect the lighting, color, and look of your show.

PRODUCTION CO:	LOLLIPOP	**GENERAL NOTES**
PRODUCTION:	GUM DROP 45" spot	MATERIAL THAT HAS NOT.
DOP:	J BEZOU	ALREADY GONE TO EDIT:
DIT:	TOM TURLEY	
		DATE: 10/12/20
FORMAT:	5dmk2 H264 / STILLS CR2 + JPEG LG	A CAM - MAG 27
FPS:	25	B CAM - MAG 25
RESOLUTION:	1080x1920	C CAM - MAGS 2,3,4
ASPECT RATIO:	16:9	
RECORDING:		ALL MARKED IN GRAY ON DRIVE

DESTINATION DRIVES: 'LOLLIPOP MASTER' + 'LOLLIPOP BACKUP'

MAG #	# OF CLIPS	STILL/VIDEO	NOTES	SCENE #	GB	LENS	STOP	filters	LH	Distance	Incline
A1	8	VIDEO		9	7.67	50	4	nd6	4'1	6'6 - 7'8	4degree down
A2	30 stills	STOP MOTION	Extended version of A1	4	.9	50	4	nd6	4'1	6'6 - 7'8	4degree down
A3	28 stills	STOP MOTION		1B	0.8	50	4	nd6	4'1	6'6 - 7'8	4degree down
A4	1	VIDEO	Disregard this, use A6	1B	1.9	50	4	nd6	4'1	6'6 - 7'8	4degree down
A5	6 + plates	VIDEO + STILL PLATE	Plates for giraffe	6	3.44	50	4	nd6	4'1	6'6 - 7'8	4degree down
A6	4x takes	STOP MOTION		14	4.78	50	8	-	3'7	2'3	14degree down
B1	5	VIDEO		4	7.62	50	4	nd6	4'1	6'6 - 7'8	4degree down
B2	1 + odd stills	VIDEO + STILLS		2	1.23	50	5.6 1/2	-	3'8	1'10	26degree down
B3	32 stills	STOP MOTION	Curtains	6	.8	50	4	nd6	4'1	6'6 - 7'8	4degree down
B4	3 takes	STOP MOTION		6	2.67	50	5.6 1/2	-	3'8	1'10	26degree down
B4	1	LIVE ACTION		2	.9	50	5.6 1/2	-	3'8	1'10	26degree down
A9	65 stills	STOP MOTION	Extended version of A8	4	1.93	50	4	nd6	4'1	6'6 - 7'8	4degree down
B5	4	LIVE ACTION		2	5.64	60	5.6 1/2	-			
A10	stills/video	PLATES	Plates for orangutan	4	.3	50	4	nd6	4'1	6'6 - 7'8	4degree down
A11	1	LIVE ACTION		8	2.6	85	4	nd6	4'3	4'9	10degree down
A12	4	LIVE ACTION		8	7.16	85	4	nd6	4'3	4'9	10degree down

DIT report for a commercial where the DIT aimed to match the look of DSLR still photos and videos.

*Color science studies how humans react physiologically and psychologically to seeing color. DPs always balance whites, so viewers perceive the white parts of images as white without a green or other color cast. They do this knowing that during color grading they can saturate or desaturate a scene.

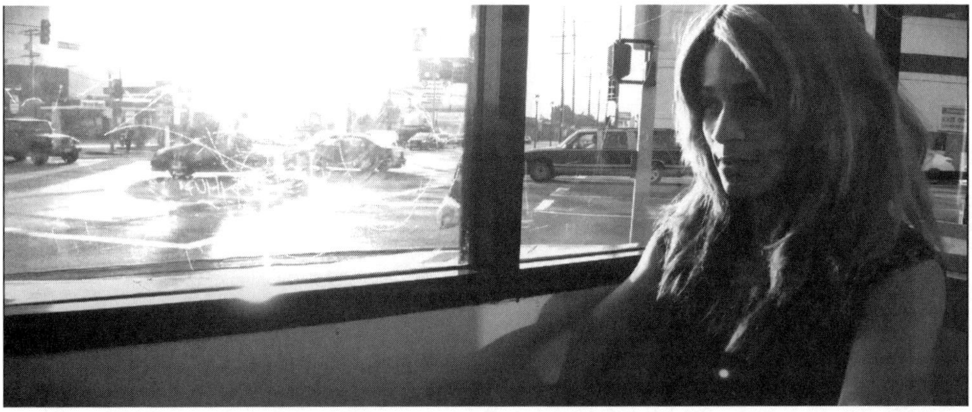

Three iPhones set at a 2.35:1 aspect ratio (equivalent to 16:9) captured the lives of two transgender sex workers in *Tangerine* (2015, a short, award winning dramedy set in LA).

Aspect ratio

Aspect ratio is the ratio of width to height in a frame. Cameras offer multiple aspect ratio choices, as do screens where viewers will watch your show. Most digital cameras shoot in 16:9, which creates a widescreen, landscape frame and is the standard for HDTV, disks, Netflix, YouTube, and other video sharing and VOD platforms. For years, aspect ratios pushed horizontal limits. Now with social media channels, aspect ratio has gone vertical; Facebook, Instagram, and Twitter accept 1:1 and 4:5, amongst other ratios.

You and your DP will decide what aspect ratio you will shoot at based not only on which screens your audience will viewing your show but on the story you're telling. Is your show an intimate character driven plot? Then you might choose 4:3, the old SDTV format. Do you want to set your characters against a wider backdrop? Or do you need as much latitude as possible to show the action or include the background? Then you'll choose 16:9. In any case, make sure the action can be viewed on all anticipated screen sizes.

Where does editorial enter in to all this? You can have editorial change the aspect ratio—software makes this possible—but why would you? You and the DP have composed all the shots to your chosen aspect ratio. Changing the ratio in post throws the planned look of your show out the window.

What K is OK?

2K, 4K, 6K, and 8K refer to the horizontal resolution of an image measured in pixels. 2K contains 2000 pixels, 4K has 4000, and so on. The higher the K, the sharper and more life like the picture. 4K, often referred to as Ultra HD or UHD, since it has four times as many pixels as regular HD, is the current standard shooting resolution.

While streaming services have offered 4K and higher for years, only 40% of U.S. theatres project 4K, and TV manufacturers are lagging, making 4K expensive and only available on larger screens. Hollywood reserves 4K for blockbusters, shooting 80% of features 2K. Of course, this is all changing; we'll likely be enjoying 10K and beyond in not too many years. But for now, when you're deciding what K to shoot at, consider the above factors along with your budget. If you shoot 4K or higher, the files are currently too big to play back, so your editor will cut with proxies—lower res files generated by the camera or the digital editing system. As part of final finishing, the editor or the post house will relink the proxies to the high-res files.

The future

Formats continue to evolve: The worlds of shooting, editing, broadcast, streaming, and projection are in flux, so stay tuned.

SOUND ADVICE: HOW TO APPROACH YOUR SHOW'S AUDIO

What sounds should I get on set? How do I know if they're the right sounds? When should I start exploring music? Sound plays a critical role in your audience engaging with your film. However, with so many other issues to tackle, directors often neglect to consider it ahead of time. This next section addresses how to anticipate and acquire the vital sounds for your show.

Create a sound vision

> ... if you encourage the sounds of the characters, the things, and the places in your film to inform your decisions in all the other film crafts, then your movie may just grow to have a voice beyond anything you might have dreamed. —**RANDY THOM**, C.A.S., sound designer and mixer, *The Revenant, Cast Away, The Right Stuff, Star Wars: Episode VI- Return of the Jedi*

Part of realizing the vision of your film is conceiving what viewers will hear. Start during preproduction. Imagine how the world sounds in your film. Anticipate the soundscape of different scenes and sections. Are they light and sprightly, cheery with an underlying sinister tone, painful yet hopeful, etc.? Will the scenes or sections clash or complement each other?

You might envision each character or object as an instrument or a theme: What do they sound like? What tune do they play? What mood do they suggest? For example, think of the roles that trains play in movies. A train rolls magically along in *The Polar Express* (2004), steams relentlessly toward revolution in *Doctor Zhivago* (1965) and screams danger and death as it pulls into Auschwitz in *Schindler's List* (1993).

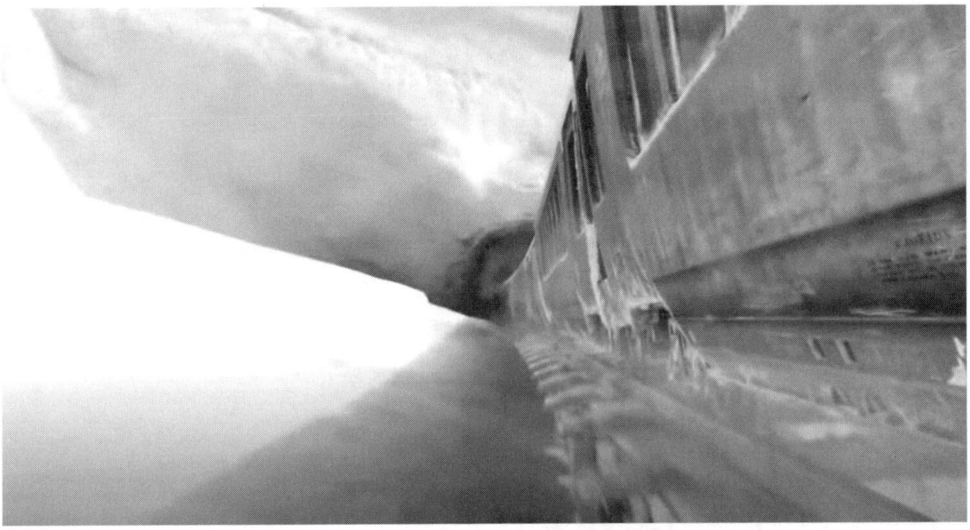

The sealed, non-stop "iron box" in *Snowpiercer* (2013) represents capitalism with each car segregated by socioeconomic class, in this dystopian drama about climate change and status.

What sound and music can say

Ensure that each piece of sound and music enhances and supports your story: Record vital onscreen and offscreen sounds. Consider using Hitchcock's approach. He believed that to "describe a sound accurately, one has to imagine its equivalent in dialogue," and gave this illustration from 1963's *The Birds*: "The flock gathers, surveys, and attacks, saying, 'Now we've got you where we want you. Here we come. We don't have to scream in triumph or in anger. This is going to be a silent murder." If a sound in your film could speak, what would it say about a location? How would it voice a character's thoughts?

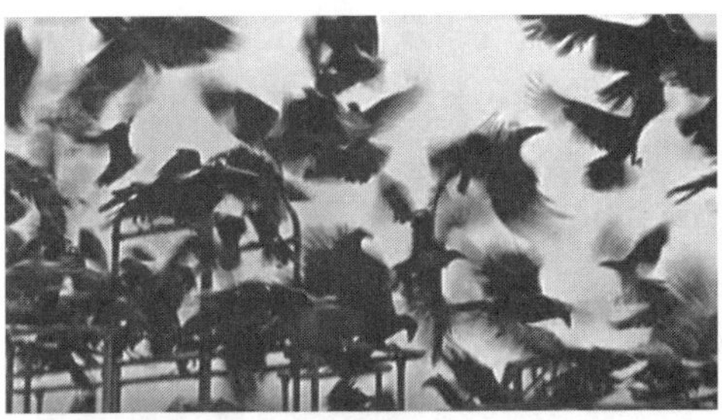

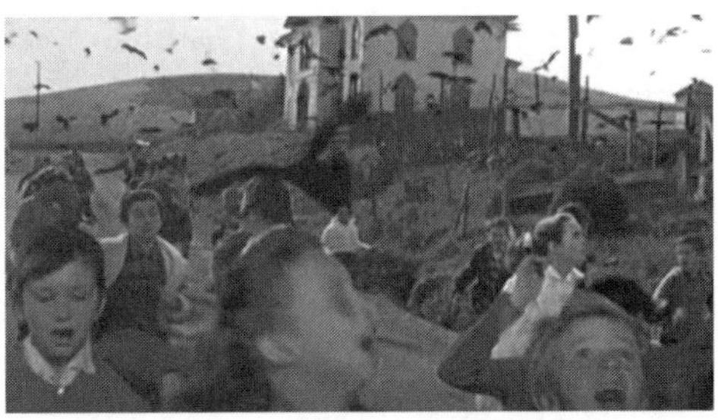

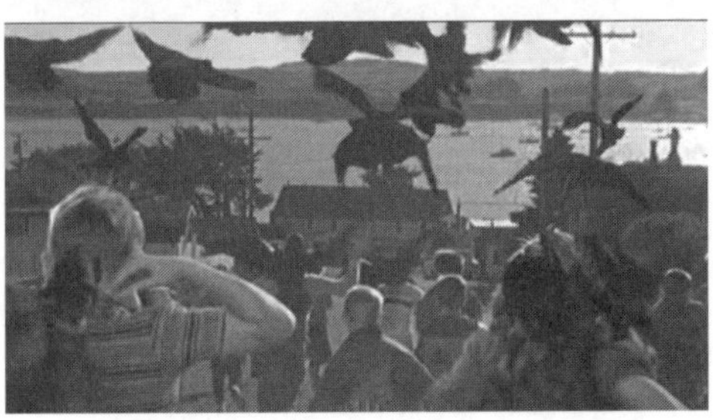

"*The Birds* is coming" was the slogan used to advertise Hitchcock's 1963 horror flick. And here they come, launching from the Jungle Jim outside the schoolhouse, and striking the fleeing children. *The Birds* relied heavily on sounds—there was no score—to sustain its birdbrained plot.

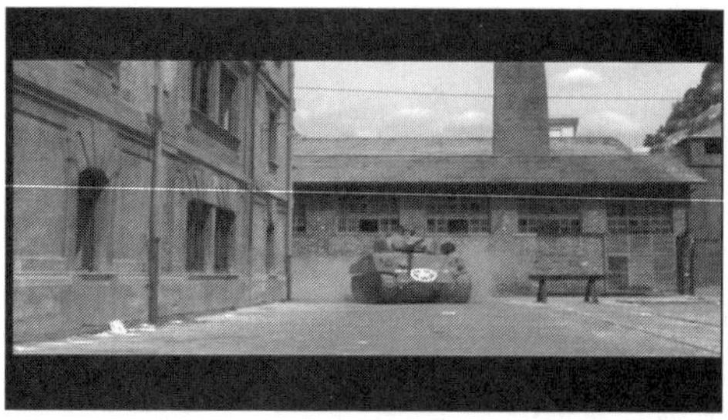
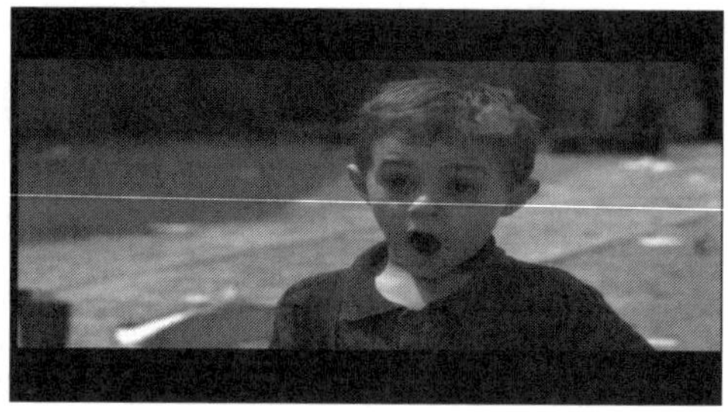
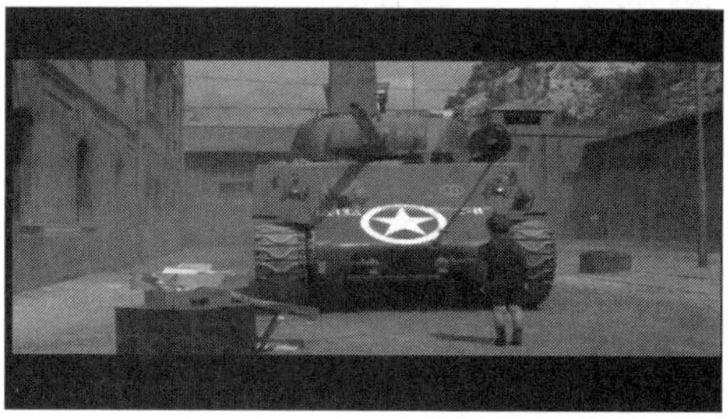

The rumble of a U.S. tank approaching at the end of 1997's *Life is Beautiful* fulfills the father's promise of freedom to his son.

Sound effects

Think about specific sounds (hard sounds) and background sound (soft sounds) and how they might work. Does the sound make us believe in the location whether it be India or Mars? Is the sound, or music recurring? Is the source of the sound onscreen or offscreen? Does it create a mood such as joy, tension, relief, sorrow, or horror or represent something important or symbolic? The goal is to get a sense of the subtle beats and grand tones of your film's sonic environment and how it supports your film's beats, characters, and themes.

Music

Music is the emotional touchstone of your film, driving how your audience reacts to what they're seeing. Well thought-out music sets the appropriate tone for your picture, clueing viewers in as to what to expect: a comedy, a romance, or a chance to rock and roll. Begin thinking about music during preproduction. Hire the composer and discuss your ideas with them so they can start experimenting, and then composing, as you send them edited scenes during production. Once you've got your music plan, be sure to allow enough time to obtain rights, record that band you're dying to use, or create it yourself.

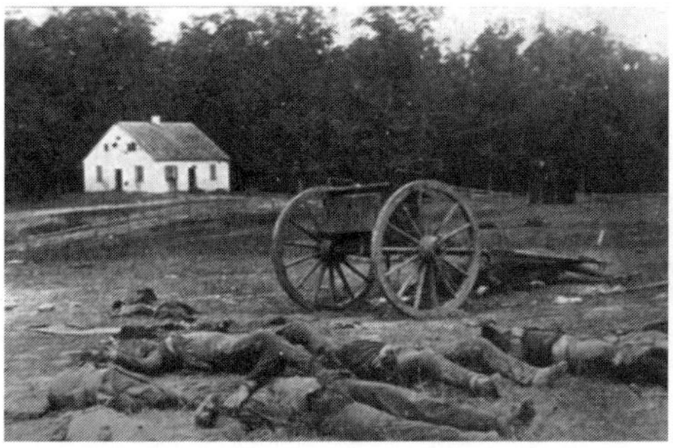

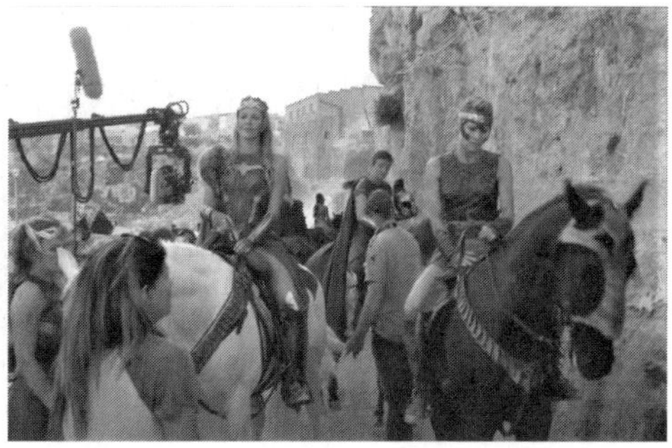

LEFT: Ken Burns' *The Civil War* series (1990) evoked the war's tragic losses with poignant renderings of the era's songs. **RIGHT:** Recording *Wonder Woman* (2017).

ON LOCATION: RECORD USEABLE SOUND

When you look at a possible location, listen to it too. Invite your sound recordist along. Planes, trains, generators, traffic, wind, dogs, and the like annihilate takes and waste precious shoot time while your cast and crew idle. Unwanted sounds on location are unavoidable at times, but if you and the recordist mull them over beforehand, you can prepare some workarounds. Do not count on bad sound being fixable in postproduction.

Record clean tracks

Be the sound editor's best friend. Record clean tracks: no helicopters whirring overhead, no doors banging, no dolly squeaking, etc. Make sure all dialogue is crisp and clear, so your audience won't miss a word. Poor sound, especially dialogue, can only be corrected so much in postproduction—and at a cost—so get it right during production!

Get RT and WT on every location and set

RT a.k.a. room tone, ambience, or presence: Record a minute of RT—wordless, noise free background sound—for every scene. Sound editors require RT to smooth out scenes, especially dialogue scenes.

WT a.k.a. wild track or wild sound: Record WT—non-sync, non-dialogue sound—on every outdoor location. Get the forest sound, the traffic, the factory—all the organic sounds. Record specific sounds that are crucial to how you want your project to sound. The sound editor can access thousands of sound effects but won't have the mating sound of the ring-tailed lemur your show is documenting. It may be impossible or costly to pick certain audio up later.

LAST WORD

There's a belief in the film industry that you "Pay it up front during production or pay more downstream during post," so save yourself time and money by getting picture and sound right, from the start. Shoot your footage correctly, so shots cut together the way you want. Put your best show forward in sound and image: Your work and your audience deserve nothing less.

WHAT DIRECTORS SHOULD KNOW ABOUT SHOOTING FOR EDITING

- ☐ Maintain an organized set. Slate each take and ensure accurate script notes and shoot logs are kept. Communicate clearly with the cutting room.
- ☐ Don't cut in the camera. Leave it to your editor to do the cutting and set the pacing.
- ☐ Plan your B-roll and shoot coverage: reaction shots, reverses, close-ups, two-shots, overheads, inserts, etc.
- ☐ Anticipate transition shots and montage shoots.
- ☐ Hold and repeat action at the start and end of takes.
- ☐ Avoid mismatches by shooting good continuity. Match angles, framing, pacing of shots, eyelines, lighting, screen direction and position, along with props, hair, and wardrobe.
- ☐ Observe the 180 Degree Rule or break it with deliberate awareness.
- ☐ Shoot with your eyes and ears: Envision your show's sound and record audio on set and location to realize it.
- ☐ Muse about music ahead. Talk it over with the composer and/or musicians you plan to hire.

2

WHAT AN EDITOR BRINGS TO THE PARTY

You may wonder, "Who is this editor-person and what exactly do they do?" If you ask them about their work, they'll probably tell you what show they're cutting, and perhaps whether it's going well or badly, not much of a clue, really. You may then think, "What is the big deal about editing? All the editor does is remove the useless frames and slap my stellar shots together: What does that take, about a nanosecond on a computer?" And you may ponder, "Why, oh why, would anyone want to sit in a dark room poring over sounds and images when they could be outside doing anything else?"

To begin answering these questions, it's important to realize that editing, like most aspects of filmmaking, is both mundane and magical, technical and artistic. It demands organization, listening to you—the director's intent—and melding it with the reality of the footage. A supple editor can shift from the intimacy of one scene to the broad view of the entire show and back in an instant.

While editors may seem invisible, concentrating on a screen in a typically windowless room away from the set, their contribution is visible in the story, the emotion, and the flow of your show. In this chapter we'll open the door to the cutting room with all its rhythms and routines, both inspired and practical, and begin to reveal what the person sitting at the digital editing machine does.

MISCONCEPTIONS OF EDITORS AND EDITING

What editors do not bring to the party constitutes a couple of common misunderstandings which are worth elaborating on to better understand what they do bring.

Removing the bad frames

The main misconception people have about editors is that in order to put a show together they simply remove the bad frames from the best takes. This is like saying a chef picks the best apples, cuts out the bad spots, and bakes them into a pie. There's a lot more to concocting the perfect pie or edited show.

Editing *is* an elimination process: The editor does leave out the bad, boring, and unnecessary frames and selects which parts of which takes to include. But this only partially defines the job. Simply put, the editor takes the raw ingredients—the film you shot, plus any archival footage—and blends them together to realize your vision of the show. While this gives us a general definition of what an editor does, we now need to refine this with the attributes—the ingredients, if we stick with our cooking metaphor—to fully describe what an editor brings to the party.

Actor's Enemy No. 1

A secondary misconception about editors—that they are the actor's enemy and leave them on the cutting room floor—is downright myth. Au contraire, I would counter, the conscientious editor is the best friend of the actor (or whoever is being filmed), dedicated to bringing out the best from everyone on camera. Editors polish great performances, upgrade mediocre ones, and rescue poor ones. While the editor should have input into dropping or recasting a character, the decision will be made by you and/or the producer or client. This cutting room floor myth is so entrenched that I was once denied a preferred rate on home insurance because the company thought an actor would sue me over it. The agent went to his boss but no amount of explaining the reality changed the company's stance.

Reality

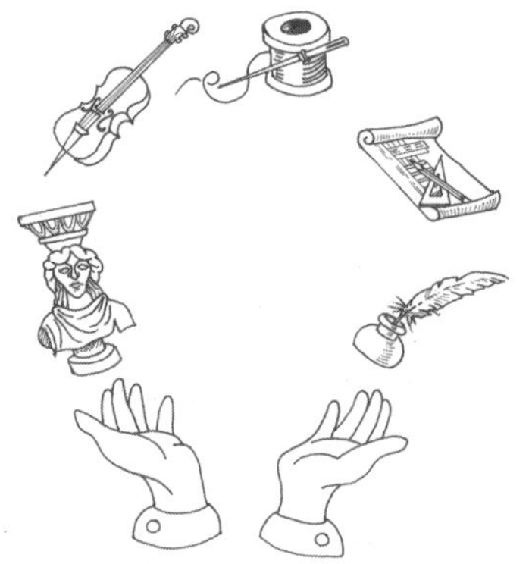

So, what is editing exactly? It has been likened to music for its rhythm and flow, beats and rests, pauses and pacing. It's also regularly compared to sculpting, since the editor works through all the footage, selecting the shots and frames necessary to tell the tale and rejecting the rest. Or is editing more like architecture; the editor builds the show from the blueprint of the script with the building blocks of the filmed shots, cut by cut, scene by scene, section by section. Or is the

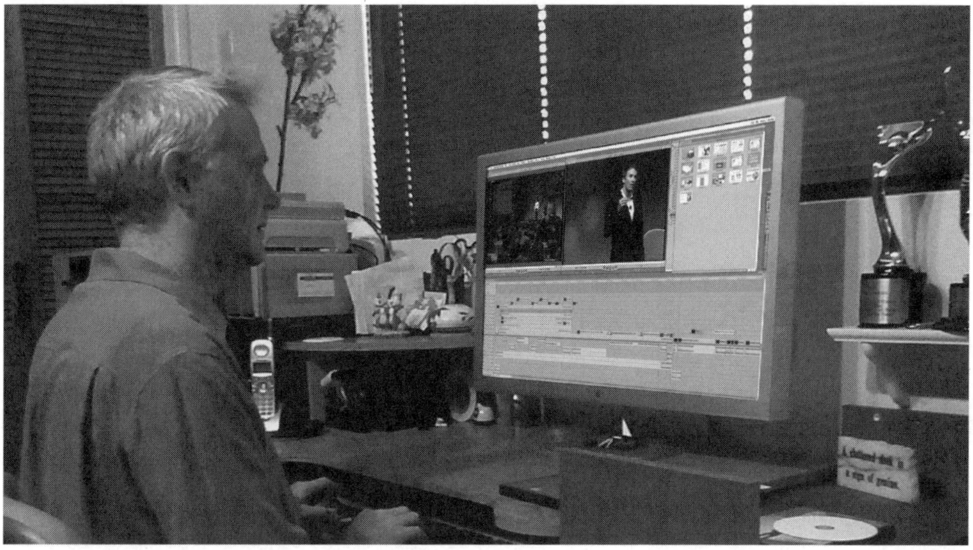

Editor and actor. *Photo courtesy of Chris Senchack.*

editor a writer, using picture, sound, and occasional subtitles to create the final, audience version of the script or outline—becoming the final writer according to many filmmakers? At times, every editor feels like a seamstress, sweating to stitch poor shots together, to make a passable show and tailoring it to others' poor visions, while dreaming of decent footage and a collaborative director for whom they can construct a superior show that dazzles the audience. Editing incorporates part of these five arts and is its own unique art.

EDITOR AS CREATIVE ARTIST

> As Kurosawa used to say, 'The only reason you write and direct is to get material to edit.' And that's exactly true. Editing is where you make the film. It's a very beautiful thing . . . I shoot to cut. —**ALEXANDER PAYNE**, director, *Nebraska, The Descendants, Sideways, Election*

Independent Eye

Like the other principal players on your film, the editor has read the script or gone over the outline for the documentary (or often created it themselves). Unlike everyone else, the editor has not experienced what you suffered to get shots: the snow or heat you endured on location, the difficulty you encountered with an actor, the standoff you had with a documentary subject who suddenly clammed up. This removed perch gives the editor special insight and a unique perspective. Their clear eye is critically important to your success.

The editor first views the show as raw footage on their screen. It is raw ingredients—groceries—but not a meal, until the editor blends everything together.

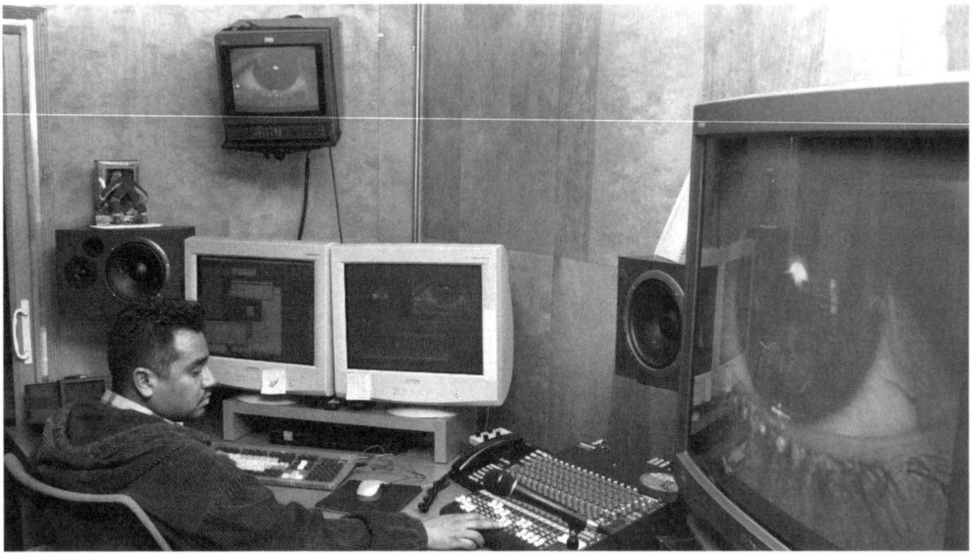

The eyes have it with the editor. *Photo courtesy of Chris Senchack.*

There's likely a recipe—the script or an outline—but these are blueprints for the editor to brew from. The editor may add some sizzle with jump cuts or quick cuts, or simply let your magnificent master sing out in one unbroken take. Cooking at the editing table is an experimental process of adding, subtracting, and moving sections around. Each successive cut shows you more of what you want your film to be.

Attentively watching your footage with an unjaundiced eye, the editor lasers in on what serves the story and winnows out what doesn't work, for reasons such as shots, lines, or scenes being repetitive, unnecessary, or not believable. The editor deals objectively and tenderly with each character or interviewee's words, looks, arc, and progression with an eye to the purpose of each scene or segment, and to your show as a whole.

In choosing what goes in and what stays out, your editor will strive to bring out the best in not only performance but also cinematography, art direction, sound, and the rest of the elements you and your crew labored so hard to capture. A magician, sometimes an alchemist, the editor forges your film with image and sound, frame by frame, shot by shot, scene by scene.

You are the ringmaster, and the editor is there to tame your film, but the editor stands apart with their independent perspective, seeing the forest and the trees. This is a unique gift to you and your project.

The Editor's Prayer

Our perfect director who art in heaven,
Showered with Oscars be thy name.
Thy Lifetime Achievement will come, thy will be done
In the editing room as it is on location.
Give us this day our dailies on time and
Forgive the missing footage as we also forgive
the person in charge of continuity.
Lead us not into frustration
But deliver us to the talented director,
For ours is the splicer, the mouse,
and the objective eye.
Forever. Amen. Rewind.

Storytelling

> And if you're not telling a story, it doesn't matter how much razzle dazzle there is. It is not about the tools. It's about the story. —**ZACK STAENBERG**, editor, *The Matrix Trilogy*

The essence of editing is not eliminating shots or making fancy cuts, it is simply making the story work. The editor is your final writer, a storyteller who composes with picture and sound. Whatever didn't work in the script, on the set, or in the dailies, must now be wrangled with and made to work. The editor reads the footage; views it, listens to it, visualizes the story, and then builds it. Like a writer, an editor sets up the story, decides when and how to reveal important information, contracts time or expands it with the length of each edit and number of edits, and structures it, to most effectively tell the tale.

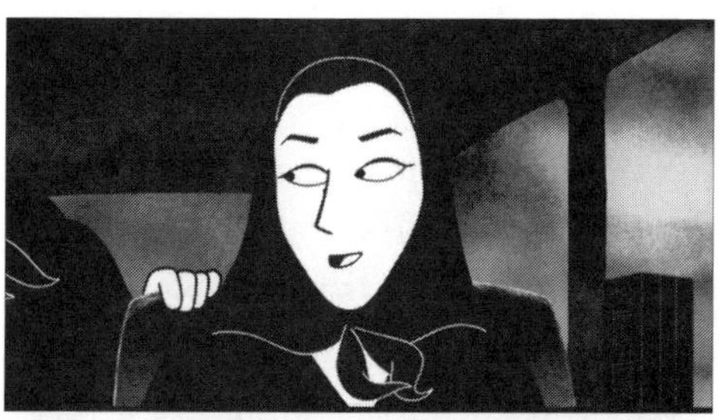

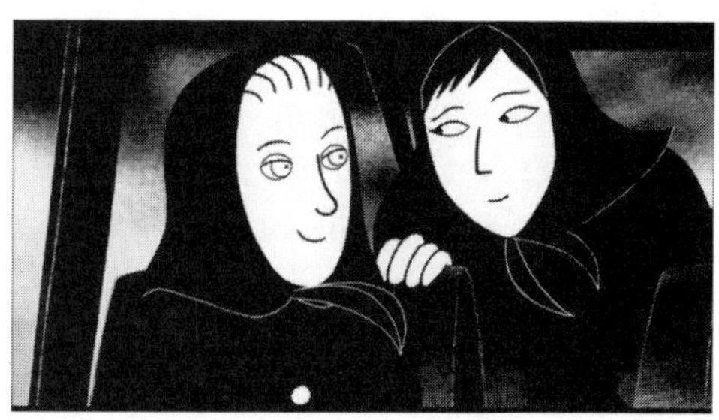

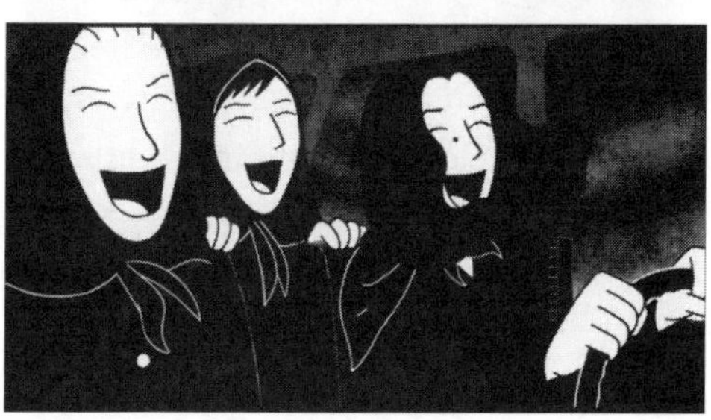

Beginning: Marjane bets her friends she'll remove her veil. Middle: They take the bet. End: She removes it and they all shriek with joy in *Persepolis* (2007).

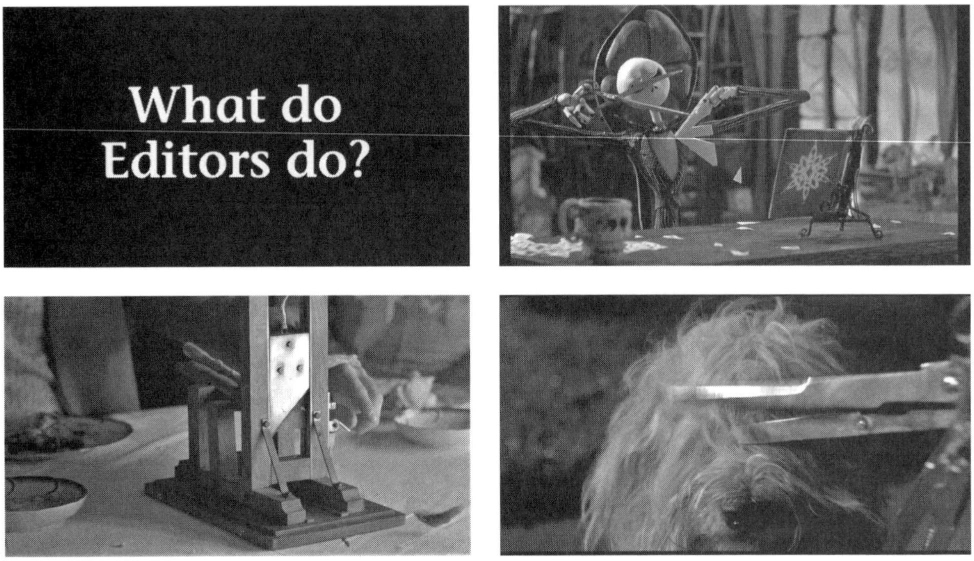

This matchless doc on editing plays with the question of what editors do starting with quick cuts of . . . cutting. *The Cutting Edge: The Magic of Movie Editing* (2004).

Just as a script has a beginning, middle, and end, so does each scene. The editor has to figure out how to get into the scene, how long to let it play, and when—on what shot—to get out of it. Consciously or unconsciously, they'll ask: Whose scene is it? Should it focus on the speaker or the listener? Which shot carries the information best and for how long? Many filmmakers consider editing the final rewrite of the script and directing of the film.

Good editing means good storytelling, sculpting what the footage and story demand, and is the crucial, inalienable skill of an editor.

Documentary storytelling

When you're making a documentary, no matter how useful the outline (and it's often incomplete or non-existent), the editor is the initial shaper of the story, as well of its visual style and sound design. Doc editing therefore can be an extraordinarily creative, collaborative, and rewarding experience for both you and your editor. You will thread together statements by interviewees and experts, drop in cutaways to bridge lines or sections, arrange images to clarify the thought process and points of view, massage gaps and segues, create a montage or two, layer in music, add narration and sometimes a few graphics or animated segments. Often the hardest part is deciding from all the stories you're keen to tell, which one(s) to drop due to length or from not wanting to overload viewers.

Story problems

> The buck stops in the cutting room. —**DEDE ALLEN**, editor, *Bonnie and Clyde*, *Dog Day Afternoon*, *Reds*, *The Breakfast Club*

The problems with a film become glaringly apparent during editing. The lead performance isn't consistent. The ending doesn't work. There are lots of fine scenes—too many—and the show stagnates. This is where you and the editor become problem solvers and collaborators to make the large fixes and small adjustments. This may involve telling the story from more points-of-view or fewer, intercutting scenes or moving them around, or rearranging or tightening lines. You and the editor will create the final story that your movie will tell.

Editor and actor

On most shows the editor seldom if ever meets the actors or interviewees. To an editor, an actor is a character, and an interviewee is a subject. Yet in many ways an editor knows these onscreen people better than they know themselves. Editors take in their looks, gestures, and the fullness of life they inject into their character or interview. The editor is affected by the actor's and interviewee's delivery and performance. Editors put themselves in the subject's shoes, and in turn affect their delivery and performance.

Editors help actors in several vital ways. They spend an inordinate amount of time studying takes to choose the dialogue readings and reactions that best reflect the character and build the scene. Editors cement character arcs and coordinate actors' timings so that their characters are consistent and support the dramatic purpose of the story. Editors can usually upgrade a poor performance, improve a lackluster one, and gild a great one by pulling out the best moments.

Editors coordinate the actors' timings and reactions so that each performance is consistent and attains its dramatic purpose. Sometimes this entails holding a beat on an actor to expand the emotion and time. Other times it calls for cutting tightly, to sustain a performance and keep a taut pace. Always, editors deal objectively and passionately with each character or interviewee's words, lines, looks, and total presentation, with an eye to the purpose of the scene and the show as a whole.

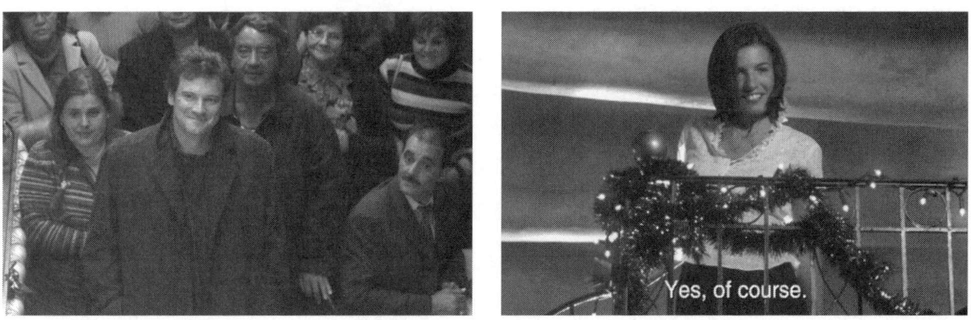

A balcony scene brings a romance to a marriage proposal in *Love Actually* (2004).

Left on the cutting room floor

When you elect to delete an entire character or interview subject, it usually isn't due to a weak performance or interview. Rather, it's because the performance or interview slowed down, got confused, or otherwise negatively impacted the show. For example, you ax or minimize a character because you've axed or minimized a scene or a plotline; you jettison an interview because the interviewee's views and experiences are covered by another interviewee or the narrator.

Stand in for Audience

> The humbling truth is that a film is made in the editing room. The most magnificent performances and the best intentions mean nothing if they don't cut. . . The director, the actor, the designer, the writer can and do become sidetracked, confused, indeed even inspired into serving two masters—the story and themselves. The editor serves only the story. As such, they are the best friend of the audience, and time and again, the salvation of the filmmaker.
> —**DAVID MAMET,** writer, at the 2002 Academy Awards ceremony, *State and Main, Heist, Hoffa, Hannibal* (screenplay)

However the editor may read the footage and weave it together, it is the edited form of the show—not the script or outline or raw dailies—that reaches the audience. Each cut, whether picture or sound or both, communicates to the audience not only content and plot, but what the characters are seeing, experiencing, thinking and feeling and how they are reacting and acting. This affects how the audience thinks, feels, sees, and reacts. The editor stands in for the audience. It's a delicate business as the audience is intelligent—has high movie IQ—and reads volumes into the subtlest gesture or look.

The editor is the eye of the audience, attuned to where it is looking at every moment. From the shots, sound, and music, the editor shapes the story and sets each scene's pace, controlling what the audience sees and hears, and when they see and hear it. Whether you call it manipulation, engagement, or just good filmmaking, it serves to give the audience a fright, a tear, or a laugh. Fiction or nonfiction, editing makes a show feel real for the audience. A sign of success is enrapt viewers who, unknowingly, breathe with the action on screen.

Film Language and the Editor

Editing, meaning the way the film is put together and plays, is, simply and profoundly, the language of the film. Editing is how the assembled footage speaks to the audience. In the over one hundred years of public cinema-going, the language has gotten quite sophisticated, a far cry from the start which Chapter 3 documents. According to film lore*, Parisians famously fled the theatre in 1896 upon witnessing a short film of a train steaming into a station. First time moviegoers in rural South America in the 1980s

* While this did not actually happen, it was an urban legend propagated at the time to alarm the masses about the seductive power of film.

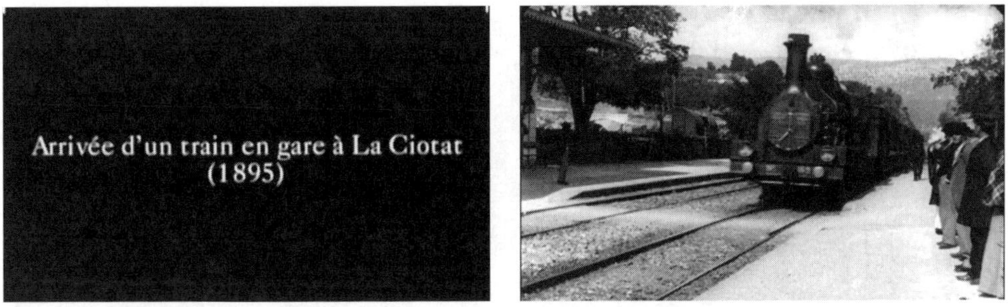

The famous 45" film shot in 1895 by the Lumière Brothers showing a train arriving at a Ciotat station near Lyons, France.

rejected a film about mosquito abatement which featured a close-up of the pest, insisting, "We don't have mosquitos that big." This reaction has been repeated elsewhere in other cultures over the years.

Editing mimics thought and is what differentiates filmmaking from the other arts. It accomplishes this with the editor's selection of shots—close-ups, wide shots, reaction shots, POVs, etc.—and their juxtapositions. The editor creates flash cuts, flashbacks, flashforwards, short and long cuts, and manipulates the "real" filmed time to do this. Editing imitates the workings of the mind, and it takes the mind to do it.

Editors speak the language of film and voice it with every frame. On each project, the director and editor develop the language anew. For example, one scene may demand expletives in the form of jump cuts that ratchet up the tension of a marital spat; the next scene may call for long sentences in the form of shots that linger in the aftermath of the couple's reconciliation. Your completed project, if well done, will equal more than the sum of its cuts, as the editing imprints its own meaning and impacts your audience.

EDITOR AS PRACTICAL PLANNER

Editors are also part librarians: They catalogue and memorize all the footage. It's a major organizational job. The editor and their assistant and apprentice—if they're fortunate to have one or both—organize the footage as well as the script and notes, schedule and workflow, and the cutting room itself. Understanding the basics of what and how editors organize will put you at ease with the components of the editing room, so when you sit in the cutting room with the editor, it will be familiar, and you'll be ready to roll up your sleeves and work.

Cutting room

It may be a dedicated suite, a cubicle, or a back house with just enough space for a couch and chair. It could be at a studio or post house, in a motel or a mobile home. I once edited in the director's closet. A music video editor I know edited on a bus for months

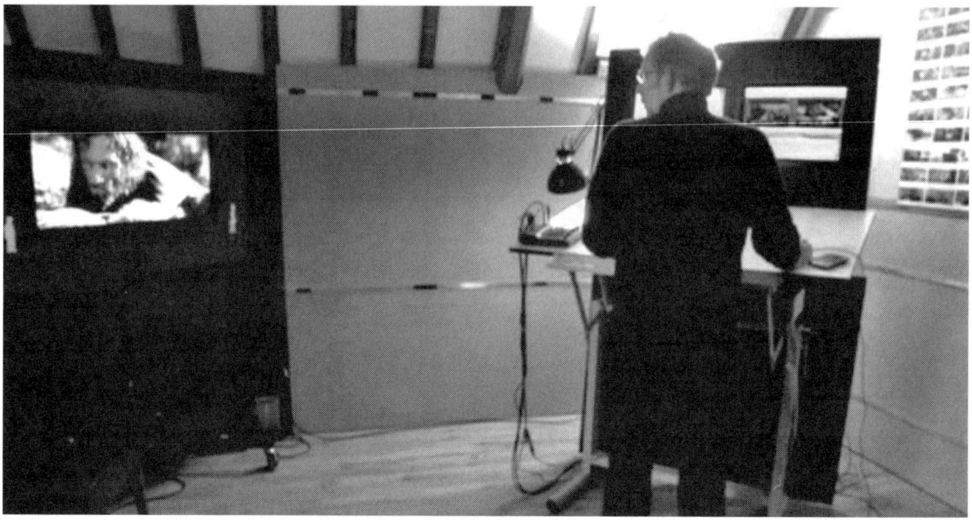

Editor Walter Murch, author of the bestselling book on editing *In the Blink of an Eye*, in his cutting room above a garage on his northern California property. *The Cutting Edge: The Magic of Movie Editing* (2004).

while touring with the band. Whatever. Wherever. The cutting room is your editor's work cave and you'll be clocking a few hours in it. Most cutting rooms don't have windows and if they do, they're darkened. Why? To best view images and scenes.

Editing is not for slobs. Your editorial crew will arrange the room so that source footage, logs, script, vital phone numbers like the pizza delivery service—everything—is readily available! A cutting room that's a pit causes tension and time lost in desperately seeking screening notes or a missing latte. Editorial will ensure there is adequate lighting, power, speakers, and temperature to create the ideal climate for viewing footage, editing, and screening your show. They'll do their best to secure a couch, a lamp, a small fridge, and an ergonomic chair.

Digital editing system

Your editor will oversee the set-up of the Adobe Premiere, Avid Media Composer, Final Cut Pro, or whichever digital editing machine they'll be using. Ideally, they will have time to put the machine through its paces to be certain that audio and video devices are functioning perfectly, software is operating properly, show settings are correct, and importing and exporting of footage from all sources—server, devices, camera card—works. Waiting until dailies arrive to discover problems starts things off on a bad note and causes stress. Lastly, the editor will gauge how much storage will be required for the expected amount of footage.

Speaking of digital equipment—Adobe, Apple, Avid—each manufacturer's editing software is complex with an ongoing learning curve as new features and software versions are released. Knowing how to operate a system, cajole it to talk to other devices,

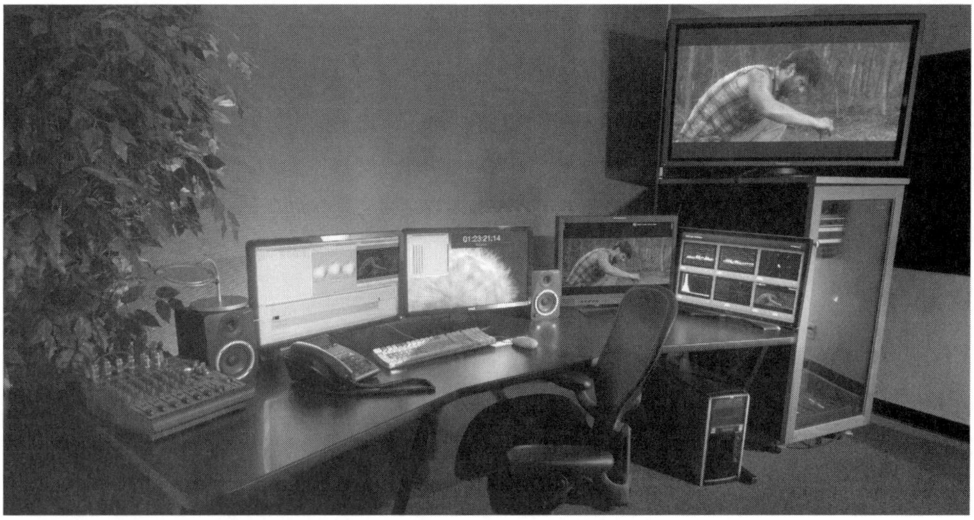

A digital editing set up at a post house. *Photo courtesy of AlphaDogs.*

and deal with crashes and freezes, constitute other skills the editor brings to the party. The editor will use the system to create VFX (from simple dissolves to complex green screens) and to add and mix dialogue, sound effects, music, and narration.

Final frame

You'll experience tense times, fun times, frustration, joy—the gamut of moods and emotions. And, hopefully, you'll create something you're satisfied with—even proud of—in the end. All in the ever-so-humble cutting room.

Workflow

Your editorial team will be clear on your show's workflow—the path the footage will take from the first frame that enters the cutting room to the exit of the final cut. The basis for any workflow is knowing the format(s) of the incoming footage—card, disc, drive, file, or tape—to be ingested (entered) into the digital editing system and knowing the format(s) the project will finish on.

There are workflows for features, dramas, and docs, for low and high budget shows, animated shows, Final Cut Pro shows and Avid shows, for HD shows and 3D shows: You name it: there's a workflow for it. Workflows are also determined by editing system, type of show, budget, and camera used (Alexa, RED, Viper, etc.). While there are common workflows, it's just as common to deviate from them.

How to make sense of it all? The flow chart on the next page shows a workflow with the basic steps every project takes to ground your understanding of the editorial process. Your show's workflow will likely diverge from it in one way or another. We will elaborate on the steps as we reach them in subsequent chapters.

Basic Workflow

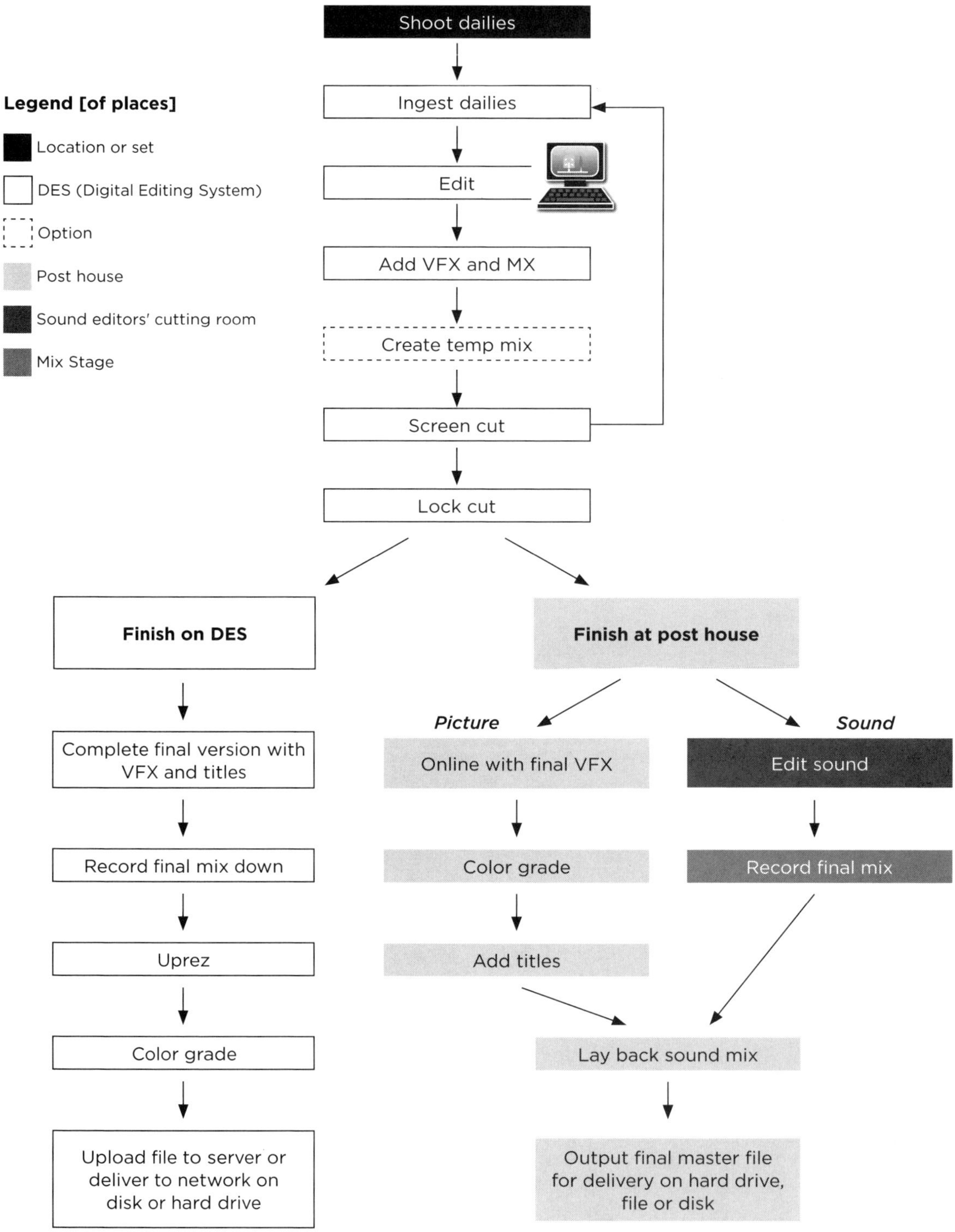

Postproduction schedule

The schedule will display a stampede of events including shoot dates and due dates for the First Cut, Director's Cut, the mix stage, delivery, etc. New dates may be added e.g., if you need to make pick-ups or re-shoot. Usually, editorial receives the schedule from the post supervisor. There may be no schedule at all, or it may be made up as you go. Don't be surprised if the schedule changes. Most schedules can and do change. Changes can give you some breathing room or force editorial to work into the night or through the weekend. Since postproduction takes place at the end of the line, if the show is running behind or the schedule gets shortened, editorial gets pushed to work harder and longer! The post supervisor will work with your editor to set and determine the schedule and keep you in the loop.

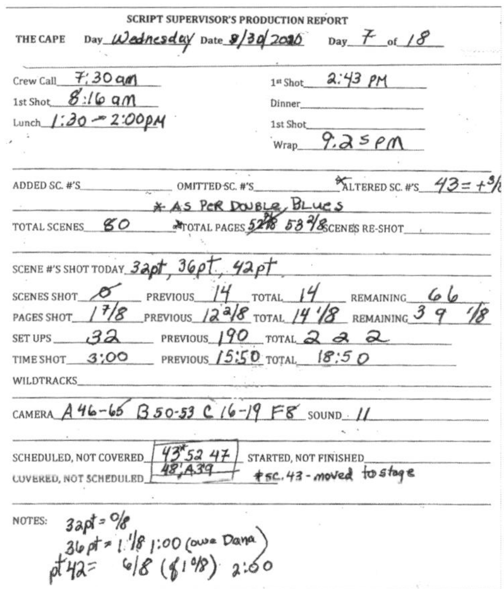

SCRIPT SUPERVISOR'S PRODUCTION REPORT

THE CAPE Day Wednesday Date 8/30/2016 Day 7 of 18

Crew Call 7:30 am
1st Shot 8:16 am
Lunch 1:30 – 2:00PM
1st Shot 2:43 PM
Dinner
1st Shot
Wrap 9:25 PM

ADDED SC. #'S OMITTED SC. #'S *ALTERED SC. #'S 43 = +3/8
* AS PER DOUBLE BLUES
TOTAL SCENES 80 *TOTAL PAGES 53 2/8 SCENES RE-SHOT

SCENE #'S SHOT TODAY 32pt, 36pt, 42pt
SCENES SHOT 0 PREVIOUS 14 TOTAL 14 REMAINING 66
PAGES SHOT 1 7/8 PREVIOUS 12 2/8 TOTAL 14 1/8 REMAINING 39 1/8
SET UPS 32 PREVIOUS 190 TOTAL 222
TIME SHOT 3:00 PREVIOUS 15:50 TOTAL 18:50
WILDTRACKS

CAMERA A 46-65 B 50-53 C 16-19 F8 SOUND 11

SCHEDULED, NOT COVERED 43* 52 47 STARTED, NOT FINISHED
COVERED, NOT SCHEDULED 48, A39 *SC. 43 - moved to stage

NOTES: 32pt = 0/8
36pt = 1 1/8 1:00 (owe Dana)
pt42 = 6/8 (1 0/8) 2:00

Script Supervisor's Production Report, a summary of the day's shoot.

Dailies

Logging dailies and all the rest of the footage—archival footage, stock shots, inserts, VFX, SFX—on the digital editing system is editorial's foremost organizing responsibility. Depending on the source format of the show (disc, hard drive, tape, film) and the type of show (scripted or non-scripted), editorial will receive some or all of the following reports: Your notes, the script supervisor's notes and reports, lined script pages, editor's daily log a.k.a. one-liner, daily production log, DIT report, lab report, camera and sound logs. If your show's shooting on film, there will also be a lab report and a telecine* report.

The editor (or assistant if there is one) will meticulously check and file the reports. They want to be certain they have all the footage you shot. An editor's nightmare is to be in a screening and hear you say, "Where's the close-up of the toaster? I know I shot it." Another reason editorial will fastidiously

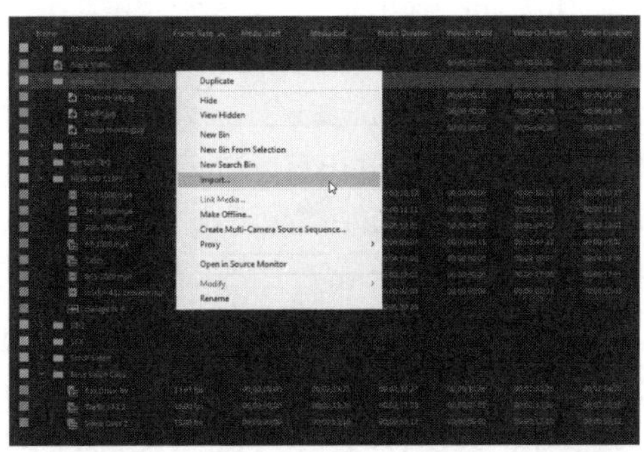

Ingest screen on Adobe's Premiere Pro editing system initiated by clicking on "Import." *Photo courtesy of Jay Scherberth.*

* Telecine: Transfer of film to tape.

organize all reports and paperwork is to ensure that info and footage are easily accessible at any time, such as when you're present and ask to view a specific take or to see dailies from a particular day or location.

Next the editor will ingest (input) the dailies into the digital editing system. They may need to sync audio and video files. Most importantly, the editor will then log each shot into the editing system's database with a description: Master, WS, MS, CU, etc. They may mark a take that you noted or they liked with an asterisk (*), or label it NG (No Good). Each shot will have a unique identity (comprised of its scene and take number and description as well as its timecode, metadata, and more), for tracking it from the editing room to your final deliverable(s).

LAST WORD

The editor is your collaborator—organizing, cutting, and re-cutting to serve your vision, bring the story in the footage to life, and enthrall the audience.

WHAT DIRECTORS SHOULD KNOW ABOUT EDITORS AND EDITING

- ☐ Editing, like the rest of filmmaking, is both mundane and magical, technical and artistic.
- ☐ The shot footage is the raw material that the editor will sculpt into the show.
- ☐ Since editors do not participate in the shoot, they have an objective eye and unique insight into the story lying within the footage.
- ☐ The essence of editing is not eliminating shots or making fancy cuts, it is making the story work. The editor is the final writer, a storyteller who composes with picture and sound.
- ☐ Editors help actors' performances by cementing their characters' arcs, coordinating their timings and reactions, so that their characters are consistent and support the dramatic purpose of the story.
- ☐ The editor stands in for the audience, aware of where their eyes are focused and affecting what they think, feel, see, and how they react.
- ☐ Editing mimics thought and is the language of film created anew by you and the editor on every show.
- ☐ Editorial has a lot to organize and keep track of: dailies, reports, notes, and other paperwork, the workflow and schedule, and the cutting room itself.

3

THE FLICKERS AND THE FRAMES

A SHORT HISTORY OF EDITING

From the start, inventors, scientists, technicians, and artists sought to portray their world to their fellow human beings by making still images move. This is why the history of film editing can be viewed through two interlocking lenses: 1) The revolutions and evolutions of editing technology and tools and 2) The integral role editing has played in the development of the language of cinema, meaning how the images and sounds speak to the audience. While this chapter cannot cover every revolution and evolution, it aims to be a whirl-a-gig ride, spotlighting key frames that led to where we are today.

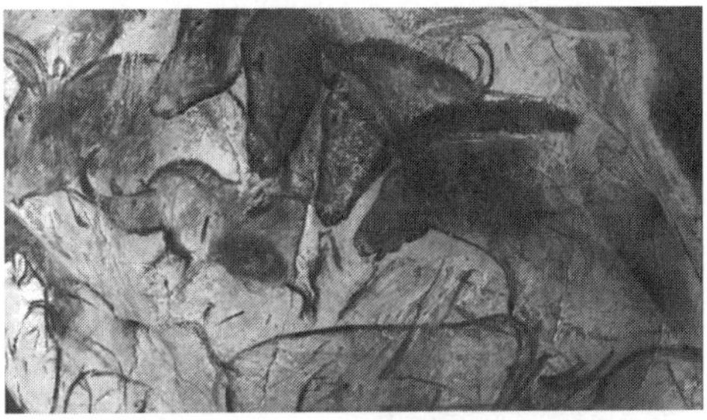

Multiple horse heads in Chauvet cave in Ardèche, France, appear to move when a light is passed over them in Werner Herzog's *Cave of Forgotten Dreams* (2010).

ANCIENT BEGINNINGS

Some 30,000 years ago, Paleolithic painters created the first moving images in caves in France, Spain, and Portugal. Created with a burin, (a flaked Stone Age tool), these superimposed images of successive, split action movements became animated when lit by a torch, depicting animals in motion such as a bison flicking its tail, a lion loping along, or a horse shaking its head. Who knows how and when these animations were shown.

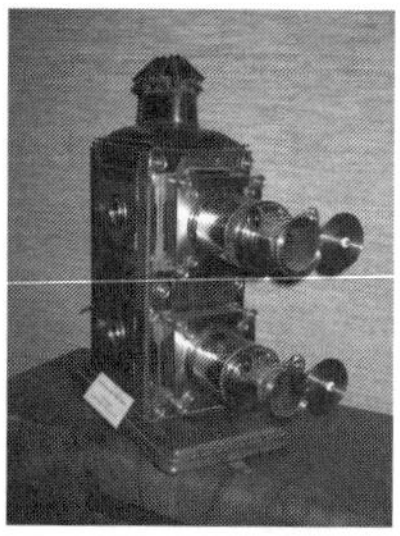

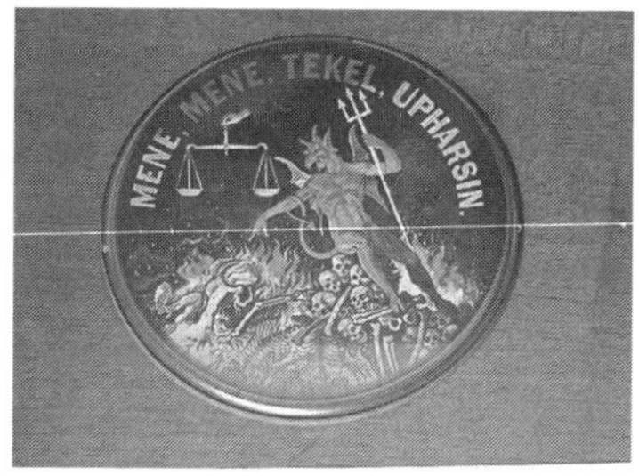

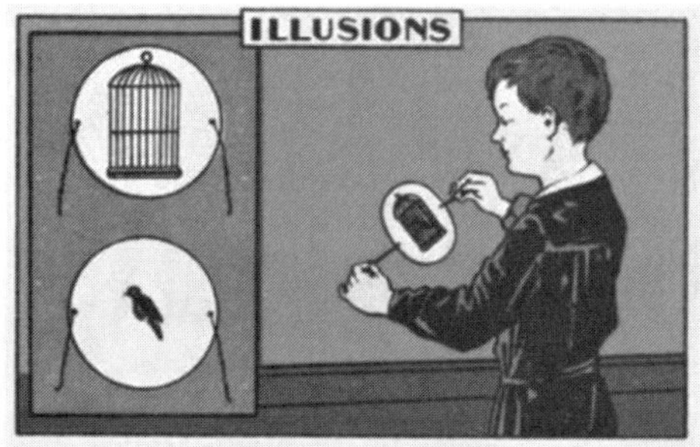

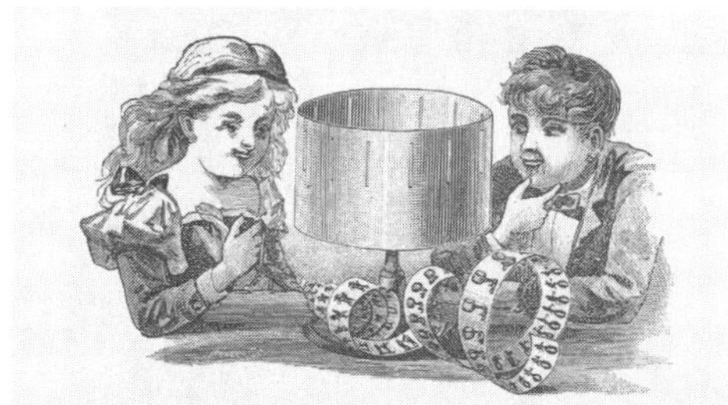

THE ZOETROPE, OR WHEEL OF LIFE.

TOP LEFT: Magic Lantern circa 1890; Collegiate model illuminated by limelight jets made by J H Steward & Co. of Strand, London. *Photo courtesy of David Evans, Secretary, Magic Lantern Society of U.S. & Canada.* **TOP RIGHT:** Hand painted Magic Lantern glass slide circa 1860 with Satan, skeletons, and a Hebrew warning, "God has numbered your days." *Photo courtesy of David Evans, Secretary, Magic Lantern Society of U.S. & Canada.* **BOTTOM LEFT:** This trade card illustrates how a Thaumatrope worked. *Image courtesy of Collection of Jack and Beverly Wilgus.* **BOTTOM RIGHT:** Viewers spin the Zoetrope and peer through its vertical slits to glimpse a sequence of pictures on a strip of paper move. *From the Milton Bradley catalogue 1889.*

OPTICAL TOYS

Flash forward to the 1600s when the Magic Lantern was developed and became the first popular device for exhibiting images that appeared to move in the 1800s. Using one to three lenses, the device projected hand-painted glass slides onto a wall lit at first by candlelight, then by oil lamp, gas lamp such as the limelight, and finally by electric lightbulb. The projectionist created dissolves between the images which illuminated monsters, mandrakes, constellations, and many other-worldly wonders before the Magic Lantern settled into edutainment, projecting anatomical diagrams, astronomical phenomenon, historical figures, and the like.

Other early picture devices were less home theatre and more novelty optical toy. The user of a thaumatrope—"wonder turner" in Greek—simply twirled two strings with a disc in the middle, each side stamped with a picture or words, to see a bird fly out of a cage, a poem, or a riddle. John Ayrton Paris created the Thaumatrope in England, in 1824 to demonstrate persistence of vision*, a necessary component in creating the illusion of moving pictures.

Other early moving picture contraptions utilized paper strips with drawings,

* How the human eye takes in a series of still images and sees them as moving pictures. Scientists and perceptual psychologists dispute this vision concept, but film theorists maintain its relevance to cinema history.

spinning disks, revolving lampshades, and cylinders that the spectator turned and that sported mysterious, technical sounding names (not unlike tools today) with Greek roots, including Phenakistoscope, Zoetrope, and Praxinoscope.

A PHOTOGRAPHIC EXPERIMENT, A BET, AND A RACEHORSE

By the 1870s, photography was fashionable but dependent on photographers; cameras were not in everyday people's hands and images were still. A bet by railroad baron and former governor of California, Leland Stanford, motivated a photographer to isolate motion in an experiment that is considered a forerunner to getting film images moving.

A popular conundrum of the day posed the question, "Does a galloping horse ever lift all four hooves off the ground at one time?" Persistence of vision doesn't allow the human eye to detect if this is true. Stanford believed it was. He already had a stable of racehorses and a track, he just needed a jockey and photographer to prove his belief and win a reputed $25,000 wager. In 1872, he hired accomplished British photographer, Eadweard Muybridge, who shot a series of photographs of thoroughbreds trotting past threads that set off camera shutters. But the horses didn't gallop, and the images were blurry.

Muybridge worked on quickening the film emulsion and shutter speeds, to create what are essentially studies of stop-motion photography. In June 1878, the press observed from the stands as jockey Gilbert Domm swung up on Sallie Gardner and galloped her around Stanford's Palo Alto Stock Farm. Muybridge had rigged 24 glass-plated cameras which fired off frames as the mare swished by and produced 12 images. He developed the negatives with the press in the darkroom to verify his veracity, then demonstrated the results in a continual action sequence on a Zoetrope. Success! The horse lifted all four hooves off the ground and Stanford won his wager. More remarkably, Muybridge had halted motion and time, then re-animated them, a parsing and transmuting of action destined to influence filmmaking and become part of the language of cinema.

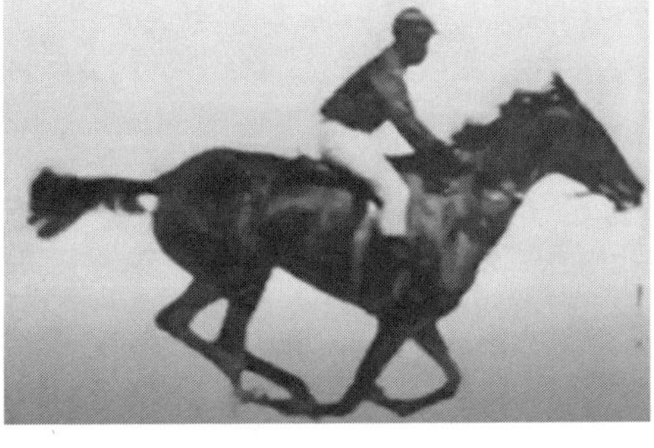

The frame that won the bet from Muybridge's 1878 stop-motion study, titled *Sallie Gardner at a Gallop* or *The Horse in Motion*. For more frames in the study see the cover of this book.

FILM IS ON A ROLL AND PICTURES BEGIN TO MOVE

So far, editing had been a matter of choosing and ordering images, and the term did not exist. In 1889, George Eastman of Rochester, New York launched celluloid film on a roll, the prelude to changing all that. In West Orange, New Jersey, photographer-engineer Laurie Dickson noticed a stitching machine in the lab of his employer, Thomas Edison, and added the sprocket holes to Eastman's roll. Dickson then ran the film through a Kinetograph*, the camera he'd designed, and film was finally in motion.

Edison

In 1893 the Edison Manufacturing Company, under Dickson's direction and Edison's oversight, began making movies in the Black Maria**, the first U.S. movie studio. Constructed of tar paper and black inside and out, the Black Maria was a quasi-sundial with an open roof, built on a turntable that men pushed to keep the lighting—the sun—constant during filming. Edison's crew filmed anything that moved—a blacksmith, a man sneezing, two theatre actors kissing, two sisters boxing, Annie Oakley—and re-enacted two executions: the beheading of Mary Stuart and the electrocution of Leon Czolgosz, who assassinated President McKinley in 1901.

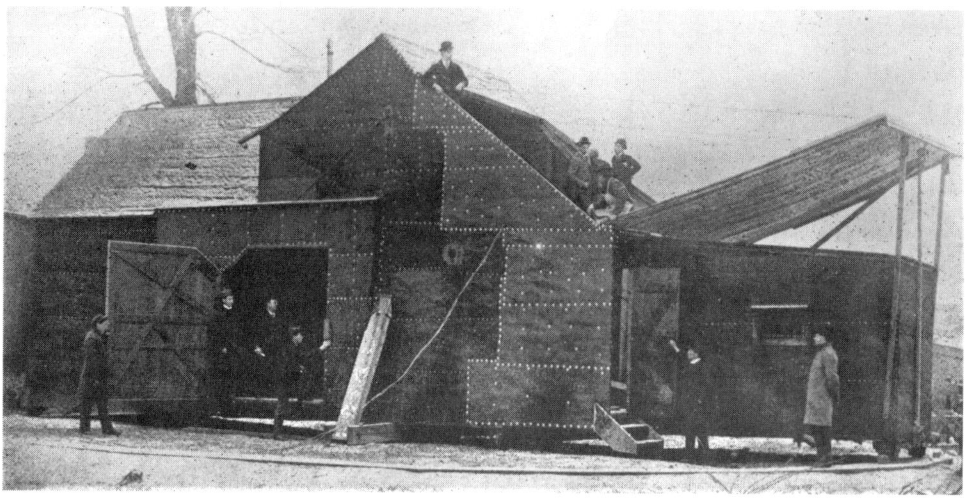

"The Kinetographic Theatre" (as the photo is titled) a.k.a. the Black Maria, the first movie studio in the U.S. ***Photo courtesy of Thomas Edison National Historical Park.***

The Lumières

Meanwhile, across the pond in Lyons, France, brothers Auguste and Louis Lumière who, like Edison, had a successful business (photography) and the capital to experiment, had invented their own celluloid motion picture machine, the Cinématographe.

* From Greek: *kineto* meaning "movement" and *graph* meaning "to write."
** Black Maria (mar·eye·uh) was a slang word for a police patrol wagon.

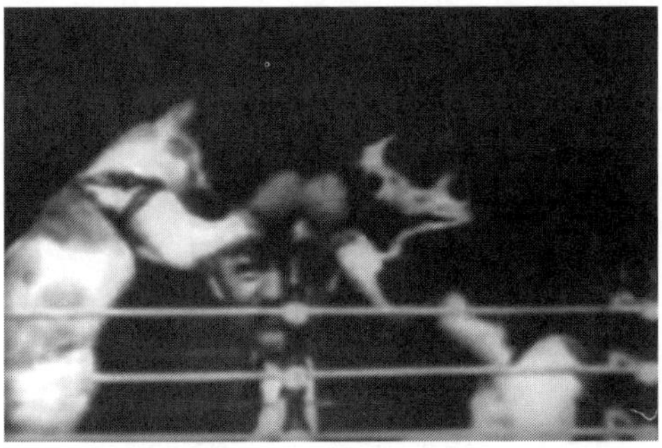

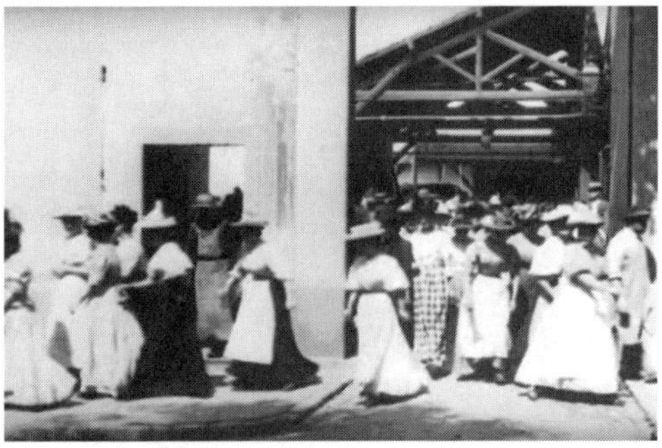

LEFT: 1894: Cats box each other in an act from Professor Henry Welton's Cat Circus shot in Edison's Black Maria studio. **RIGHT:** 1895: Workers exit the Lumière Brothers' photography factory in this actualité, the first screened in their Paris program.

The Lumière frères started filming "actualités"*—local scenes of a train arriving at a station, gentlemen drinking and playing cards, a couple feeding their baby and the like. They then sent camera operators around the globe to capture military and official events as well as stage shows and everyday life. On December 28, 1895, the Lumières took their Cinématographe—which was both a camera and projector—to the Grand Café in Paris, charging one franc to see a 20-minute program of ten of their actualités. It's considered the world's first public screening.**

Now the images were moving, but how were they going to move audiences?

Early Theatres

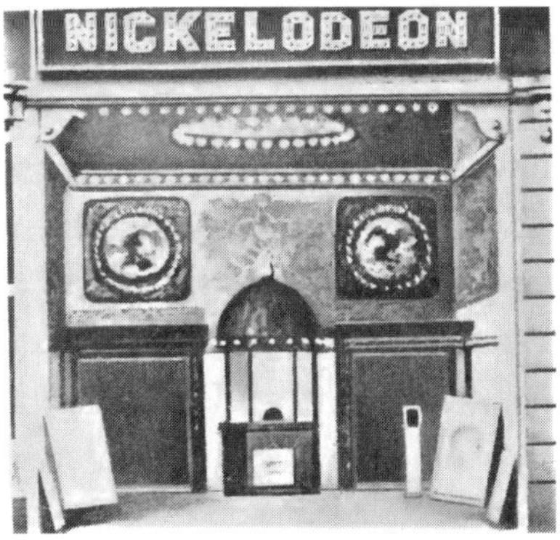

Nickelodeon in Pittsburg, PA circa 1905. *Photo courtesy of Forsher Collection.*

The public was first introduced to and entertained by Edison's and others' short films at music halls, where they were part of vaudeville line-ups. Soon folks were flocking to converted storefronts furnished with hard, wooden seats, plunking down a nickel to see an entire program of films. The curtain had risen on the short-lived era (1905-1913) of the Nickelodeon. Actually, Nickelodeons had no curtains: Owners projected the films on a back wall to the accompaniment of a piano or a drum. By 1910, there were over 10,000 Nickelodeons frequented weekly by an estimated 30% of the U.S. population. It was a business propagated for and often by immigrants who numbered 13.5 million and accounted for 14.7% of the population.

Competing with this crowd pleaser was Edison's Kinetoscope. Designed for

* Although the Lumière Brothers, Edison, and other producers abandoned actualités by 1908, they formed the roots of newsreels, documentary, reality shows, and YouTube videos.

** Visiting the Institut Lumière (the Lumière Cinema Museum) in Lyon and the Thomas Edison National Historical Park in West Orange, which contains the Black Maria painstakingly reconstructed by his son in the 1950s down to the identical nails and tarpaper, was a thrill for this filmmaker and is highly recommended.

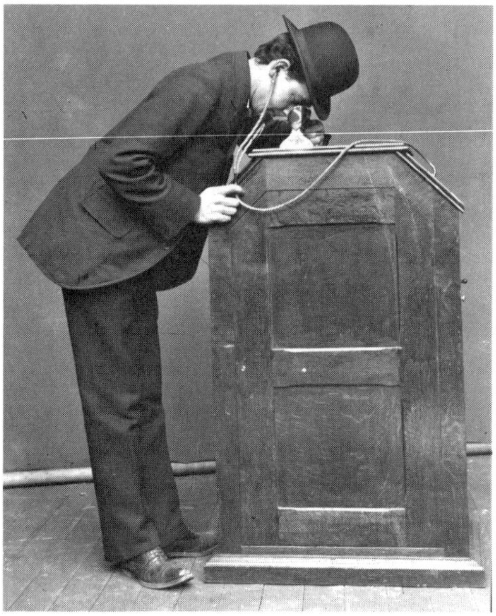

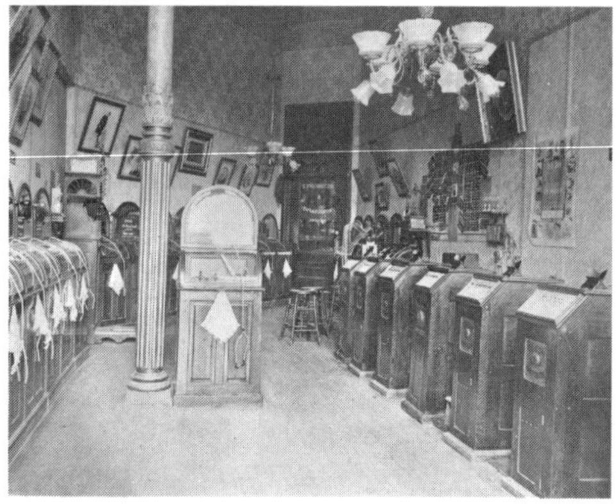

LEFT: Viewing a short on Edison's Kinetoscope, engineered by Laurie Dickson. *Photo courtesy of Thomas Edison National Historical Park.* **ABOVE:** Kinetoscope parlor in San Francisco, 1895. *Photo courtesy of Thomas Edison National Historical Park.*

individual viewing, Kinetoscopes populated penny arcades, game parlors, and amusement parks, the video arcades of their day. The viewer inserted a quarter in a slot and hunched over a peephole to see a string of the many shorts Edison was cranking out at his new glass-roofed studio erected on top of a nine-story building in Manhattan.

First Edits

Up until this time most films consisted of a single shot or several shots that were created and edited in the camera. The operator (often the director) hand cranked the film to record the first shot, stopping at the edit point to reposition the camera, then cranking it forward for the next shot. However, around the world groups and individuals were experimenting with the budding technology. And phantom ride films—a fleeting fad—were giving spectators a thrill ride atop a steam train via a long POV shot captured by strapping a camera operator to the roof of the train. In 1899, A.G. Smith, a member of a group in Brighton, England dubbed the Brighton School, cut a phantom ride shot of a train entering and exiting a tunnel in two, and inserted a shot filmed on a stage of two actors stealing a kiss. Audiences accepted that the smooch took place while the train was in the tunnel.

A Kiss in the Tunnel is notable for being one of the earliest edited sequences, and because it connects two shots filmed in different locations at different times: Moviegoers had no trouble seeing the shots as one event in one place: They made the time-space connection.

Most films at this time were composed of a long take or two and conceived like stage plays, the camera keeping its distance from the action in a wide shot, standing in

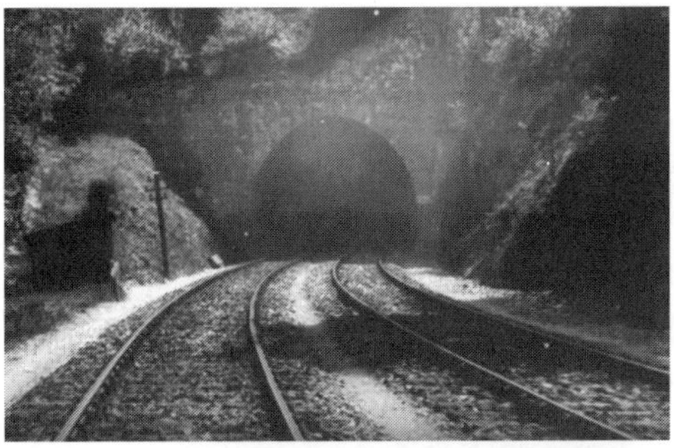

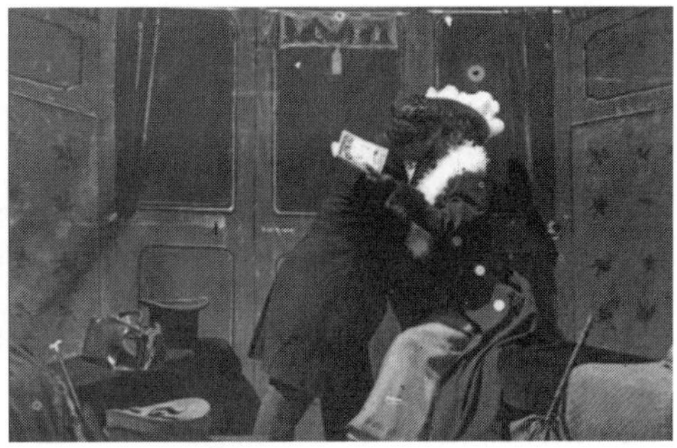

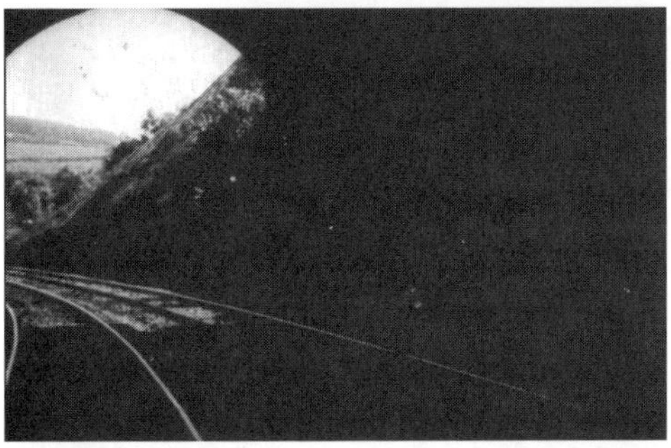

A Kiss in the Tunnel (1899), AG Smith's 38" phantom train ride film, consisted of three edits: a POV shot from atop train as it enters a tunnel, a kiss, and a POV shot of train exiting the tunnel.

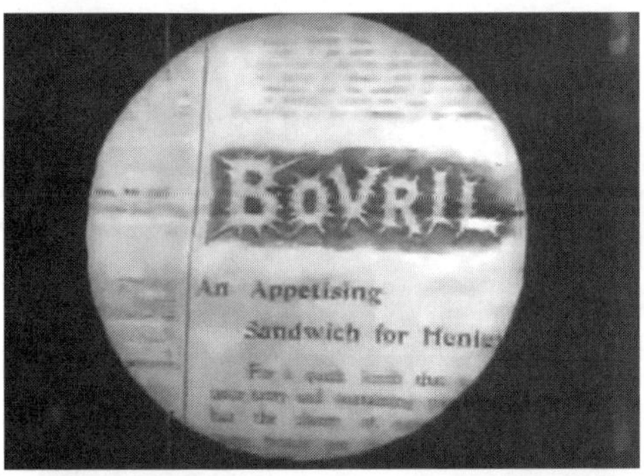

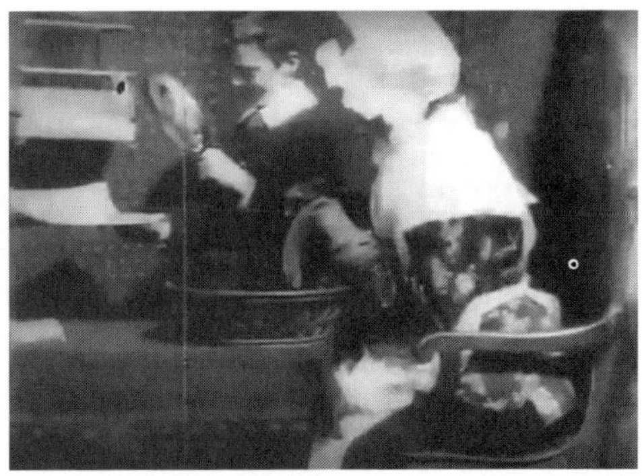

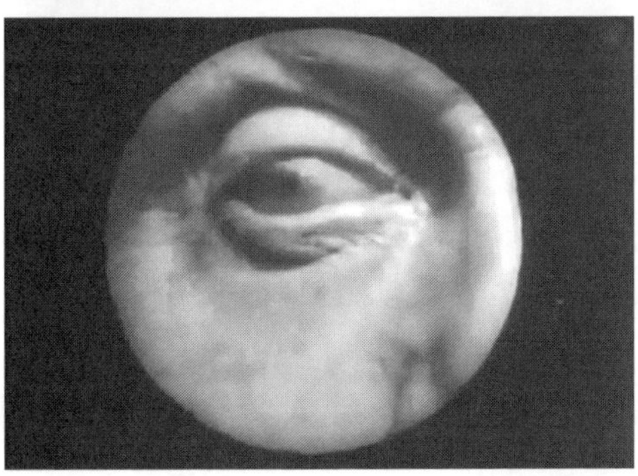

Grandma's Reading Glass (1:19) begins with a POV close-up of a newspaper ad as it follows the curiosity of a boy exploring his grandmother's world through her magnifying glass.

for a theatregoer sitting in an orchestra seat. In *Grandma's Reading Glass* (1900) Smith countered this, using a wide, stage shot intercut with close-ups and POV shots of a boy playing with his grandmother's looking glass.

FOUR PIONEER FILMMAKERS

Georges Méliès shoots for the moon

In 1902, one director shot a stage play film, forwarding editing and influencing directors and filmmakers to this day. The director was Georges Méliès and the film was *Le Voyage dans la Lune* (*A Trip to the Moon*). With nearly 400 films under his belt before starting, Méliès called on all the tricks and techniques he'd learned as a filmmaker, actor, illusionist, and stage producer.

In his glass walled and ceilinged studio constructed in a Paris suburb, Méliès labored for three months on mechanized stage sets, spending 10,000 francs to shoot this 14 minute sci fi spectacle—a big budget and lengthy film and production schedule for its time. He relied on mattes and multiple exposures throughout *A Trip to the Moon* to contrive different events such as a lunar snowstorm.

Editing

Méliès pioneered editing outside of the camera. He used substitution splices a.k.a. a stop trick or stop motion. This meant stopping the camera to reset the scene and achieve a transformation of some kind. He employed match cuts and color tinting to disguise these substitution splices so that the film's 50 plus edits are not always visible.

More importantly, the narrative of *Trip to the Moon* is both linear and nonlinear. Most of the story evolves linearly from one scene and set of real time actions to another. But Méliès covered the lunar landing itself, twice, in two nonlinear, instant replay scenes. First the bullet-shaped space capsule crashes onto the man moon face (an actor in a moon mask) in the film's most famous shot. Then the action repeats as the capsule comes to rest in the duff of the lunar terrain.

Reception

All Méliès' efforts paid off. Audiences worldwide were transported to the moon and back by his sci-fi fantasy. The French embraced the theatrical, exotically hand-tinted adventure, the antithesis of a black and white actualité. Americans loved it so much that producers, including Edison, broke copyright law to pirate it, siphoning off much of Méliès' Star Company's profits.

Impact

With *A Trip to the Moon* and other films such as *L'Affaire Dreyfus* (*The Dreyfus Affair*), Méliès enthralled audiences and influenced editing and his peers, notably directors Edwin S. Porter and D.W. Griffith who stated, "I owe him everything." In 2011, Martin Scorsese directed his first and only 3D feature, *Hugo,* an homage to Méliès' story, which included scenes from the film. Yet Méliès' career dwindled, his Star Company went

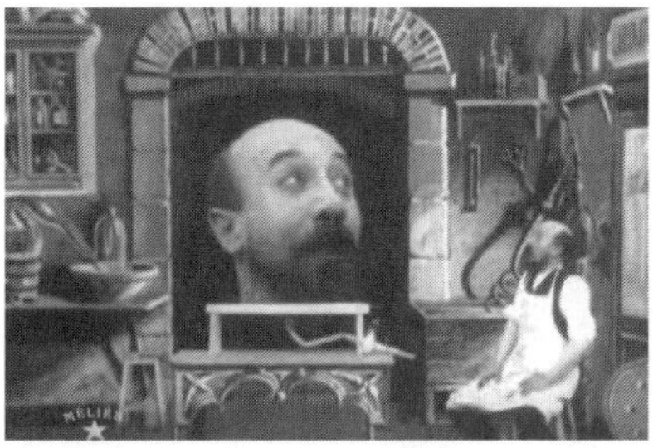

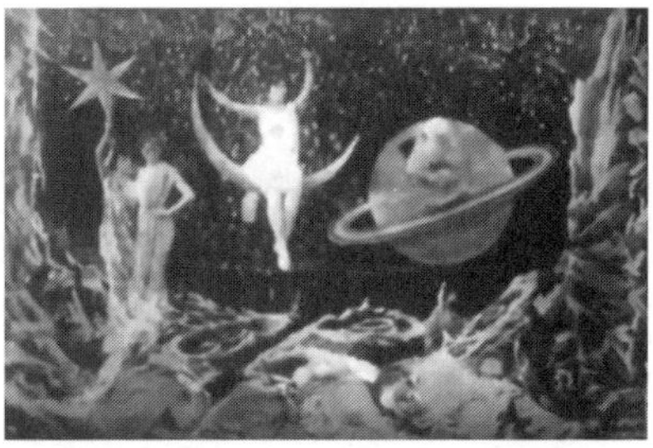

LEFT: Georges Méliès himself, directing and playing two parts in *The Man with the Rubber Head* (1902). **RIGHT:** Lunar snowstorm in Méliès' *A Trip to the Moon* (1902). Following earth rise, six astronomer-astronauts sleep as snow sifts down and other planets appear including a new moon.

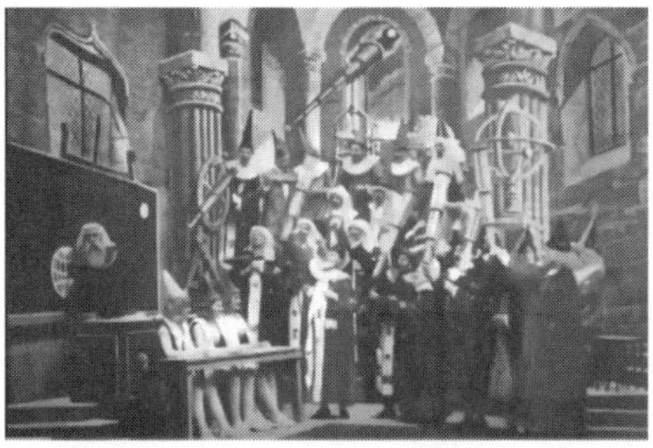

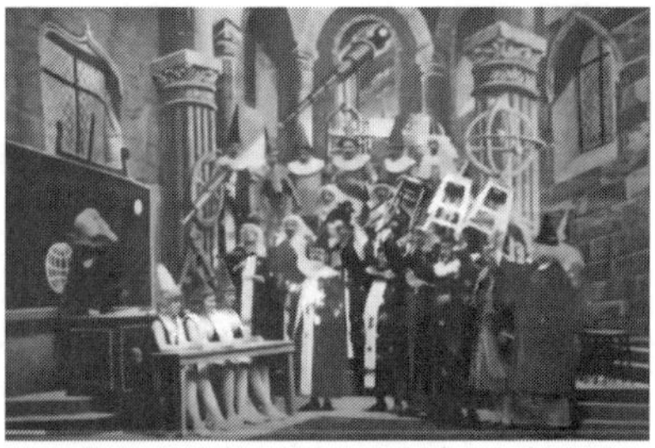

The head astronomer on the left (played by Méliès), directs the astronomers to raise their telescopes which then morph into chairs via a substitution splice combined with a match cut which Méliès achieved with scissors and glue in *A Trip to the Moon* (1902).

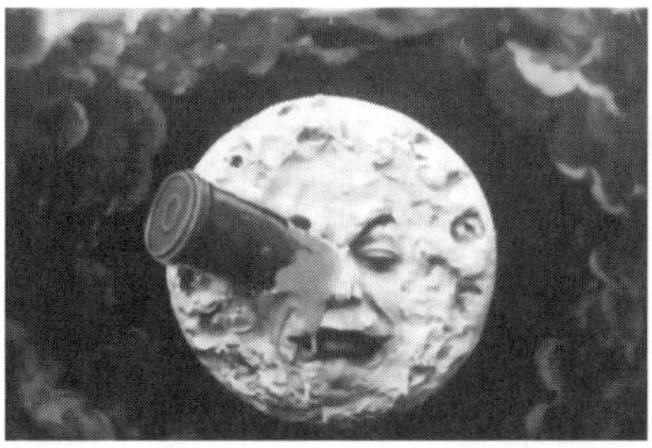

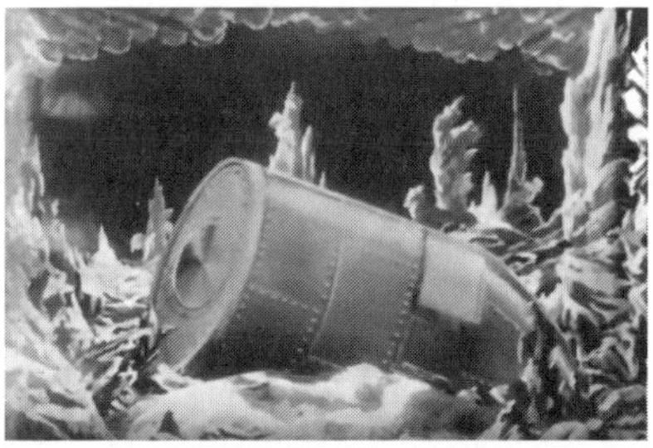

The iconic image from Méliès' *A Trip to the Moon* of a rocket landing with a splat on the eye of the man in the moon. The action repeats in a closer shot as the capsule plows into the moon's surface.

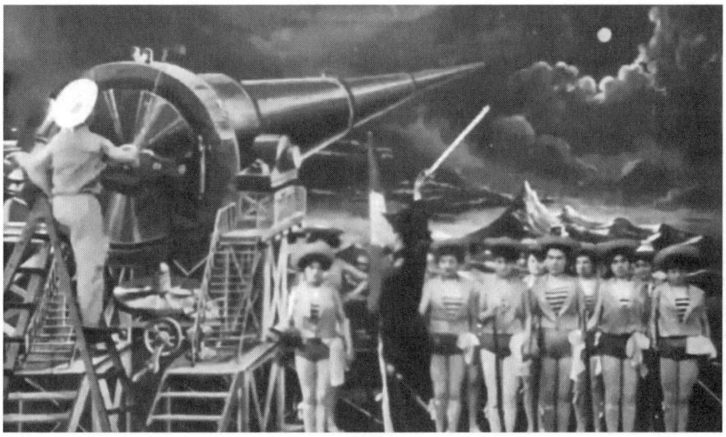

LEFT: Shooting for the moon: Preparing the launch vehicle—a giant telescoping cannon—for the moonshot in Méliès' film, *A Trip to the Moon*.

bankrupt, and he made his last film in 1913. For decades, prints of *A Trip to the Moon* deteriorated, were destroyed, or were believed lost as was the score Méliès had hired a composer for.* Then a couple of incomplete prints were located. Twelve years and a half million dollars later, a digitally restored print debuted at the opening night of Cannes in 2011 with a new score by Air. Although many films of Méliès and others from this early period are gone, the groundbreaking hard work that resulted in *A Trip to the Moon* has been preserved.

Alice Guy Blaché adds narrative

When the Lumière Brothers unveiled their Cinématographe and screened their first film at an industrial event in March, 1895 in Paris, a 21-year-old secretary observed the demonstration. She then scrutinized the films her employer, the Gaumont Film Company, was churning out. She went to Léon Gaumont, her boss and founder of the company, and told him she could do better. Gaumont assented, but only if she kept up with her secretarial duties. In 1896, that secretary, Alice Guy-Blaché, shot *La Fée aux Choux* (*The Cabbage Fairy*), a single shot 48" film on her lunch hour. It charmed audiences and Blaché became Gaumont's head of production, directing 300 films and supervising 300 more. By 1910, she'd relocated from Paris to Fort Lee, New Jersey, a then booming film town on the Palisades across from Manhattan, and founded Solax Company, a state-of-the-art studio, where she made another 325 films.

In those early days, the director commonly did everything: write, shoot, direct, edit, and project. Blaché acted too, but she did not shoot and always hired camera operators, the first director to do so. She directed films of all genres and budgets from comedy, actualités, and Westerns, to dance, vampires, suspense, and religious dramas. She made films sympathetic to abused women, immigrants, and Jews along with *A Fool and His Money* (1912), generally acknowledged as the first narrative film about African Americans.

Editing contribution

Blaché was the first female director and studio founder and a film pioneer. She used Gaumont's Chronophone** to create 100 early sound films and employed the special effects tricks of the day such as mattes and double exposure. Additionally, she ran film backwards, used depth of field ahead of the Americans, and cut in dramatic close-ups and reverse angles. But what set her apart from other director/editors, and caused Gaumont to promote her, was her adaptation of fictional storytelling to film narrative.

* Almost from the beginning, "silent films"—those shot without sound from the mid-1890s to the late 1920s—were not intended to be viewed in silence. Many were narrated or had dialogue voiced by actors behind the screen, and most were accompanied by a pianist who used sheet music or improvised. Luckier audiences enjoyed the stylings of the "Mighty Wurlitzer" organ which could imitate an orchestra or simulate sound effects such as galloping horses, gunshots, thunder, lightning, and more. As films became popular, studios sent out composed scores to city venues for small orchestras.

** Sound was pre-recorded on the Chronophone's wax cylinders and then synced to the film.

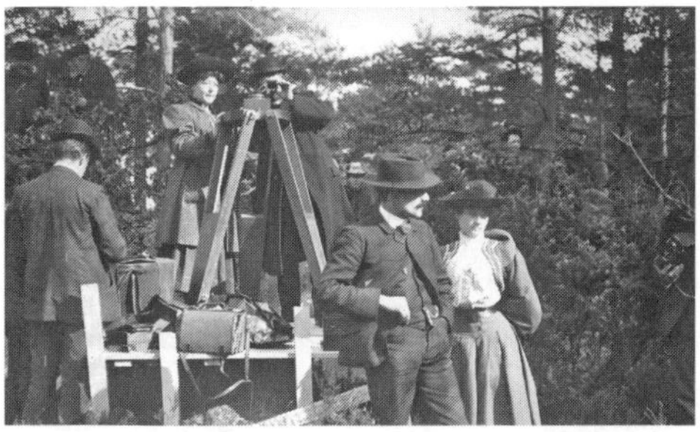

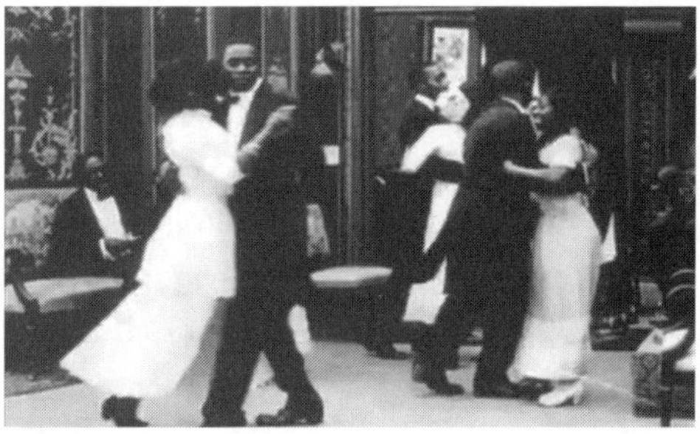

LEFT: Alice Guy Blaché directing at Solax, her studio in Fort Lee, NJ circa 1911-1913. *Photo courtesy of Ally Acker, Reel Women Media.* **RIGHT:** White actors balked at working with black actors, so in 1912, Blaché filmed *A Fool and His Money* with an entirely black cast.

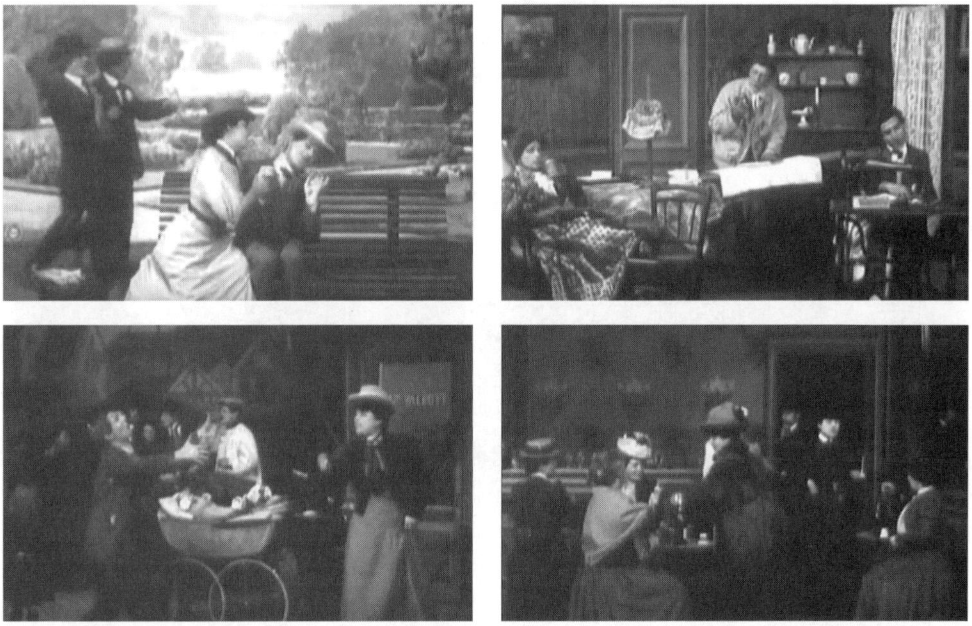

Les Résultats du Féminisme (The Consequences of Feminism). In this 1906 social satire, Blaché reversed gender roles: women pursued men, lounged around at home, were beseeched by their pram-wheeling husbands to stop drinking and come home, and enjoyed each other's company, in a women only bar.

Blaché was attuned to the audience, the story, and the way it was told. The mother of film narrative, she crafted movies with realistic characters that audiences believed.

Alas, as with Méliès, Blaché's career had a premature end. As the industry moved to California, she was forced to sell Solax. She shot her last film in 1919 and relocated to Hollywood, which shut her out, along with other female directors such as Lois Weber*. In 1953, France presented Blaché with the Légion d'honneur, the country's highest non-military award. In 2011, lobbied by the Fort Lee Film Commission, the Directors Guild of America (DGA) posthumously bestowed membership to Blaché and granted

* Weber, who also took on social issues and was the first U.S. female to direct a feature film and start her own studio, directed over 100 films, trailblazed the split screen effect, and died in poverty.

her a Special Directorial Award for Lifetime Achievement, which Martin Scorsese presented, along with a tribute.

Edwin S. Porter—Cross-cuts

By 1905, the Lumière Brothers had stopped making films and had divested themselves of their film accoutrements to pursue other inventions. Edison occupied himself more with securing patents on his inventions. After being judged in violation of anti-trust laws in 1918, he sold his company and got out of the movie business but not before launching the career of Edwin S. Porter.

Porter's trajectory mirrored Méliès' and Blaché's: He shot the first of his 250 films in 1901 and the last in 1915, becoming a popular filmmaker and making vital contributions to editing, then declining, as the freewheeling DIY days of filmmaking gave way to a standardized industry. Porter created a succession of crowd pleasers starting with *The Great Train Robbery* in 1903, a 12 minute one-reeler,* a long movie for its time. It was the first Western (though it was shot in northern New Jersey and looks it) and exhibits some trailblazing editing.

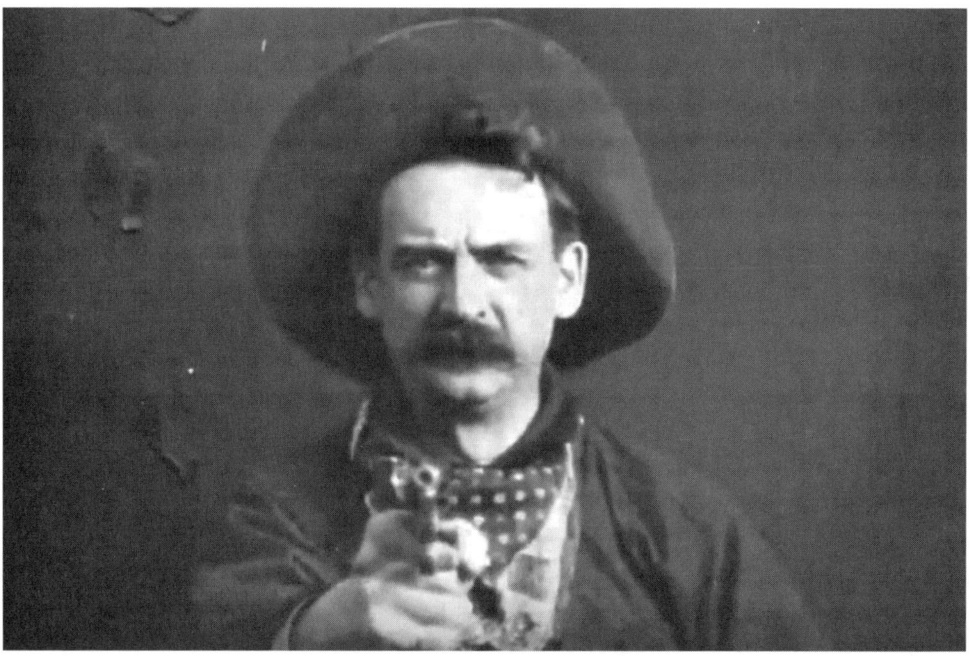

Porter's *The Great Train Robbery* (1903) began or ended (according to the theatre owner's whim) with this medium shot of a bandit in a hand tinted polka dot kerchief and green shirt, shooting at the audience.

* A thousand feet of 35mm, or slightly more, was all a projection reel could hold then. A one-reeler ran 10-12 minutes. Shows were measured in reels: One-reeler, two-reeler, etc. A four-reeler was called a feature as it was the main show: In 1914, U.S. audiences could see over 400 features.

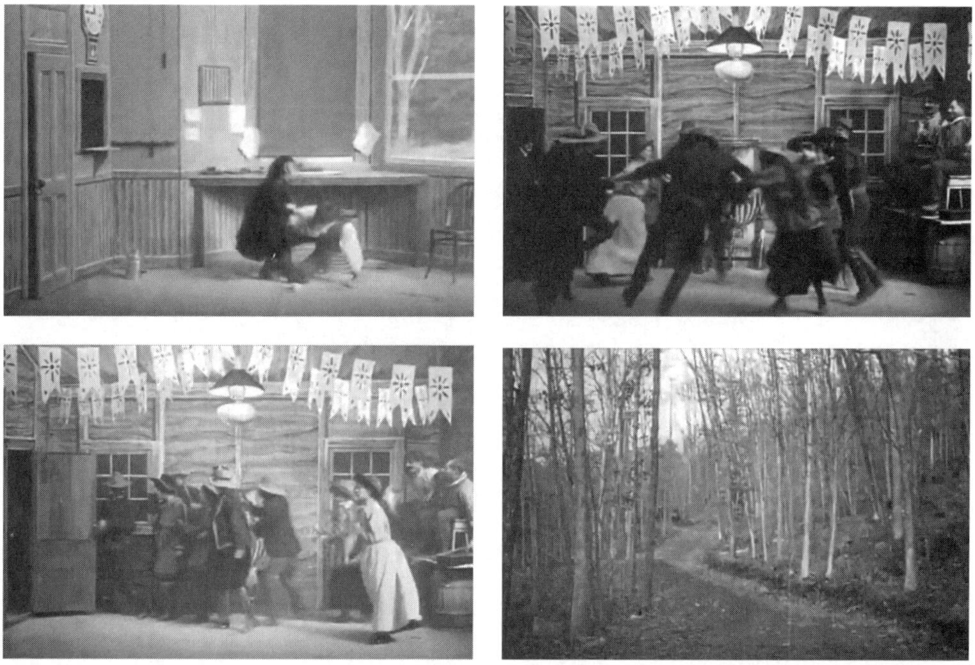

Primitive cross-cutting in *The Great Train Robbery* (1903). Frame 1: After being tied up by the robbers and unbound by his daughter, a telegraph operator rises to alert law enforcement of the train heist. Porter cross-cuts to a dance hall (Frame 2) where after a full 10" of dancing, the telegraph operator enters. Once every last member of the instantly formed posse exits (Frame 3), he cuts to the bandits (at the top of Frame 4) galloping down the hill with the posse (after another 10") in pursuit.

Splicing edits

Film splicers had been around since films were first exhibited in the 1890s, created for and often by projectionists to string the era's single-shot films into full programs. The projectionist could scissor out the very first shot in *The Great Train Robbery* and splice it at the end, depending on where the theatre owner chose to give moviegoers a fright. Either way, it stood out as the only close shot in the movie and broke the fourth wall by showing an outlaw firing a shot directly at the audience.

Creating action and cross-cutting

The Great Train Robbery stands out for other editorial reasons. While there are no cuts within its fourteen linear scenes and each scene, whether an interior or exterior is a wide shot, Porter varied the angles, performed a few short slow pans and tilts, and moved the actors around to create more action within the frame. Most significantly in terms of editing, he shortened time between scenes, creating some of the first cross-cuts,* though basic and slow placed.

* A cross-cut occurs when you edit two (or more) dependent lines of action together—characters, settings, or subjects—that interact directly and are aware of each other.

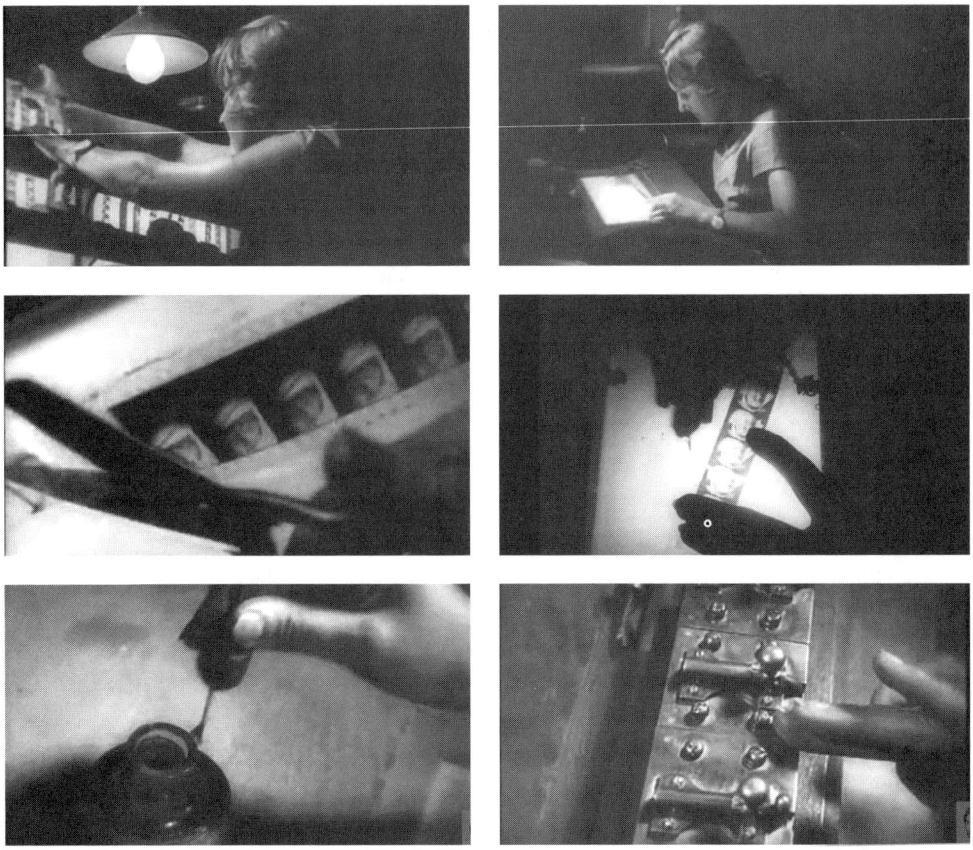

The painstaking work of selecting a shot, viewing it over a light well, scissoring it, and scraping the emulsion off a frame in preparation for gluing it to the previous shot in the splicer is depicted in the documentary *Man with a Movie Camera* (1929).

D.W. Griffith films the first full length feature

Now the public was flocking to the flickers,* absorbing shifts in time and place with fewer interstitials (title and narration cards), and ripe for longer, narrative films. The novelty of one-shot films and scenes was wearing thin, just as filmmaking was transitioning into a structured industry with budgets, schedules, departments, and department heads. The first editors were young men who scissor cut the negative film right out of the camera, clipping out the slates and the fogged frames. There were no editing machines. Directors viewed the film with a magnifying glass or over a light box and made notes for cuts and interstitials.

Early editors

As the business developed beginning around 1910, camera operators and directors were required to be on the set at all times. Directors stopped editing their films. Film

* Films flickered on the screen in the early days for several reasons including: 1) Rudimentary projector shutters and lamps. 2) Projectors being hand cranked (as were cameras). 3) Different film stocks of varied fps.

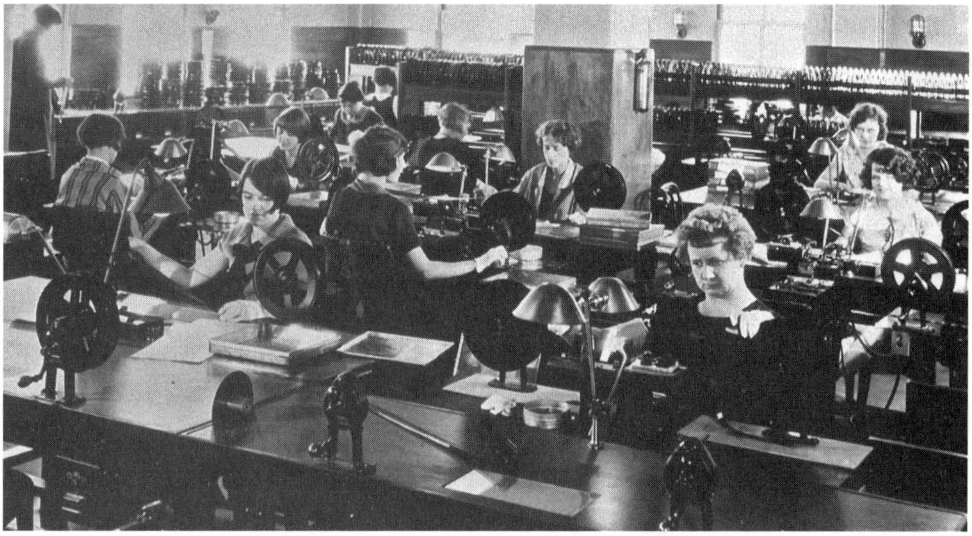

Film patchers a.k.a. film joiners in the back rooms of the newly regimented film industry. *Photo courtesy of Ally Acker, Reel Women Media.*

labs began striking positive prints and women were hired for the tedious, eye-splitting, low paying labor of cutting. Called patchers or joiners, they cut and joined scenes by hand, winding through hundreds of feet of film to locate shots, or as time went on, referring to a continuity script they'd created on set. Dailies began to be projected after the day's shoot.

One director who screened and essentially edited in a small theater with a projection booth was DW Griffith. Pausing a frame of film in a projector could set the booth on fire due to the nitrate base of 35mm then. So, when Griffith spied a cut point, he buzzed the booth and a projectionist marked the point by inserting a piece of paper into the take-up reel. In this manner along with two editors in the theater, he screened and edited the world's first 12-reeler, the three-hour long *Birth of a Nation* (titled *The Clansman* until near release). Reprehensible for its fabrication of Reconstruction history and racist view of miscegenation, the film would be forgotten today, if it weren't for its editing techniques and influence on future features.

Griffith's editing

Griffith employed multiple angles—overheads, reverses, close shots, side angles—and intercut them as no one had before. His intercutting of *The Battle of Bull Run* gives an engrossing "you are there" feeling. In a soberly scored segment which starts with a title card "War's Peace," he interweaves static, blue-tinted shots of corpses with active, red-tinted flashbacks of the battle.

Griffith picked up the pace of film narrative by tightening cuts—using fewer frames to end one cut and start the next—which shortened actions and time. He also made

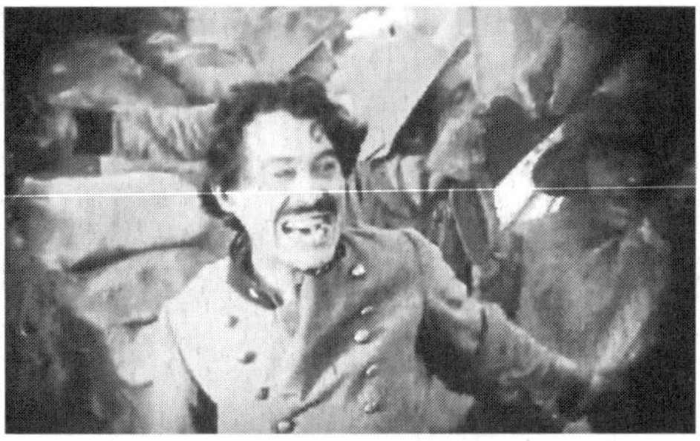

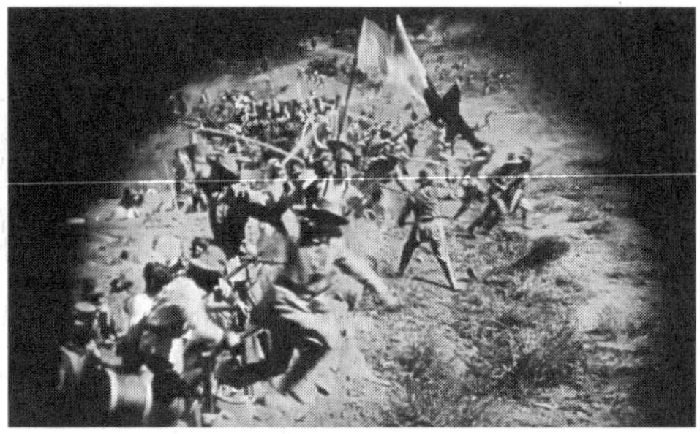

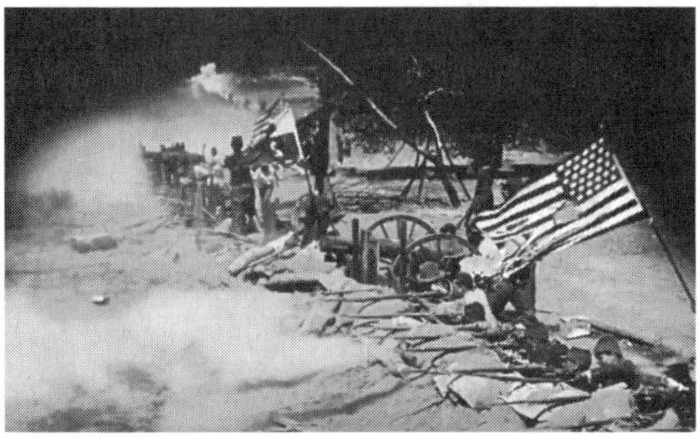

The son of a Confederate colonel, Griffith dramatized the chaos and pathos of war like no one before him, in *Birth of a Nation* (1915).

tighter and more frequent cross-cuts than his predecessors, cross-cutting between not only scenes but between shots. A major addition to editing and storytelling was his match cutting on movement, a.k.a. an action match. Griffith match cut mundane movements e.g., characters' entrances and exits as well as climactic actions such as when John Wilkes Booth cocks his pistol and prepares to assassinate President Lincoln. Today action match cuts are routine, and they continue to tighten as audiences grasp information ever more quickly.

Birth of a Nation aftermath

Despite protests by civil rights groups, politicians, and newspapers and being banned in three states, *Birth of a Nation* was a blockbuster and played a part in the resurgence of the KKK. In addition, it was the first film to include an intermission and to list editors—still called cutters—in the end credits. Griffith made a few more hit features—none as successful as *Birth of a Nation*—then he was left behind, as the Hollywood studio system took over and independent directors lost their clout.

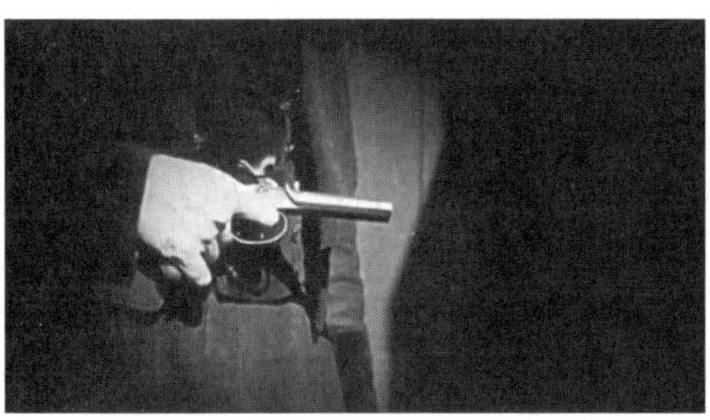

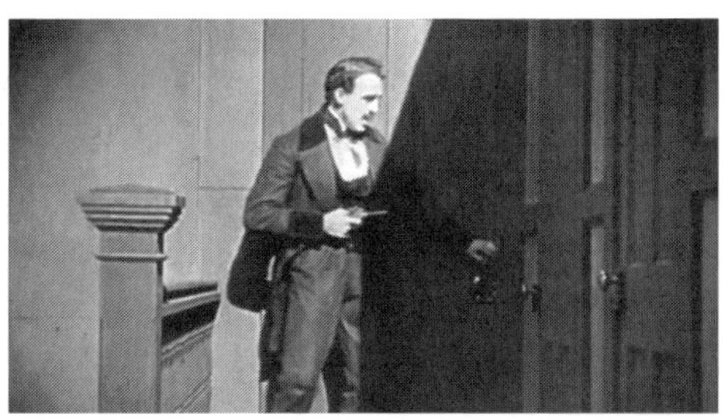

In this action match cut, John Wilkes Booth prepares to carry out his infamous deed. *Birth of a Nation.*

THE 1920S: THE FILM INDUSTRY TAKES ROOT

Hollywood

In the 1920s, as Hollywood boomed and companies consolidated, the filmmaking process was systematized, and its tools refined. Cameras became lighter, allowing for more free-roaming shots and editors got their first editing machine.

Moviola debuts

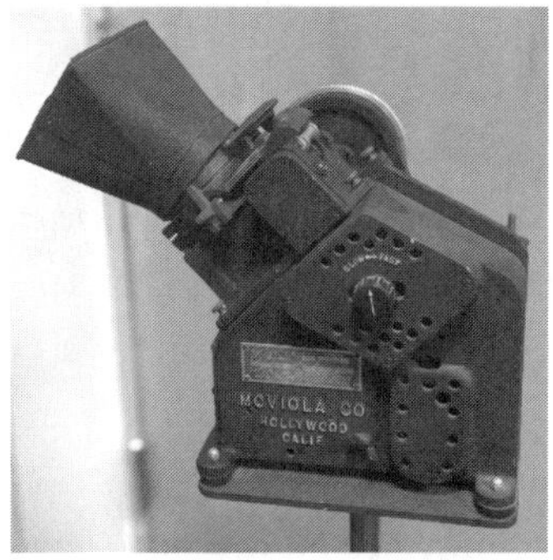

Early Moviola pre sound. *Photo courtesy of Sharon Smith Holley.*

In 1924, an electrical engineer, Iwan Serrurier, happened by a room of patchers and was inspired to improve their work lives. He outfitted a small, hand-cranked machine with two reels, a viewing lens, and a lamp house and bolted it to a bench, deriving its name from the Victrola. He sold the first Moviola to Douglas Fairbanks for $125.

Although it made a racket and sometimes chewed the film (like all later models), cutters instantly took to the Moviola because they could: 1) Stop on a frame and mark cut points with a grease pencil. 2) View footage more easily and at different speeds, which made for better scene pacing. 3) Become one with the footage and crank out (literally!) more and better movies. A few editors, notably Robert Wise and Orson Welles, considered the Moviola a musical instrument orchestrating the rhythm of films.

Audience and editing

By 1920, editors and audiences alike were discovering the language of film. They were appreciating establishing shots for their setting of locale and time, reacting to the emotion telegraphed by close shots, grasping reverse angles and cross-cutting between people, places and time periods, enjoying colorization for its look and mood accentuation, and growing accustomed to iris ins at the start of scenes, dissolves, and other basic transition effects. Editing was slowly transitioning from being a background player to a major influencer of the finished film.

Enter the Russians to shake it all up and add theory.

Russian revolt

> The crazy Russians started f*ing around with images and juxtaposing them, and creating different emotional effects. —**QUENTIN TARANTINO**, writer/director, *Once Upon A Time... in Hollywood, Pulp Fiction, Reservoir Dogs*

The 1917 Russian Revolution terminated Czarist rule and replaced it with a Bolshevik ideology that nationalized every segment of society including filmmaking. The new

Soviet state was long on propaganda and short on resources such as film stock. Teachers at the Moscow Film School—founded in 1919 and the first in the world—had to be creative when training the next generation. Students took apart and re-cut American movies. They studied D.W. Griffith. They shot with short ends. The result was Soviet Montage Theory, which emphasized how pieces of film were put together to compose a film and how this editing impacted the proletarian audience who needed educating in Bolshevik beliefs. Soviet filmmakers believed that individual shots when edited together created a larger meaning—that the whole is greater than the sum of its parts.

Kuleshov effect

With their school and films, the Soviets began proving their theories. One teacher, Lev Kuleshov, conducted an experiment with leftover film. He intercut three shots—a bowl of steaming soup, a girl in a coffin, and a languorous woman on a chaise longue—with a deadpan close-up of a man (a popular white Russian actor who had fled). Kuleshov's audience made a connection between each pair of shots: They thought the man was hungry seeing the soup, sad after seeing the dead girl, and amorous after seeing the woman. In actuality, the reaction shot of the man was the same shot cut in three times. Kuleshov's experiment, repeated by other filmmakers and psychologists over the years, reached the same conclusion: Viewers infer meaning from shots edited together, regardless if the meaning was intended.

Eisenstein

Another teacher at the state school, Sergei Eisenstein, built on Kuleshov's theories, and famously wrote his own montage treatises, and then made films based on them. Eisenstein's montage theory combined the Hegelian Dialectic—thesis, antithesis, synthesis—with Marxist philosophy: Czar oppresses workers, workers revolt, Czar represses revolt, but workers win more for their cause. Eisenstein thought shots should be juxtaposed to collide against each other and ensure that the audience fully feel the frames. Eisenstein's legendary Odessa Steps sequence in *Battleship Potemkin* (1925) with the drumming cadence of the advancing soldiers, contrasting with the teetering roll of the baby carriage, perfectly illustrates his beliefs.

Vertov

Dziga Vertov formed Kino-Eye (cine eye), a production company which aimed to capture Kino-Pravda (cine truth) by showing everyday life—unstaged, unacted, and untitled. Vertov, his fellow kinoks (camera-eye men), and his editor (his wife) accomplished their goal in 1929 with his masterpiece, *Man with a Movie Camera*. Shot over three years in Kiev, Moscow, and Odessa, the film documents urban life and runs 68

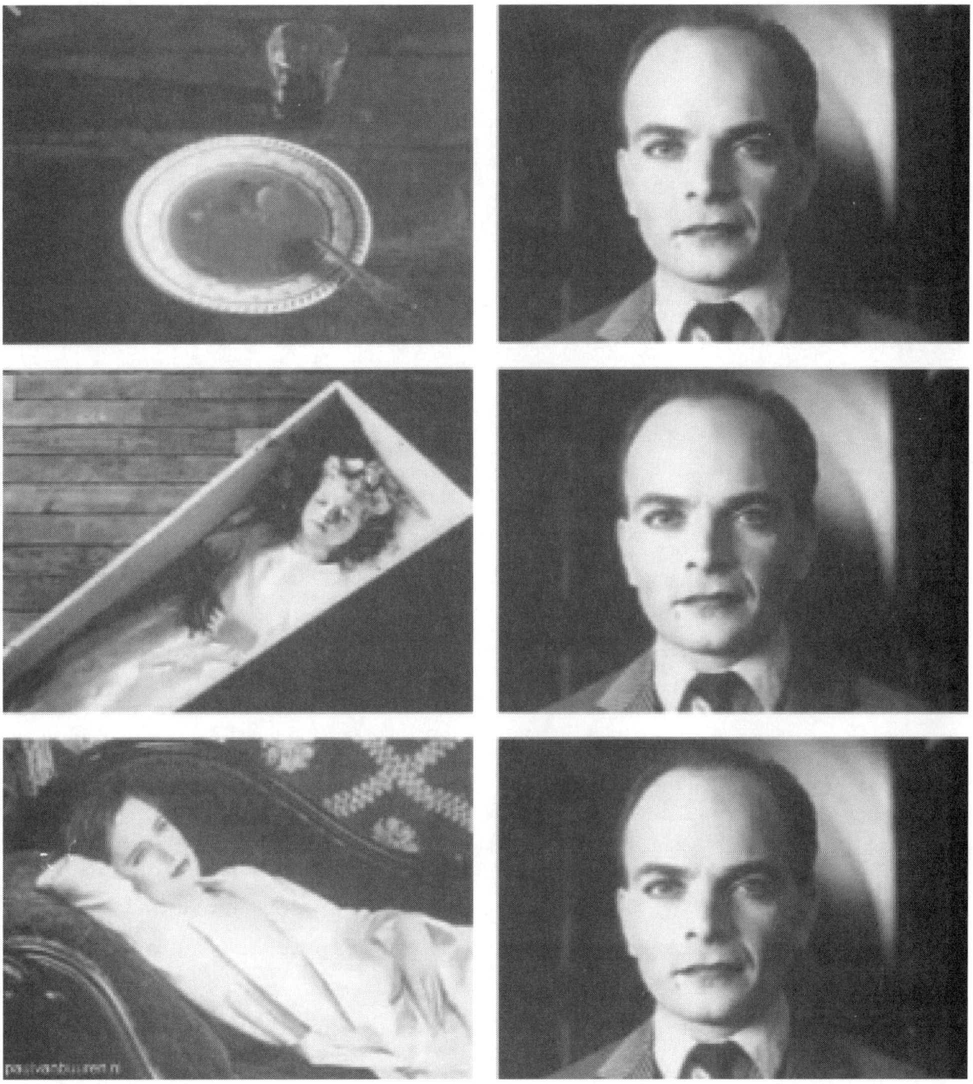

Kuleshov Effect: With these six frames, Kuleshov famously demonstrated that shots take their meaning from being intercut with other shots, regardless of when and where the shots were filmed.

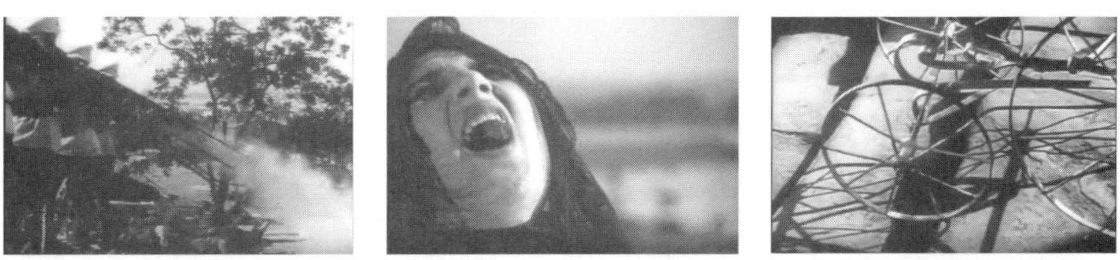

These three cuts in the Odessa Steps sequence from *Battleship Potemkin* (1925) were directed and edited by Eisenstein and demonstrate his montage theory: The soldiers shoot the mother who while dying, lets go of her baby carriage which lurches down the steps, setting off a frenzy of reactions from fleeing bystanders.

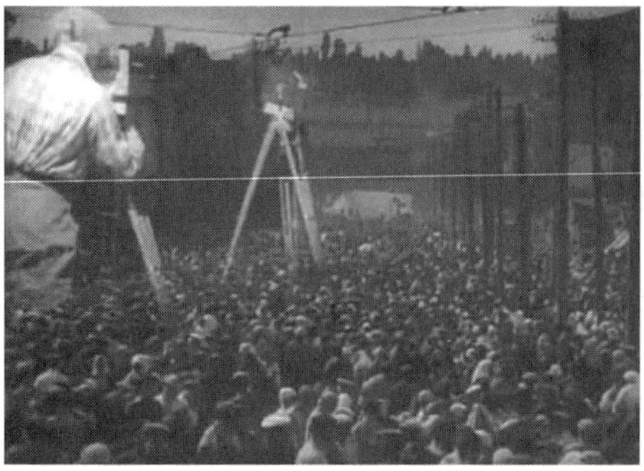
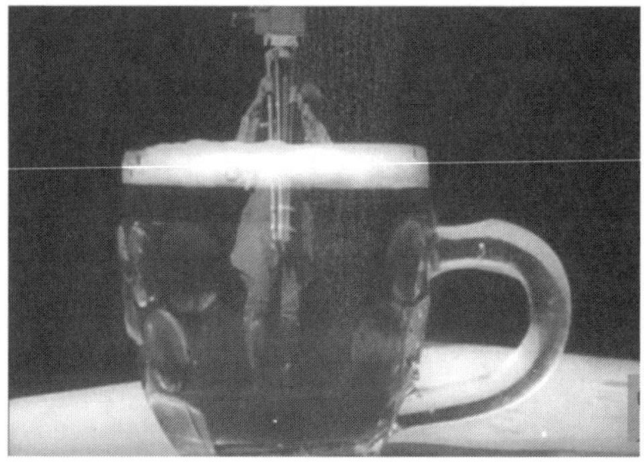
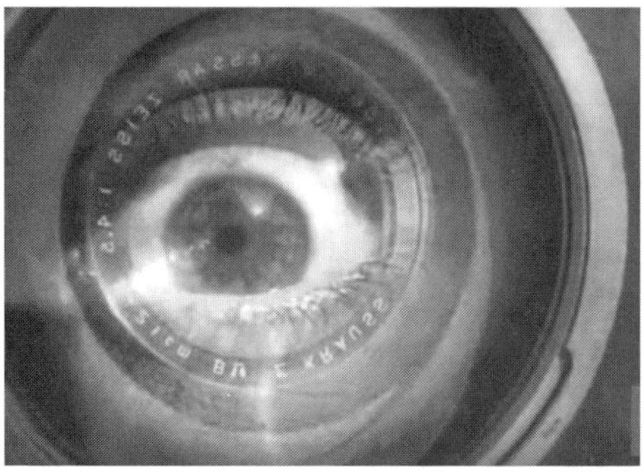

Vertov inserted the cameraman cranking the camera into *Man with a Movie Camera* (1929) to expose filmmaking, and demonstrate that it is work like every other vocation. The middle frame of the cameraman in a beer mug initiated a beer hall sequence. The last frame, a Kino-eye rising out of the camera's shutter, ends the movie.

minutes. Its avant-garde style anticipates Leni Riefenstahl's Nazi propaganda films in the 1930s, French Cinéma vérité in the 1950s, and modern music videos.

Man with a Movie Camera has a musical pacing that builds, ebbs, and flows with staccatos, rests, frenzied sections, and parts that breathe normally, like ordinary life. The film accomplishes this pacing with freeze frames, stop motion animation, speed ups, black flash frames, split screens, and varying angles (overhead, low, and tilted). Vertov also employed multiple exposures, different types of match cuts, such as action and shape matches, and repeating frames. The ASL (average shot length) in 1929 was 11.2"; today it's 2.5". *Man with a Movie Camera* had an ASL of 2.3".

In addition to its superlative scenes which range from recording childbirth to documenting death, divorce, marriage, work life, and recreation, the film integrates the making of the filming process into the film itself, revealing the cameraman shooting, the editor editing, the projectionist operating the projector, and the theatre audience watching.

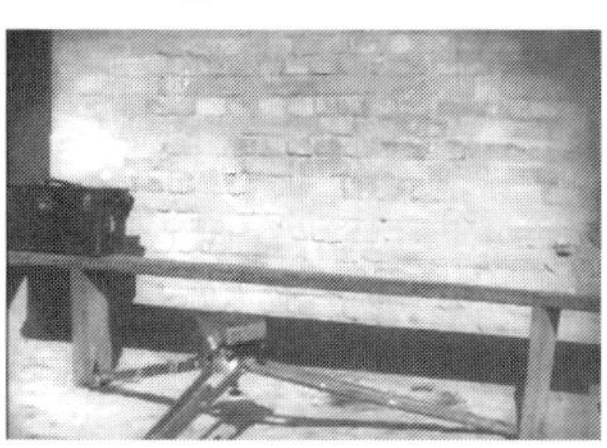
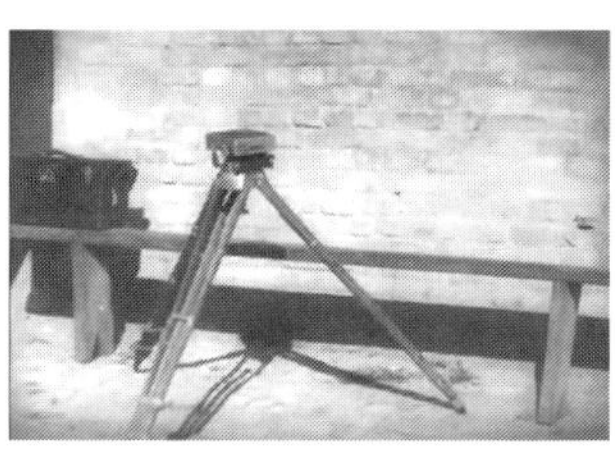
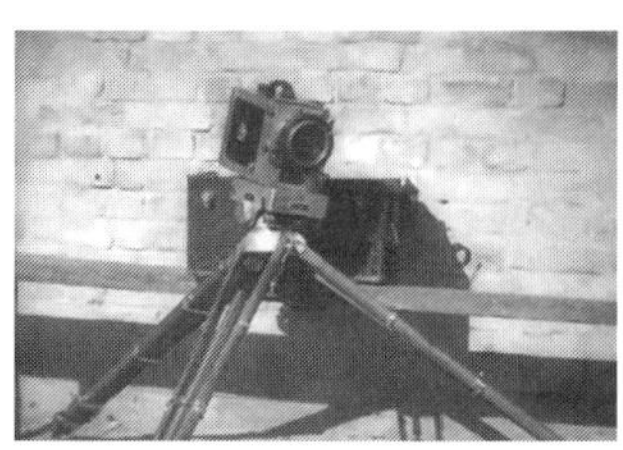

Camera sticks grow and acquire a camera in this stop motion sequence from *Man with a Movie Camera* (1929).

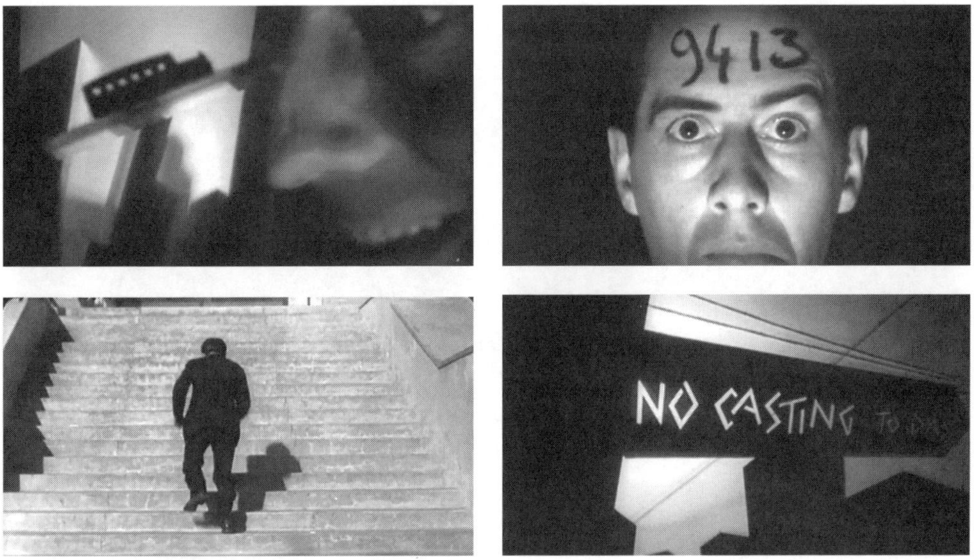

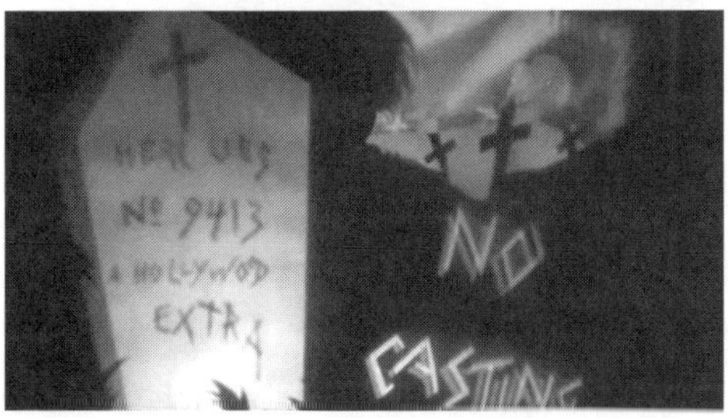

Director Robert Florey, editor Slavko Vorkapich, and cinematographer Gregg Toland collaborated on this 1928 expressionist short, *The Life and Death of 9413: A Hollywood Extra.* Using miniatures, repeated shots of the character trying to climb the stairway to success, action match cuts, split screens, multiple exposures, and LA exteriors they spent $97 ($1,415 today). Set to "Rhapsody in Blue," it was both avant-garde and popular.

THE 1930S

Hollywood

Meanwhile, back in the epicenter of movie making, genres were becoming established: comedy, drama, gangster, horror, musical, romance, suspense, war epic, western, and a new category—Hollywood on Hollywood.

You ain't heard nothing yet

Technicolor was advancing in the late 1920s, but more significantly, a technology that would dramatically change everything was materializing. Sound! Engineers had been trying to marry audio to film since the 1890s but were stymied by perfecting sound that would stay in sync with the picture and that could be recorded reliably and easily, edited efficiently, and heard clearly in theatres.

In 1927, a few sound films were ready for release. One film allowed viewers to see and hear the sound effects of Charles Lindbergh's taking off from New York on the world's first transatlantic flight; a second, F.W. Murnau's drama *Sunrise,* treated them to sound effects and music. These films were popular, but the smash hit was *The Jazz*

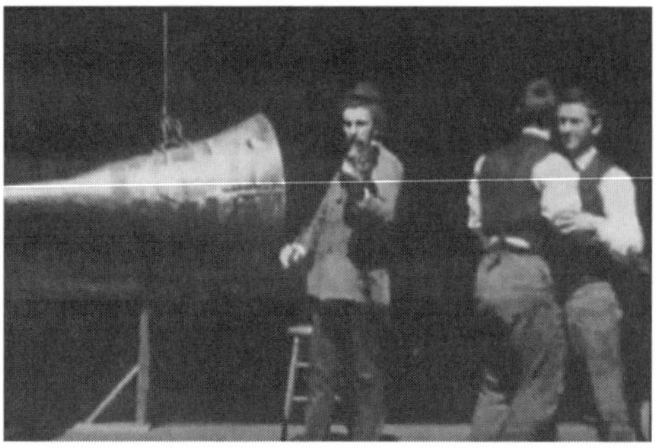

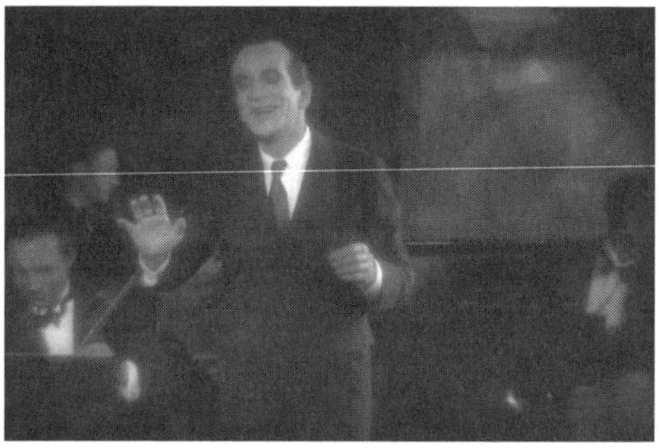

LEFT: In 1894 Laurie Dickson made a 17" test film of Edison's Kinetophone, recording a violinist playing a folk tune into a metal cone—the mic—and recording it onto a wax cylinder. Seventy years later the original cylinder was rediscovered and in 1998 Academy award winning sound editor Walter Murch re-synced the sound on digital equipment. **RIGHT:** Al Jolson utters the famous first words "Wait a minute. Wait a minute. You ain't heard nothing yet," in *The Jazz Singer* (1927).

Singer, the first feature to show people talking. The first words audiences heard were Al Jolson's character promising a cabaret crowd, "Wait a minute. Wait a minute. You ain't heard nothing yet." Released in two audio versions—with sound on a record and sound on film—this first "talkie" delivered only two dialogue scenes but snared audiences' ears and tastes, changing films, filmmaking, and editing forever.

At first, shooting these popular dialogue scenes proved problematic, due to the recording equipment's stationary mics which required stationary actors and cameras. Every set had a "Monitor Man," the sound recordist who gave a thumbs up or down to each take. These drawbacks were mitigated by innovative workarounds such as the sound blimp and the barney, which were overcome by technical advances within a year or two. But initially they caused some film critics to disparage talkies over "silent" films and predict that talkies were a passing fad.

Enter sound editors

The Moviola, now run by an electrical motor, was updated with a magnetic sound head and a built-in speaker to play reels of picture and sound via electrified foot pedals. Sound was recorded on the edge of the film as an optical track read by the exciter lamp in the projector, making 24fps the uniform frame rate. More meaningfully, the advent of sound created new editing rooms for new jobs: sound editing! Now there was dialogue, sound effects, and music to add, edit and mix. There was also vocal doubling (shortened to "dubbing") for foreign films, looping* to replace dialogue lines that were flubbed or technically compromised, and Foley**. Sound editors deciphered sound by ear and by eye, learning to read the squiggles on the optical track to make their cuts.

* The sound editor made three film loops—a picture loop, a guide loop (with the line to be replaced), and the record loop (for recording the actor speaking the replacement line). Looping is called ADR (Automatic Dialogue Replacement) today and is a digital process.

** Sound effects recorded during post to sync with specific actions on screen such as footsteps. Named after its inventor, director Jack Foley.

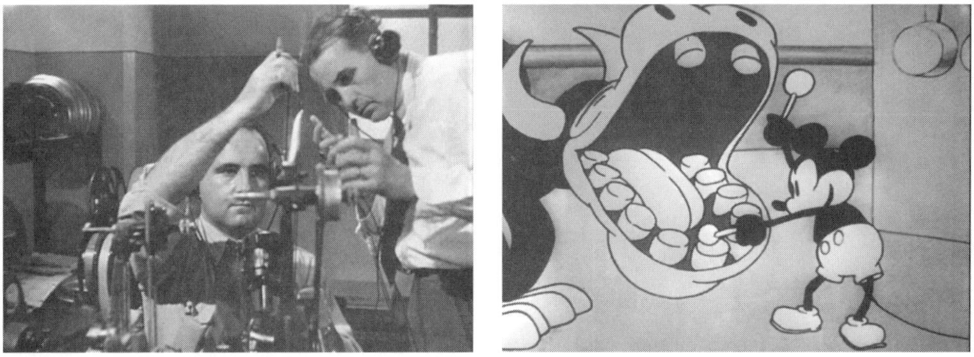

LEFT: Early sound editing. *Making Waves: The Art of Cinematic Sound* (2019). **RIGHT:** Mickey Mouse makes his debut in *Steamboat Willie* (1928), 7:46 long.

Early sound movies and theatres

In 1928, Mickey Mouse made his debut in Walt Disney's *Steamboat Willie,* a "sound cartoon" as the end title card reads. It was the first film to use voice (animal grunts and sounds), sound effects, and music that were all created during postproduction, the standard for all animated films since.

By 1930, half the movie theatres in the U.S. were fitted for sound with the record system losing out to sound on film. Led by Hitchcock, Welles, Lang, and other directors who swiftly grasped and implemented sound's power, the decade saw the development of sound's abilities to tell stories and reveal people's inner thoughts and emotions.

Awards for editing

The Biltmore Hotel in downtown Los Angeles hosted the seventh Academy Awards ceremony in 1935. For the first time, an award was given for (picture) editing: Conrad Nervig, *Eskimo,* beat out Anne Bauchens for the first *Cleopatra* epic. It would take another 28 years until sound editing was recognized: In 1963, Walter Elliott won Best Sound Effects Editing (category later renamed Sound Editing) for *It's a Mad, Mad, Mad, Mad World.* In 1937, two picture editors and a sound editor formed the Society of Motion Picture Film Editors, known today as the Editors Guild or more precisely as IATSE Local 700. The initial guild consisted of 571 picture and sound editors, along with assistants, apprentices, and film librarians.

T S E I A 700

The Editor's Guild logo a.k.a. the union bug for IATSE Local 700. IATSE (International Alliance of Theatre Stage Employees Moving Picture Technicians, Artists and Allied Crafts) formed in 1893 to represent stagehands. The IA, an umbrella union of cinematographers, gaffers, props, etc., boasts 140,000 members and growing.

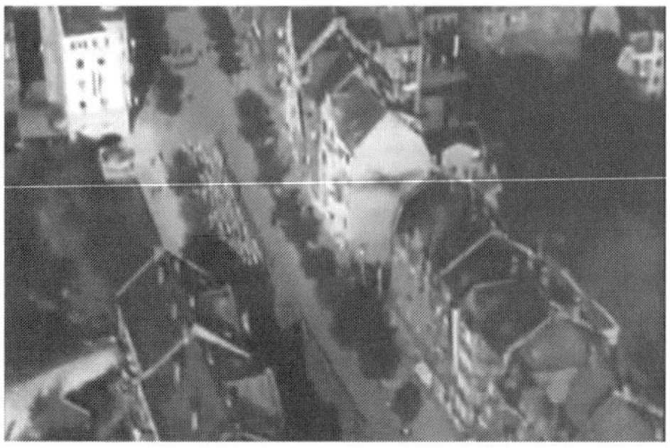

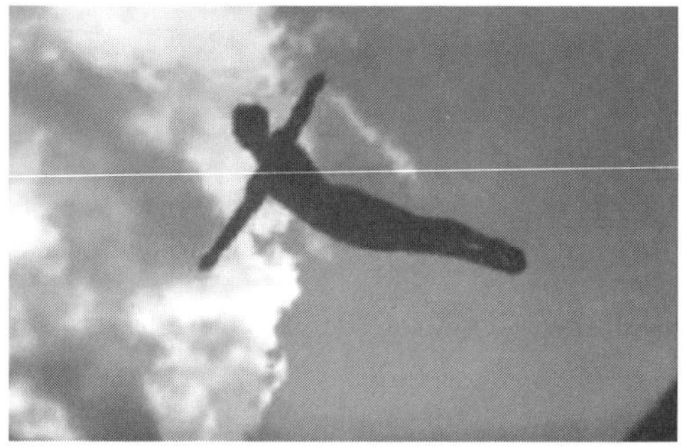

LEFT: Hitler's plane descends on Nuremberg, sending a shadow in the form of a cross onto the white side of a tall building in *Triumph of the Will* (1934). **RIGHT:** A diver-god framed against the clouds from *Olympia*. Despite Riefenstahl's acclaimed filmmaking and her undying protests that her allegiance was to film, not the Fuhrer, her collaborations with Nazis on five films proved the downfall of her career.

German propaganda

The 1930s also saw newsreels become a staple in movie theatres and the rise of propaganda films created by director-editor Leni Riefenstahl. In 1934, a Nazi rally in Nuremberg was staged for her to shoot *Triumph des Willens, (Triumph of the Will).* With the nation's resources at her disposal—crew, cameras, architect, and Hilter's input—she delivered a documentary that artistically elevated the Fuhrer to a Christian messiah (he arrives through the parting of clouds in a plane, which gives off a cruciform shadow), and helped unify Germans for his Third Reich regime. In 1936, Riefenstahl documented the Berlin Olympic games in *Olympia*. In its famous high dive sequence, she intercut competition and staged footage, besting Busby Berkeley's swim numbers, and creating a balletic series of swan dives punctuated by slo-mo splashdowns.

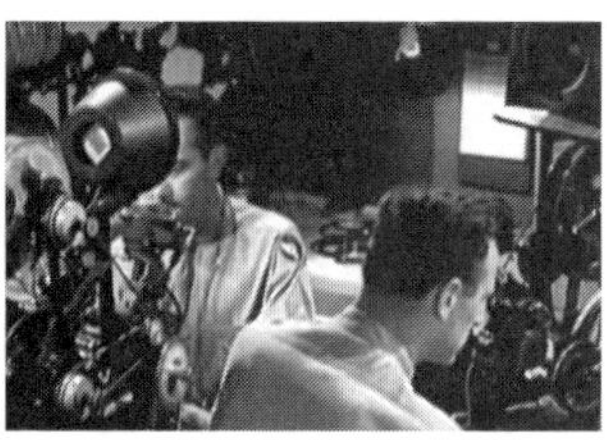

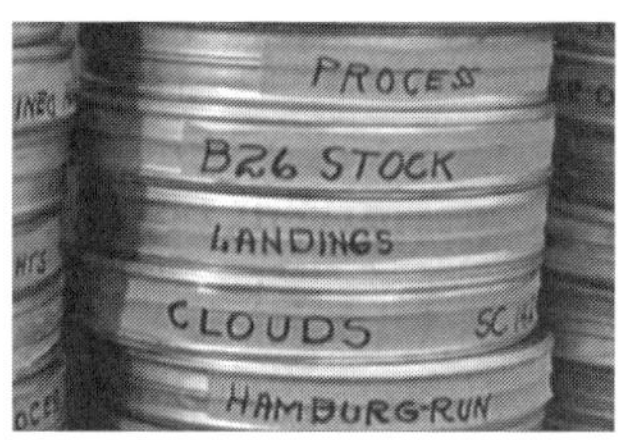

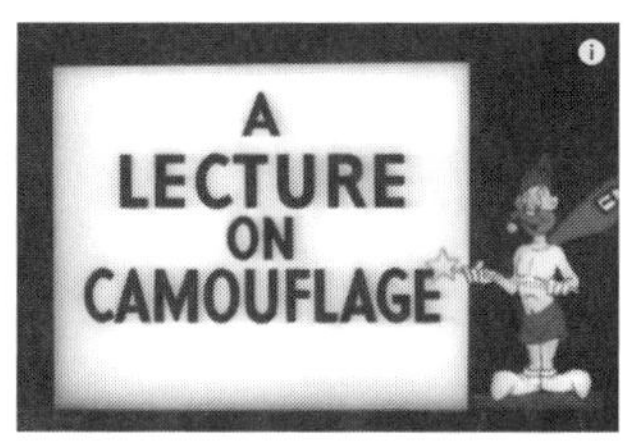

Editors on their Moviolas during WWII, stationed at Hal Roach Studios in Culver City, CA from *Hollywood Goes to War: The Army Air Forces 1st Motion Picture Unit* (1944). RIGHT: Popeye instructs in *Private Snafu—A Lecture on Camouflage*, a 1944 AAF cartoon.

THE 1940S

During WWII, if your CO was Jack Warner or Ronald Reagan or William Wellman, you were a member of Motion Picture Unit 1 of the Army Air Forces (AAF). As a "Celluloid Commando" your motto was "We kill 'em with fil'm" and you worked at "Fort Roach" (Hal Roach's studio in Culver City), pumping out over 400 training, informational, and entertainment films.

Some short films enlisted Bugs Bunny, Daffy Duck, Porky Pig, and Woody Woodpecker to spoof the enemy, others used models and simulations to help bombers navigate foreign terrain, and one, *Beyond the Line of Duty* with Ronald Reagan, won an Oscar in 1942.

RKO 281

Born in 1915, Orson Welles was a filmmaker of the second generation. He worked in theatre and radio—directing, acting, and doing just about everything else—but when he set his sights on directing a film, he studied his predecessors: Eisenstein, Renoir, Clair, Capra, and Ford (he viewed *Stagecoach* a reputed 40 times), among others. All this in preparation to direct *RKO 281,* which premiered in 1941 as *Citizen Kane*. Welles' deep dive into the heart and soul of an American newspaper tycoon with its meshing of old and new filmmaking techniques—famously DP Gregg Toland's use of deep focus—has kept the drama ranked the number one American film for decades.

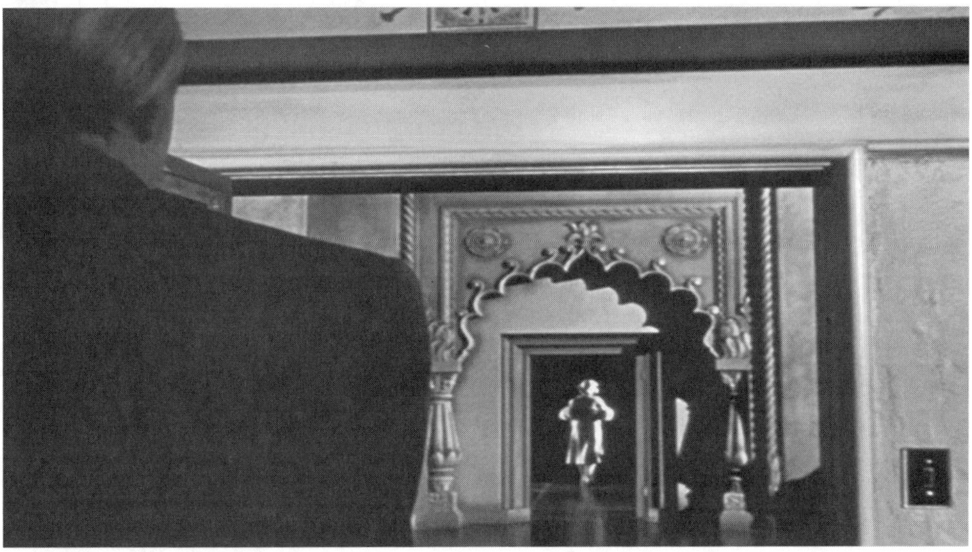

A deep focus shot over the shoulder of Charles Foster Kane (Welles' character) shows his second wife walking out on him. *Citizen Kane* (1941).

Editing

What *Citizen Kane* pioneered in terms of editing is multifold. First, Welles used flashbacks and flashforwards to tell a nonlinear story narrated by the three people closest to Kane: his business manager, his best friend, and his second wife. Second, Welles condenses time to progress Kane from a dying man to a young boy and back. Third, coming from a radio background, Welles applied his sound techniques to the screen, editing tight dialogue that cut off or was overlapped to inject scenes with heat and energy. He

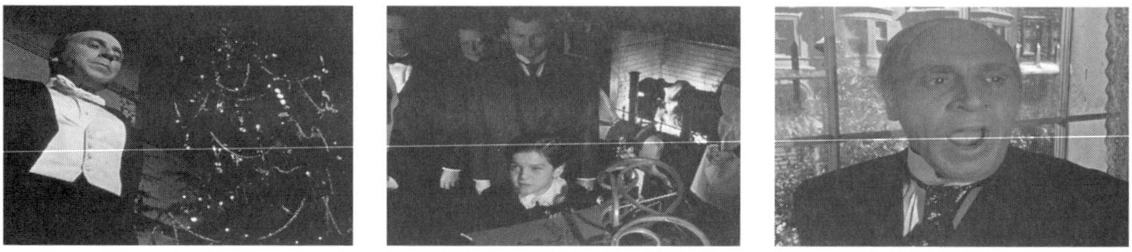

In this scene's first two shots, young Kane listens to his guardian wish him "Merry Christmas . . ." In the third shot his guardian, now visibly older, adds, ". . . and a Happy New Year." Thus, we witness Kane turn from a boy to a man (off camera) in a mere three picture cuts, and one overlapped line of a familiar holiday greeting. *Citizen Kane* (1941).

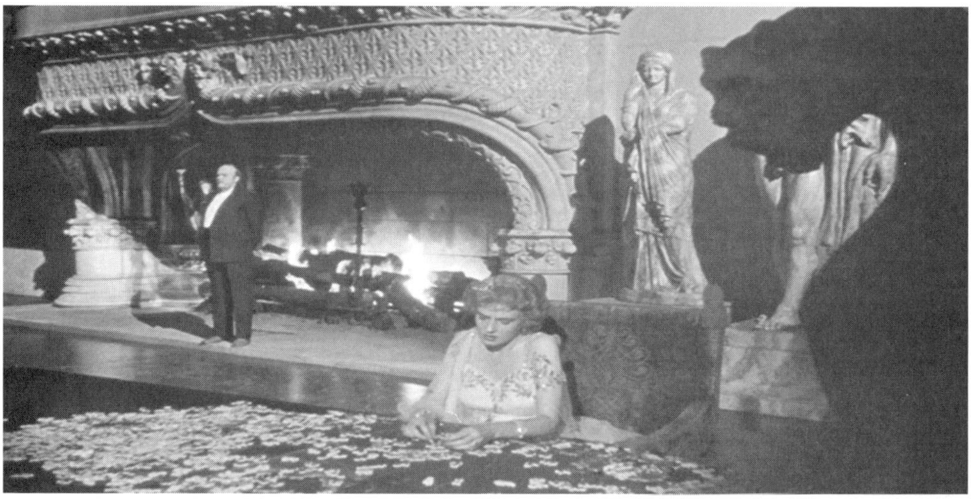

Another deep focus shot with echoey voices portrays life at Xanadu castle. *Citizen Kane* (1941).

created aural montages with layered sound that underscored, heightened, and at times dominated the visuals. Eschewing RKO's Sound Library, he and his crew generated all the film's sound effects, designing a soundtrack that bared relationships between characters. For instance, he created a cavernous Xanadu castle where Kane and his wife lived their deadened lives.

Welles also knew the value of silence, employing it like rests in music to give pause during critical reveals and to expose the bitter desperation weighing down life at Xanadu. Wisely, he hired Bernard Herrmann, embedding him during the shooting and editing of the film, with the result that Herrmann not only composed, but did his own orchestrations and conducted the score. Lastly, Welles created picture montages that eclipsed time and showed Kane's trials and tribulations. The acclaimed breakfast sequence takes 24 cuts and less than three minutes to depict the disintegration of Kane's marriage to his first wife. By the end, she's reading the rival paper to his sensationalist rag and the distance between them is palpable.

Just as Welles studied *Stagecoach*, filmmakers and film lovers continue to study and revere *Citizen Kane* today.

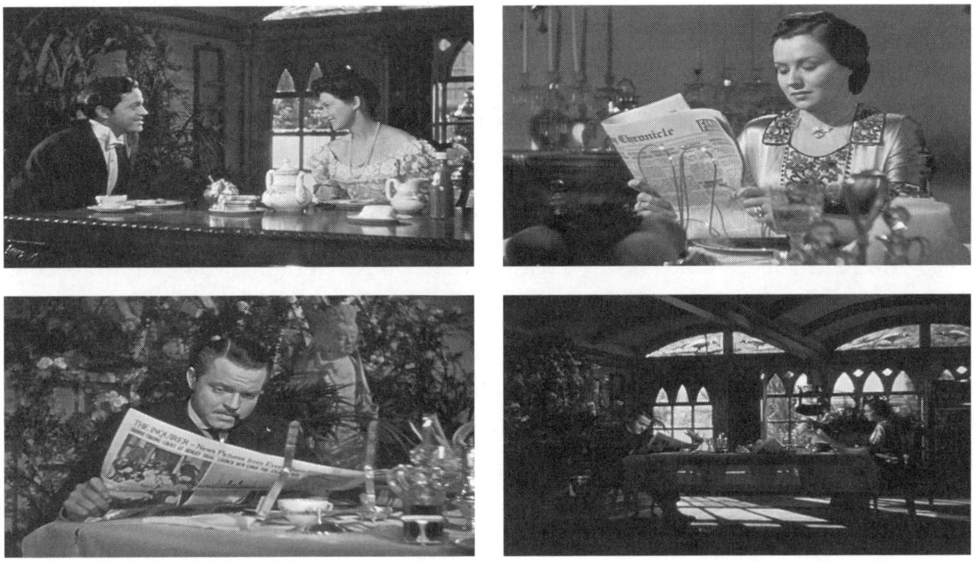

In the breakfast montage, Welles intersperses swish pans between medium singles of the Kanes as they age. In the final shot the camera pulls back from him to reveal how the closeness and familliarity in the first shot has dissolved. *Citizen Kane* (1941).

TWENTIETH CENTURY: SECOND HALF

The 1950s

TV and sitcom

The post war decade witnessed the invasion of TV into households and with that, the birth of sitcoms. Some shot with multiple cameras to speed up production and fly prints out to make weekly airdates. While this made for fewer continuity problems in editing, it brought in three times as much 35mm footage for syncing, coding, and cutting. In those days, editors marked cutpoints with a grease pencil and assistants cut the film and spliced the show reels together. Dann Cahn, editor of *I Love Lucy,* was the first to interlock reels and cut on "the monster" Moviola which sported three picture

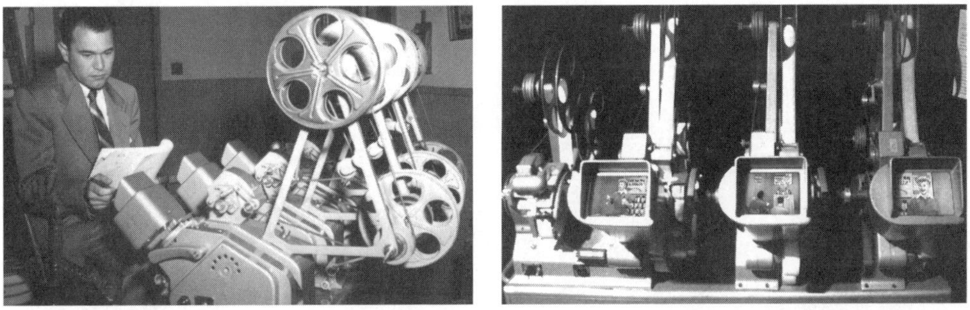

Dann Cahn at the gargantuan Moviola he dubbed "the monster" and different camera angles of the Vitameatavegamin commercial in the monster's three picture heads. *Photos courtesy of the Dann Cahn Estate.*

heads and one sound head. Multi-cam shows—primarily sitcoms and music concert shows—continue to interlock reels on digital systems today.

The French New Wave

As television postproduction was settling into new routines, editing itself had settled into what is now termed the traditional or classic style of cutting. Good editing meant linear stories and "invisible editing," with the cut points designed to be unnoticeable. The accepted pattern was for an editor to start a scene wide with a master shot or a long shot (to establish time, place, and geography of characters and objects), then move into coverage with a pair of over-the-shoulder shots and drill down to close-ups as the drama ramped up and exposed the characters' emotions.

French filmmakers and film critics were fed up with this conventional editing and being deluged with U.S. films. As much as they adored certain American directors such as Welles and Howard Hawks, who exemplified their Auteur Theory*, they were anxious to create a new national cinema which focused on the everyday lives of common people, not just the bourgeoisie. In 1951, they launched *Cahiers du Cinéma,* a film critique and theory journal which sparked La Nouvelle Vague—The New Wave.

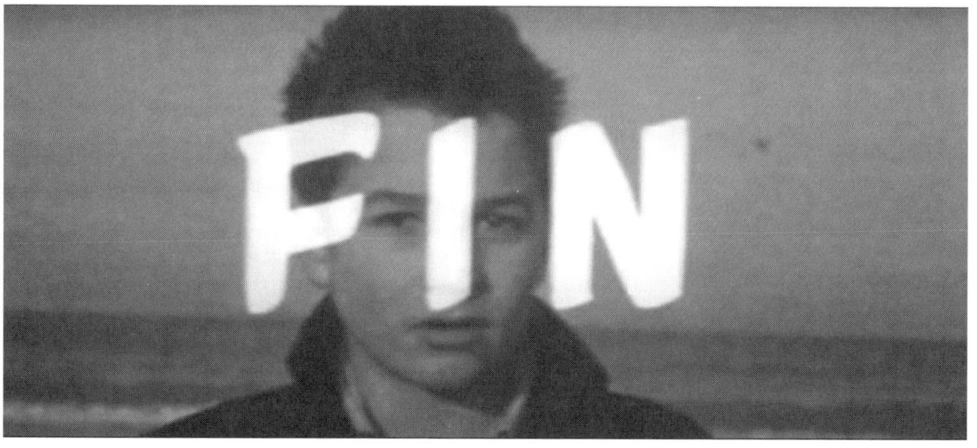

Movies did not end on freeze frames until 1959 when Truffaut zoomed in and froze on his protagonist for the final frame of *Les Quatre Cent Coups,* a French idiom for "Raise hell" but exhibited in the U.S. as *The 400 Blows*.

New Wave editing is characterized by the use of jump cuts**, catalyzed by Jean-Luc Godard's *À Bout de Souffle,* meaning "out of breath" and titled *Breathless* in English. However, jump cuts were just one way to counter Hollywood and make editing cut points visible. The New Wave filmmakers told stories in a nonlinear manner,

* The Auteur Theory (Author Theory) holds that the true author of a film is not the screenwriter, but a director with a distinct style, Hitchcock being a prime example.
** A jump cut occurs where objects or characters appear to jump because the shots are too similar. Technically, this is due to the camera angles of the two shots being less than 30 degrees apart.

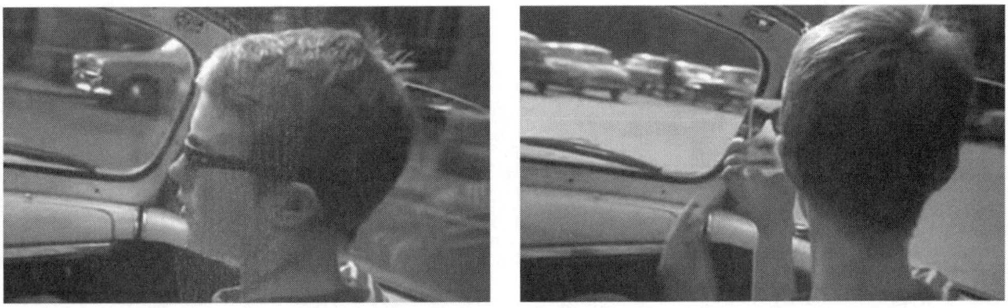

A jump cut shortens one of Godard's many long takes and maintains the tension as an aimless young couple drives through Paris in *Breathless* (1960).

and improvised plot and dialogue (reportedly daily on *Breathless*). Eschewing sets, they shot on location with handheld cameras (in part due to the lack of Hollywood budgets and resources such as dolly tracks), and added sound in post, all to impress upon cinema goers that they were simply watching reels of celluloid running through a projector.

Affected by existentialist philosophy, post war living, and Godard's beliefs that "film is truth twenty-four times a second" and "a film should have a beginning, a middle and an end, but not necessarily in that order," New Wave filmmakers aimed for realism and honesty. This extended to their documentary filmmaking, Cinéma vérité, which had its roots in Vertov's Kino Pravda, both translated as "film truth."

The 1960s

Honorary editing societies

> The objects and purposes of the American Cinema Editors are to advance the art and science of the film editing profession; to increase the entertainment value of motion pictures by attaining artistic preeminence and scientific achievement in the creative art of film editing; to bring into close alliance those film editors, who desire to advance the prestige and dignity of the film editing profession. —THE ACE CREDO

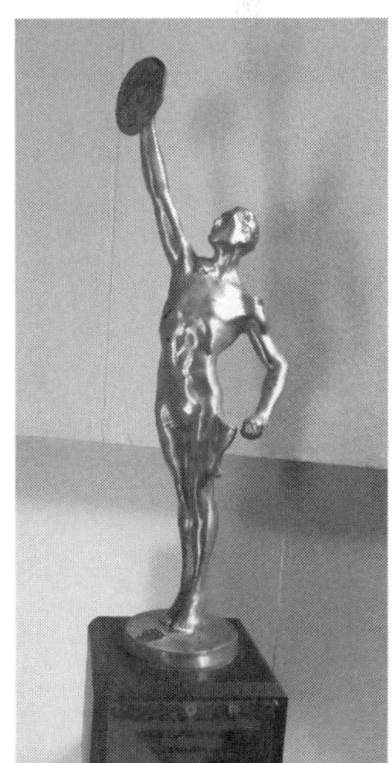

Annual ACE Eddie award. *Photo courtesy of Victoria Rose Sampson.*

Founded in 1950 by two editors, ACE, an honorary club of American Cinema Editors, handed out its first Eddie award in 1962 for best edited feature to Philip W. Anderson for *The Parent Trap.* The Eddies, which now include TV, animation, docs, and comedies, are held every January at a black-tie dinner ceremony.

MPSE (Motion Picture Sound Editors) began in 1953 and is "dedicated to improving the recognition of its members by educating the public and the rest of the filmmaking

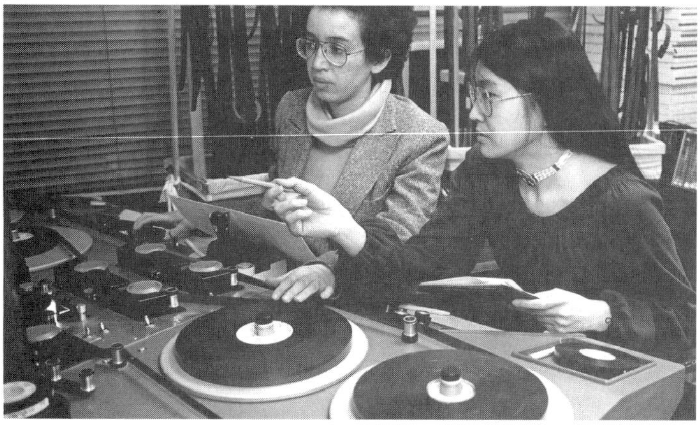

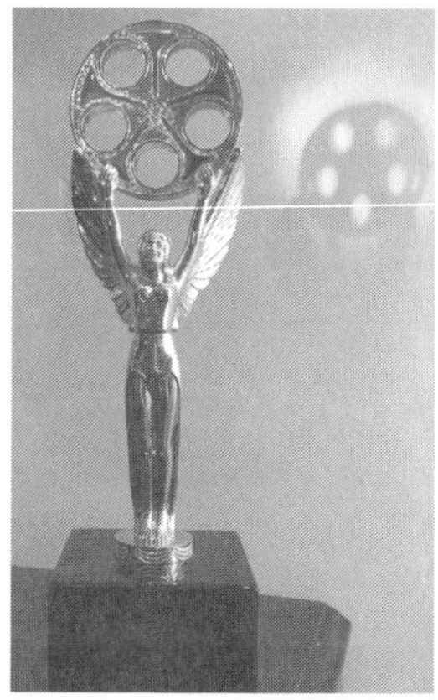

LEFT: An assistant editor and a director at work on a 16mm flatbed with two trim bins in the background. *Photo courtesy of Marty Barkan.* RIGHT: Annual MPSE Golden Reel Award for Sound Editing. *Photo courtesy of Victoria Rose Sampson.*

community as to the artistic merit of sound editing." It also hosts an annual gala dinner, presenting Golden Reel awards in over thirty categories of sound editing.

Editing machines and edits

The 1960s brought a new tool for American editors, the flatbed, which was normally referred to by its German manufacturer's name: KEM or Steenbeck. With a monitor four times the size of a Moviola's and three tracks of sound to the Moviola's one, flatbeds ran on horizontal reels which allowed for viewing more footage.

The decade also brought some spectacular films that changed editing. A memorable edit in David Lean's three hour *Lawrence of Arabia* (1962) was whittled down during editing and turned from a dissolve into a cut. It changes time and place in a breath and is a "match cut" due to its prop.

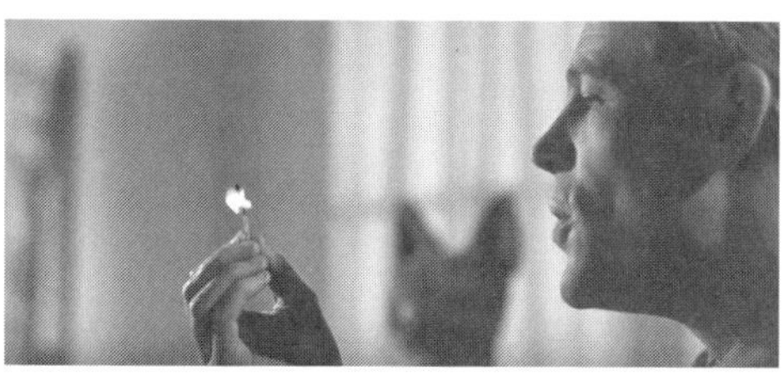

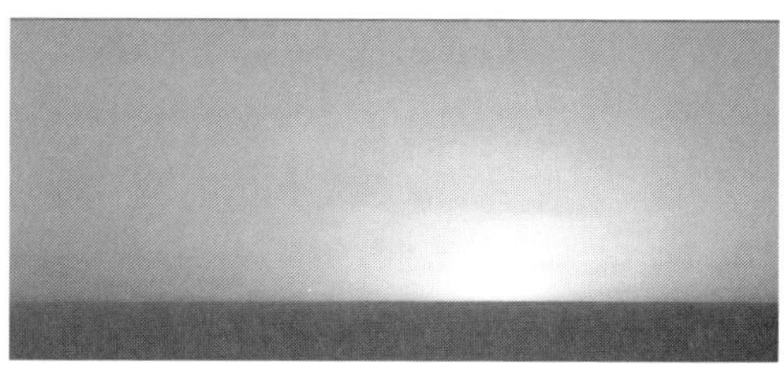

The famous "match cut" by editor Anne V. Coates, who won the Academy Award for editing *Lawrence of Arabia* (1962).

Another iconic 1960s time-place cut, can be seen near the beginning of *2001: A Space Odyssey*: A bone descends from a Stone Age sky in slo-mo and becomes a satellite in outer space.

It is a double match cut, matching shape and movement.

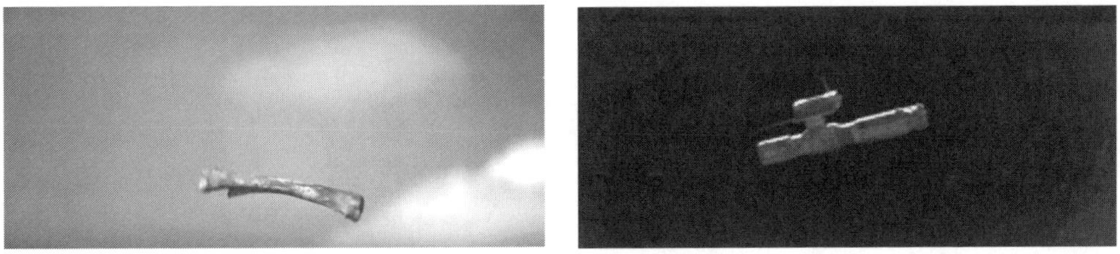

Shape and motion match cut from *2001: A Space Odyssey* (1968).

But beyond these famous cuts, two very different U.S. movies were impacted by the French New Wave and shook up editing.

The Pawnbroker

Influenced by Left Bank director Alain Resnais' *Hiroshima Mon Amour* (1959), director Sidney Lumet and editor Ralph Rosenblum constructed *The Pawnbroker* in 1964. One of the first films to grapple with the Holocaust, *The Pawnbroker* evoked a survivor's broken, tortured life, relying on what the director-editor pair termed "memory cuts." These consisted of flash cuts (many less than a third a of second), sound matches (the screeching of a subway becomes the shrieking baby in a cattle car), and the recurring sound of a barking dog.

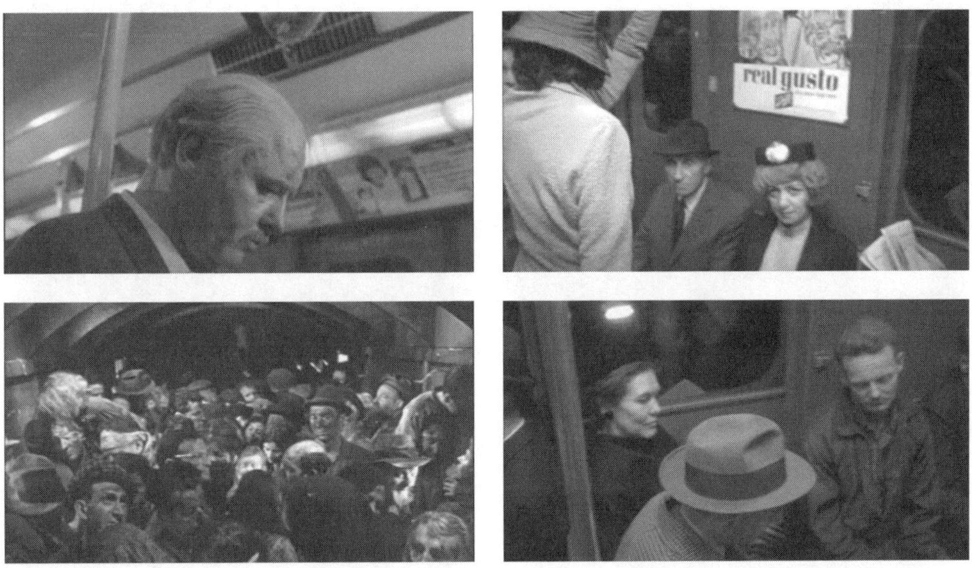

Harrowed by his WWII experiences, NYC pawnbroker Sol Nazerman (Rod Steiger) looks around the subway and is transported back to a cattle car via flash cuts in *The Pawnbroker* (1964).

Bonnie and Clyde

A tale of cop-crossed lovers on a crime spree, interwoven with a road trip through Texas and Missouri, *Bonnie and Clyde* (1967) is most remembered for its final scene in which the outlaws are gunned down by Texas Rangers. Accompanied only by the rat-a-tat-tat of the bullets, this one minute scene of 50 cuts combines regular and slow-mo shots, along with jump cuts to effect a death scene that is simultaneously shocking and balletic, felt and observed, quick and elongated. Silence follows (except for ambient sounds), as the Rangers creep out from the bushes; a heavy silence which carries to the end of the film.

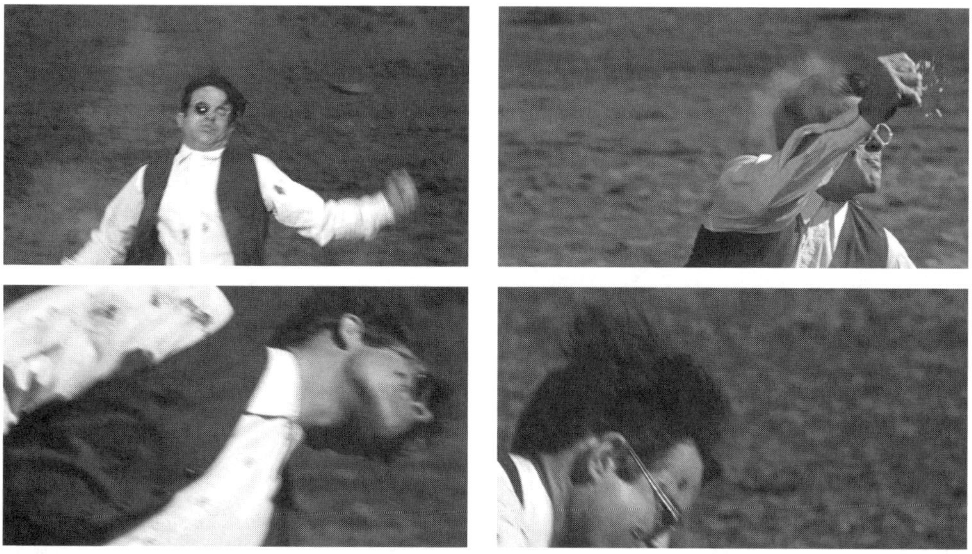

Clyde Barrow (Warren Beatty), falls to his death in a series of slow mo, regular motion, and jump cuts in *Bonnie and Clyde* (1967).

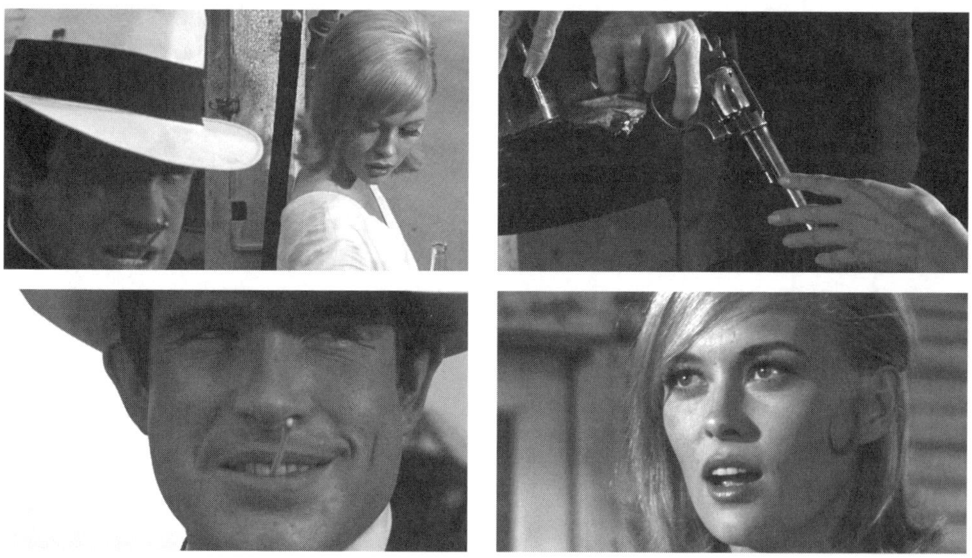

In four close shots, we see what captivates Bonnie (Faye Dunaway) about Clyde when they first meet.

In addition to the impact of the New Wave, Dede Allen, editor of *Bonnie and Clyde,* said that she was influenced by her work cutting commercials in Manhattan. Allen countered the Hollywood style of editing and changed it by cutting instead of dissolving between scenes, and by setting up characters and scenes with close-ups and jump cuts.

The 1970s

The decade ushered in multiplex theatres and a new generation of directors to supply them: Coppola, Spielberg, Lucas, and Scorsese to name but a few. Nowhere was safe in the 70s: the streets (*The Godfather,* 1972), the sea (*Jaws,* 1975), or the sky (*Star Wars,* 1975). And the countryside was not immune either, as the residents of Mt. Bethel, New York found out in July 1969 when a music festival overtook their rural community.

Woodstock

With its three-hour running time (whittled down from 120 hours of 16mm film), the movie *Woodstock* depicted the event and the times. The documentary's evocative montages, interviews, and split screen edits of musicians, festival goers, and townspeople continue to give audiences the sensation of being there. Editor Thelma Schoonmaker was nominated for the Academy Award for Best Film Editing (exceptional for a documentary) and went on to have a stellar career working primarily with Martin Scorsese, *Woodstock*'s assistant director.

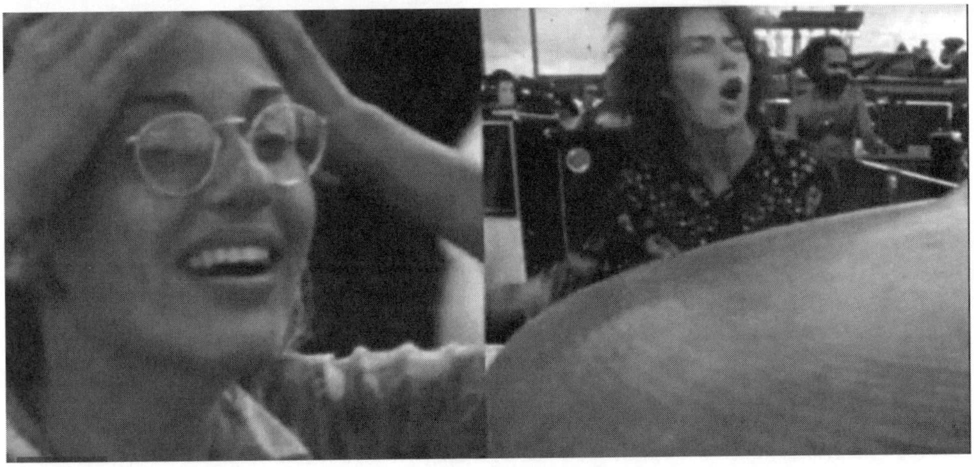

Using freeze frames, superimpositions, multiple angles (from 16 cameras), and split screens created in post, *Woodstock* helped create the legend of the festival. In 1971, it won the Academy Award for Best Documentary.

Apocalypse Now

In 1979, the decade closed out with a nightmarish contemplation of the war in Vietnam four years after it ended: *Apocalypse Now*. A tour de force of picture and sound editing, the nearly three-hour film begins with a sound match cut, as the sight and sound of helicopters clipping the screen morph into the chopping whirr of a ceiling fan in the hotel room of the central character, Captain Benjamin L. Willard (Martin Sheen). Nominated for an editing Oscar, the film won the Academy Award for Best Sound.

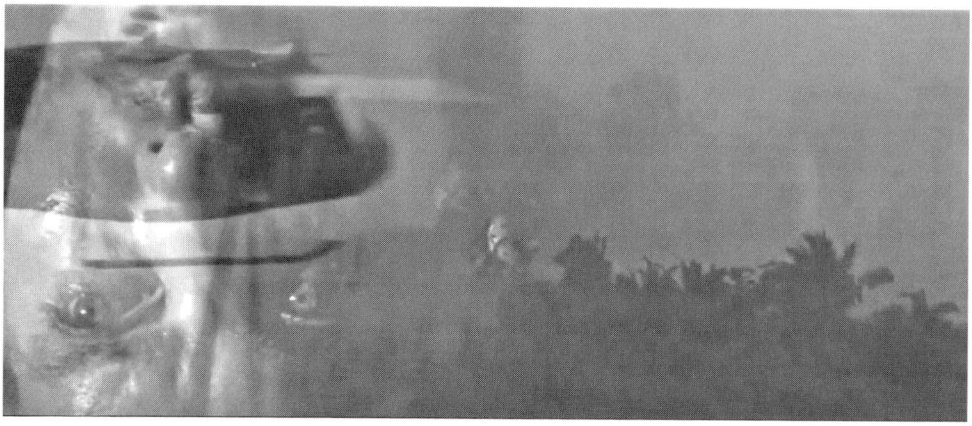

Discarded film made up the opening helicopter shots that dissolve in and out of the overhead shot of the main character in his Saigon hotel room in *Apocalypse Now* (1979).

The 1980s

Raging Bull

Thelma Schoonmaker received her first Academy award for cutting *Raging Bull* in 1981. The drama is a study in how a great editor working with a great director can create the rhythm of a film. Schoonmaker and Scorsese composed fast and slow sections, skips and staccatos, pauses and rests to create a symphony of a film that viewers breathe with.

The movie chronicles the rise and fall of 1940s middleweight champ, "Raging Bull" Jake LaMotta (Robert De Niro), getting inside his head as he boxes (often violently) with everyone in his life, both inside and outside of the ring. During the fight scenes, the editing jabs and pulls back in fast and slo-mo cuts like the boxers themselves. Skip frames* heighten and speed along the brutal action. The movie's only scene in color is comprised of distressed footage designed to look like happy home movies, setting a new trend. Additionally, there are slo-mo subjective cuts such as when Jake falls for his second wife at a neighborhood dance as well as tense interpersonal scenes like the one in the kitchen with his brother-manager and their (mostly silent) wives and children.

* Removing a frame within a cut at repeated intervals (e.g., removing every third frame) to achieve a stuttering (skipping) movement.

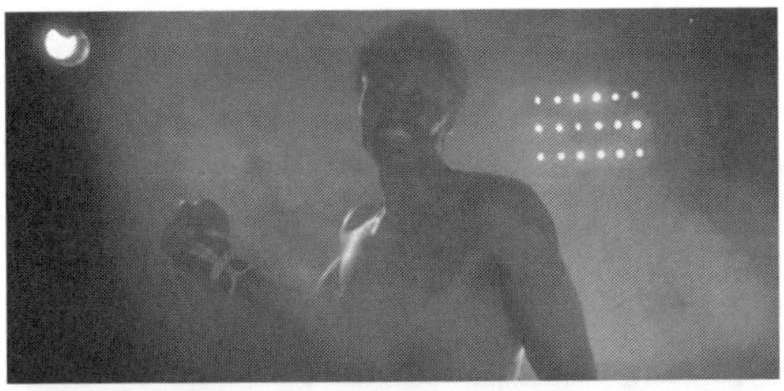
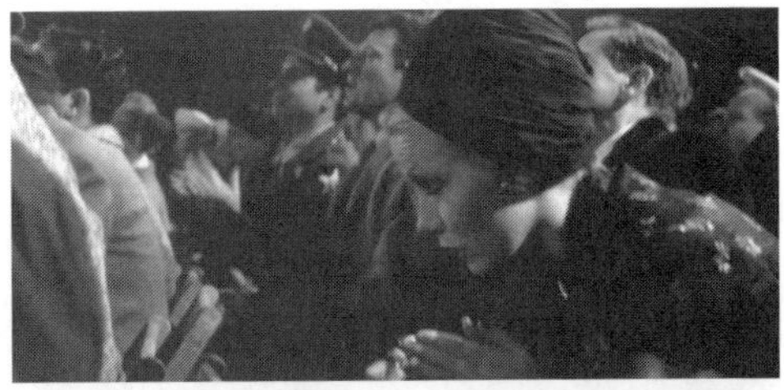
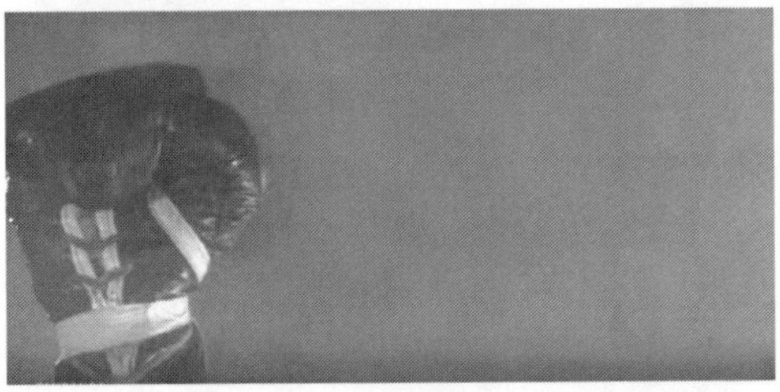
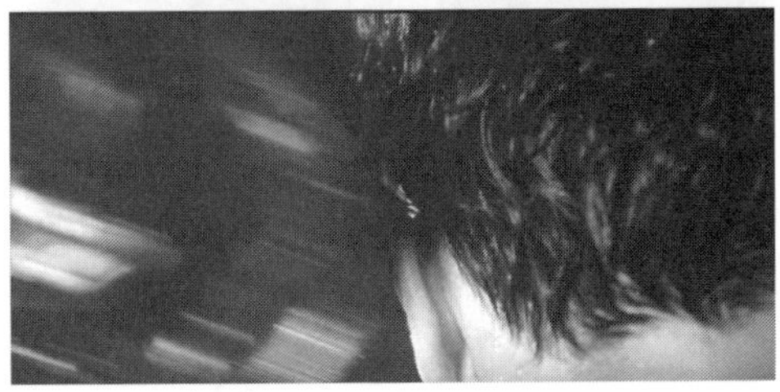
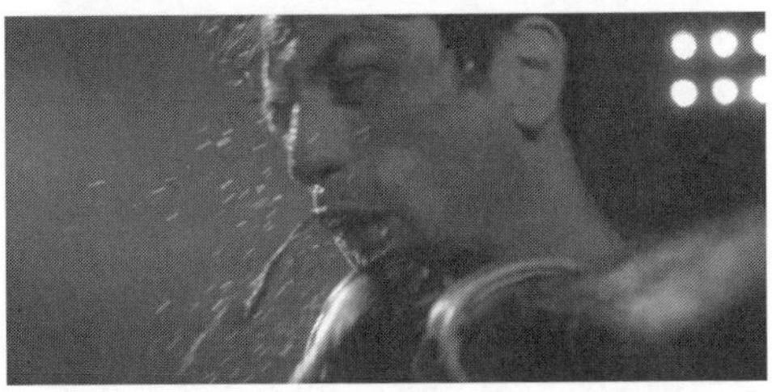

A mid fight, slo-mo interlude with Jake on the ropes concludes when Sugar Ray Robinson winds up for the punch, the crowd braces, and the cuts fly as he pummels Jake in *Raging Bull* (1980).

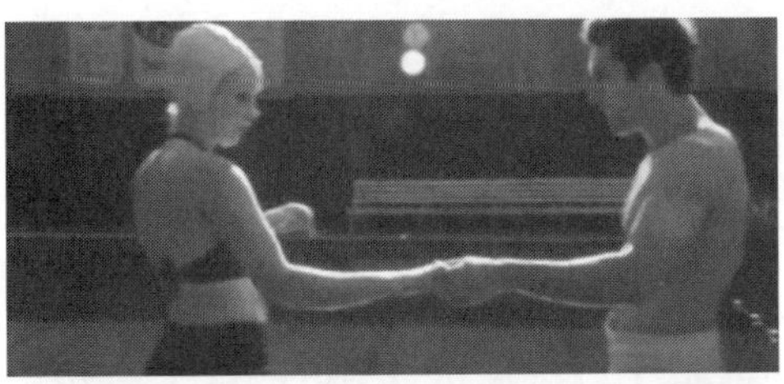
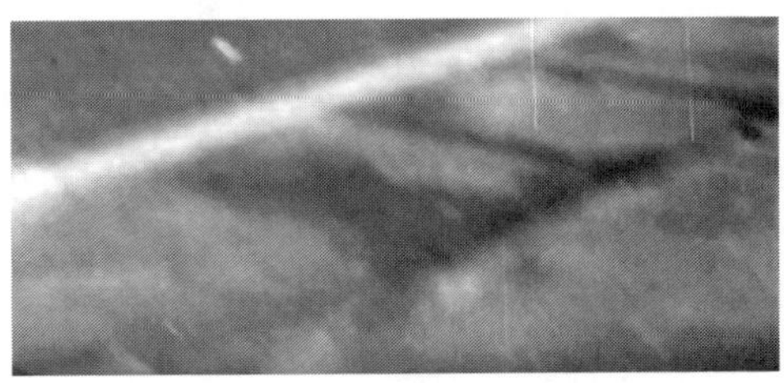
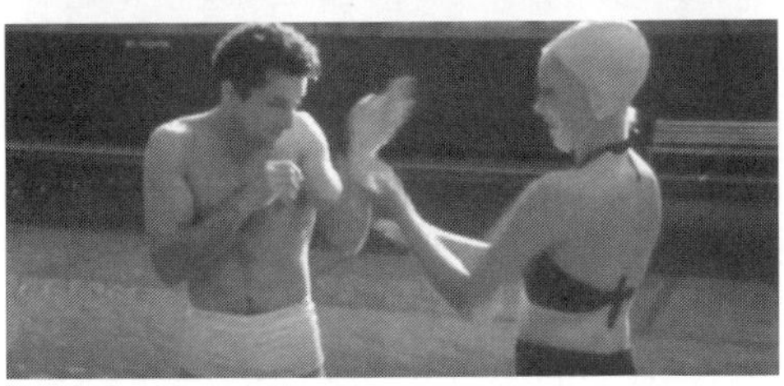

Jake and second wife Vickie (Cathy Moriarty) horse around and mock-fight near a pool, intercut with a flash frame of a blurry camera move of the pool. *Raging Bull* (1980).

MTV effect

The cutting in *Raging Bull* anticipated the first broadcast of MTV on August 1st, 1981 and the music video era which helped solidify the "modern style" of editing. Since the channel's inception, filmmakers have been debating, deriding, and embracing the "MTV effect" on cutting. But what is it? One music video editor defined it as "freaking the footage." An ill-defined term, the MTV effect can summarily be described as speeding up ASLs (average shot lengths), infusing scenes with handheld, line crossing camera movements, and multiple everything—cuts, VFX, and story lines—while eliminating dialogue and letting music dominate the (sometimes thin) story.

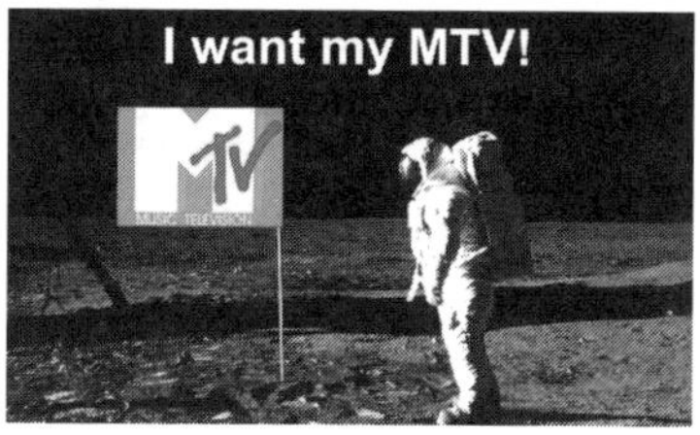

Editing on video tape

Early in the 1980s, non-feature editors began editing on linear video tape machines on which each edit was created and recorded sequentially—linearly—from the beginning of the show to the end. Operated by joystick, console, or keyboard, linear machines eliminated splicing and other tedious film cutting room tasks, allowing edits to be previewed from a source material tape before being recorded to the show tape. Tape footage still required logging and organizing but now online suites replaced film labs for producing the final show.

By the end of the decade all TV shows were editing on NLEs—nonlinear editing systems which allowed edits to be created non-sequentially—in any order (like film)—and ran on tapes or laser discs.

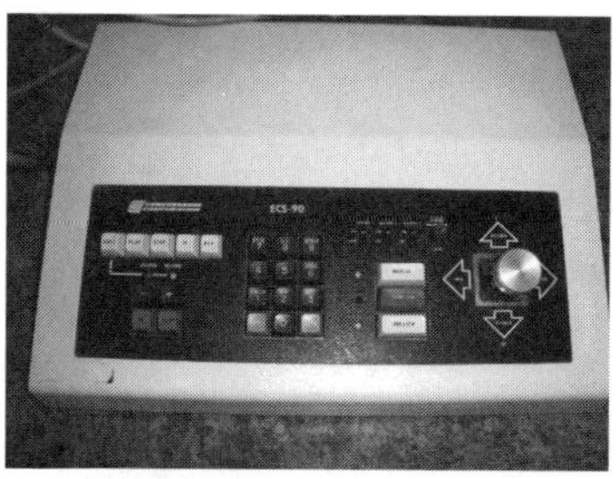

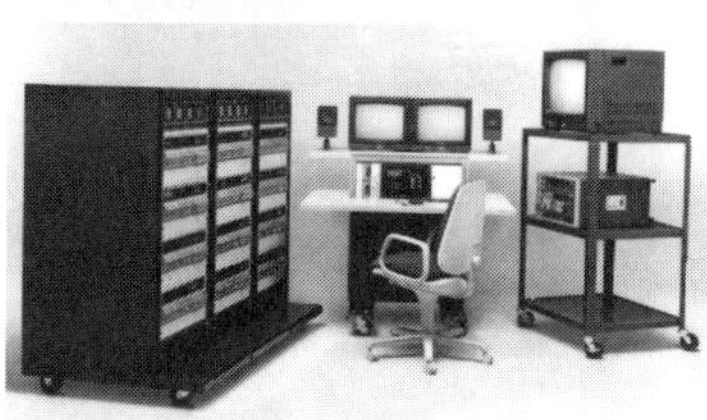

TOP: The ECS 90, a linear tape machine, was a workhorse operated by a joystick. Editors created freeze frames by unplugging the power. **BOTTOM:** Ediflex, a popular NLE tape system for episodic TV, turned the grease pencil into a light pen which the editor used to make edits and command the system to playback from a dozen VHS tapes in a dozen tape decks. *Photo courtesy of Tony Schmitz.*

The 1990s

Technological evolutions are driven by budget, attitude (openness to change), access, and the project's demands (amount of footage, schedule, and finishing format); they do not happen overnight. The 1990s began with editors cutting on two different mediums and three different types of machines: Feature editors on film flatbed machines, TV editors on nonlinear tape systems, and documentary,

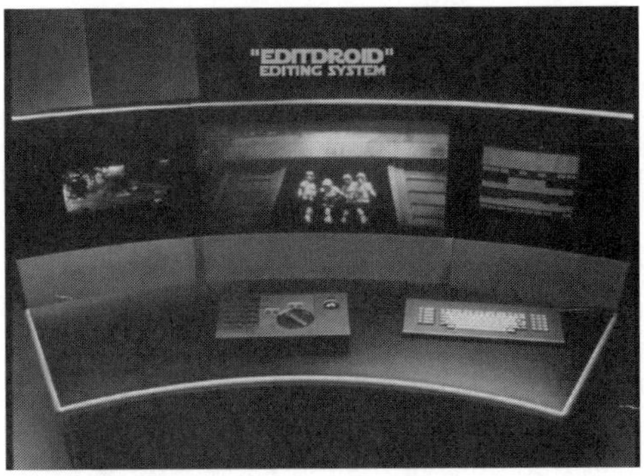

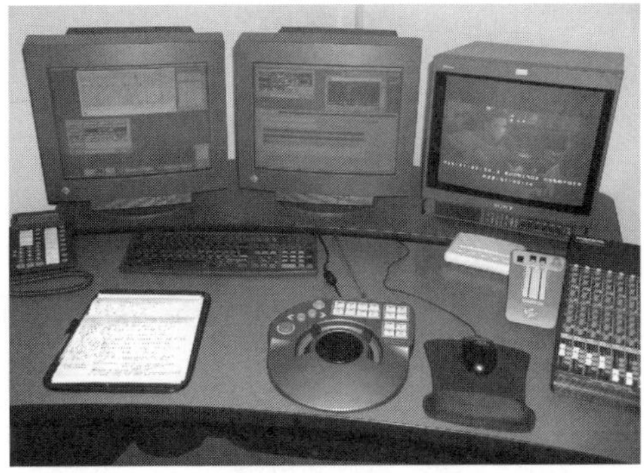

LEFT: EditDroid, designed by Lucasfilm, fittingly, relied on laser discs. Editors clicked on a scissors icon to make a cut and Darth Vader materialized if they did something the Droid didn't like. *Photo courtesy of Droid Works.* **RIGHT:** The Lightworks Digital Editing System turned the flatbed's controls into a roundish editing console. *Photo courtesy of Lightworks NLE.*

news, and corporate editors on linear tape machines. Mid-decade, digital systems appeared, revolutionizing all phases of the industry from preproduction to shooting to postproduction. Now all film and tape formats could be turned into digital images and edited together with digitally captured images on NLE digital editing systems. As software improved and acceptance spread, editors from all sectors of filmmaking began to migrate over.

Digital systems have given editors more freedom than they've ever had to trim and extend shots, cut and re-cut, make different versions of scenes, add and mix sound effects, narration, and music on unlimited tracks, create VFX (video effects) and titles, and speed up and slow down picture and sound.

Reality TV effect

Concurrent with the digital revolution was the inception and proliferation of Reality TV. Faced with tons of non-scripted, non-blocked footage with little continuity and few if any logs, reality show editors learned to plow through dailies at high speed to extract the story. In pioneering this new show format, they altered editing to this day.

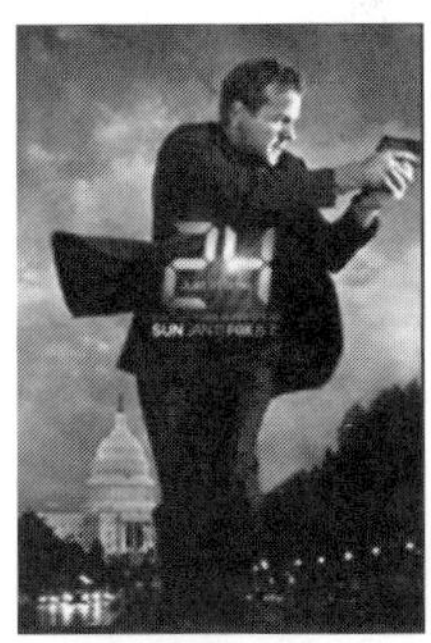

The reality TV series *24* followed counterterrorism agent Jack Bauer (Kiefer Sutherland) in real time; each one-hour episode covered one hour of his life, adding up to 24 hours every season from 2001-14.

Reality editors piece together the limited dialogue, speed up and cheat shots, and deploy jump cuts, flash frames, and transition FX to juice the show. They don't worry about match cutting or if the editing is obvious. Their editing and the shooting style make the shows seem real and is what the audience not only believes but expects.

TWENTIETH-FIRST CENTURY

Reality TV, hand in hand with MTV and digital technology, brought us what is referred to as the "modern editing style."

*ASL research**

> Modern movies may be more engrossing—we get "lost" in them more readily—because the universe's natural rhythm is driving the mind.
> —**JAMES CUTTING, JORDAN DELONG, AND CHRISTINE NOTHELFER,** Cornell University.

Cognitive psychology professor, James Cutting, and two of his grad students studied "Hollywood style" editing and filmmaking defining it as the invisible style that ". . . is designed to suppress awareness of the presentational aspects of the film, while promoting the narrative." They measured the duration of each shot in each scene from 150 popular Hollywood movies filmed between 1935 and 2005 in five genres: action, adventure, animation, comedy, and drama.

Applying a concept from chaos theory—the 1/f fluctuation—which describes a pattern of attention that occurs naturally in the human brain, the trio found that films made after 1980 matched the 1/f pattern of the natural rhythm of the mind. They deduced that this pattern developed during the life span of filmmaking as the edited rhythms of shot sequences succeeded or failed to create clear and engaging movies. Action flicks, they discovered, are closest to the 1/f pattern, followed by adventure, animation, comedy, and drama. The researchers predicted, ". . . over the next 50 years or so, and with action films likely leading the way, Hollywood film will progress toward a shot structure that more generally matches the 1/f patterns found elsewhere in physics, biology, culture, and the mind."

Modern style editing

So, what does the research, the MTV Effect, and the Reality TV Effect combined with the ever-expanding capabilities of digital systems add up to in terms of editing today? Anything goes, really. Many films—both fiction and non—are cut in the traditional style with linear plots, invisible match edits, a slower pace (longer ASLs), and music inserted to enhance certain moments or scenes. Many others cut in the more modern style, with lots of in-your-face edits and VFX accompanied by multiple plotlines, a nonlinear structure, a faster pace (shorter ASLs), and liberal use of songs and music. The following frames from *Slumdog Millionaire* (2008), nominated for its editing and winner for Best Picture in 2009, comprise an outstanding example of the modern style.

Most shows, no matter how traditional or modern the editing looks, combine both

* A 2011 study by Magliano and Zacks used an MRI to examine how different parts of the brain react to classical continuity edits vs. discontinuity edits and a 2017 study by Heimann, et al used an EEG. See Bibliography for complete reference to these studies.

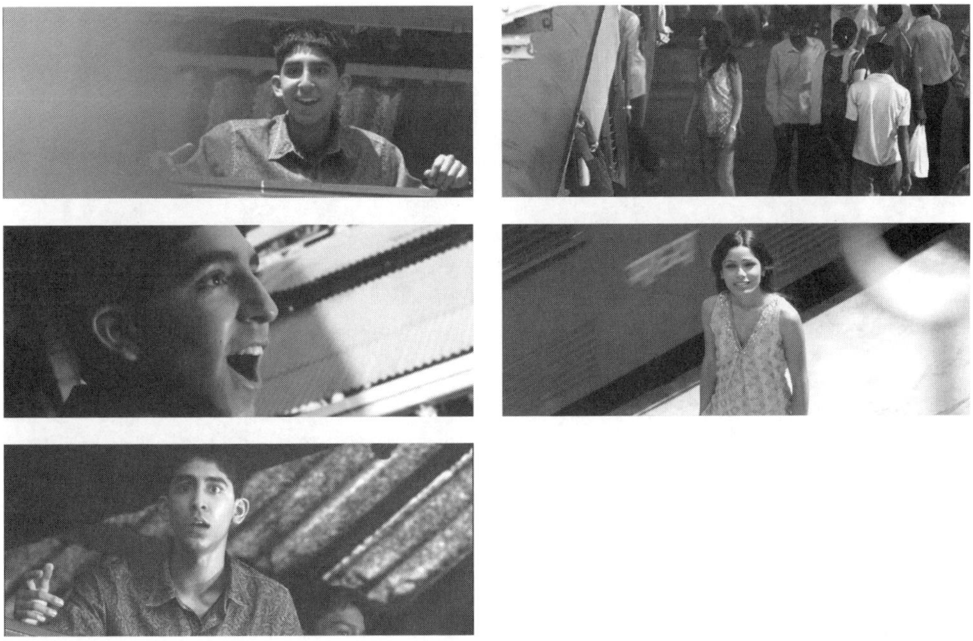

This short scene starts with a shimmer of a cymbal, which melds into the hum of a packed train station as Jamal Malik (Dev Patel) glimpses Latika, his lost beloved (frames 1 and 2). "Latika!" he cries out, which is the scene's main dialogue, other than her brief, low response "Jamal" as she notices him (frame 4). Flash frames (omitted) and music, along with station sounds prolong the moment between them. Then fear strikes (in the last frame) as he spies her pimps closing in. The music crescendos, the angles skew, and the pace turns frenetic as he races to save her. *Slumdog Millionaire* (2008).

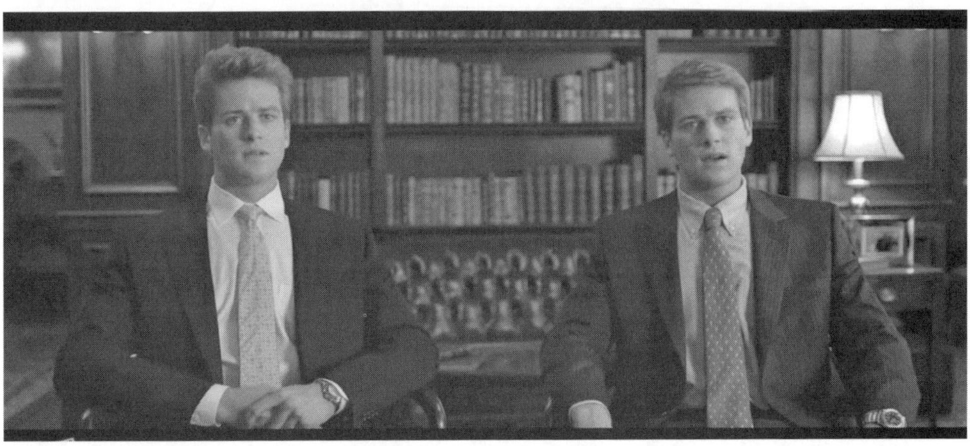

Garnering Oscars for Best Directing and Best Editing in 2011, David Fincher's, *The Social Network* (2010), a dialogue film primarily, seems to be cut traditionally. However, two actors (Armie Hammer and Josh Pence) played the Winklevoss twins, but one lost his head (Pence) which was digitally replaced by Hammer's. The movie has nearly 1000 VFX including the face replacements and digital matte paintings.

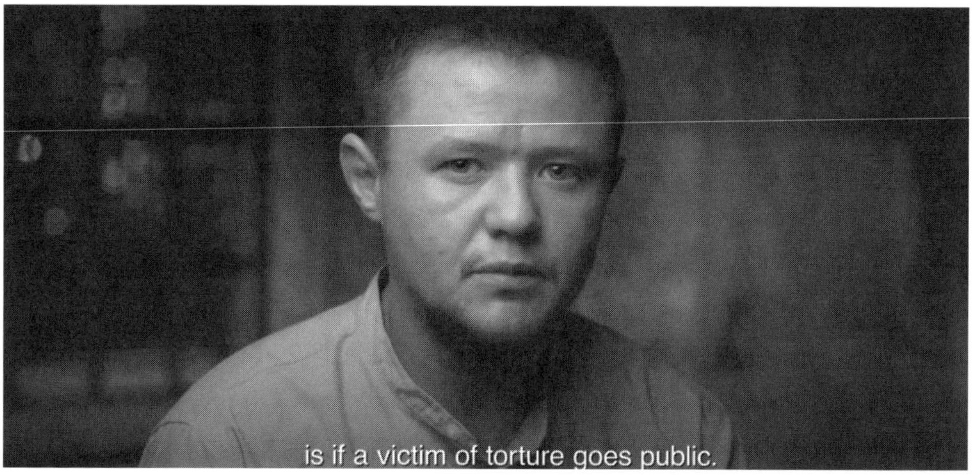

The documentary *Welcome to Chechnya: The Gay Purge* (2020) created 23 digital faces to protect the identities of rescued LGBTQ people and preserve their authentic voices, bodies, and emotions.

styles. For instance, a show may appear to be cut straightforwardly in the classic style but contain layers of VFX that aren't noticeable.

We expect digital characters in sci-fi movies such as *Avatar,* but they are proliferating in dramas, comedies, and docs as well. 2019 saw Robert De Niro's character in Scorsese's *The Irishman* digitally aged along with lots of digital stitching of shots in Bong Joon-Ho's *Parasite,* both nominated for Best Editing. Digital deception has become more than an artistic controversy as fraudulent uses of digital faces are proliferating in the form of deep fakes that harm and defame.

LAST WORD

It has been a long ride from pictographs to magical toys to film, tape, and digital images viewed in caves, salons, homes, theatres, TV screens, and computer screens. No matter what technologies, genres, or platforms next arise, footage will continue to show up in the editing room and be shaped into the final story.

WHAT DIRECTORS SHOULD KNOW ABOUT EDITING HISTORY

- ☐ Editing—how shots and sounds communicate to and affect the audience—has played a major part in the evolving language of cinema and continues to do so.
- ☐ Part of the history of editing is the development of narrative. A critical step in film narrative was the audience's ability to view shots filmed in different locations, at different times, as one event in one place and make a time-space connection.
- ☐ Directors were the first editors.
- ☐ Technical revolutions and evolutions affect how shows are edited.
- ☐ The advent of Talkies—dialogue on film—along with other sounds gave birth to sound editing and mixing.
- ☐ Eisenstein and other Russian revolutionaries developed their montage theories based on studying how juxtaposing shots affected viewers.
- ☐ French New Wave filmmakers and theorists broke down traditional Hollywood editing patterns and freed editing and filmmaking to be visible.
- ☐ Film audiences, theorists, cognitive psychologists, and filmmakers continue to look at how the lengths and rhythm of edited shots affect cinema.
- ☐ MTV, Reality TV, the internet, and digital editing systems have affected editing today by speeding up shots, commonly making the editing more visible, and gaining acceptance for multiple story lines, nonlinear structure, and more VFX.

4

HIRE A COLLABORATOR

THE DIRECTOR–EDITOR RELATIONSHIP

You've slaved for months to get the show off the ground and shoot it. Now it's time to turn the footage over for editing to someone you've heard of or know casually or a stranger you just talked to during an interview. Maybe you've been assigned an editor. Optimally, you'll have input into their hiring. However you are brought together, you may think, "Why should I trust this person to deliver my baby? Will the editor support my vision? How will we get along?" This chapter gives you guidelines for what to expect when working with an editor, and how to hire the right person for you and your show. But first, we'll start with a perennial question: Why do I even need an editor?

WHY CAN'T I HIRE MYSELF: PROS AND CONS OF EDITING YOUR OWN SHOW

Have you ever edited before? If not, you will have a steep learning curve on a digital editing system, and classes can be pricey. Whether or not you have editing experience the preeminent reason to leave the editing to an editor is that they bring that independent, fresh eye, along with the storytelling and problem-solving talents we discussed in Chapter 2.

Of course, many beginning directors do edit their films (often due to budget constraints) and they turn out fine. And many accomplished directors edit to keep control: Frederick Wiseman, the Coen brothers (as Roderick Haynes), Akira Kurosawa, Gus Van Sant, Steven Soderbergh (under his mother's name), and Robert Rodriguez, to

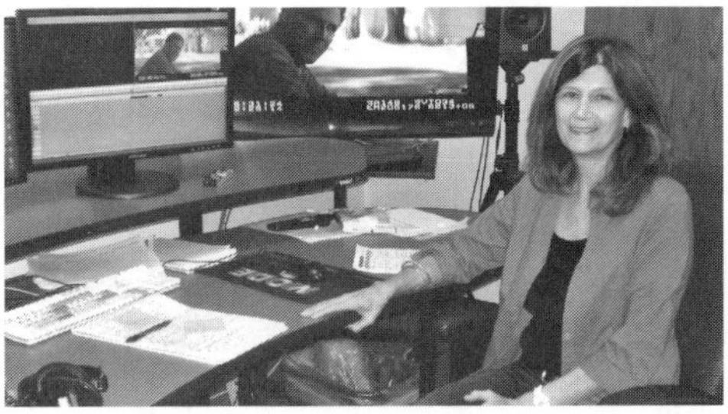

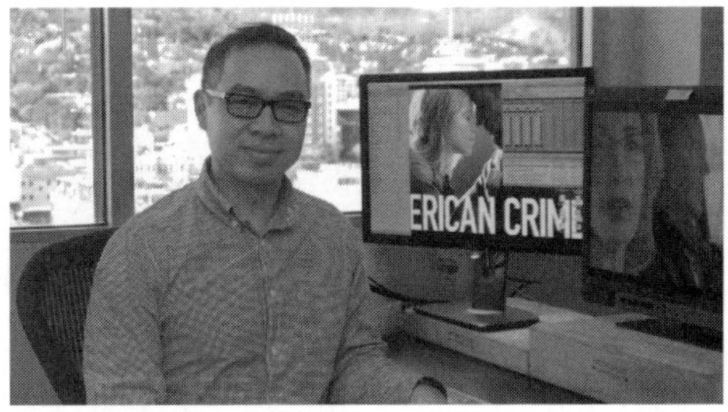

LEFT: *Photo courtesy of Sandra Adair, ACE.* RIGHT: *Photo courtesy of Luyen "Lu" Vu, ACE.*

name a few. So, if you do decide to edit your own show, you'd be in good company for putting on your editor's hat and cutting the picture you want to put in front of the audience. You can hire an assistant for the technical and organizational duties and create your own focus group of family, friends, and filmmakers for screening cuts and getting feedback. Make sure to allow yourself the time you need to get it right.

WHAT TO LOOK FOR IN AN EDITOR

> We share moments in which we show the most vulnerable state of the movie. We share the most uncertain future. You are up and down with them. And this makes editors true partners.
> —**GUILLERMO DEL TORO**, director, *The Shape of Water, Crimson Peak, Pan's Labyrinth*

First and foremost, you want to hire someone you can trust to support your vision of the show. Even though you may not discuss your vision directly, you must be certain that the editor understands your intentions for the film. You need an editor who is dedicated to working with you to solve all the problems, er challenges, that arise in this crucial finalizing phase of your project. You want someone willing to experiment and try your ideas, even the crazy-wild ones. A good editor will reflexively try and get inside your head to figure out your way of seeing things.

Second, you want to hire an editor who will fight for the show and story with every frame, scene, cut, and screening. This doesn't mean that they will agree with all your ideas. Since editors possess the independent eye and, like your eventual audience, are unaware of what happened on the set or location to get a certain shot, they are in a unique position to focus on performance and the story, and wrest the best from your footage. When you're unsure of something, you want someone you can rely on to diplomatically tell you what's working and what isn't, and to collaborate with you to come up with solutions. For instance, if your show is running long, what scenes can be dropped or truncated? If a scene is sluggish, can lines be dropped, cuts tightened, or can it be intercut with another scene or scenes?

Third, it's critical that you find a knowledgeable, informed editor. They should be familiar with the script if your project is a fiction piece, or the intention and the outline if it's nonfiction. They should be competent on the digital editing system, well versed in the editorial process, and super organized so they can call up shots, scenes, and cuts quickly. They should be aware of the needs of the sound and music departments as well as those of the visual effects (VFX) folks and the assistant editor, who they depend on for much of the organization.

Fourth, look for someone you feel compatible with. You'll be living with this person through a lot of cuts, work sessions, screenings, and probably a meal or two. You want someone you feel at home with.

Fifth, hire an adaptable person. As much as you plan and anticipate, every show is different and takes a path of its own. No editor can say exactly how they'll cut the footage until they wade into it. Most shows bring new territory for you and your editor so you want to pick someone who can field new or unexpected situations. You can't always express yourself clearly because you don't always know what you want. As you develop a relationship, a good editor will read beneath the words and laser in on your intent and vision.

Finally, make sure the person is available and can stay for the duration of the show. Once you're used to working with someone, it takes time to adjust when they leave and a new person takes the reins.

> There is a brotherhood in filmmaking . . . between the film editor and the film director -It's a brotherhood of trust and interdependence, and it is a sanctuary. It is for me where the filmmaking really gets started, and it's where I feel most comfortable. —**STEVEN SPIELBERG**, director, *Schindler's List, Saving Private Ryan, Jurassic Park*

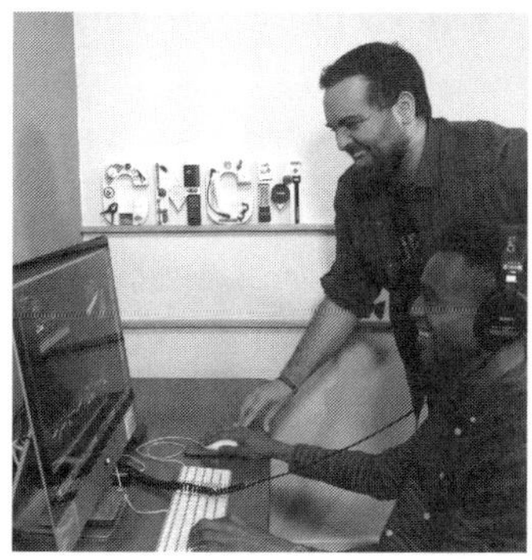

Photo courtesy of the Community Media Center County of Marin, CA.

How do I find out who's good?

The interview should tell you what you need to know.

Prior to that, ask other directors as well as producers, associate producers, production managers, and postproduction supervisors. You can familiarize yourself with an editor's work by viewing their reel or by watching a show they've edited.

Genre typecasting

Like actors, editors can get typecast: "Rowan is a comedy cutter. Harper is *the* music video editor. Trillian's got big action feature credits. Nico's received three nominations for best documentary." Don't fall for this. A good editor can cut any type of show. Just as directors don't like being slotted into a genre in their careers, neither do editors.

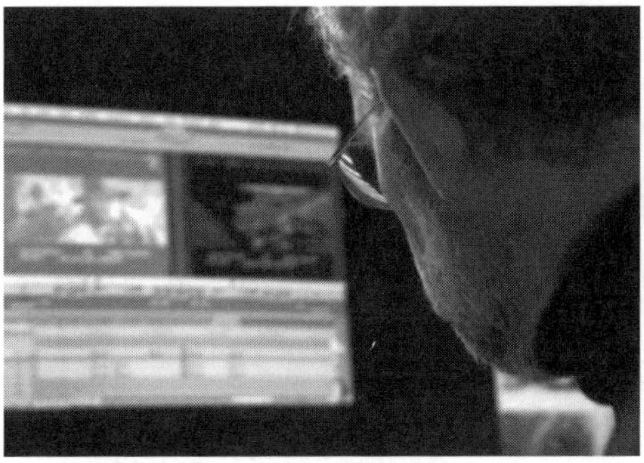

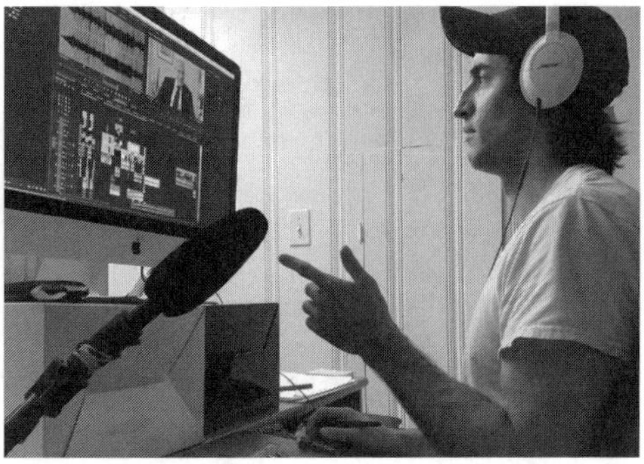

LEFT: Editor Walter Murch from *The Cutting Edge: The Magic of Movie Editing* (2004). RIGHT: *Photo courtesy of Matt Orfalea.*

Which should I hire: An Older Editor or a Younger Editor?

> I have learned the most that I have about directing from editors, from hanging around them in the *Rawhide* days and watching them work. —CLINT EASTWOOD, director, *Gran Torino, Million Dollar Baby, Unforgiven, Pale Rider*

Whether you hire an older or younger editor, both of you need each other, should have each other's back, and can learn from each other.

Older editor

A common practice over the years has been for a young director to hire an older editor due to their experience. An unflappable old hand can be a steadying, calming force who understands your concerns as a director, can reinforce your instincts and ideas, and be counted on to keep you on track. Well-seasoned editors have saved many a director and show. Also, it's likely an older editor has directed at some point themselves. Now they have no directorial aspirations and are at ease with and committed to the vicissitudes of the editing room. Editors with years of credits and a variety of shows under their belt are used to being a sounding board for both inexperienced and experienced directors.

Younger editor

A young editor will be steeped in all things digital and most likely have edited a music video or two. They may have fewer preconceived notions than a senior editor and be willing to follow your lead and experiment more. On the negative side, they may not read you or the footage. Worse, they may not have an opinion at all. Or they may be reluctant to tell you what they think. (This can be true of older editors as well, who are tired of not being listened to.) A good, less seasoned editor will be tirelessly dedicated to you and determined to put in the time and effort to cut the show as you intend.

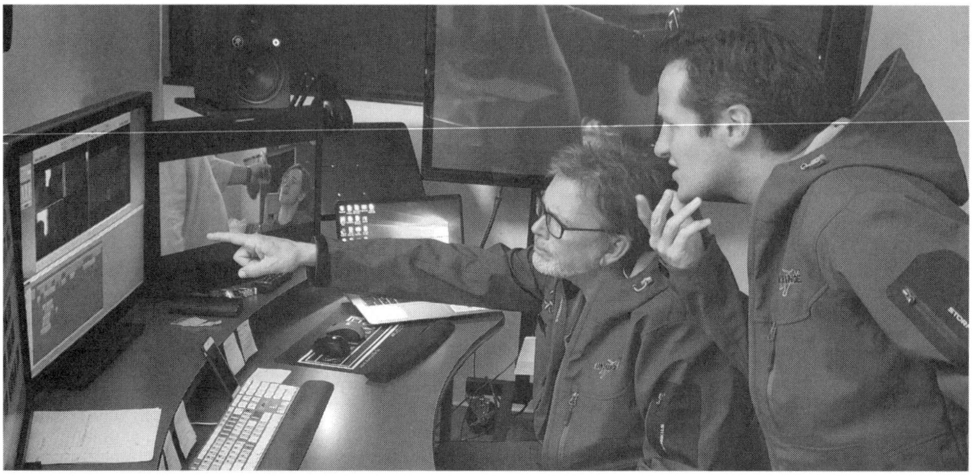

Editor and assistant on *Unhinged* (2020). Photo courtesy of Steve Mirkovich and Bart Brevé.

When do I hire an editor?

The editor is the last one to the party, correct? Yes and no. Yes, editors can't edit until you've shot the material. Yes, the postproduction phase of filmmaking follows the production phase. But TV series and most Hollywood films bring on the editor and assistants before the shoot start so they can set up the cutting room and be ready to pounce on the footage the second it rolls in. On 3D and VFX-driven shows editors are onboarded during preproduction to cut the filmed storyboards as part of the planning phase called previz (previsualization). Similarly, on animated films, editors are brought on during previz to cut the storyboard footage and the characters' dialogue tracks. Once those are locked, they then cut the story reel, which marries the storyboard and the dialogue tracks.

Conversely, on low budget shows or shows shot over long periods of time with long intervals of no shooting, the editor may arrive in the cutting room with all the footage shot and waiting. In any case, you'll want to talk to the producer, associate producer, or UPM (Unit Production Manager) to schedule onboarding the editor.

THE DIRECTOR-EDITOR RELATIONSHIP

> [the editor is...] the end of the relay race, and she and her director share one certain knowledge that binds them in a way no screenwriter can ever be: They both know they're on the Titanic together . . . —**WILLIAM GOLDMAN**, screenwriter, from his book *Adventures in the Screen Trade*

You'll likely spend more time with your editor than with any other crew member. You're on the ship together and will weather different seas and winds to co-pilot it to shore.

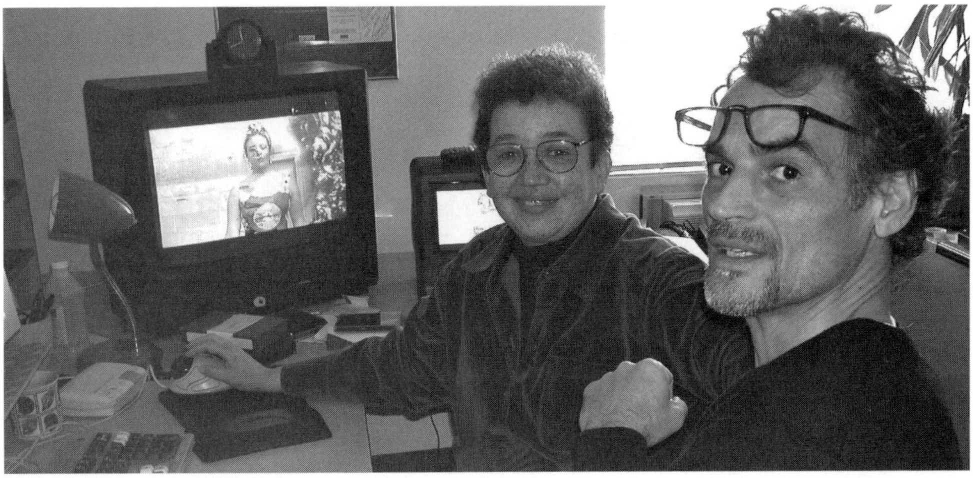

Editor and director. *Photo courtesy of Joe Staton.*

While you are the captain and have the final say, ideally you and your editor are creative partners, co-parenting the show through delivery.

The director-editor relationship is a marriage or at least a great affair. While you'll most likely work with a lot of different editors, especially if you work in TV or on independent or short projects, you may wish to work with the same editor or set of editors exclusively. There are famous director-editor pairs who have worked together for years. A current short list includes Martin Scorsese and Thelma Schoonmaker, Steven Spielberg and Michael Kahn, Ang Lee and Tim Squyres, and Spike Lee and Barry Alexander Brown.

Nightmares and Dreams

Another way of understanding who you want to collaborate with as an editor is to know who you don't want to hire. So, here's the horror show version—the relationship from hell you both want to avoid. While this bad dream may sound exaggerated, all these things have happened: Forewarned is forearmed.

Editor from hell

The editor of your nightmares makes a hash of your footage. They fail to honor your concept of the show and its scenes and sequences. This editor simply does not get the show and your view of it. They pick the wrong takes and worst shots. Their edits lack rhythm and pace—they're too short or too long—and spotlight the wrong character or place at the wrong time. A nightmare editor will not listen to you or communicate well. They lack initiative, exude negativity and doubt, balk at making changes or experimenting, and have to be overseen cut by cut to complete the show. They are an arrogant

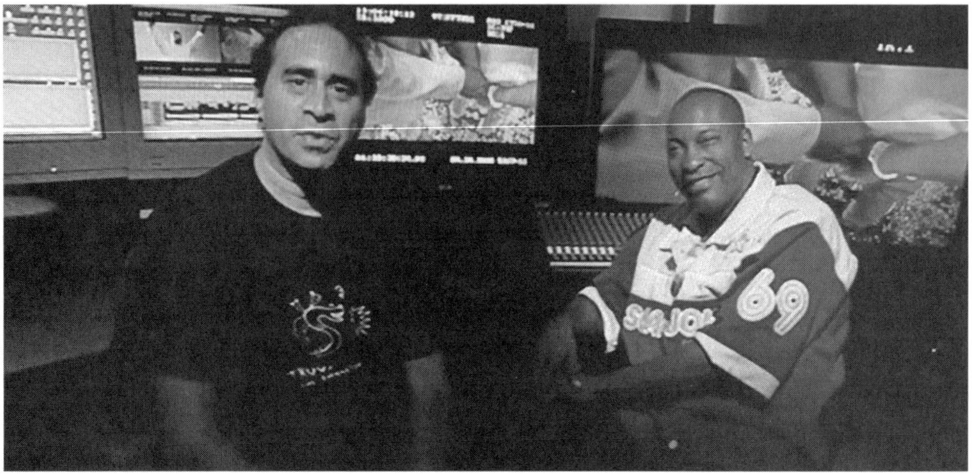

Bruce and John worked together for decades until John's untimely death in 2019. *Photo courtesy of Bruce Cannon and John Singleton.*

know-it-all who treats their assistant and everyone else crassly. They conspire with producers or clients against you.

Director from hell

A nightmare director does not understand or respect what an editor brings to a show. They want everything yesterday and have no concept of nor could care less about how long things take. Editing is a mechanical job, not a creative one to them. This director won't listen to or respect the editor. They oversee every cut, snapping their fingers at cutpoints and turning the editor into a pair of hands—a lowly droid executing each edit on the digital editing system. This director sees nothing wrong with jumping on the system themselves to make cuts. Or bringing in others to screen cuts behind the editor's back. The nightmare director shouts impatiently and treats everyone poorly. They use the cutting room as an office to make phones calls, and carry out other business, ignoring that it is the editor's work den.

OK. Breathe! You're awake now and realize it's all been a terrifying dream. The following job descriptions encapsulate your newly hired editor:

Director's dream editor

The stellar editor understands your intent, perceives the show's theme and message, and works to co-create a film on schedule that exceeds expectations.

Editor's dream director

Encouraged and respected by you, the editor feels free to engage with the footage to reflect your ideas and sculpt the show.

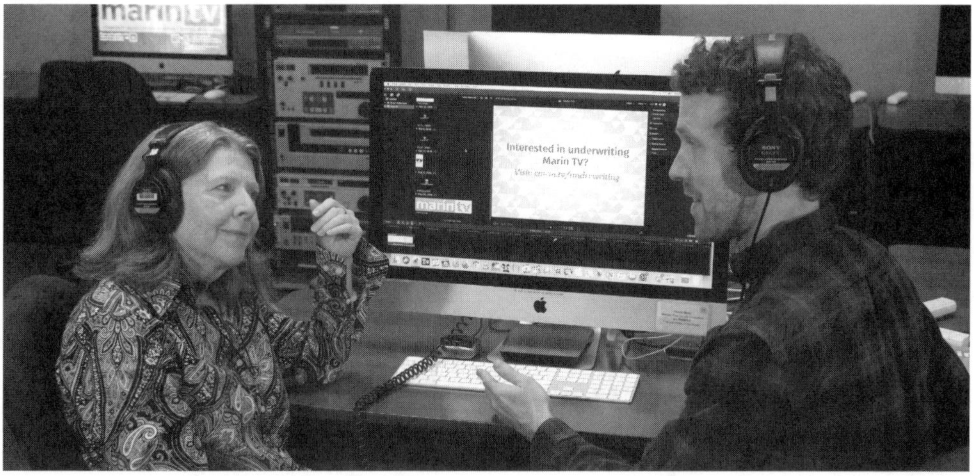

A director works with her editor. *Photo courtesy of the Community Media Center County of Marin, CA.*

LAST WORD

Keep in mind the insightful words of editor-author Walter Murch (*The English Patient, Apocalypse Now*, and many more): "Editing is not so much a putting together as it is the discovery of a path." Discover the path together with your editor.

WHAT DIRECTORS SHOULD KNOW ABOUT HIRING AN EDITOR

- ☐ Choose an editor you trust to support your vision of the show.
- ☐ Hire a person who will fight for the story all the way.
- ☐ Pick a problem solver you can rely on to tell you what's working and what isn't, and to collaborate with to create solutions.
- ☐ Ensure the editor knows the postproduction process and the digital editing system and is well informed about your show (has read the script or outline).
- ☐ Look for someone you feel compatible with who gets what you're expressing.
- ☐ Hire an adaptable person who can field new or unexpected situations.
- ☐ Make sure the person is available and can stay for the duration of the show.
- ☐ Hire for or against genre expertise.

5

EDITING
WHAT AN EDITOR DOES

. . . but you gotta know the territory. —**CHARLIE COWELL**, salesman in *The Music Man*

Since you'll be sitting with the editor in the cutting room staring at screens full of the images you shot and watching cuts play on monitors, you want to understand what the heck is going on. Like Dorothy landing in Oz, you've entered an unfamiliar land with different players and places. And a quasi-foreign language. How do you lead if you don't know or understand the territory? This chapter decodes how editors speak, think, and approach the footage, and demystifies match cutting, overlapping, cheating shots, and a host of other actions editors take daily.

PREPARING TO CUT

As dailies stream in, editors make themselves super familiar with the footage.

Screening dailies

The practice of director and editor screening dailies together along with the DP and other crew members is a rare occurrence today. The norm is that you two are in different locations and streaming dailies on an iPad (you) and on the digital editing system (the editor). You send notes of preferred takes, etc., to the cutting room via the script supervisor, email, or phone. Before starting to cut a scene, the editor reviews your notes, views the footage, and makes mental and/or written notes about shots, lines, angles, and cutting ideas. If the project is a documentary, the editor goes over the shot logs and rereads the outline or paper cut—or adds to it, if they're creating it.

Cutting Room Terms

As editing has evolved from cutting and splicing physical film to pushing buttons on video tape machines to mouse-clicking and key-pressing on today's digital systems, old terms have lived on and new terms have been added. Even though images and sound are no longer physically cut on film, editing is still referred to as cutting and the editing room continues to be called the cutting room. Picture and sound—film terms—are freely mingled with video and audio—tape terms—in today's digital domain. Since most movies are shot, edited, and projected digitally, perhaps in the future we'll go to the theatre to see not a film but a "digi." But for now, film, video, and digital terms are interchanged in the cutting room and everywhere else in postproduction.

Picture editor, a.k.a. the editor or the cutter. Editor who puts the show together.

Edit (noun). A portion of a take or shot put into a show.

Cut (noun)

- A series of edits.
- Cut and edit are used interchangeably: An edit can be made up of cuts, a cut can be made up of edits. Compounding the confusion, the words are both nouns and verbs. For consistency's sake, this book will use the noun *cut* to stand for a series of edits except for a few instances where its meaning will be clear within the context.

Cutting room. Room where the editor puts the show together. It could be anywhere: at a hotel, a garage, a studio lot, a corporate cubicle, a kitchen table.

Postproduction a.k.a. editing, editorial, or post. Final creation phase of a show during which all editing and finishing work takes place. Once through post, a show is ready for distribution and exhibition.

Post house. Postproduction facility that offers a range of services to the production company including film scanning (telecine), offline and online editing, editing rooms and system rental, screening rooms, etc. Big post houses are usually affiliated with a film lab and offer VFX, color grading, and graphics design services as well.

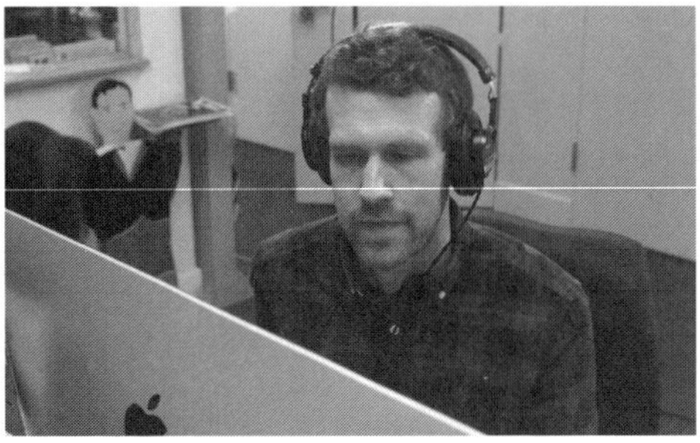 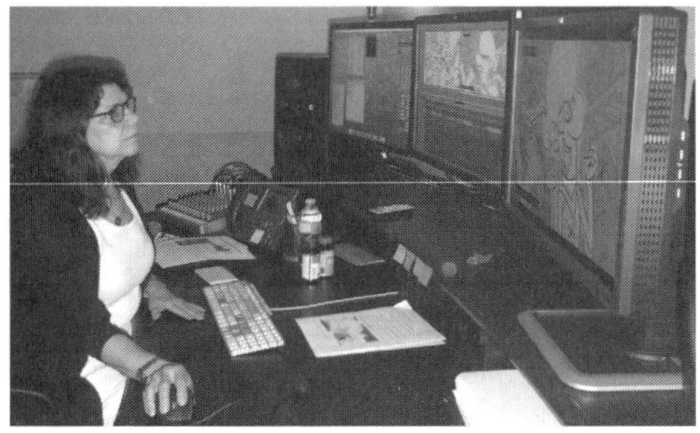

Contemplating the canvas. LEFT: *Photo courtesy of Community Media Center County of Marin.* RIGHT: *Photo courtesy of Nancy Frazen.*

BEGINNING TO CUT

> The art of editing occurs when the combination of two or more shots takes meaning to the next level—excitement, insight, shock, or the epiphany of discovery. —**KEN DANCYGER**, *The Technique of Film and Video Editing*

When editors approach cutting a scene, they consider the scenes before and after it and ask: "What led to this scene? What does this scene lead to?" Doc or drama, editors want to know where they're coming from, and where they're going to before diving into a scene. To make the First Cut (and every cut) editors evaluate four main factors for which shot and take to use. They select for:

1. Action = Take that most clearly tells the story.
2. Dramatic quality = Take that is best acted/experienced/felt.
3. Pace = Rate that most suits the flow of the story.
4. Technical quality
   - More critical: camera, lighting, sound, composition, continuity.
   - Less critical: hair, makeup, wardrobe.

Picking the first frame

> I've often felt that editing is a process akin to painting . . . As I selected shots and clipped out the 'good bits,' I couldn't help but feel that I was assembling a series of rich palettes with which to work . . . The screen . . . was my canvas, but what was more fun was that my "painting" was in not two, but four dimensions . . . height and width, naturally . . . then movement within these two and in the implicit screen "depth." However, the dimension unique to editing was time-space, and I sometimes imagined this dimension as one that extended out of the screen towards me and beyond . . . —**MATTHEW TUCKER**, documentary and fiction editor

After deciding which take to use, the editor determines the right place to start—the in point. They choose the frame where the drama starts, where something begins to happen, where information is given out, where the story starts. To end the cut—pick an out point—the editor plays the shot and notices where it stops being interesting and effective. They then ponder, "What do I want to see, know, learn, or reveal next?"

There is no set answer as to when to end a cut and begin another, because there is no single way to put a show together, no fixed rules for editing. However, there are more effective and less effective ways to cut. When editors cut for the right reasons and in the right place they:

- Sustain the viewer's interest, involvement, and investment in the show.
- Set a pace other than the real time pace established by the master shot.
- Maintain continuity: The cut will appear seamless to viewers even though it's a change in angle or framing.

Motivating a cut

> At all times, my editing is driven by story, not by style. —**JILL BILCOCK**, editor, *Moulin Rouge!, The Road to Perdition, The Dressmaker*

"Each cut should be motivated" is an oft-repeated caveat in editing and means that each cut should advance the story, the action, the flow, and the thought process. Good editors don't put a shot in solely because it looks grand, arty, or cool or cost a hefty amount of time and/or money. They make sure each cut links to the cut before and after it to knit the story together, edit by edit. The editor must tell the story with each edit in every scene. So why does an editor cut? Answer: to move the action forward.

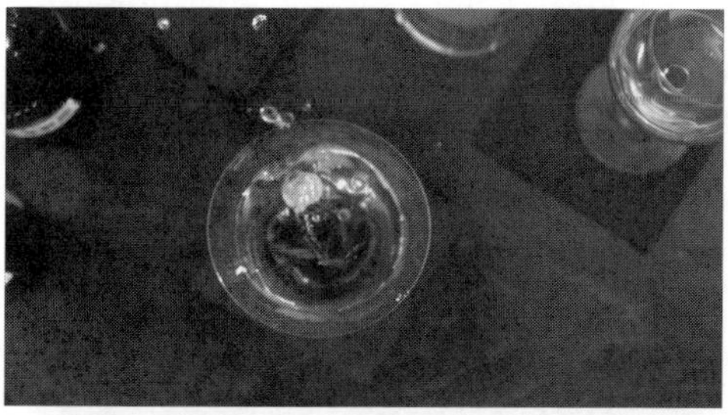

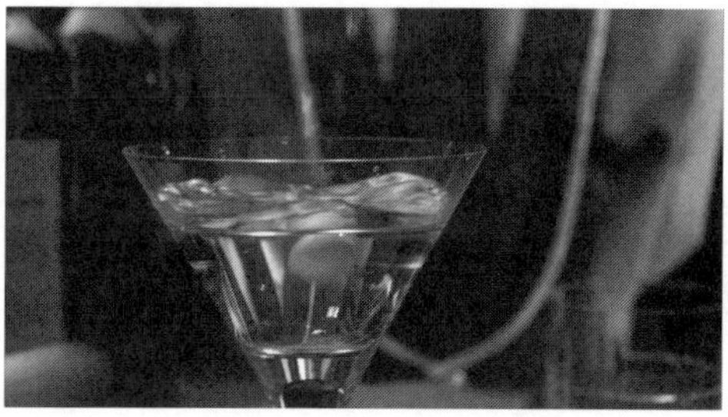

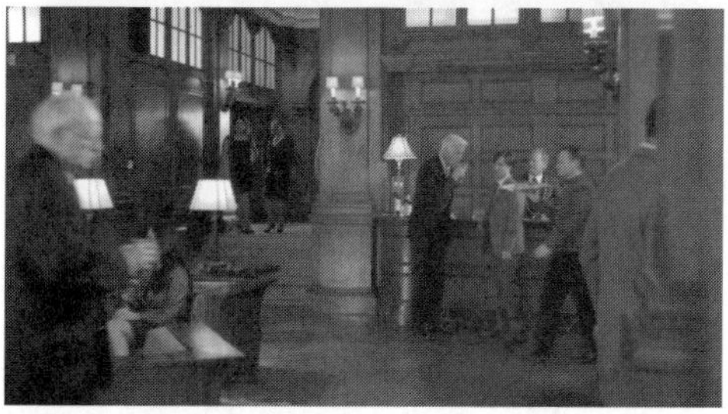

With the drop of an olive from above, in three inventive, economical cuts we're plunked into the start of this comedy episode of *Bored to Death* (2009).

Cut from the gut

This is not to give the impression that editing is a strictly cerebral endeavor. On the contrary, most editors go with their gut more than their head when cutting. They don't dryly reason out each edit. They use their heart and instinct to cut. Sergei Eisenstein reflected on the *Battleship Potemkin*: "The filmed material at the moment of editing can sometimes be wiser than the author or editor. I realized the emotive scenes as the Holy Scriptures say, 'without seeing my creation' that is, I realized them thanks to the feelings which the events inspired within me."

Smooth cutting angles

You may be worrying, "Is my stuff going to cut?" Or you may be confident, thinking, "I shot it. It will cut together like butter." Either way, it's good to know which angles cut together—match—more seamlessly than others as the chart below makes clear.

Type of Angle	Best Match to
ELS, LS, WS	FS, MS, MCU, CU, insert shot.
Full shot	MCU, CU, ECU, insert shot.
Medium long shot	MS, MCU, CU, insert shot.
MS and CU	ECU, insert shot.
Angle on left Angle on right	All angles on right. All angles on left.
Moving shot: pan, dolly, tracking, or crabbing shot	Cut to themselves if pacing and visual continuity match.
Overhead shot	Cuts to almost anything. Minimizes continuity problems.
Over the shoulder or raking shot	Cut to each other in matching pairs and to CU, insert, MLS, LS, and WS.
POV shot	All shots with matched eyelines and directions.
Two-shot	CU, insert, LS, WS or two-shot of different people.

How to get here from there: Transitions between shots and scenes

Usually, an editor uses a cut to make the transition from one shot or scene to another. However, it's also routine to use an effect such as a dissolve or wipe to move from one shot or scene to the next. Once again, it all depends on what the doc or drama demands. Have you just completed a desultory expository scene and now you want to bang into the next scene with a smash cut? Or has this been an emotionally turbulent scene, and you want to give the audience a breather in the form of a long, luscious dissolve to a new locale?

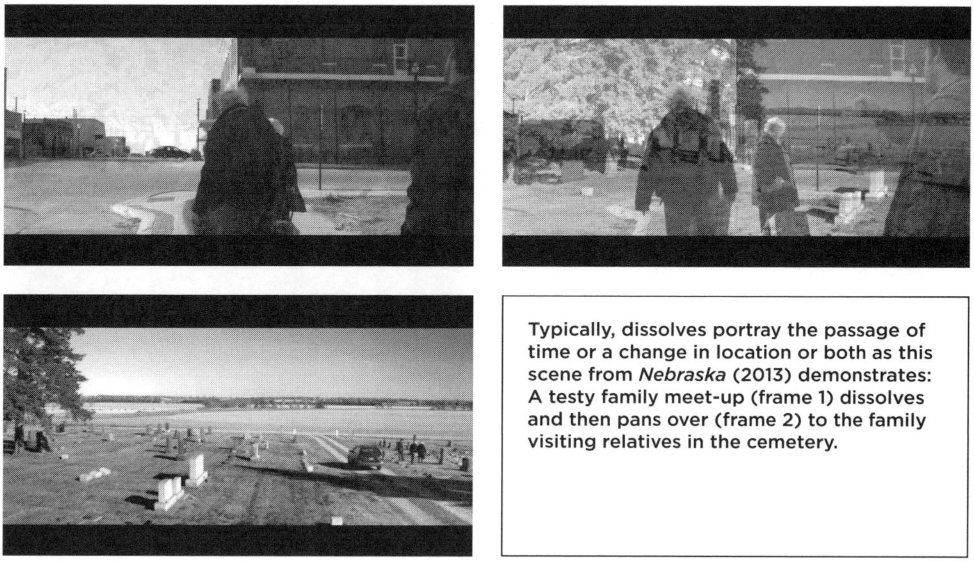

Typically, dissolves portray the passage of time or a change in location or both as this scene from *Nebraska* (2013) demonstrates: A testy family meet-up (frame 1) dissolves and then pans over (frame 2) to the family visiting relatives in the cemetery.

Alternatively, your editor may insert a few frames of white (a "white out") or black (a "black out") before cutting or dissolving to the next scene. Or they may dissolve *to black* (fade out) or *from black* (fade in). Some transition effects are common, some are inventive, some underscore the emotional intensity of a scene, and all must pass the test of serving your film and advancing the story.

MATCH CUTS: HOW AND WHY EDITORS MAKE THEM

When looking for the best place to cut, editors habitually look for a match point—a place in the first shot that is duplicated in the second shot. The primary elements to match are: action (movement), screen direction, eyeline, camera angle, and framing. The secondary elements to match are: props, sound, weather, wardrobe, hair, makeup, lighting, and color. Why? Because these secondary elements can be improved later in post (lighting, color, weather) or masked (the rest) by the skillful matching of other elements.

Match cutting on movement

Cutting on motion makes for smooth yet dynamic cuts. Editors freely match actions to prod the story along or prolong moments. The motion can be as grand as a horse galloping along a beach, as simple as someone exiting a car, or as subtle as a character turning their head.

When editors cut on action, they not only move the story along but also affect time by either shortening or lengthening it. Here are a couple of examples:

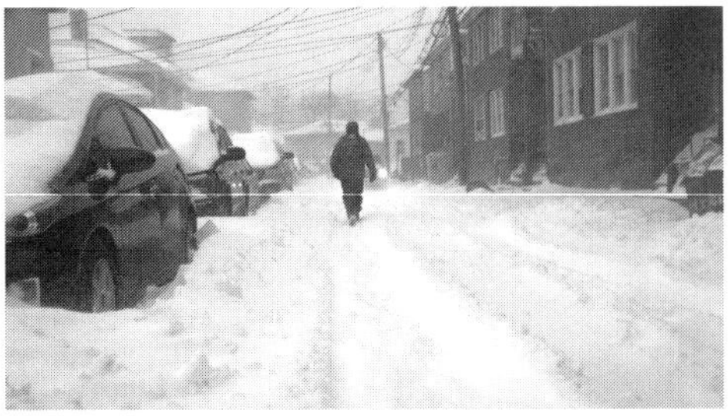

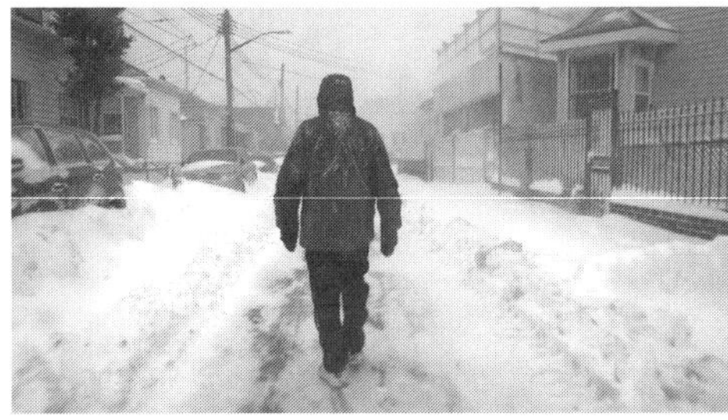

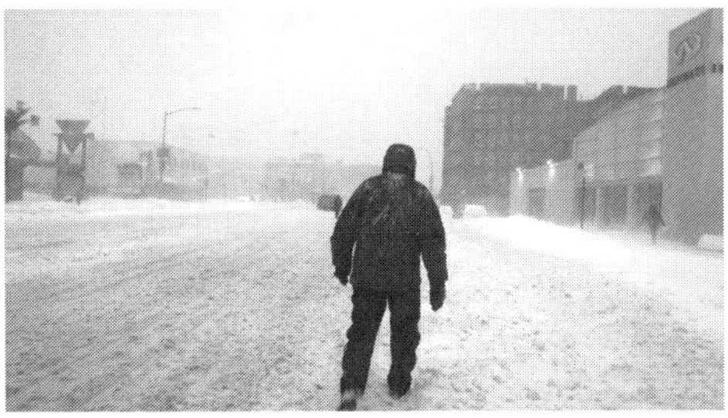

These three cuts from the documentary *The World Before Your Feet* (2018) show Matt Green striding through Brooklyn on his quest to walk every street of every borough of NYC. The cuts forward his story by matching action, background, screen direction, and the sound of the winter wind.

Cutting on movement to tighten the action—compress time

Example: A character goes through a door to enter a building.

The editor shortens the action of a character entering a building by starting them in an exterior wide shot, then cutting to an interior (reverse) shot as they begin to open the door. With the push of the door, this action match cut literally and figuratively pushes the action forward and into the building.

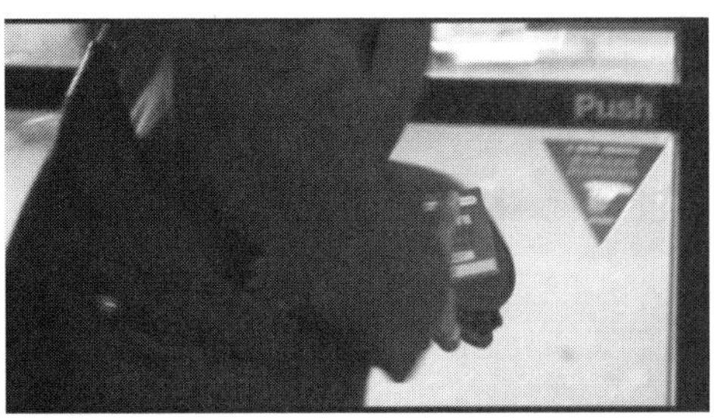

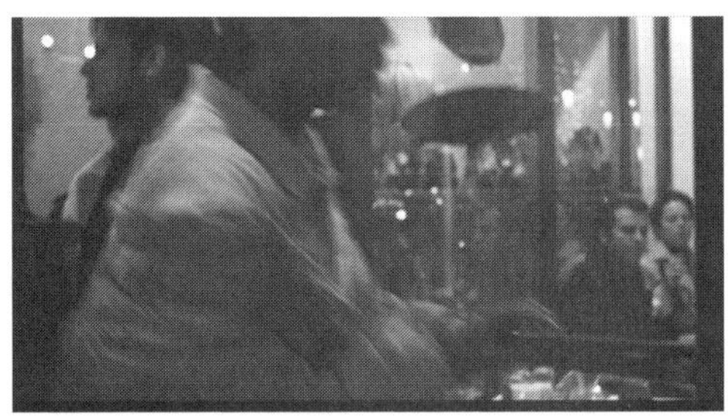

Normally, an action match on a door opening takes a character from inside to outside (or vice versa) or from one room to another. This exceptional door opening match in *Crash* (2004) cuts between two scenes and two characters: It shows one character leaving a store during the day and another character exiting a cafe at night.

Cutting on movement to prolong the action—expand time

Example: Two people kiss.

The editor increases the duration of the kiss by playing it as long as it lasts in one shot, and then cutting to a second shot where it's just started.

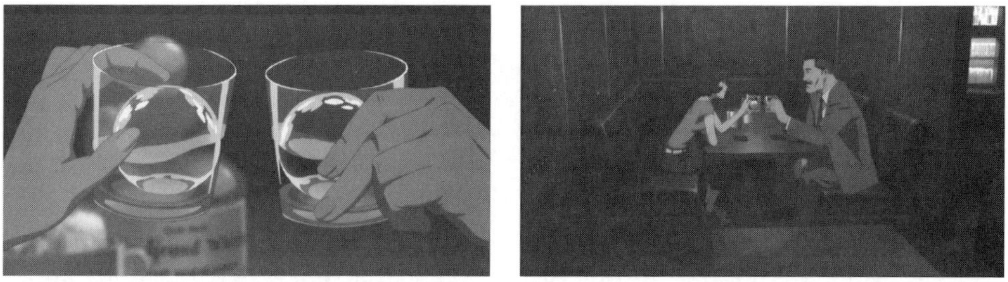

Drinking toasts are regularly extended by action match cuts of glasses clinking as this scene from the anime *Paprika* (2006) demonstrates.

The importance of matching eyelines

> I have a theory about matching, which is; if the eyes are right and if the attitude of the actor is right, the cut should work. —**DEDE ALLEN**, editor, *Bonnie and Clyde, Dog Day Afternoon, Wonder Boys, The Breakfast Club*

Eyes convey emotion and vital reactions. When two characters interact, the audience follows where their eyes are looking—their eyelines. Matching eyelines means the editor makes cuts so the characters are looking at each other. Eyeline matches are workhorse cuts that portray characters' emotions and reactions to each other and their environment. Matching eyelines keeps characters connected and interacting with each other. If eyelines are mismatched and the characters aren't looking at each other, viewers may infer the wrong meaning from their interaction. So, if eyelines don't match, it had better be what you and the editor intend. Usually, nonmatching eyelines mean the characters are avoiding or disregarding each other or distracted or disconnected for some reason that is part of the story.

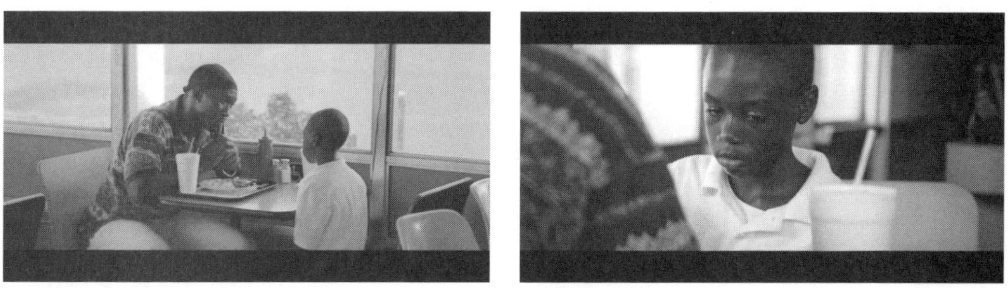

The man tries to get the boy to open up, but the boy's nonmatching eyeline telegraphs his refusal to trust in *Moonlight* (2016).

Match cuts and invisible editing

> An editor is successful when the audience enjoys the story and forgets about the juxtaposition of the shots. If the audience is aware of the editing, the editor has failed.
> —KEN DANCYGER, *The Technique of Film and Video Editing*

Match cuts constitute the majority of the cuts that editors make. Why? Because they push the story forward and preserve the continuity—physical relationships of characters, geography, props, etc.)—of its action and narrative flow. Viewers don't notice these smooth match cuts. This "invisible" editing as it's called, leaves them engrossed in the story and its players—precisely you and your editor's intention!

This seamless, invisible editing is what filmgoers are used to. Just as the symphony audience hears the orchestra and seldom singles out individual instruments, so does the movie audience view the film, taking in the whole show and not the individual edits. Now and then the audience may notice a cut, distinguish the oboe, but most of the time it takes in the whole, be it a film or Beethoven's Fifth.

When cuts don't match you risk losing viewers who may become disoriented, if only momentarily, or drop out of your show. You want to keep them engaged. This does not mean that every cut must match. Good editors make flash cuts, jump cuts, and other noticeable edits as the show demands. They do not make conspicuous cuts to prove anything or because they're the latest, hottest cut, but to support the movie's essence—its theme, story, rhythm, and meaning.

Invisible editing is not the rule; I differ with Dancyger's statement above. Serving the story and the shot material is the rule and means that most frequently, the editing, like the editor, is invisible.

HOW EDITORS DEAL WITH MISMATCHES

Everyone has gleefully spotted a mismatch during a movie, but many more have been put over on us than we have ever detected. Mistakes in continuity and getting around them are a fact of life for an editor. Here are common types of mismatches:

Mismatch	Example
Eyeline	A person looks right and down in one shot and left and up—in a totally different direction—in the next.
Lighting, makeup, hair, or wardrobe	Eyeglasses on in one shot and off in the next.
Pacing of shots	The camera tracks, pans, or dollies faster or slower in one shot than the other.
Position of limbs or props	A bag is in the left hand in one shot and the right hand in the next.
Screen direction	A person or an object does not exit from the right side of one shot and enter from the left of the next shot, so they appear to have jumped across the room.
Screen position	People or objects on the right side of the screen in one shot are on the left side in the next shot.
Sound	The wording, volume, or pacing of the dialogue or sound changes from one shot to the next.
Weather	It rains in one shot and doesn't in the next.

All editors make mismatches, even those who win Academy Awards. We miss these mismatches because we're pulled into the film and don't see the cuts. The skillful editor cuts for drama, pacing, and story which means mismatches occur and usually fly by.

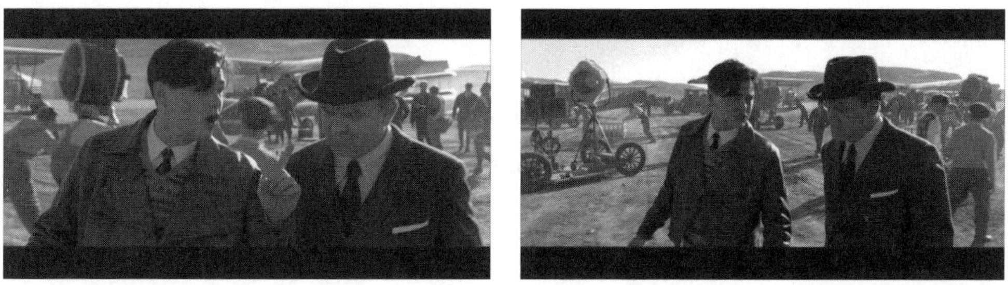

There are three mismatches in this cut from *The Aviator* (2014) which took the Academy Award for Best Editing. Can you spot them? See footnote for the answer.*

*Mismatches: Background (BG) action, hand position of actor on left (Leonardo DiCaprio), and body position (varying distances) between the two actors. These mismatches go unnoticed due to the characters' brisk movement and dialogue and the continuity of the BG sound.

Mismatched angles: Why shots don't cut and how editors fix them

Invisible editing calls for angles that match, but not all do, which you will see if you observe editing or try it yourself. So which angles don't match? The table below lists them along with editors' solutions.

Shots that don't cut together	Reason they mismatch	Solutions
Shots with too similar angles.	Too similar angles make for obvious jump cuts, mismatches, no new information, and a lack of visual variety.	Use angles that cut together (see previous table). Enlarge—blow up—one shot to a cuttable close-up.
Shots with drastically different framing.	They look poor, unsettle the viewer, and can make a person appear to be a giant or a dwarf—be disproportionate.	Cut to a MCU, CU, LS or overhead shot before going to the angle.
Two-shot to two-shot in a three-person scene.	The person common to both shots will appear to jump and most likely will cause a continuity problem.	Bridge two-shots by cutting to a MCU, CU, LS, or an overhead shot.
Moving shot of moving subject to static shot.	Subject will appear to jump.	Before cutting to the static shot allow the: - Moving shot to stop. - Subject to stop moving. - Subject to exit frame.

Tips and Tricks: How Editors Finesse Mismatches

Primarily, to mask a mismatch, editors act like magicians, intuiting where the audience's eyes will be. Audiences notice movement and will overlook the mismatch. More specifically, editors mitigate mismatches in several ways: 1) They cut earlier or later, where there is a better match point. 2) They make an overlap*: Sound and picture cutting in different places assuages the mismatch, smooths the transition to the next shot, and keeps the story moving. 3) They cut away to another shot such as an insert or close-up. 4) They fix sound mismatches such as uneven volumes across shots and scenes or unwanted noises by equalizing the volume levels, covering them with ambience or music, or making audio dissolves (cross fading).

* Cutting to the sound of an incoming shot before cutting to its picture or vice versa; cutting to the picture of an incoming shot before cutting to its sound. Editors habitually overlap, regardless of a mismatch.

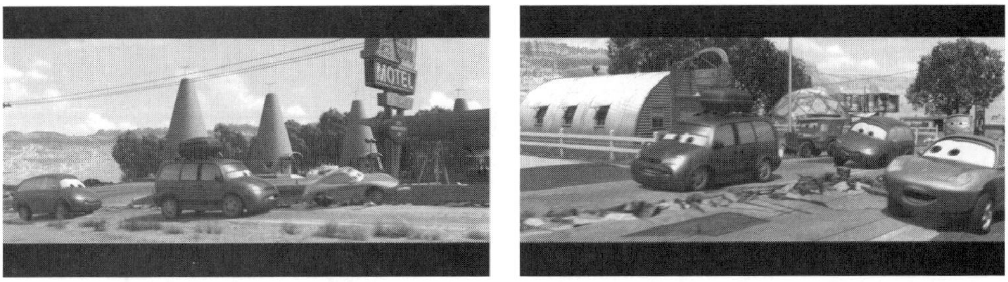

This cut from *Cars* (2006) is mismatched four ways: Screen direction, screen position (sports car), background, and foreground. The motion of the sports car surging to the front of the line helps keep the focus off the confusion.

When are mismatches acceptable?

Mismatches are an expected part of the drama in battle and other chaotic scenes. Mismatches are part of editing, and at times, the only possible cut or the best cut. In the words of director-editor Edward Dmytryk, "Always remember that film is the art of illusion, and the most unlikely things can be made to seem real." The real, underlying question is: "What is a bad cut?" A bad cut is one that takes your viewers out of the show. A brief disengagement isn't a worry, but if your audience doesn't hang with your show and drops out, you've got more serious storytelling problems.

EDITING RHYTHM

> It's the editor who orchestrates the rhythm of the images . . . For me, the editor is like a musician, and often a composer. —**MARTIN SCORSESE,** Director, *The Irishman, The Wolf of Wall Street, Hugo, Taxi Driver*

Everyone talks about rhythm in editing but what do they mean? Rhythm is the duration of shots and the number of shots in a sequence e.g., short and many or long and few. Rhythm is the pace of the cuts and is similar to music, in that it varies over the course of the picture. Some scenes will tick . . . tick . . . tick . . . Others will tick, tick, tick. And still others will ticktickticktick.

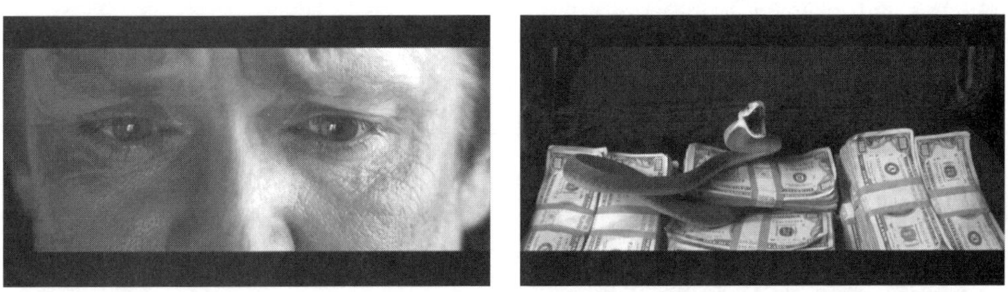

Budd is not counting on the fatal payoff of this lightning-quick smash cut. He's as shocked as the audience in *Kill Bill: Vol. 2* (2004).

Just as musicians refer to beats in a composition, editors talk about beats in a scene. To editors, a beat is a plot point or an action—where something happens or changes in a scene. A beat may be subtle as an eyeblink or as stunning as a long lost sister unexpectedly appearing on the horizon. There are beats of action within every scene; for example, soldiers advancing and retreating or a character making an increasing mess in the kitchen.

Expanding and contracting time using rhythm and pacing

> There are things an editor injects into a film: structure, pace, symmetry, the little gaps in between cuts. All of this is a rhythm. —**MICHAEL KAHN**, A.C.E., *West Side Story, Saving Private Ryan, Schindler's List, Jurassic Park*

The power of editing is clearly witnessed in the way editors deal with time. "We listen to the footage," they like to say. Editors live and breathe with the footage ahead of the audience or anyone else, taking in its pulse and altering its filmed timing. An editor can build a fast-paced chase scene—compress time—that has viewers' pulses racing. Battles can be fought and lost, and a 100-year war can be over in two minutes or less. It's all in the pacing of the footage, the timing of the cuts—the dance of the movie.

Conversely, an editor can hold a shot or series of shots—expand time—causing the audience to inhale a sublime sequence of images, say of the sun rising over a city. We've all seen the time-stretching sequence where the basketball leaves the shooter's hands just as the buzzer goes off at the end of a tied game. Will the ball go in the basket? The shot is slo-mo. The editor cuts around to the bleachers, the coach, the players. The moment is extended, time almost stops . . . and the basket whooshes through the hoop.

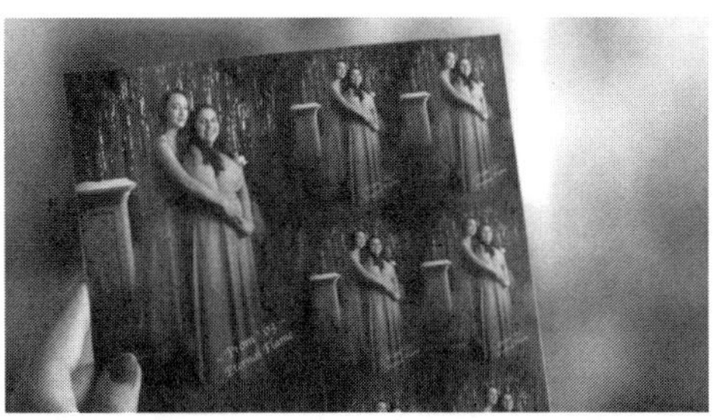

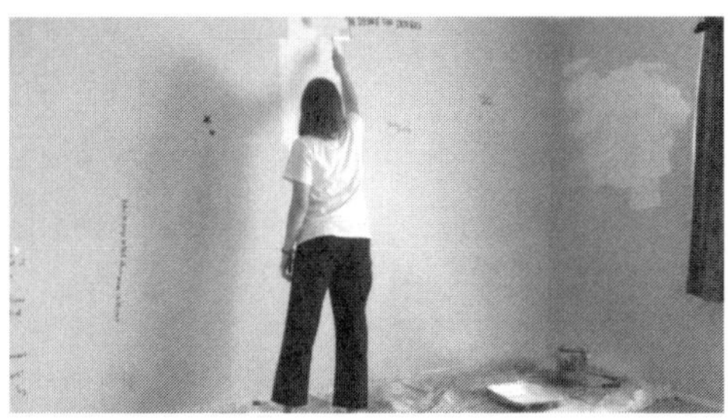

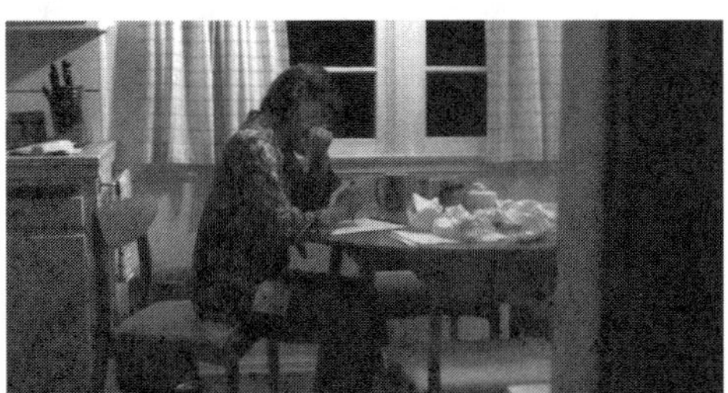

The summer goes by in a few cuts as Lady Bird (Saoirse Ronan), the main character in *Lady Bird* (2017), prepares for college.

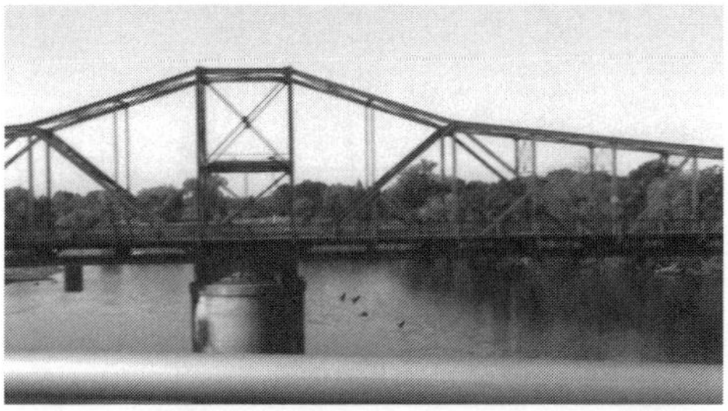

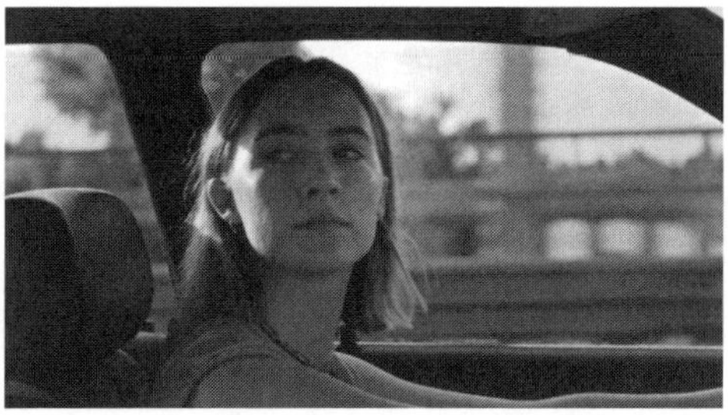

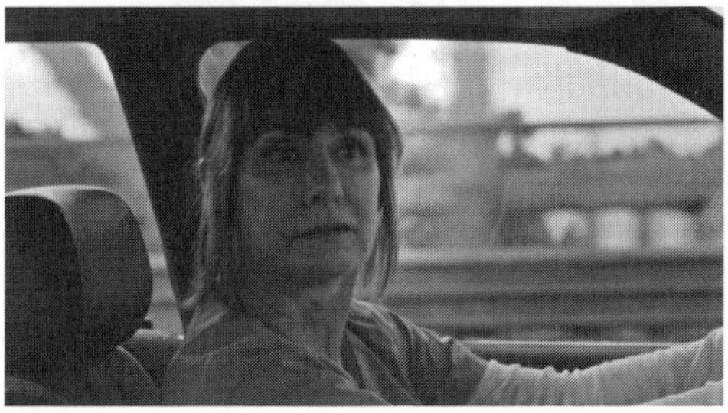

Time slows down as Lady Bird leaves home and a contentious relationship with her mother near the end of *Lady Bird* (2017).

Cut tight or cut loose

When editors leave little room between actions or "pull the air out of" lines of dialogue and narration, they are cutting tight. When they open up a cut, line, or scene to insert a breath or beat, they are cutting loose. The tightness or looseness of a scene affects its rhythm and is dictated by the action and purpose of the scene and the show.

Cut tight

Expository scenes are often tightly edited in order to deliver information rapidly and hook the audience. Commonly, editors cut tight to sustain a dialogue scene or to keep a taut pace of an action scene.

Cut loose

Just as composers write rests into their music, so editors prolong a shot or shots within a scene or add an establishing shot after a frenzied scene to give the audience a breather. Reflexively they hold a beat on an actor to expand the emotion and time e.g., on a comedy to let the audience recover from a laugh. Editors also vary the length of the cuts—short, medium, extra short, long—so that just as viewers relax, a monster alien jumps out, or vice versa, just when the audience tenses up on the edge of their seats, a troupe of clowns rolls out of a barrel.

THE POWER OF CUTTING IN REACTION SHOTS

Be aware: A reaction is worth a thousand words. The reaction can be a wide shot of Cary Grant trying to outrun a crop duster, a medium shot of Kate Winslet, arms

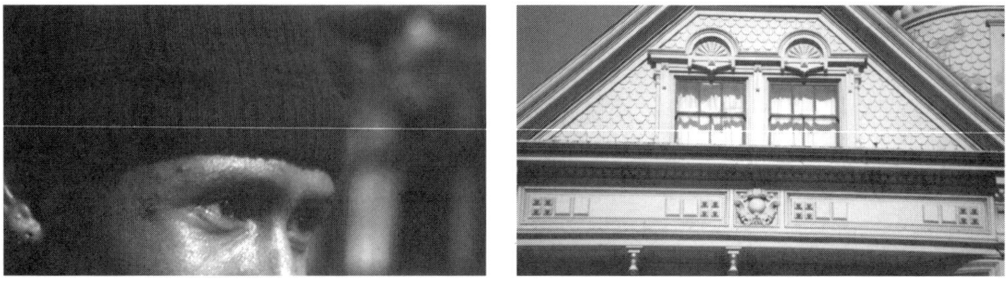

Jimmie eyes his family's former home in the drama *The Last Black Man in San Francisco* (2019).

outstretched, on the prow of the *Titanic*, or a close-up of Meryl Streep, who, with her face alone, can communicate more than a page of dialogue. Editing in actors' reactions or the reactions of people in a documentary can be extremely powerful and key moviegoers' emotional responses: Should they hold their breath? Or laugh, cry, worry, or rage against the system?

Frequently, it's more important to show filmgoers how a person, group, or crowd of people is reacting, rather than to cut to what's happening. This means that at times you and your editor may decide to play part or all of a scene on the listener-reactors instead of the speaker. For instance, it may be less important to see the dictator ranting and more important to see how the citizens are reacting. Will they string up the tyrant or blindly obey him?

In addition, reaction shots and other cutaway shots can serve you in very practical ways. They can bridge locations and continuity gaps, speed up slow sections, and skip over unwanted action bits. On documentaries, editors reflexively deploy them to leap from one part of an interview to another. On a scripted show, if you've re-ordered or deleted lines, a reaction can cover the gap.

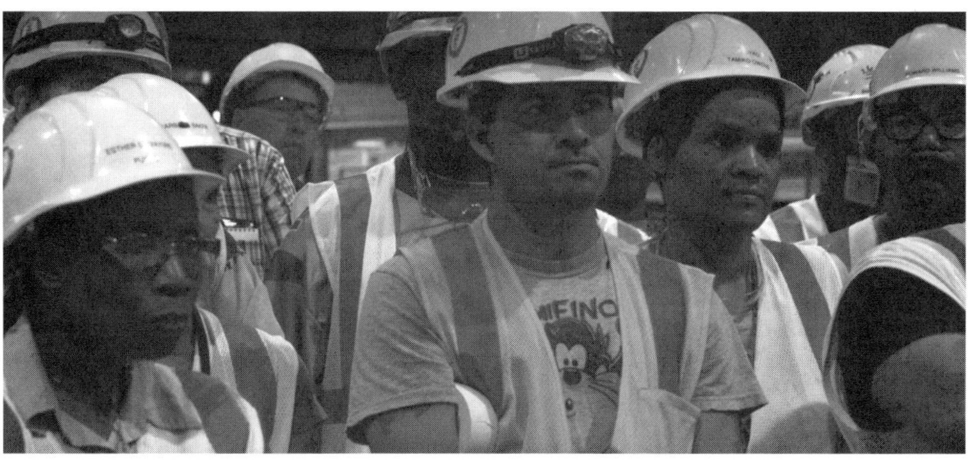

Glass workers react to meeting new management from China in *American Factory* (2019), Academy Award winner for Best Documentary.

CHEATING SHOTS

Editors often take reactions and other shots and cut them into places you didn't shoot them for. This is known as *cheating* or *stealing* shots. For example, they:

1. Use an actor's reaction to line seven for line twelve.
2. Take a shot from before you say "action," at the start of scene or from after you say "cut," at the end of the scene.
3. Freely mix crowd reaction shots from several courtroom scenes.
4. Construct action and montage scenes from shots taken on different days and in different places.

Cheating dialogue

From time to time your editor will cheat dialogue to "put words into the actor's mouth," as it's referred to. They do this to overcome a technical difficulty with the audio or to marry the best picture and sound performances.

Cheating on documentaries

It's acceptable to substitute shots and reactions on a doc if the cheat accurately portrays people's responses and the situation. If it doesn't, this is unethical. For instance, showing Reverend Pat Robertson performing a same sex marriage would be a lie—perhaps a fantasy or a comedy! You and your editor must maintain integrity on non-scripted pieces with every image, dialogue, and narrative choice you make.

EDITING THE ACTION SCENE

> ... however good the director's raw material, it is the editor who makes or mars a sequence of action. —**KAREL REISZ AND GAVIN MILLAR** from their seminal book *The Techniques of Film Editing*

"All hell breaks loose when the crowd realizes the banker has run off with the till," reads the script. "A series of shots of the climbers summiting Everest," says the paper cut. Drama or doc, the action scene is but a vision and perhaps a storyboard until the editor creates it. Propelled by images, an action scene is often accentuated by music and punctuated by sounds and words, but not reliant on dialogue which it may lack entirely.

Many action scenes land in the editing room with tons of footage from multiple cameras. How does the editor deal with this overwhelming amount of footage to select images and carve out the drama? This section throws light on editing action scenes so you can understand how to perfect them with your editor.

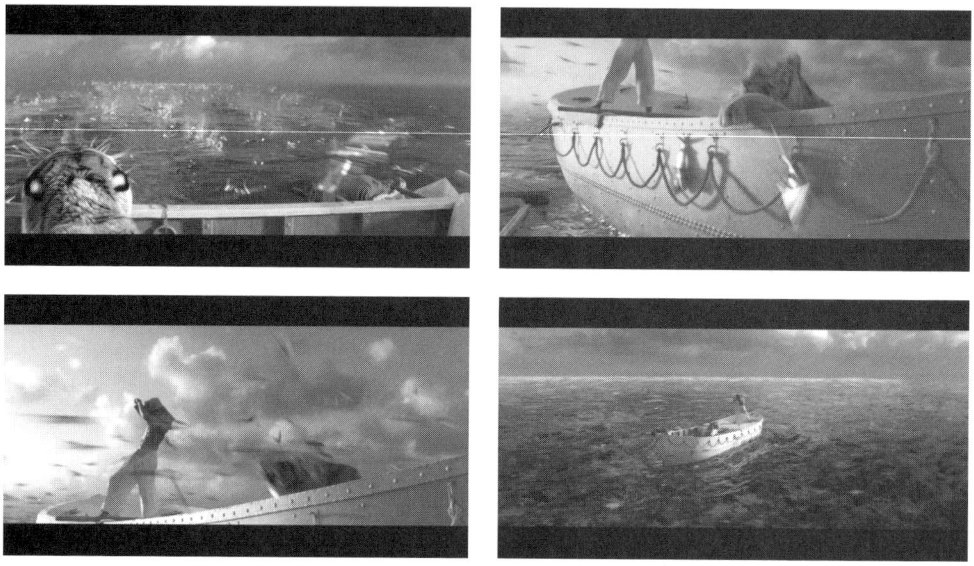

This gloriously outlandish scene of flying fish from *Life of Pi* (2012) consists of multiple angles and sounds: the thuds and plunges of the fish and the grunts of the tiger and the boy.

Pacing the action scene: what makes the action scene move

> . . . while it's great to talk about how revolutionary *Avatar* is, we were still making a movie . . . all this technology is just there to make the images more compelling and to tell the story better. Ultimately, we're asking the same questions editors always ask: Does this shot work? Does this scene serve the story? It's all about performance and story. —**JOHN REFOUA**, A.C.E., co-editor, *Avatar*

The pace of the action scene is produced by the type of shots (LS, CU, etc.), their length, and their placement. Inexperienced camera operators sometimes believe that keeping shots in motion by shifting the camera around creates the pace of a show. Not true. Pans, dollies, and zooms don't usually move at the same rate and if cut together may result in a gut-wrenching scene of the wrong kind. The editor sets the pace from a series of static and moving shots.

Shots and the information they convey

Long shots and wide shots contain more information, so to make them register, editors hold them on screen longer. Since viewers absorb close-ups and medium shots more quickly, editors cut them shorter. Intercutting wider and closer shots affect a scene's pace and heighten the dramatic tension to put your audience on the edge of their seats.

The cutting and pacing of an action scene is similar to music, with its fast and moderate tempos, staccatos, and rests. To get a cutting rhythm going, some editors crank up the rock music; others turn off all sound and cut in silence. As the action moves along, the edits tend to get shorter and the angles closer. Wham! The editor cuts back for the next strike, the next score, the next pratfall. The notorious shower scene in Hitchcock's *Psycho* (1960), lasts two minutes and contains 50 cuts, for an ASL (average shot length) of 2.4". Many scenes in modern films have even shorter ASLs. But it's not the number of quick cuts that make an action scene effective. Buster Keaton's famous train sequence in *The General* (1926) spans 18 minutes and 160 cuts. It's the juxtaposition and duration of shots—short and close, long and wide—that determine the show's pace.

Think of an action scene as a mini story; each cut, no matter how long or short, must be motivated and advance the story.

Repeating the action

Editors frequently repeat the same action in two or more angles to milk the big event: the bomb blast, the bridge collapse, the train smash, etc. By intercutting different angles and slo-mo shots of the same action, the editor spins out the action. Usually, the repeating of action is obvious as the editor duplicates longer or different portions of the action over a series of shots. This overlapping of picture amplifies the action for dramatic or comic impact and expands time. Editors also regularly repeat frames between cuts because viewers' eyes don't instantly catch up between certain shots. For instance, if you repeat a few frames of the action at the tail of a long shot and the head of a close shot, the result is a smooth cut that viewers perceive as a continuous motion.

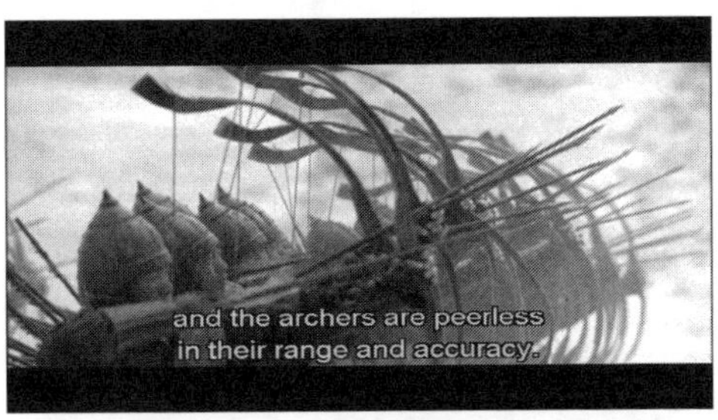

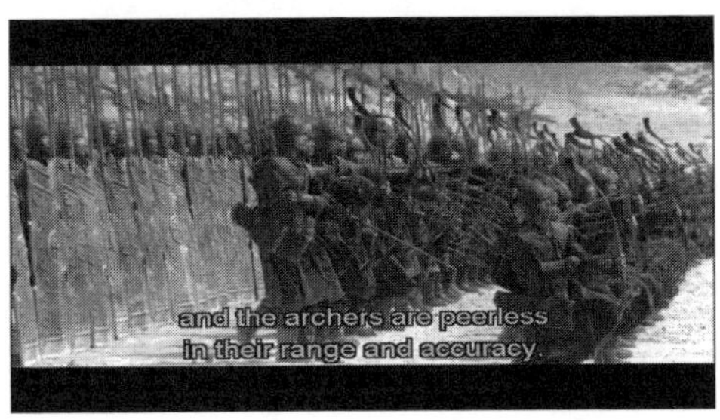

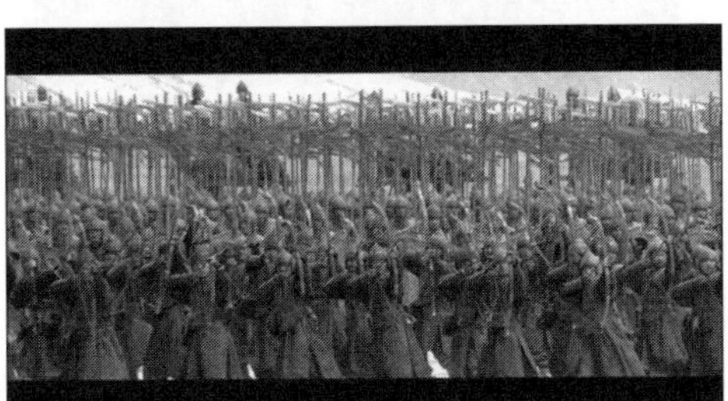

The archers repeated bow lifting actions draw out the wait for the battle to begin in *Hero* (2002).

Putting the people in action scenes

> All the scenes in *The Hurt Locker* are intimate character scenes, even the big action ones. That's what sets this apart from other films that just have random things that go "boom" in them. We had to keep the character drama alive during the action sequences, just as much—if not more—as in the quieter, more intimate moments.
> —**CHRIS INNIS AND ROBERT MURAWSKI**, winners of the Academy Award for Best Editing for *The Hurt Locker*

Compelling characters + well shot scenes = best action scenes

Cutting in characters' reactions heightens the emotional intensity of an action scene. It also forwards the drama, as characters respond and act to send the plot in unexpected directions. Often, you'll want to show reaction shots of minor characters and bystanders as well as the main character(s) in a scene.

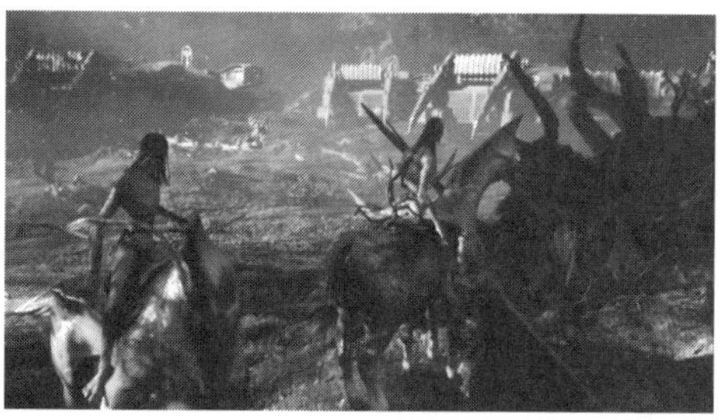

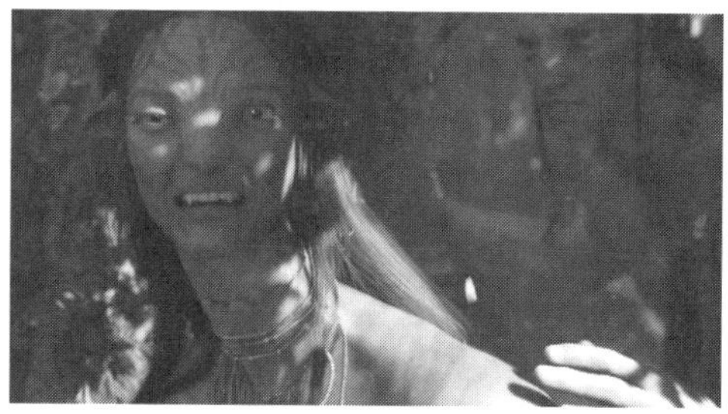

The action drops back for a reaction in *Avatar* (2009).

Reaction shot saves the scene

I was the assistant editor on a sitcom with Dann Cahn, a television editor famous for his innovative comedy editing on *I Love Lucy*. We worked on an episode where a boy got a tractor going and couldn't stop it until it smashed into a partially constructed house. There were many cameras and takes of the action, but no reactions of the boy. Dann caught this omission and brought it up to the director. The director agreed but said it was too late—there was no time to go back to the location. "Put him in a chair," Dann persisted. So, the crew went outside the sound stage, hoisted the actor in a chair above their heads, and wiggled it from side to side against the sky while the camera caught him in a close-up. When cut in, the boy's reactions made all the difference in the scene.

EDITING IN 3D

> You don't cut a 3D movie just like you don't write a 3D movie or compose shots in 3D. There are some small accommodations to the stereo that need to be made, but they should always be downstream of the dramatic edit. I don't think we shifted one cut because of it. More people are going to see *Avatar* in 2D anyway, so the edit is the edit; it has to stand on its own.
> James Cameron, director and co-editor on *Avatar*

Nowadays, feature films and TV shows—including action, dialogue, and animation pictures—regularly rely on CGI (computer generated images), complex VFX, and/or computer modeling. Even though 3D's popularity waxes and wanes, a number of shows continue to shoot 3D or bump from 2D to 3D, keeping it a fixture in today's cinematic landscape. So how does 3D affect editing?

Editors and 3D

Due to 3D being so costly, editors are onboarded during the storyboard phase of pre-production so they can put together sequences and aid in the creation of the characters, lines, and the story as well as the previz. They collaborate with you, the writer, cinematographer, production designer, lay out, and others. Collaboration as well as organization are key on 3D shows within editorial itself because there are so many editors: picture, VFX, sound, assistant editors, etc. Other factors of 3D editing include:

- Master shots are cut longer than usual so moviegoers can take in the action and the world being created.
- Camera movement must be well-defined because fast paced, blurry camera moves are too much for viewers to take in.
- More time is allotted for editing due to:
  - Large amount of footage such as VFX, CGI, 3D modeling, and virtual capture.
  - Having to create multiple versions: 2D, 3D, and IMAX 3D.

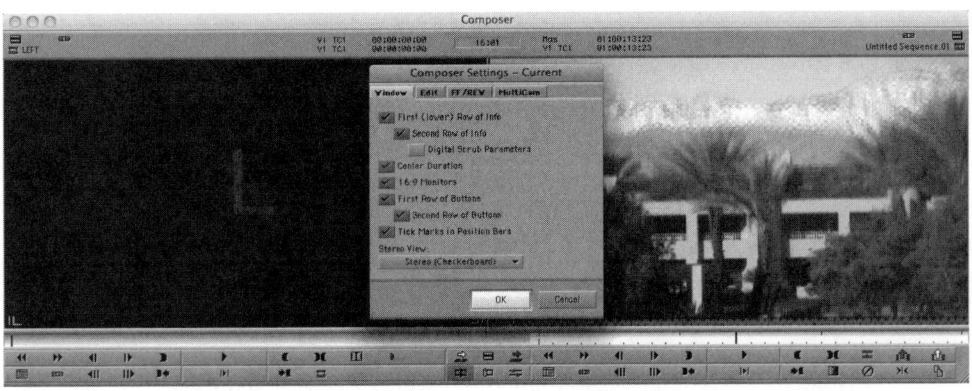

Editor's eye view of 3D: A 2D view screen which synchronizes both eye images, left eye on top, to simulate 3D. *Photo courtesy of Avid.*

Editing 3D on the digital system

Since stereo (3D) projection works by converging two images—one for each eye—that have been captured at slightly different angles, editors must view the two images properly converged in 3D. Most editors cut in 2D lower res proxy versions, then screen scenes and cuts in 3D due to the tremendous amount of storage 3D devours.

JC Bond, additional editor on *Alice in Wonderland* (2010), reflects on the difference between cutting 2D and 3D: ". . . you get used to the fact that you're looking at something in stereo. And then you just cut it like a regular movie. There's no major difference beyond that. There are minor considerations. You can do some cheats in 2D where you may cross the line, and things like that are a bit more jarring in stereo. But from a creative standpoint, you should try to avoid those things—even in regular 2D."

3D is part of the continuum of the melding of the technical and theatrical worlds to immerse the audience evermore deeply in the world they're seeing. 3D is another aid to storytelling that lets viewers experience your show in more emotional and sensory ways. If the story's good, and well done, 3D will enhance it. If the story's no good, no amount of 3D or HD will help—it will just deserve a plain old D.

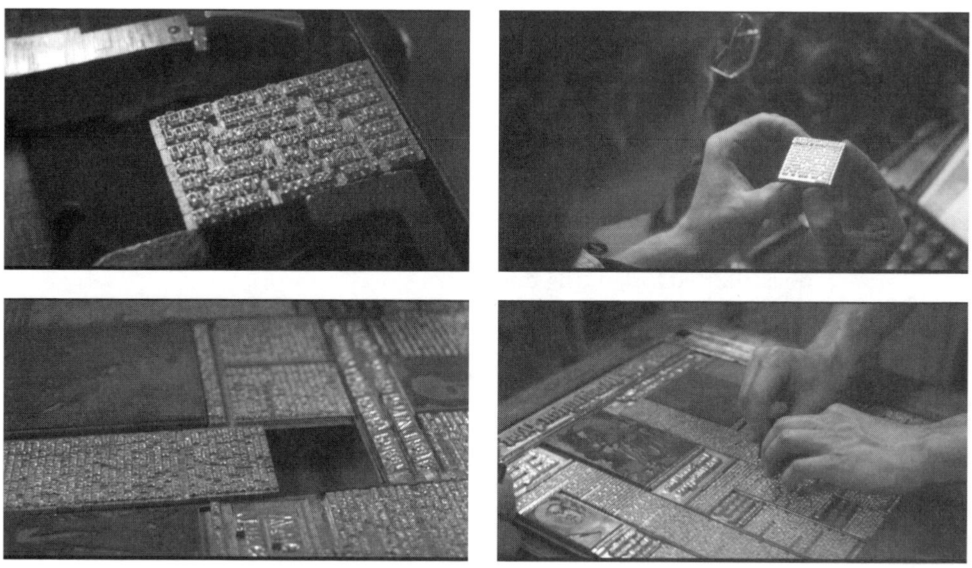

In *The Post* (2017), two short, fast paced montage scenes portraying the linotype set up of the newspaper are intercut with tense decision-making scenes as to whether to publish the *Pentagon Papers*.

CUTTING MONTAGE

What exactly is a montage? Answer: A succinct, self-contained interlude of images inserted to convey or recap facts, and feelings. Montage scenes regularly pop up under opening credits and are commonly expository or function as bridges between dialogue or action scenes. Documentaries, commercials, infomercials, dramas, and comedies—all genres use montages.

A montage can be one of three types: dramatic, comic, or informative as the table below describes.

Type of montage	Example
DRAMATIC	
Grief or Recovery	The character walks the old, familiar path on the beach or in the city, stares out the window on a rainy day, or lies in bed unable to move. After the montage, the character returns to life by taking a first step or making a choice of some kind.
Love	Two lovers enjoy sunsets, romantic dinners, rolls in the hay, etc., before emerging from their cocoon and confronting the realities lurking around the corner.
War	A platoon goes through the travails of boot camp, setting the scene for battle and the testing of the soldiers.
Success	A rock band jams in a garage and by the end of the montage is playing at Madison Square Garden.
COMIC	
Job	A college grad is interviewed by a series of bizarre employers.
Dating	A woman goes out with a string of off-the-wall dates.
Clothing	A man tries on a succession of ridiculous ties.
INFORMATION	
History	Immigrants arrive in Manhattan and erect the city.
Process	A mayfly hatches, grows, mates, and dies.
Search	A reporter travels to different holy sites, seeking enlightenment.

Putting a montage together

The montage arises from the script, the outline, you, or the editor. A script or outline for the montage typically reads like these examples:

- A series of shots as Jack and Jill go up the hill.
- A montage of newspaper headlines condemning the murder.
- Archival footage of tornadoes in the Midwest.

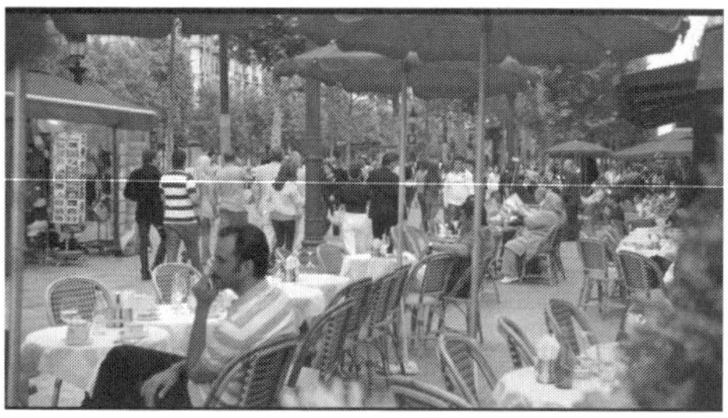

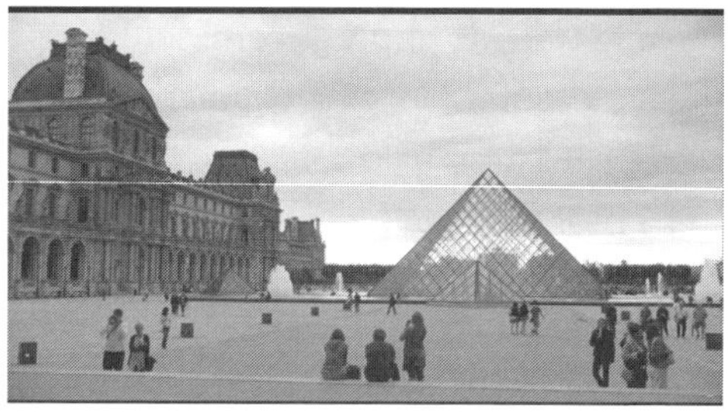

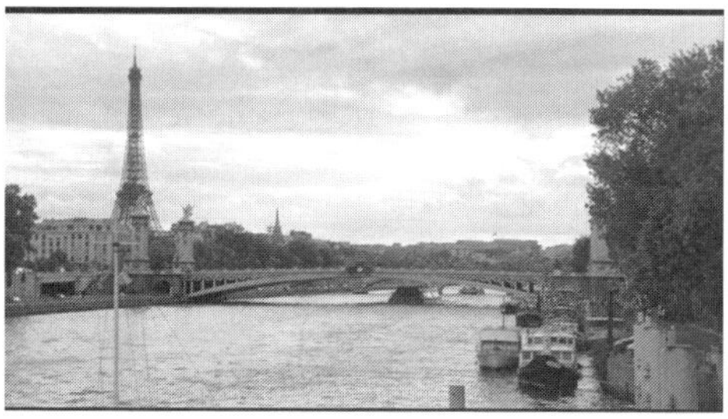

A nearly four-minute opening montage set to a languid jazz melody establishes the pace, place, and time in Woody Allen's *Midnight in Paris* (2011).

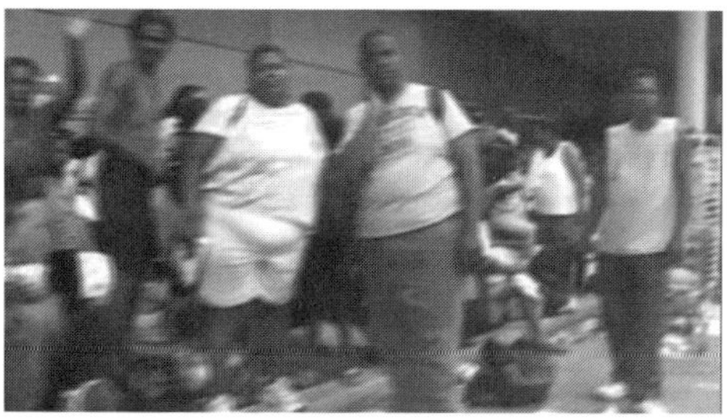

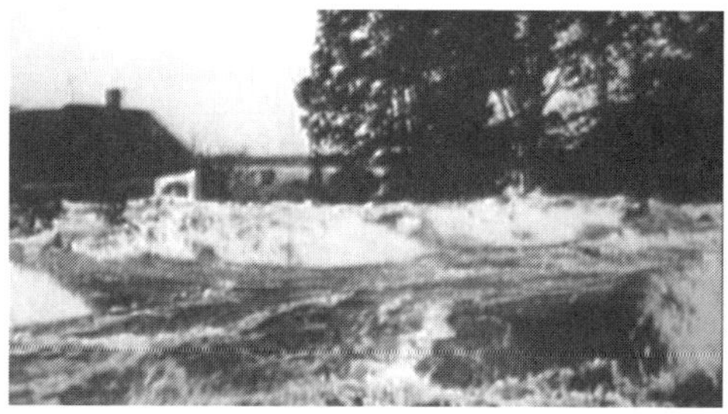

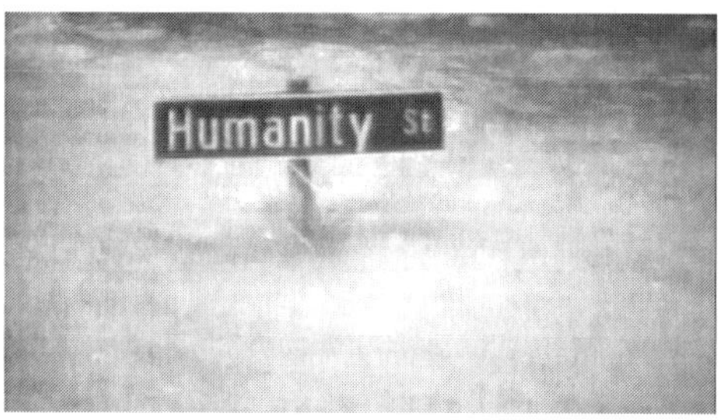

Spike Lee's three-minute montage at the start of *When the Levees Broke: A Requiem in Four Acts* (2006-2007) serves as an elegy to New Orleans.

The rules for cutting a montage are the same as for cutting anything else. The main difference is that cuts are usually separated by dissolves, wipes, or other transition effects. Commonly, the cuts tend to get shorter as the montage progresses. Few montages are silent: Most contain little or no sync dialogue or narration and are set to music, though some use wild sound or deliberate, recurring manufactured sounds. Editors often cut a montage to a piece of music but just as often they add the music or narration afterwards.

A montage typically consists of a collage of images from different times, places, and sources. If you and your editor end up creating one together, you may stumble across random unexpected connections. When you've finished editing the montage, you may delight in having created a scene that is bigger than the sum of its shots.

CUTTING DIALOGUE

Dialogue is a pulse editor's cut to and can drive a scene or even an entire show. While spoken words are important, it's the interactions between people, be they real or fictional, that keep your audience engaged. A dialogue scene forges relationships between characters using the actors' words and looks. These relationships, whether they wither or thrive, are integral to the development of your show, and must be carefully constructed.

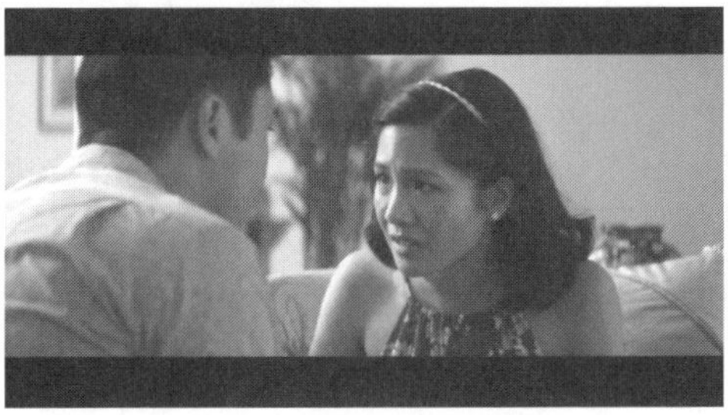

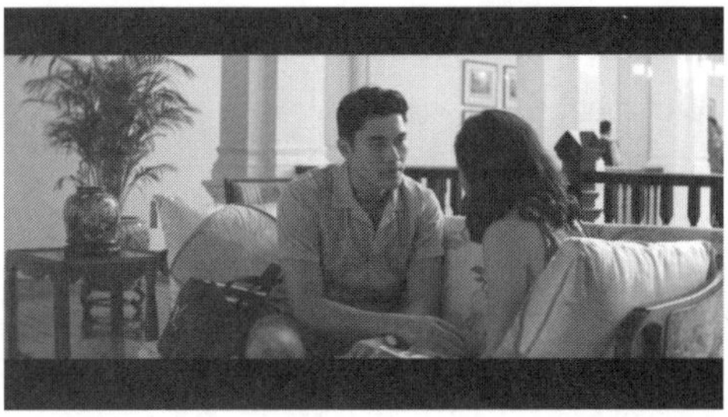

A couple quarrels in *Crazy Rich Asians* (2018).

Arc and pacing

With narrative and dialogue scenes, building the growth and movement—the arc—of each character or documentary subject is vital. This requires cutting the looks and words at the pace each scene demands. The words set the pace 80% of the time in dialogue scenes. Proper pacing requires tightening words and lines in some places and loosening them in others. This is particularly true when cutting comedy, but also applies to drama. When you and your editor are absorbed in editing or re-editing a dialogue scene, you'll become keenly attuned to this subtle but crucial pacing and will live and breathe with your characters.

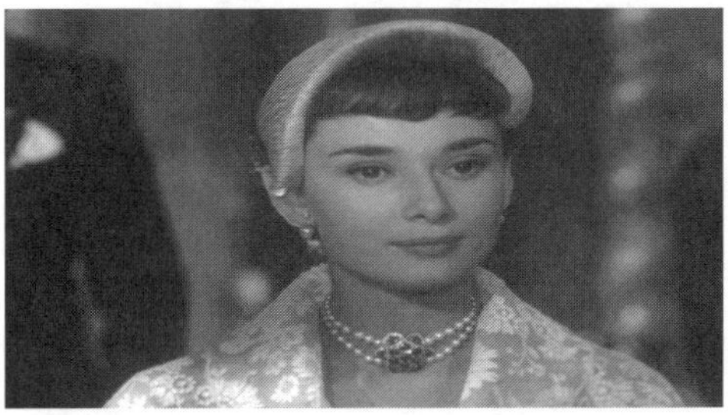

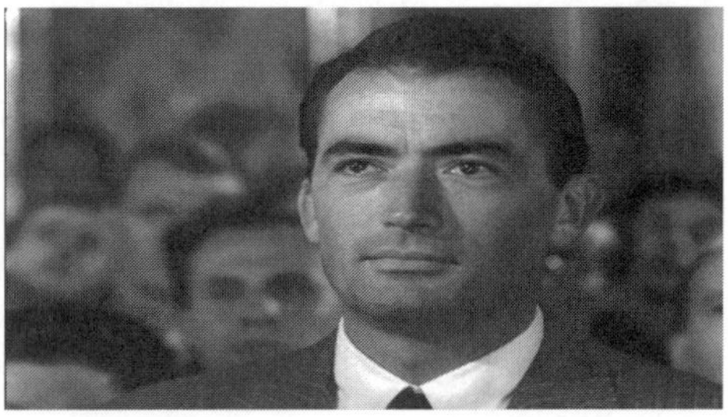

The state-crossed lovers share their final glances in *Roman Holiday* (1953).

CUTTING NARRATION

For editing purposes, narration is defined as a speaker's voice that is heard but not seen while visuals play. It's also referred to as voice over narration, voice over, or VO. Editors edit narration in two ways: 1) They cut the picture and add the narration track later or 2) They lay out the narration then drop in the pictures. Both approaches necessitate some frame adjustments after the second element is added to make sound and picture mesh perfectly.

Approach 1: Cut picture, add narration

Ordinarily, editors cut the picture first. Once the narration has been written, they record and lay in a temporary narration track referred to as the *scratch track*. The scratch track narrator can be you, the editor, the producer, or someone else recruited for their suitable speaking voice. A scratch track is immensely helpful for timing visuals and making certain that they dovetail with the written narration and have the desired impact. Due to expense, the final narration is recorded by a professional narrator and laid in after you've screened a few cuts and the show is in solid shape or locked.

Approach 2: Cut narration, add pictures

On documentaries, editors often start by stringing together the words of the person being interviewed or the narrator speaking. They cut and paste sentences, phrases, and words and may jump around parts of the interview or between takes of the narrator. Since they're ignoring the picture for the moment, some people call this a *radio cut*. While constructing a radio cut, they'll "pull out the air"—remove pauses, false starts, and the "ums" and "uhs." Their goal is to knit together a coherent, well-paced VO that accurately states what the interviewee or narrator said. Once the narration is complete, they'll drop in appropriate visuals, and likely have a few anchor points where the interviewee speaks on camera.

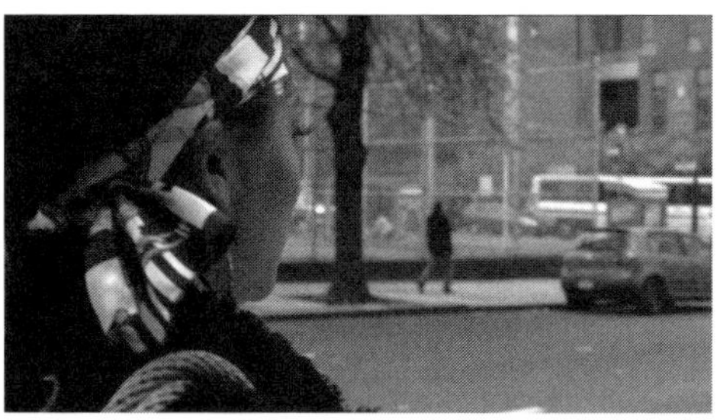

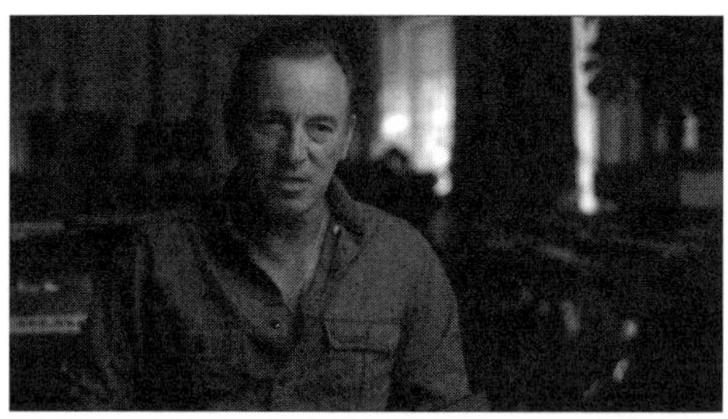

20 Feet from Stardom (2013), a doc that illuminates the lives of backup singers, begins with the VO of Bruce Springsteen and then cuts to him on camera.

CUTTING MUSIC

> When you work with sound, you have to think about what works for the picture and how to manipulate the audience's emotions. I love to intertwine music and sound effects to create a 'soup' that is very atmospheric—so you can't tell the difference between the music and the effects. —**CHRIS DICKENS**, editor, *Rocketman, Les Misérables, Slumdog Millionaire*

It's always amazing to experience what laying in the right piece of music does to a scene. Suddenly your documentary comes alive. The shots in your montage flow together. Those boring seconds where the shero crosses the hall have life and purpose and finally seem joined to the rest of the picture. Serendipity! A song can boost a film and, if over end credits, leave a positive final impression of the show. We can all think of at least one film where the theme song was more memorable than the movie. Tom Bullock writes in his book, *Sound Editing Nuts and Bolts,* "As far back as silent movie days, film music has always been used as the 'cosmic glue' to save scenes that are not happening pix-wise." Many shows go overboard with music, spreading the cosmic glue everywhere, but there's no denying that music can keep a show alive and breathing, like an audible heartbeat.

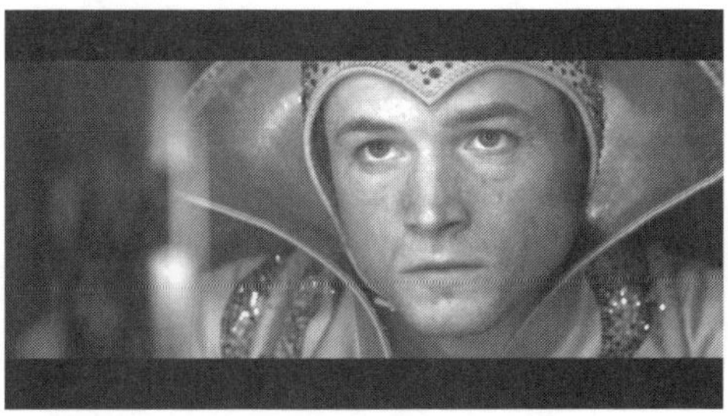

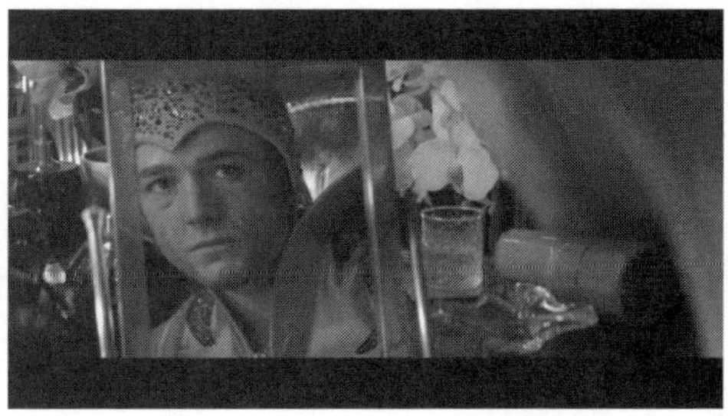

The music in *Rocketman* (2019) drives the movie as much as does the story of Elton John's life.

Cutting in music

Time and again when your editor lays in a song, you'll be astonished at how key actions miraculously fall on beats. Sound engineer, Tomlinson Holman, the "TH" in THX sound, asserts in his book, *Sound for Film and Television*: "Music imposes its own order on a scene, whether the picture is cut to the music or not. It is surprising how many times music will be laid underneath a scene of someone walking, for example, and the walk appears to be 'on the beat.' Somehow our brain searches for order out of chaos and imposes it finding order where none was intended."

Which comes first: Picture or music?

Just as with folding in narration, editors can cut the picture first, and add the music later or lay down the music and then add the visuals. It all depends on when the music is available and a variety of other reasons, as the table below makes clear. Whichever cutting method your editor uses, as with adding narration, they will likely fine-tune the picture afterwards. Also, editors frequently finesse music by dropping out or repeating stanzas or lines, creating invisible aural cuts.

	Scenario	How it's handled
Cut pix to MX	Pre-approved MX with rights secured or not needed.	When a specific piece is definitely going to be used in the final show the editor lays MX in and cuts to it.
	Temp song or piece of MX. FYI: Sometimes temp MX is preferable to final MX but rights are unobtainable.	Editor adds temp music to help a scene, section, or montage. Temp MX occasionally becomes or leads the way to the permanent choice.
	Musical, dance number, MX video, or MX concert piece.	You decide on a song or music before shooting the picture.
	Promos, commercials, and documentaries.	You select the MX before the picture is shot or cut.
Cut MX to pix	A montage or scene is already cut.	Editor adds temp MX before screening the show for you.
	Temp mix.	Any MX is possible because the show is still a work-in-progress.
	Picture is locked.	Scenes are timed for MX and the composer composes or the MX editor hunts down music and cuts it in.

PARALLEL ACTION AND CROSS-CUTTING

cross-cutting. Editing two (or more) *dependent* lines of action together —characters, settings, or subjects—that interact directly and are aware of each other.

parallel action. Editing two (or more) *independent* lines of action together —characters, settings, or subjects—that do not interact directly and are unaware of each other.

Cross-cutting and parallel action create conflict and intrigue and are seen in all genres. Parallel action regularly kicks off films, revealing strangers going about their separate lives, unaware of each other, and leaving the audience wondering what they have in common and itching to see them meet. Well, most of the time, as the example at the top of the next page exemplifies.

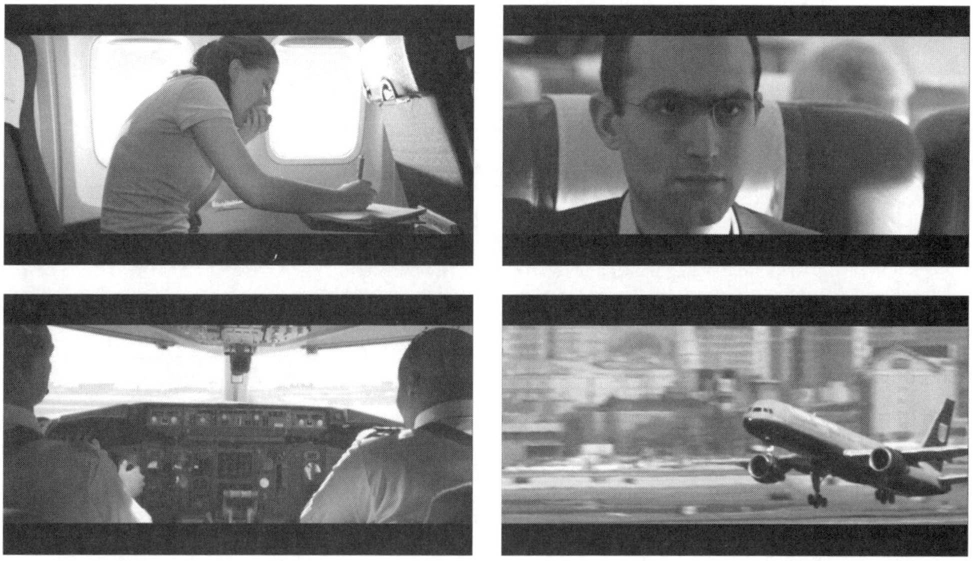

On 9/11 passengers, terrorists, and pilots were living parallel lives when their flight took off. *United 93* (2006).

Cross-cutting is used after the strangers have met or are aware of each other. We watch the characters react to each other or a situation in separate scenes. Cross-cutting invariably tightens the pace and ratchets up the conflict toward a climax or resolution of some kind.

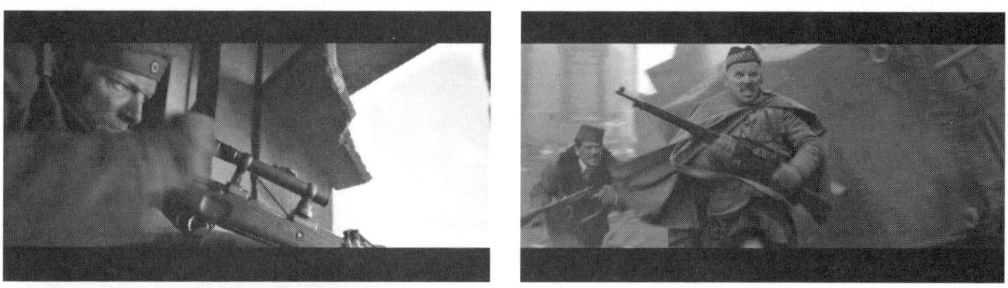

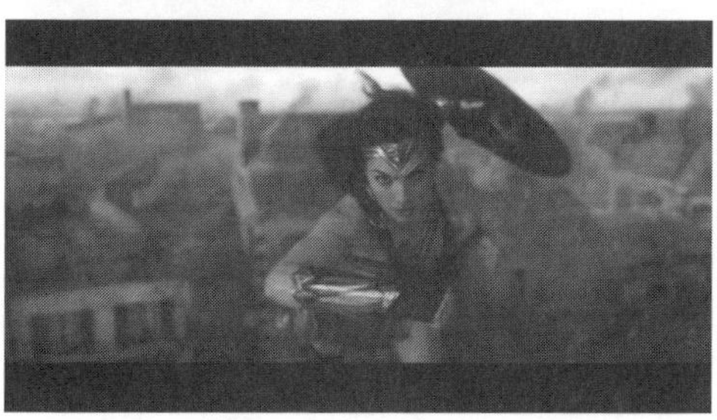

This scene from *Wonder Woman* (2017) cross-cuts between a German sniper, the Allied soldiers, and Wonder Woman.

The table below summarizes parallel action and cross-cutting and gives examples of each.

	Description	Movie example
Parallel action	Editing two (or more) independent lines of action together where characters, settings, or subjects do not interact directly and are unaware of each other. Scenes run independently of each other and rely on viewers to make the connection.	***Obit***—non-scripted Parallel lives, or rather deaths, are shown through the daily travails of the *New York Times* writers who write obituaries. ***BlacKkKlansman***—scripted This Spike Lee crime drama uses parallel action to show undercover Colorado Springs cops and the local KKK chapter along with disparate elements such as footage from *Gone with the Wind, Birth of a Nation*, and the Charlottesville white supremacist car slaughter.
Cross-cutting	Editing two (or more) dependent lines of action together so that the characters, settings, or subjects interact directly and are aware of each other. Scenes are dependent on each other and don't function without being cross-cut.	***American Factory***—non-scripted This 2019 Academy award winning doc, set in an Ohio glass factory, cross-cuts between American workers and their Chinese managers as the two cultures intersect, conflict, and try to resolve their differences. ***Parasite***—scripted Wealthy employers and their desperate, poor employees live parallel lives in the same household as depicted by cross-cutting, which shows them increasingly interacting until the film's climax.

LAST WORD

Now that you're familiar with editing practices, it's time to enter the cutting room in Chapter 6 and start to work with your editor.

WHAT DIRECTORS SHOULD KNOW ABOUT HOW EDITORS EDIT

- ☐ To make a cut, an editor evaluates four main factors for which shot and take to use: story action, performance, pace, and technical quality.
- ☐ When an editor cuts for the right reasons and in the right place, it sustains viewers' involvement in the show and sets a pace, other than the real time pace set by the master shot.
- ☐ Editors strive to ensure that "every cut is motivated," meaning it advances the story, the action, the flow, and the thought process of the show.
- ☐ Editors habitually look for a match point—a place in the outgoing shot that is duplicated in the incoming shot—for the best place to cut. Match cutting creates invisible edits, but is not the rule. The rule is making motivated edits that serve the shot material and forward the story.
- ☐ Like magicians, editors mask mismatches by intuiting where the audience's eyes will be, cutting earlier or later for a better match point, overlapping, or bridging to another shot such as an insert or closeup.
- ☐ The editor deals objectively and passionately with each character or interviewee's words, lines, looks, and total performance with an eye to the purpose of the scene and the show as a whole.
- ☐ Cutting in reaction shots is vital for showing human feelings and thought and keying your audience's emotional response in all types of scenes and shows, including action scenes and documentaries.
- ☐ A montage consists of a collage of images from different times, places, and sources and can be a powerfully evocative scene that is bigger than the sum of its shots.
- ☐ Your editor may cut the picture first and then add music and narration or vice versa. Afterwards they will adjust frames to mesh picture and sound.
- ☐ You use cross-cutting and parallel action to create conflict and intrigue in all genres: drama, documentary, comedy, thrillers, etc.

6

IN THE CUTTING ROOM PART 1

FROM DAILIES TO FIRST CUT SCREENING

The postproduction process proceeds in three stages: 1) Editing, which creates the final, locked cut; 2) Sound and music, which are combined to make the final mixed show; 3) Finishing, where the final mix is married to the final color grading, VFX, titles, and credits, to produce the deliverable—your finished show! This chapter launches the Editing stage (which completes in the next chapter) and escorts you into the cutting room to familiarize you with what your editor and editorial crew do to prepare the show for the First Cut for screening with you.

IT'S A ROUGH CUT LIFE

The first time a show is edited and screened it's solely for you, the director, and it's called the First Cut, the Editor's Cut, or the Editor's Assembly (contractually required on a union show). This First Cut is also commonly referred to as the *rough cut*. Editors have never considered their work "rough" as they have always worked hard to perfect character, story, action, and dialogue to make the smoothest, best First Cut. The First Cut *is* rough in the sense that it lacks final VFX, stock footage, titles, and the sound mix. But this is true of every cut until the show is locked, and then finished, in the post-editing phase. With digital editing equipment, an unlimited amount of sound and video tracks are available, so rough cuts have become highly polished. Therefore, to be accurate and respectful, we will refer to them as the First Cut.

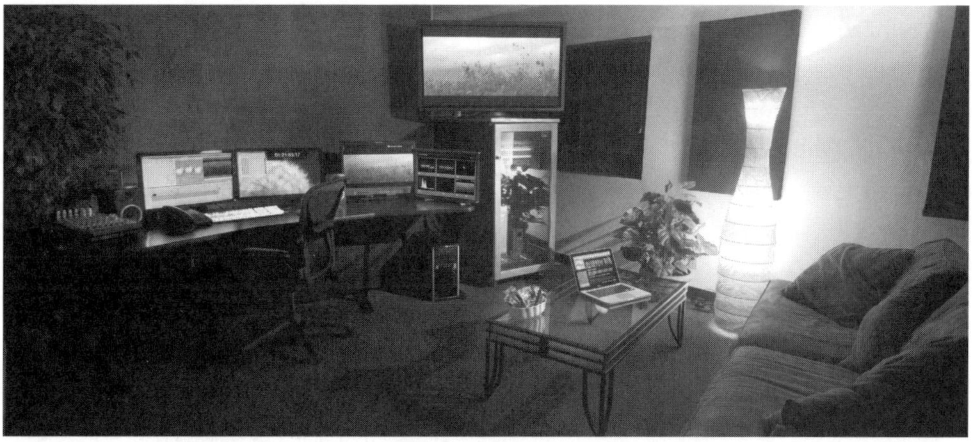

Post house editing suite. *Photo courtesy of AlphaDogs.*

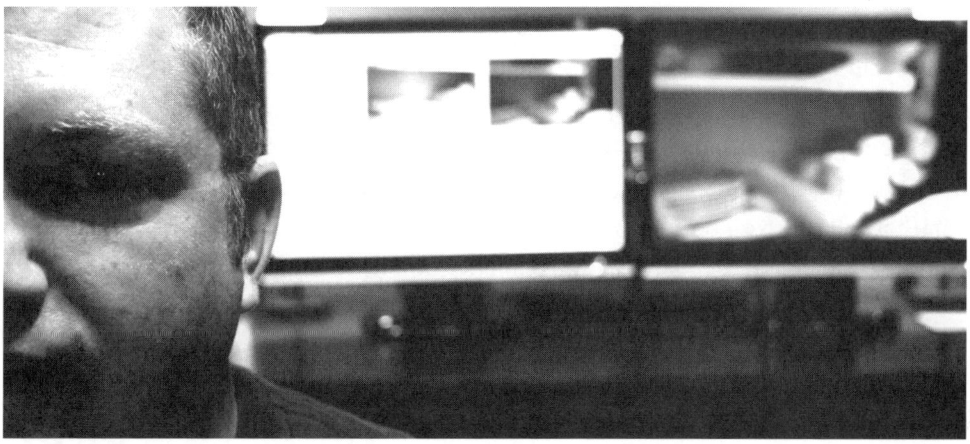

Photo courtesy of David Mallory.

The First Cut is the springboard for all the rest, from Director's Cut to locked cut. The editor will be making them all, so in a sense they're all the editor's and director's cuts.

FIRST CUT

While you're shooting, the editor is putting together the First Cut, perusing any notes from you and the script supervisor, and following the script or an outline that you or they have created. On shows with tight schedules such as TV series, editors aim to stay *up to camera,* meaning they cut each day's dailies before the next day's arrive. On shows where the editor is hired after you have everything in the can, they will cut sequentially. Either way, heed this Public Service Announcement: Stay out of the room while the editor is making the First Cut. You have been living with the footage, the editor has not.

The editor needs time and breathing space to engage with the footage and laser in on the best shots, lines, and story to pull out of it. You need time to decompress and get away from it all so you're rested and can view the First Cut with fresh eyes and an open mind. Be sure to give yourself adequate time to distance yourself mentally. Force yourself to step back to clear your head before embarking on the next stage of the process.

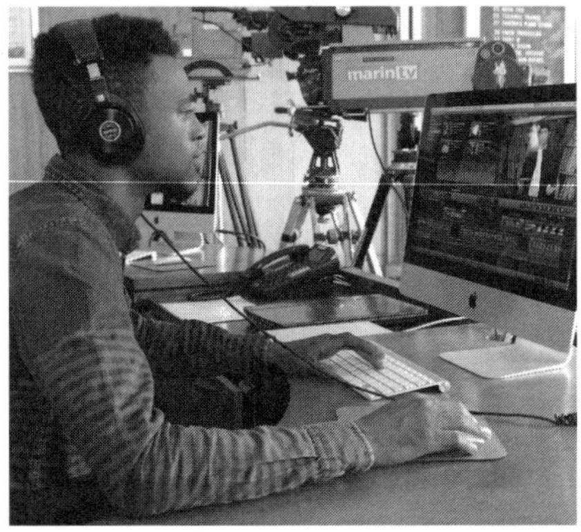

Photo courtesy of the Community Media Center County of Marin, CA.

You may or may not have viewed dailies with your editor, but you have likely discussed them or sent notes directly or via the script supervisor prior to the editor beginning to cut. And you may have already viewed a few cut scenes for various reasons such as 1) you or the editor's concern that a scene isn't working (for instance it's missing shots or the talent is shaky) or 2) continuity (e.g., you're returning to a location and need to pick it up correctly). You two have established good communication and rapport. Now is the time to let the editor absorb the footage along with your input and create a First Cut that will start you both on a good path toward creating the best show possible. The editor has the simultaneously daunting and honorable task of being the creator and first viewer of the entire show in time continuity.

While the editor is doing this, we'll talk about what goes into creating the First Cut and preparing it and subsequent cuts for screening. To start, we'll go over a few technical facets of the editing room that influence decision making, budget, and how images will be treated throughout postproduction. Shedding light on these editing practices will help you feel more at home with what goes on in the cutting room.

Preparing for the First Cut

The first order of business for the editorial crew is to ingest dailies. The assistant editor* (if your show has one) will bring all your source footage—dailies, stock footage, music etc.,—into the digital editing system. If source material is on different digital formats, they may *transcode* it—convert it from one digital format to another.

Part of the genius of digital systems is that they can ingest all formats of material —film, tape, digital- from multiple types of sources such as camera cards and disks. Legacy and new formats meet up in the digital editing system for editing together. The number of formats grows each year as engineers and IT techs write more algorithms, invent more devices, create new apps and protocols, and establish new standards.

*A word of praise here for the assistant editor, the unsung hero of the editing room, who keeps the digital ship afloat and you can rely on for updates on just about everything. Most editors begin as assistants or apprentices; the extensive organizing work and long hours the job demands only increase the desire to move up to editor.

Shots, clips, and files

Once ingested into the digital editing system, a shot (called a "clip" on many systems) comprises two files: 1) A media file consisting of the clip's picture file and/or sound file (or sound files as it could have more than one track) and 2) A data file containing the clip's critical data and metadata*.

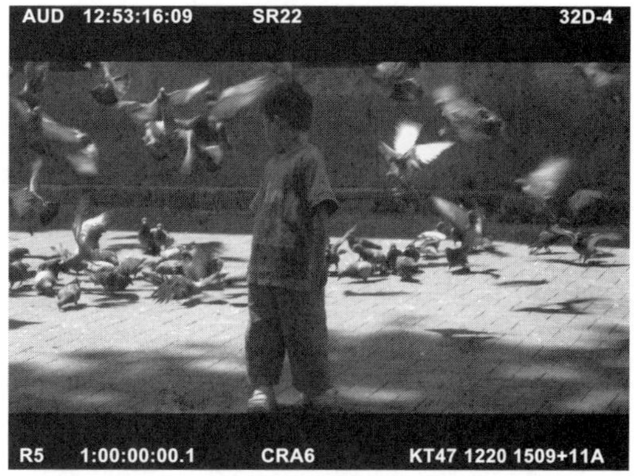

A film frame scanned to disk and ready for ingest. *Photo treatment courtesy of Chris Senchack.*

Labeling

Labeling and logging are like locking and loading: Skip it, and you can fuggedabout locating shots easily or editing efficiently. Your show may not be a huge enterprise like *Star Wars* or *Star Trek,* but your editor will have an increasing amount of footage to keep on top of as the days go by. This is why editorial obsessively labels everything: projects, source material, tapes, disks, hard drives, film reels, notebooks, shelves, and the cutting room door.

Logging

> Logging has always been a part of editing, but the big difference now is that a database is created. This makes retrieval of footage a simple matter. —**ALAN MILLER**, editor and VP at Moving Pictures, a post house in NYC.

As with labeling, not a shot gets by editorial that isn't logged. In the days of film, huge tomes—logbooks—carried heaps of handwritten data that apprentices or assistants labored to keep current and accurate. In today's digital domain, editorial relies on databases that they create or receive from the post house along with dailies on a hard drive.

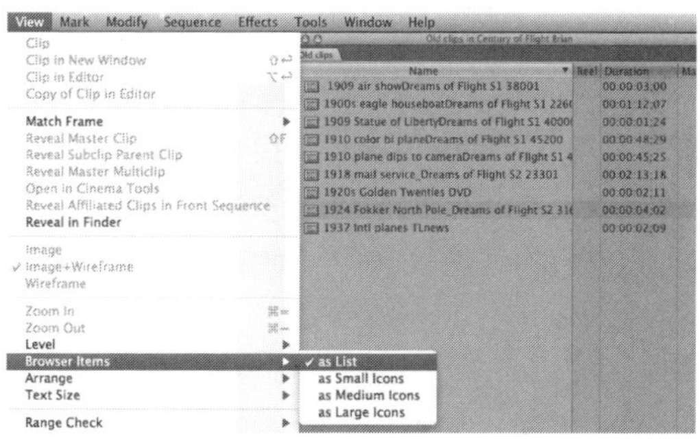

Database view of clips and their logged descriptions in Final Cut Pro. *Photo courtesy of Chris Senchack*

Editorial crews log everything that enters the digital system: dailies, tapes, inserts, animations, music, graphics, stock footage wild lines, SFX, and VFX. This is critical for not only locating media but also for reproducing the cut after it is locked and making the final, deliverable(s) for your show.

---

* Summarized as, "the data about data," metadata is the background information that identifies the condition, content, and other qualities of data. In film and video, this includes time code, frame rate, aspect ratio, sync, and descriptive data about clips such as the location of their media and effects layers.

What data is logged and why?
Shot logs and databases routinely include the shot's scene and take number, angle, shoot date, time, and location, timecode, film keycode, metadata, and source. Editorial often marks an asterisk (*) to denote a preferred take or adds other comments such as "FS" (False Start) or MOS for a soundless take. At some companies a "logger" is a starting or contracted position.

On small projects as well as those with mountains of footage or accelerated schedules, it's tempting to skip logging and just plunge into editing. This is short sighted for many reasons. Taking the time to log footage upfront saves search time and tempers down the line, and permits your editor to swiftly locate every line, look, cutaway, and frame of your show. Logging also familiarizes editorial with your footage and enables the crew to feel on top of it and not snowed under. If your show is short on media storage or time, and not going to ingest all the production footage, logging is a necessity as it helps determine which footage not to ingest. Lastly, if your show will be sharing the footage in the near future or archiving it for posterity, it must be logged.

Organizing in bins

Bin is a term and tool carried over from editing on film when footage was organized in physical bins. On a digital system, a bin sports a folder icon and is the basic organizing container for all shots and cuts (referred to as *sequences* on several systems).

Every project dictates its own bin organizing strategies, but ordinarily editors on scripted shows create a Scene 1 bin, Scene 2 bin, and so on. On non-scripted shows, editors make an Interviewees bin and Subject bins, e.g., a Chile marathon bin, Kenya marathon bin, etc. Editors often copy clips into several bins. For example, the master you shot of a hummingbird hovering over a fountain in a Sicilian town square may be copied into a Sicily bin, Bird bin, and Village bin. Routinely, editors make bins for storing dailies, sequences, stock footage, B roll, graphics, VFX, SFX, promo, music, and titles.

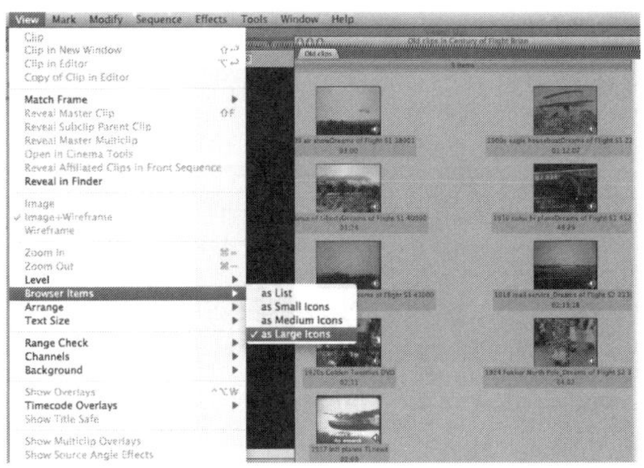

Thumbnail view of clips (shots) in a bin labeled "Old Clips" on Final Cut Pro.

Going native vs proxy editing

On small projects, editorial ingests all the digital footage in its native format, meaning in the high quality* format you shot. The clips are played back and edited natively and

* Quality includes *resolution* (basically the sharpness, clarity, and detail of the image) and color.

the editor outputs the originally ingested media for the final deliverable(s). However, on many projects (4K and above for instance), editing natively is not practical. And not just for storage reasons: The digital image files are just too big to playback or edit in real time. Editors work with proxies—lower quality files that the digital system creates during ingest or imports from the camera*. When it's time to output the final deliverable, the editor or your post house will relink the edited clips to their original high-quality format. This relinking can also be performed for screenings prior to show lock.

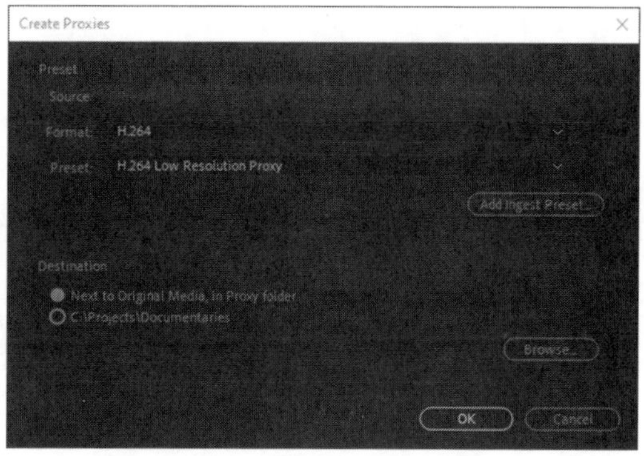

Creating proxy files with ingest on Adobe Premiere Pro. *Photo courtesy of Jay Scherberth.*

Why does any of this matter to you? Proxying is a necessary technical step which gives you the creative freedom to view and try out edits. If proxies weren't possible, the digital system would need to render** images just to audition footage or play back scenes. With proxy editing you're not waiting for the editing system to catch up with your ideas. Warning: Proxies may be good looking, but don't fall in love with them. You and the DP will color correct and finalize all images after picture lock during the final editing phase.

Editing the First Cut

All this organizing along with viewing dailies serves to familiarize the editor with your footage and get them ruminating about how to edit it. Working off the lined script, transcript, or paper cut, the editor will cut the footage you shot and may add stock shots, VFX, music, narration, and more, as this next section delineates.

Scripts and transcripts

Scripts

On scripted shows the lined script is your editor's blueprint for cutting. Many editors place the script in a script stand—a homegrown affair akin to a music stand—and keep it handy on their desk.

** Many cameras capture proxy files and hi-res files simultaneously.

*** When a clip (or series of clips) can't be played back, the computer must render it—create new media for the clip—which takes seconds, minutes, or longer and slows the flow of editing.

Transcripts

On non-scripted shows that can afford it, a transcriber creates a transcription of interviews. There are also software transcription programs that are roughly accurate. Ideally, the transcript includes the time code for every minute of speech; if not, editorial can add it. Your editor enters the time code into the digital system to swiftly locate content. They can also highlight key lines in the transcribed interviews and make other comments such as noting shot type or audio dropouts.

Paper cut

A *paper cut* is an outline that provides the initial order of subjects, segments, topics, lines, shots, and sounds for editing a documentary or other non-scripted piece. You provide the paper cut or your editor creates it themselves. The transcript shot log from the field and notes from viewing dailies serve as the basis for a paper cut. A paper cut is useful for getting a handle on the footage and story and will change with each cut.

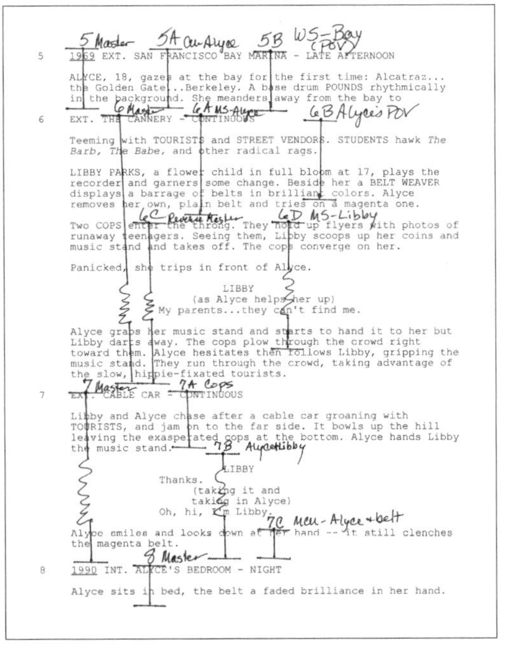
5 Master 5A CU-Alyce 5B WS-Bay (POV)

5 1969 EXT. SAN FRANCISCO BAY MARINA - LATE AFTERNOON

ALYCE, 18, gazes at the bay for the first time: Alcatraz... the Golden Gate...Berkeley. A base drum POUNDS rhythmically in the background. She meanders away from the bay to

6 Master 6A MS-Alyce 6B Alyce's POV

6 EXT. THE CANNERY - CONTINUOUS

Teeming with TOURISTS and STREET VENDORS. STUDENTS hawk *The Barb*, *The Babe*, and other radical rags.

LIBBY PARKS, a flower child in full bloom at 17, plays the recorder and garners some change. Beside her a BELT WEAVER displays a barrage of belts in brilliant colors. Alyce removes her own, plain belt and tries on a magenta one.

6C Reverse Master 6D MS-Libby

Two COPS enter the throng. They hold up flyers with photos of runaway teenagers. Seeing them, Libby scoops up her coins and music stand and takes off. The cops converge on her.

Panicked, she trips in front of Alyce.

LIBBY
(as Alyce helps her up)
My parents...they can't find me.

Alyce grabs her music stand and starts to hand it to her but Libby darts away. The cops plow through the crowd right toward them. Alyce hesitates then follows Libby, gripping the music stand. They run through the crowd, taking advantage of the slow, hippie-fixated tourists.

7 Master 7A Cops

7 EXT. CABLE CAR - CONTINUOUS

Libby and Alyce chase after a cable car groaning with TOURISTS, and jam on to the far side. It bowls up the hill leaving the exasperated cops at the bottom. Alyce hands Libby the music stand.

7B Alyce+Libby

LIBBY
Thanks.
(taking it and
taking in Alyce)
Oh, hi, I'm Libby.

7C MCU-Alyce+belt

Alyce smiles and looks down at her hand -- it still clenches the magenta belt.

8 Master

8 1990 INT. ALYCE'S BEDROOM - NIGHT

Alyce sits in bed, the belt a faded brilliance in her hand.

The script supervisor's lined script is an intersection of takes and script, which the editor receives every day with dailies. A squiggly line denotes a character's dialogue. *Photo courtesy of Chris Senchack.*

Selects reels

To help wrap their head around the footage and following a time-honored film editing practice, editors often make select reels (digital sequences) composed of your and/or their selected takes or parts of takes. This winnowing down aids in breaking the scene into workable parts (particularly on scenes with mondo footage) and serves as a basic assembly.

Stock shots, slugs, and banners

Your editor will insert stock shots in the cut. The shots will be temp and likely have time code and/or text running through them. Once the temp shots are approved and paid for, the editor will replace them with the final version. If a stock shot is undecided or unavailable (normal at the start of a show), the editor will *slug* for it—insert black from the digital system's menu as a placeholder until the shot is obtained. Instead of a slug, they may insert a *banner*—a placeholder with text that announces, "stock shot missing," "scene missing," insert commercial," "insert main title," etc.

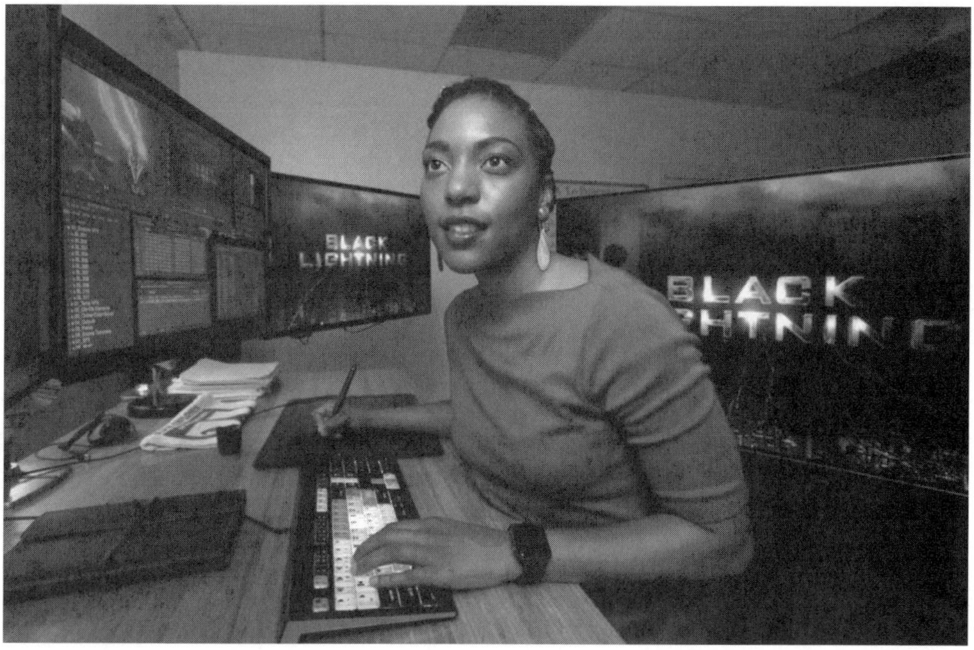

Editing VFX. Notice the drawing pen and tablet. *Photo courtesy of Anedra Edwards.*

VFX

Like many digital terms, VFX (visual effects) has evolved from a film term*, has other abbreviations (EFX, FX, or F/X), and has definitions that vary, depending on where you're working—the cutting room, post house, or special effects house. For our purposes, VFX will stand for all effects, no matter how simple or complex.

From garden variety fades and dissolves to jaw dropping multi-layered effects, every show involves some level of VFX. Why? Because they help tell the story. Editors make many or all of a show's VFX on their digital editing system. Super complex VFX require a special effects house, which creates the VFX with your input and the oversight of a VFX producer and editor. The special effects house sends the VFX files to the cutting room for the editor to drop into the cut. You can expect to see temp versions in cuts as you and the special effects house refine, update, and finalize the VFX. So, what kind of effects can you expect the editor to create and what effects would the special effect house take on? Here's the full picture:

* Until the digital computer age, VFX were called opticals, and created by reproducing the film negative and employing an optical printer at a film lab. Today, film opticals are made using the DI (Digital Intermediate) scanning process. Optical printers are mostly out of commission but still used in film restoration, for educational purposes, and by a few experimental filmmakers.

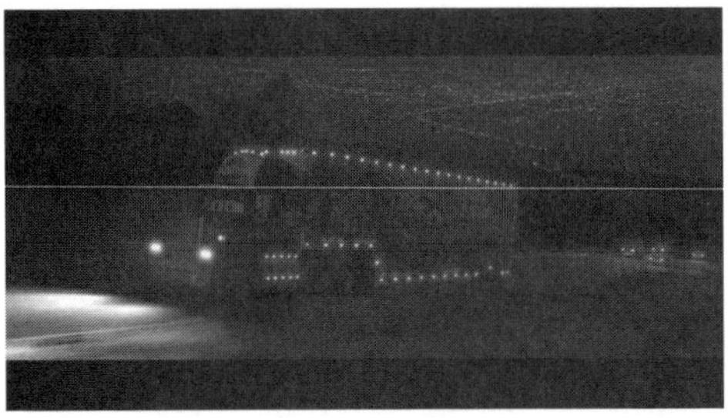

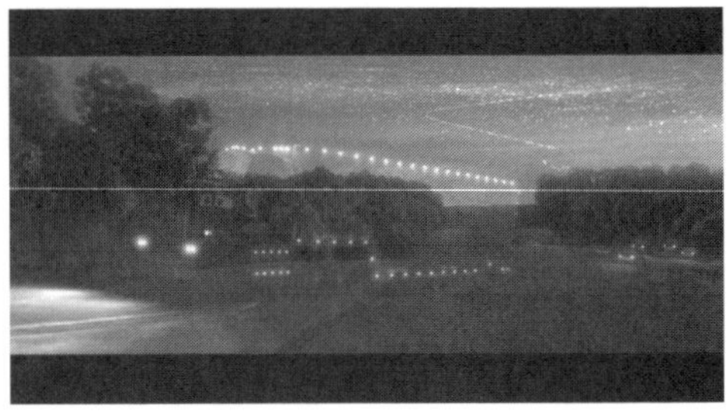

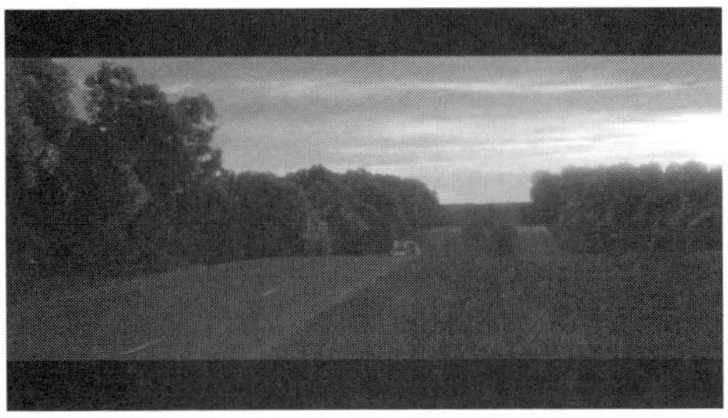

Night becomes day for a cartoon trucker via a *dissolve*, a basic transitional effect that editors make daily. Dissolves typically portray the passage of time or a change in location or both, as this dissolve from *Cars* (2006) illustrates.

Categories of VFX

VFX can be categorized by the time and money they suck up:

Simple VFX

- Include transitions, flips, and filters.
- Most common.
- Created on the digital system by the editor.

Complex VFX

- Consist of two or more shots and perhaps some text and a dissolve or superimposition a.k.a. a *super*.
- Are created during production and/or postproduction using off-the-shelf software (2D) as well as specialized compositing software and 3D animation software.
- May involve keyframes.
  Example: A ball (or other) object needs to move within a shot. For each place the ball moves, the editor sets a key frame so that it follows the desired path of motion.
- May require rendering.*
- Editor creates on the system or by using Adobe After Effects (AE) or other motion graphics software and imports into editing system.
-

* A "real time effect" can be played back instantly after being created. If a VFX can't be played back in real time, the computer must render it.

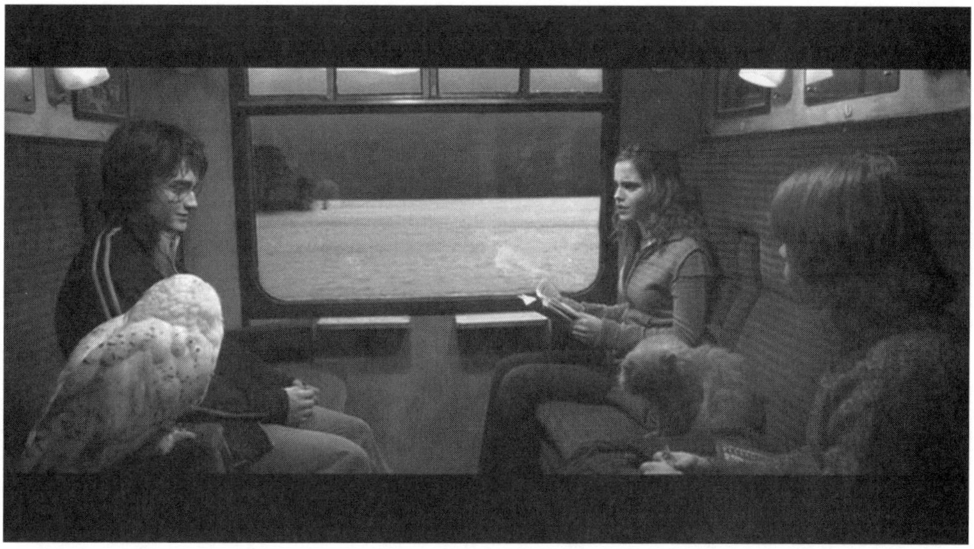

A *matte* a.k.a. a *key,* is a more complex yet routine effect in which the editor creates a hole in a shot and places (keys) another shot in that hole. The editor makes the matte effect or selects the shots to be matted for the post house or special effects house to complete. Windows are perfect holes for keying in shots. Here, Harry Potter and his chums travel to the Hogwarts School of Witchcraft and Wizardry and the scenery is matted in through their train window. *Harry Potter and the Goblet of Fire* (2005).

- May be outsourced to the post house (e.g., for wire removal—painting out wires used to make actors fly—and other routine VFX) or to the special effects house (for original, more involved VFX).

Super complex VFX

- Combines many types and layers of effects.
- Are designed during preproduction and shot in the camera during production using a variety of methods such as live plates, models, CGI, motion capture, step framing, etc.
- Can include live shots, 3D, CGI, and animation.
- Are created at a special effects house by a team of artists, craftspeople, and editors using compositing, motion graphics, or 3D animation software, such as 3ds Max, AE, Maya, and Nuke.
  - Turnover. Editorial crew turns over (provides as needed) a description of the VFX plus shot data, source media, and copies of the cut.
  - Mickey McGovern, VFX producer and editor on *Forrest Gump, Star Wars episodes* 5 and *6, Contact,* and *Speed,* explains, "I receive the script which I break down into VFX shots. I determine how the elements of each shot will be made . . . With the help of production coordinators, I track each shot. I know how much each shot costs, and the schedule for completing each shot."

The table below describes the most common types of VFX from the simplest to the complex.

Type	Description	Example(s)
Transition	Shifting from one shot to the next without using a cut.	Dissolve, wipe, fade-in, fade-out, or white-out.*
Varispeed	Altering the frame rate of a shot by slo-mo-ing it, speeding it up, or reversing it.	Reversing the action so that a car squeals to a stop, before hitting the baby, instead of moving backwards from the baby as filmed.**
Flop **a.k.a. Mirror**	Rotating a shot horizontally.	To correct a POV error: The boy now looks from right to left, instead of left to right.
Flip	Rotating a shot vertically.	A girl standing on her feet, now stands on her head.
Repo	Repositioning an object within a frame by moving the object or the frame.	Adjusting a target so it's at the correct angle to get hit by projectiles.
Resize	Changing the size of an object or the entire image within the frame by enlarging or shrinking it.	A blow-up.
Color or texture	Changing the color or texture of a shot.	Desaturating a scene to make it reflect the past.
Matte **a.k.a. Key**	Cutting a hole in a shot and placing (keying) another shot in that hole.	The witch, chickens, etc. Dorothy sees through her window during the cyclone in *The Wizard of Oz*.
Motion	Moving an object within a frame by setting it on a path, and/or by making it spin, rotate, or become animated in some fashion.	An object such as a book, arrow, or a title moves through a frame.
Composite	Combining two or more images, titles, and/or other VFX into a single, composite image.	Giant spiders attack the White House. Adding or subtracting buildings from landscapes.

* When a shot dissolves or cuts to white instead of black, it's termed a white-out.
** If you reverse a shot, be aware of lettering on signs, shirts, etc., as the letters will be reversed.

Type	Description	Example(s)
Green (or blue) screen* a.k.a. Chroma key	Compositing two shots, by keying the foreground shot (subject) over the background shot (green or blue screen).	1) Weather reporter (subject) points to the approaching cold front on the map (background). 2) An explorer (subject) flies over Jupiter (background).
Superimposition a.k.a. Super	Compositing two shots or more images full screen on top of each other. Also achieved by double exposure in the camera.	Titles and end credits are superimposed over a variety of backgrounds, including black and other solid colors, animations, freeze frames, and live action footage.
Rotoscope	Creating animation imagery or mattes, frame by frame via tracing or otherwise referencing live footage to create new images or repair images.	Light sabers in three original *Star Wars* movies. *Undone*: This entire TV series is rotoscoped.
CGI	Computer generated imagery. Digital effects created on computers that compose an ever-growing array of visual possibilities for both animated and live action footage.	*The Matrix* films (morphing i.e., shape changing), *The Lord of the Rings* trilogy, and *Avatar* (performance capture).
3D	Blending layers of shots on an XYZ axis into one shot, so it appears to have three dimensions: height, width, and depth.	*Wonder Woman* (live action) and *Onward* (animation).

* Green screens are frequently used effects because 1) they save the expense of going on location and 2) editors can readily produce them on the digital system.

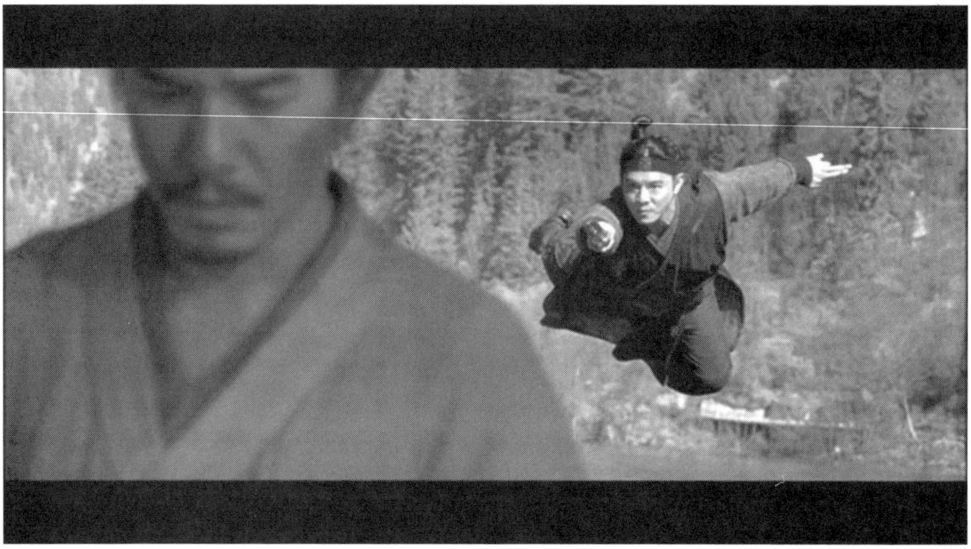

A super complex VFX which composites 1) a live action shot of a forested lake with 2) a green screen shot of a sword fighter thrusting at his opponent from *Hero* (2002).

VFX summary

Some shows exhibit such stunningly original effects that they ignite a creative revolution and make their designer the unsung *auteur* (author) of the film. Conversely, many complex, painstaking effects go unheralded, such as wire removals and composites, but contribute mightily to the film. Whether simple or complex, VFX play a part in most every show. Now that you understand how they're created and the role post plays, you are ready to work with them.

PREPARING FOR THE SCREENING

Once the editing of the First Cut is complete, the editor prepares it for screening by polishing the presentation of the images and sound.

Color grading

If a scene shot over several days results in a noticeable lighting mismatch from edit to edit and your editor has the time, they will *color grade* a.k.a. *color correct* the shots to balance the lighting. The digital system's color grading tools includes video scopes for measuring *luminance* (brightness and contrast), *chrominance* (color), broadcast acceptability, and other image properties. The editor can also use filters to *desaturate* (pull the color down) on say, a flashback scene or make it sepia or B & W (black and white). They can do the reverse; super saturate a scene such as a death, dream, or fantasy sequence. Once the cut is locked, the editor finalizes the color grading or the post house takes care of this after the show is onlined. (More about this in Chapter 10: Finish and Deliver.)

Sound work: Editing in sound and music

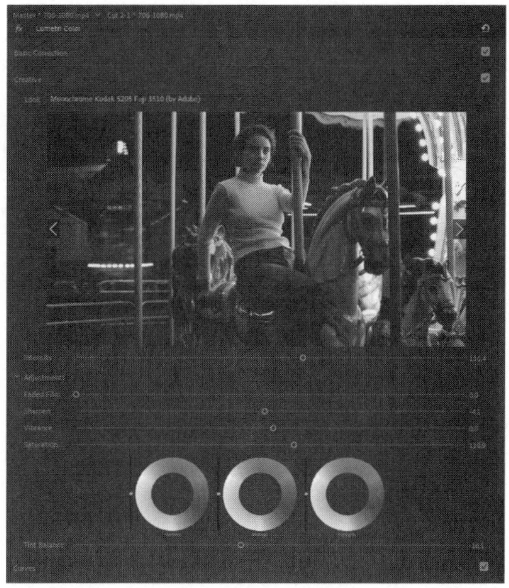

Color grading tool on Adobe Premiere Pro. *Photo courtesy of Jay Scherberth.*

Editors want their work to sound as well as look the best it can. For this reason, many editors cut in sound effects and music to help you and the producer or client better envision the show. Music and sound effects underscore your story and add believability to a cut. They also add more tracks which increases the editor's time and labor in updating them and maintaining sync as you make changes during re-cutting. Your editor will evaluate how much sound work can be accomplished for each screening. On some shows they won't have time or the budget to do much; on high budget shows sound editors may be brought in for temp mixes in order to preview the show or sell it.

Narration

If the narration is available, the editor will record a scratch track.

Wild lines

Wild lines—characters' non sync lines—are recorded during production and postproduction. These lines of dialogue are usually integrated into the soundtrack during the sound editing phase but your editor may receive some wild lines or you may create your own to cut in during the picture editing phase. Wild lines beef up scenes or cover up plot holes, especially those created when you delete scenes or parts of scenes during editing. Typically, the editor cuts in wild lines on the character's back or over another character so being in sync is not an issue. On live action, talking animal movies like *Dolittle, Christopher Robin,* and *Babe,* a major part of the dialogue will be wild lines.

Sound effects

It is common for an edit to be motivated by a sound effect such as a gunshot causing a crowd to duck. Your editor may cut in the sound effect so everyone at the screening can see that the edit works. Time and budget permitting, they will also add specific effects like phone rings, glass smashes, and body slams obtained from online SFX libraries.

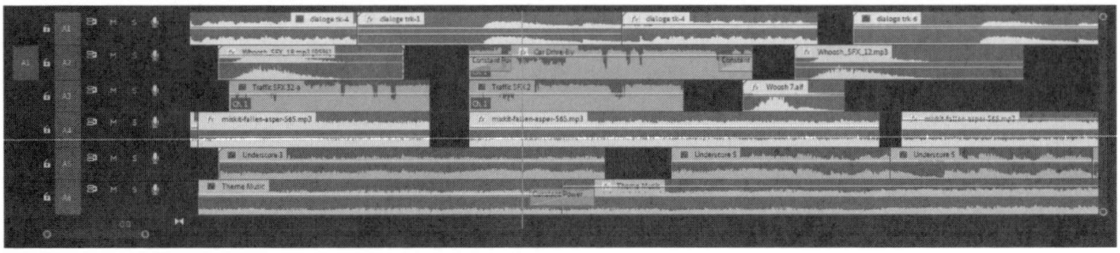

Color coded tracks laid out on Adobe Premiere Pro in typical order from top to bottom: dialogue, SFX, music. *Photo courtesy of Jay Scherberth.*

Music

Editors routinely add music to their digital cuts. Sometimes the music they pick will be used in the final mix but normally it is replaced. If your show has a music composer who was brought on early, they may receive some of the real music to cut in. When a scene or a show depends on music, e.g., a musical or music video, your editor should get the final music from the start. (We'll cover music editing and design thoroughly in chapters 8 and 9.)

Cleaning and filling tracks

The sync dialogue track, a.k.a. the production track, is the main soundtrack. For the First Cut and each subsequent cut and screening, your editor will ensure the production track (and all tracks) can be heard clearly. They will *clean the tracks,* meaning they will remove extraneous, unwanted sounds such as dolly squeaks, dish rattles, plane noises, and your voice, as well as the voices of crew members. Removing these undesirable sounds causes a drop in the audio, which is referred to as a *hole in the sound* or *dead sound*. It can kill the energy of a scene and disengage your audience. Even if these sound holes are destined to be covered by music, the editor will fill them with ambient sound, usually from within the take.

Replacing and filling track is part of the editor's job—within reason. They won't have time to fill every hole in the track, particularly when the hole is less than a second long. Bear in mind that all this track filling is only temporary since all holes will be filled during sound editing and mixing after the cut is locked.

Balancing levels and adding audio effects

If your show's dialogue, music, and sounds can't be heard correctly at one volume setting, it will sound amateurish. Your editor will adjust levels from section to section, shot to shot, within a shot, and across tracks (production, narration, music, and SFX). Digital systems are capable of a good amount of high-quality sound editing and mixing: Tracks can be panned (placed left or right), EQ'd (bass and treble balanced), and cross faded. All sorts of audio effects can be added such as *reverb* (echo), *futz* (making dialogue sound like it's coming through a telephone), and *varispeed* (speeding up or slowing down the audio).

Show timings

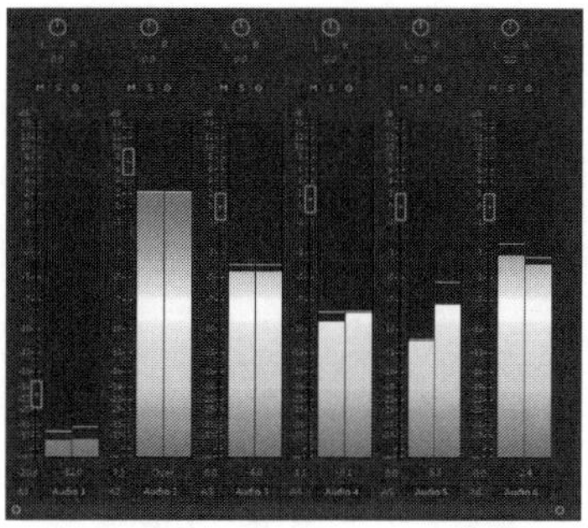

Sound mix tool on Adobe Premiere Pro. *Photo courtesy of Jay Scherberth.*

How long does your show run? As part of preparing for a screening, the editor will use the digital system's timeline to determine your show's TRT (total running time). You may have an exact or ideal TRT that you need to or would like to hit. For example, a feature film normally fits in the 90-120 minute range, but can run from 70 minutes (like *Duck Soup*, 1933) to 209 minutes (*The Irishman,* 2020) or longer. A documentary can be any length, as long as it holds the audience, but it should fit exhibit standards for shorts or features in order to be seen in theatres and on TV and considered for academy and festival nominations and awards.

The editor knows you want to see all the scenes you've shot (unless you've told them otherwise) in the First Cut, so the expectation is that it will run long. For the First Cut and each successive screening, the editor will tell you the show's running time (RT). If your show is broken into acts, segments, or reels your editor can provide these timings too. Anything can be measured with a couple of mouse clicks, including scenes, which is helpful when you need to shave time during re-cutting. Below are some additional considerations for specific types of shows.

TV timings

TV shows are divided into acts by the screenwriter, each act playing between commercials. Your editor will follow this structure initially; you may change act timings during re-cutting. There are seven acts on an MOW (movie of the week), four acts on a one-hour show, and two acts on a half-hour show. Actually, one hour shows run from 42-47 minutes and half-hour shows from 20-23 minutes due to commercials. In its delivery requirements the network specifies the exact length of a show as well as the minimum and maximum length allowable for each act. You need to be mindful of these specifications as eventually you will have to cut the show "to time"—the exact number of minutes the network requires.

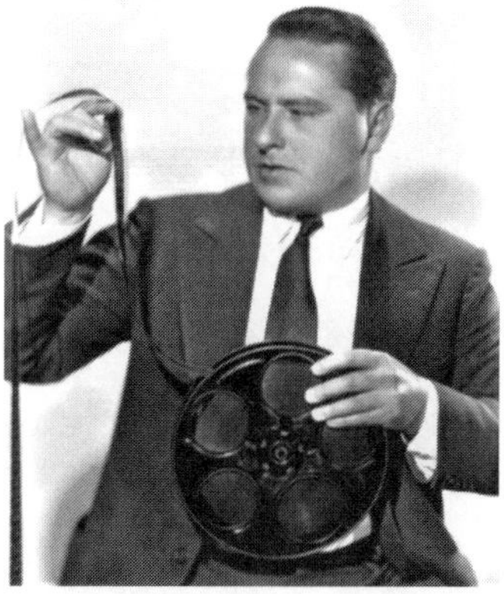

Measuring the old fashioned way—in film reels. *The Cutting Edge: The Magic of Movie Editing* (2004).

Film reels

If your show is screening on film, your editor will break the show into reels of 2000 ft (35mm) or 800 ft (16mm) for projection purposes.

Continuity sheet

The continuity sheet lists your show's scenes in the order they are edited along with a descriptive phrase or sentence about the scene's action and its RT. Continuity sheets help you measure and assess your show. Knowing each scene's RT comes in handy when you must drop or cut down scenes to shorten a show's TRT. Editorial can create new continuity sheets for each screening, so that everyone can see not only the order of scenes but which scenes have been moved, dropped, or have footage coming.

Having a continuity sheet is also helpful when you are switching scenes around during re-cutting. The continuity sheet may start out in script order i.e., scenes 1, 2, 3, 4, 5 and end up rearranged, as cutting and re-cutting progress, as scenes 3, 1, 2, 4, 5. The example below is for a TV drama episode. It works for shows measuring in time. (A film show would include reels and measure in feet and frames.)

CONTINUITY		**Show Party for Two, Ep. 14** **Cut # 2**	**Page 2 of 5**	
Act # 3	**Date** 4/7/21	**Comments:** Sc 24 split in two, sandwiching Sc 23.		
Sc #	**Time**	**Description**	**Running time** **Old**	**New**
20	N/X	Bluebird café. Slugged: Waiting for stock shot.	:02	:02
21	N/I	Robin runs into Sandy, inside a café.	1:01	1:01
22	N/I	Love scene at Robin's loft.	2:23	2:01
24 first half	D/I	Sandy ignores Robin at the press conference.	3:48	2:44
23	N/I	The aftermath at the loft: Sandy storms out.	4:13	4:13
24 last half	D/X	Robin exits conference early, upset.	Part of Sc. 24	1:26
Key D/I = Day Interior D/X = Day Exterior **N/I = Night Interior N/X = Night Exterior**			**RT** 11:26	11:06
			Gain/loss	-:20

Leaders and pops

Originally part of film syncing practices, leaders and pops have become digital like so many other parts of post and continue to fulfill the same critical sync functions. Before we discuss how and why editors add leaders and pops to your show, a few definitions.

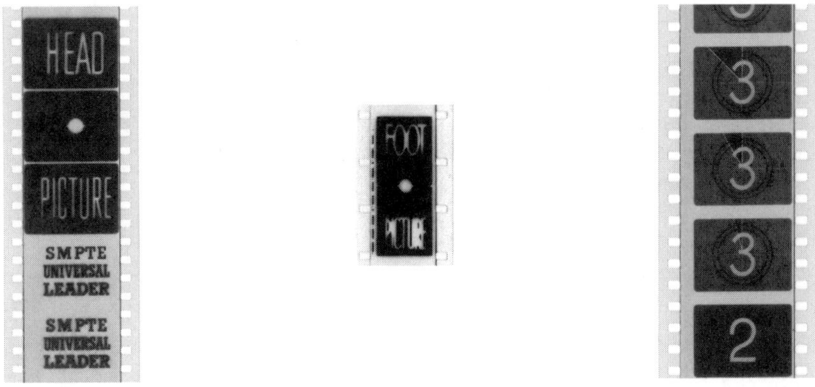

LEFT: Academy leader on 35mm, which digital leader replicates. **MIDDLE:** Tail leader on 16mm, which digital leader replicates. **RIGHT:** 2-pop frame at end of head leader. *Photos courtesy of Chris Senchack.*

Academy leader a.k.a. SMPTE leader or countdown leader*

Leader is a piece of film or tape or a digital clip attached to the head or tail of a show for the purpose of maintaining sync between picture and sound. Head leader counts down from eight to two in less than eight seconds (12 feet) in a clockwise wipe pattern (or sometimes 12 to 2 without the wipe pattern). The last frame of a head leader is the #2 frame, a single frame which is always followed by the FFOP (first frame of picture).

Tail leader runs for a few seconds after LFOP (last frame of picture).

Sync pop

A sync pop is a 1000 Hz beep tone placed on the audio track at designated spots on head and tail leaders to keep sync during screenings, sound editing, and sound mixing.

Head pop a.k.a. 2-pop. A head leader always has a sync pop on the audio track aligned with the #2 picture frame which is why it's nicknamed the 2-pop.

Tail pop. A tail leader has a sync pop on the audio track two seconds in, which usually corresponds to the frame with the word "End" printed on it.

Adding leaders and pops

For film projection, head and tail leaders are mandatory and unseen by the audience. When screening a digital cut, you don't need leaders, but if the editor inserts a head leader—which the audience *will* see—it gives everyone time to settle into the show and looks professional.

Now that the cut is ready to roll, let's enter the screening room.

* Society of Motion Picture and Television Engineers. An international technological society which invented time code in 1967, SMPTE recommends and often effectively sets the standards manufacturers worldwide use for tape, film, and telecommunication applications.

SCREENING

> DGA Basic Agreement of 2017: Only the Editor and the Editor's immediate staff may view the Editor's Assembly before you. You have the right to view the Assembly as soon as it is finished and may request that no other person, except the Editor and Editor's staff, view the Assembly for 24 hours after you view it. If it is not promptly completed, it will be held up to two weeks, for your availability. (7-505(c))

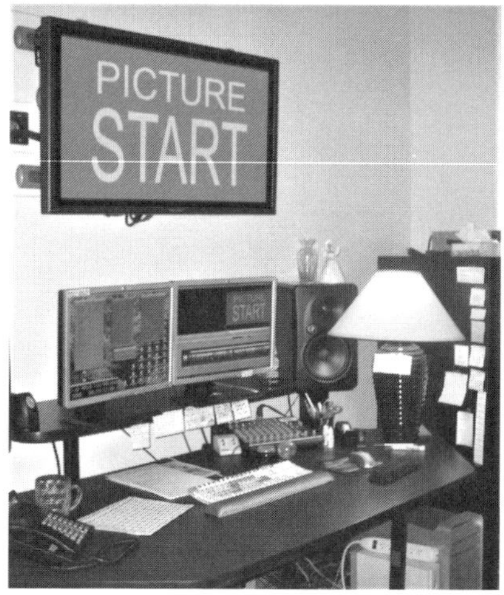

Ready to screen in the cutting room. *Photo courtesy of Sue Odjakjian.*

Normally, the First Cut (the Editor's Assembly as it's referred to above) is screened for you alone. The screening can take place in a screening room, in the cutting room on the editor's system, or remotely at your home or elsewhere via a company server or a download from the internet. Then you and the editor hunker down to create the second cut—your cut—known as the Director's Cut. (More about that in the next chapter.) Here's what to expect from the screening:

When the lights go down

You and the editor and assistant editor will view the show all put together for the first time. Everybody will see what the planning, writing, directing, shooting, and editing have accomplished. Let the darkened room work its magic. The best approach is to watch with an open frame of mind. Typically, you run the show straight through without stopping or commenting.

When the lights go up

After the screening, the editor will run the cut from beginning to end, stopping whenever you want so you can give notes and talk about the changes you would like. This après screening session can be long or short, depending on how much work there is to do and how close or far off you are from your set or ideal TRT, among other factors. It can take place immediately following the screening or the next day when you've had time to digest things.

LAST WORD

Once you've seen the First Cut of your show, you will have all sorts of thoughts, ideas, and questions. Now the real collaboration begins with your editor. It's time to make your show sing out and shine for your audience, starting with creating the second cut, the Director's Cut, which is where the next chapter picks up.

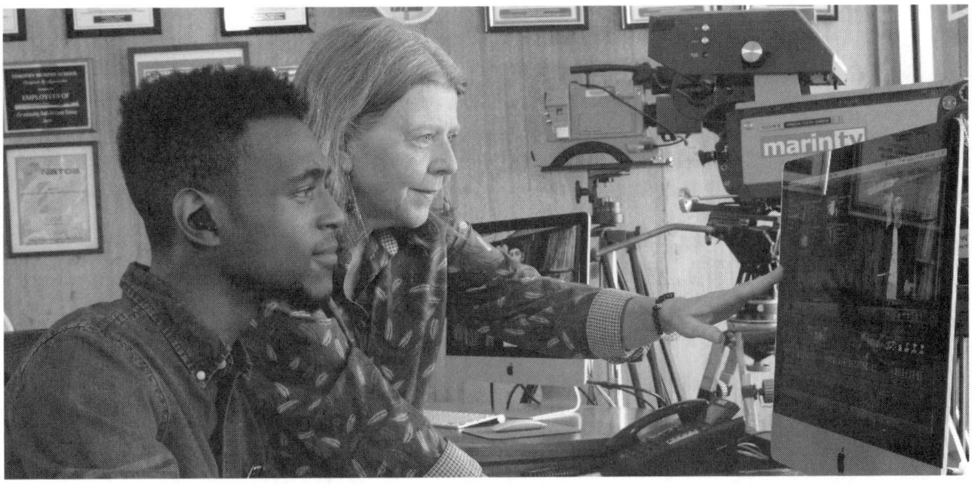

Screening a cut. *Photo courtesy of the Community Media Center County of Marin, CA.*

WHAT DIRECTORS SHOULD KNOW ABOUT HOW EDITORS EDIT THE FIRST CUT AND WHAT TO EXPECT FROM THE SCREENING OF THE FIRST CUT

- ☐ While the editor is creating the First Cut, stay out of the cutting room and leave them alone so they can best engage with the footage and laser in on the best shots, lines, and story to pull out of it.
- ☐ The editorial crew meticulously organizes the shots—called clips once imported into the digital editing system—into bins for quick access during cutting.
- ☐ The editor builds the show each day, as dailies roll, adding stock shots and VFX as they are available.
- ☐ Proxy editing gives you creative freedom to view and try out edits, but don't fall in love with their looks: You and the DP will perfect all images post picture lock during the finishing phase of editing.
- ☐ The editor slugs—inserts a few seconds of black—for missing shots or scenes.
- ☐ Editors makes a variety of VFX on the digital system and drop in complex effects created at the post house or VFX house as temp and finished versions are completed.
- ☐ Time permitting, the editor will add scratch track, wild lines, SFX, and music to cuts, as well as clean and fill tracks, balance the audio, and mix the sound.
- ☐ Editorial creates a continuity sheet of a show's scenes and keeps on top of its TRT.

7

IN THE CUTTING ROOM PART 2

FROM DIRECTOR'S CUT TO LOCKED CUT

Certainly, no director can claim to be an 'auteur' unless he can edit or fully supervise the editing of his own films . . . —**EDWARD DMYTRYK**, director/editor, from his book On *Film Editing: An Introduction to the Art of Film Construction*

You will now become a regular in the cutting room with a new co-pilot and crew—the editor and their editorial crew*. Hopefully, you will feel at ease in your new second home, where you and your editor will spend time shaping the show. This chapter familiarizes you with the steps—re-cutting, fine tuning, and preparing for screenings—that you two will take to get from your Director's cut to a completed "locked" cut. To begin, we'll take a quick tour of the cutting room to make you at home with its important components, starting with its star player, the digital editing system.

DIGITAL EDITING MACHINE

It may go by its brand name, Avid or Lightworks, or by a shortened form of it: DaVinci (for DaVinci Resolve), Final Cut (Apple's Final Cut Pro), or Premiere (Adobe Premiere Pro). Whatever your editorial crew calls the digital editing system (DES), it's a computer with software, hardware (hard wired and plug-in), and features that have the same editing and organizing functions with fairly universal terms. The system's internal hard

* The makeup of the crew depends on the size and budget of the show and whether it's a union and/or heavy VFX show. Normally the team consists of an editor and an assistant. On big features in addition there will be an apprentice, a PA, possibly an extra assistant or apprentices, and, on a short schedule, an additional editor or two.

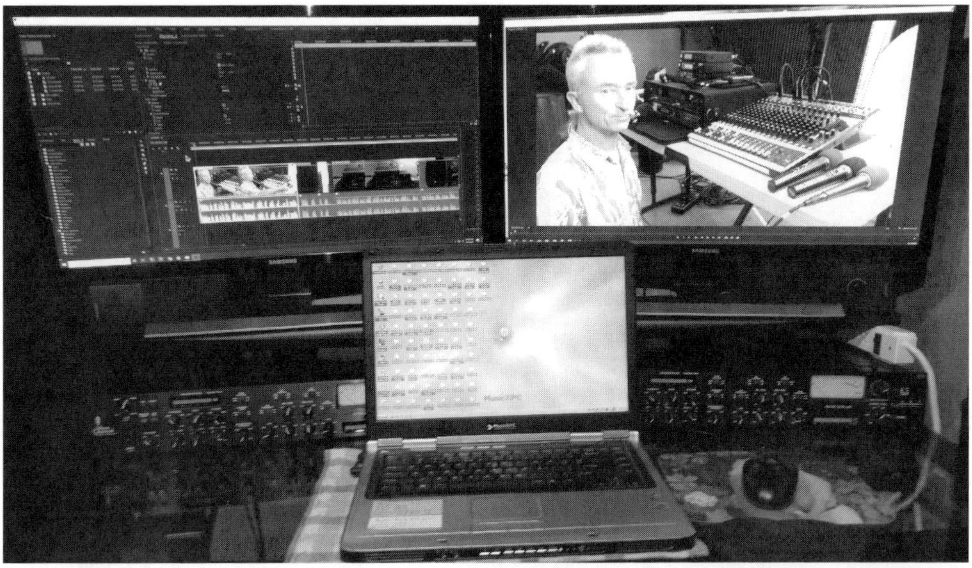

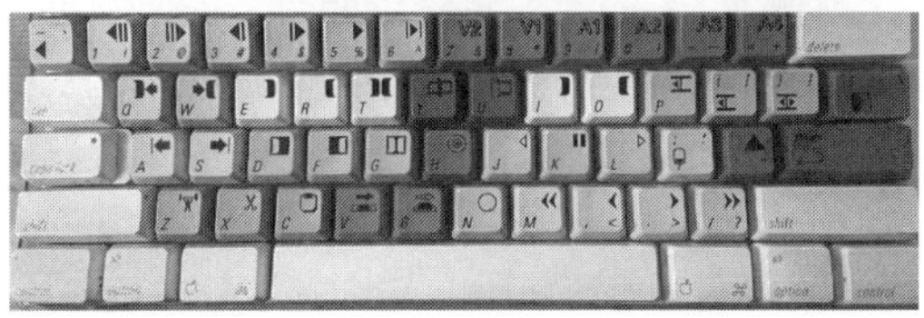

ABOVE: Adobe Premiere Pro digital editing system. *Photo courtesy of Lloyd Minthorne, Synoptic Productions.* **RIGHT:** While a regular keyboard will do, most manufacturers offer candy-colored keyboards like this one, from Avid, with pictographic keys dedicated to editing functions. *Photo courtesy of Sue Odjakjian.*

drive holds data about shots, edits, cuts, and media (on small projects). On most projects media is stored on an external hard drive(s) or on a shared server. Additionally, a digital set-up often includes a mixer for monitoring and adjusting audio input and output and recording VO. A DES can be hooked up to a variety of devices such as legacy tape decks for importing video.

The joy of a Digital Editing System (DES)

> Media Composer is my most valued tool as a film editor. My brain and my heart are the only other processors I need. —**CHRIS INNIS**, A.C.E., *The Hurt Locker,* Academy Award for Best Editing

Digital editing systems work as fast as your brain (except when they're rendering VFX or hanging or crashing like any other computer). Once the editor decides on the edit, making it is instantaneous. Undoing or moving an edit—or a slew of edits—is equally quick. Since digital systems are nonlinear, you can edit non-sequentially—skip from cutting Scene 46, to cutting Scene 9. Your editor has random access to footage and scenes, so they can add or remove a shot or shots at any time in any place.

Nonlinear + random access = Experimentation to your heart's content.

A digital system is a tool that you and your editor harness to collaborate and create your vision down to the last frame and sound edit. Its most important components for you to know are the ones you'll be staring at most: the monitors. Being familiar with

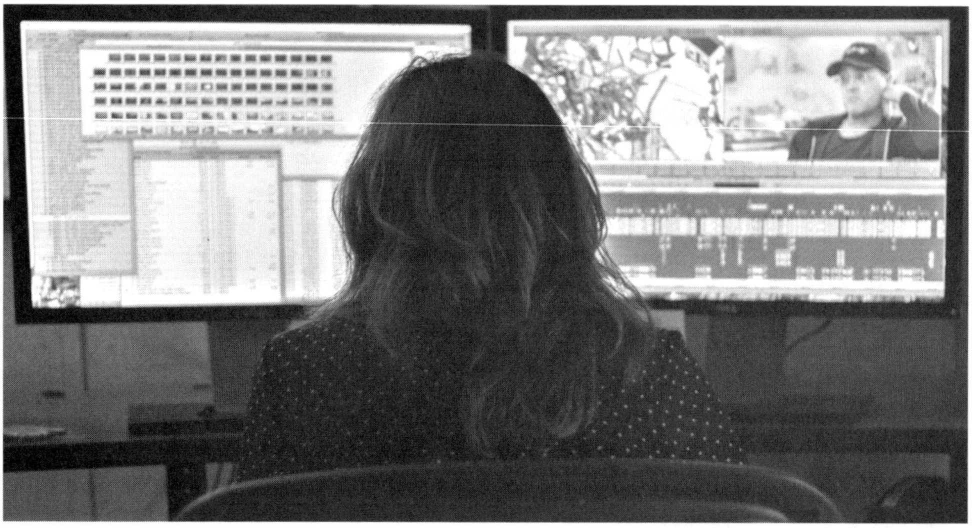

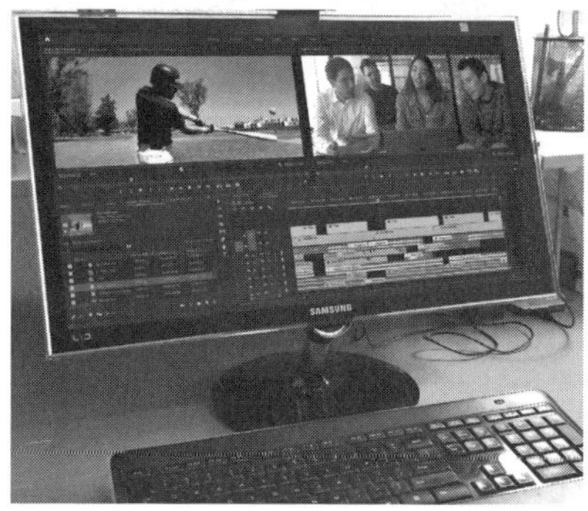

ABOVE: Two graphics monitors; organizing bins with clip names on left, editing windows and timeline on right. *Photo courtesy of Sandra Adair.* **RIGHT:** Graphics Monitor. *Photo courtesy of Jay Scherberth.*

the monitor's viewers and timeline will help you understand what's going on and where you are in the editing process.

Monitors

A DES is tethered to two types of monitors—a video monitor (optional) and a graphics monitor.

Video monitor

This monitor plays clips and *sequences* (DES term for cuts) as if they're on a TV screen. This is advantageous as you can view footage and cuts full screen. With proper calibration, a video monitor can display the images the way they will appear to a broadcast audience.

Graphics monitor

This icon laden screen is where your editor clicks on buttons and menus, to make editing and computer system choices (e.g., file saving). Many shows use two graphics monitors: One for displaying bins and organizing clips (the digitized shots); the other devoted to editing. Having two graphic monitors is a necessity on multiple-camera shows, such as rock concerts and sitcoms, and on shows with huge amounts of footage. On low budget set ups the editor makes and views all cuts on the graphics monitor, and there are no other monitors of any kind.

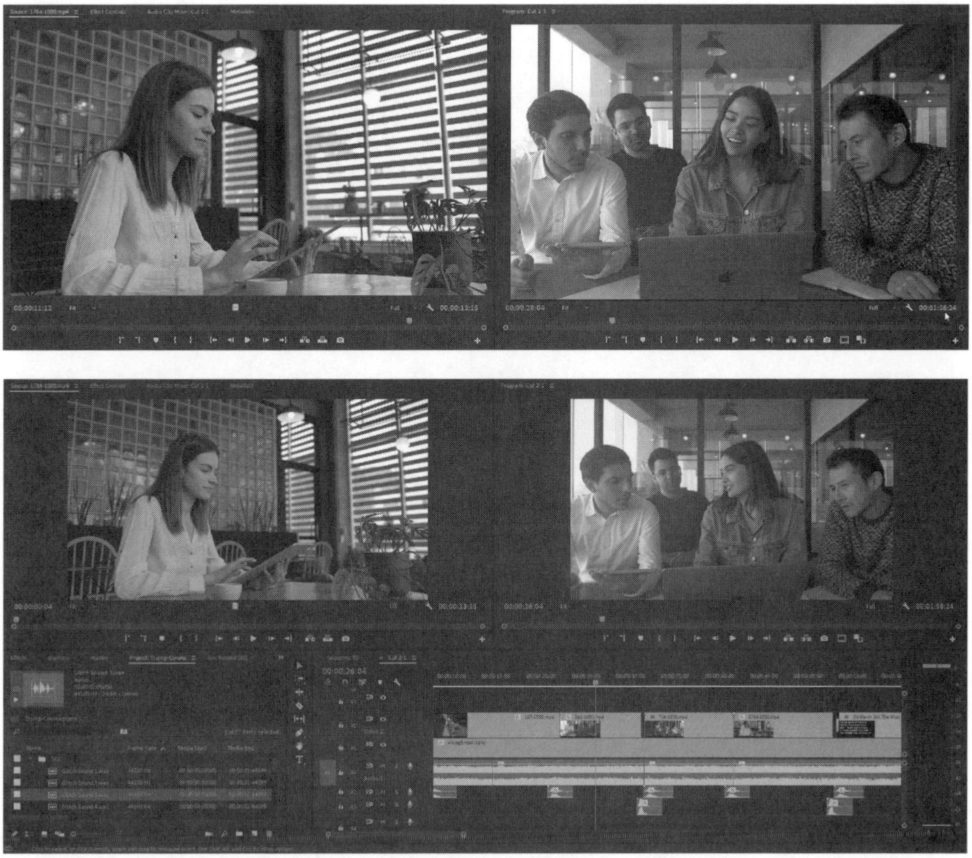

TOP: Source viewer (left) and record viewer (right). **BOTTOM:** The timeline is below the source and record viewers on the right. Notice that the video track (on top) shows a thumbnail image of each clip. *Photos courtesy of Jay Scherberth.*

The first feature on the graphics monitor most likely to catch your eye is the source and record viewers. In the *source viewer* you and your editor will view and audition clips: dailies, stock footage, music, etc. In the *record viewer** the editor will screen sequences and build new ones. Both source and record viewers can display time code and other metadata, depending on the settings the editor selects.

Timeline

A distinguishing feature of every digital system, the *timeline,* is a horizontal bar graph of all the edits in the sequence. The record viewer shows you visually where you are in your cut sequence; the timeline shows you graphically. The timeline reads left to right, from first edit to last.

Each bar of the graph—called a *track*—represents a video or audio series of edits.

* Record viewer is a repurposed term: you don't record any edits. The term has hung on from video editing, where every edit was recorded and viewed on a physical record monitor.

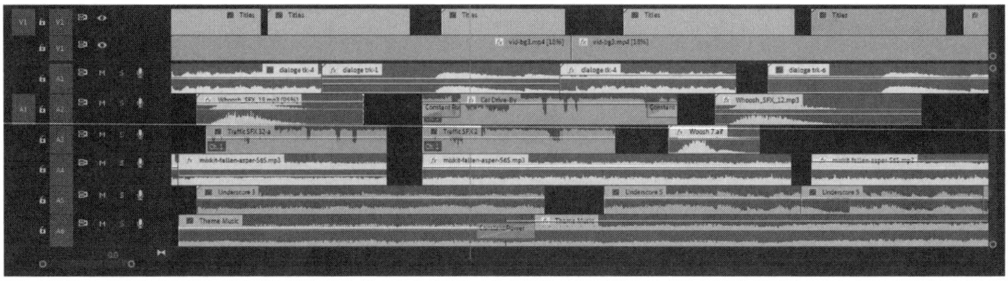

Timeline with labeled tracks and clips. *Photo courtesy of Jay Scherberth.*

The editor labels each track e.g., titles, video 1, SFX1, music, narration, etc. Each edit within a track carries its clip name e.g., "CU-Michelle," "Honolulu Aerial 5," "firecracker SFX," etc. Video tracks can show a thumbnail image of the clip if the editor selects that setting. Some editors also color code clips by character, interviewee, camera angle, B roll, musical number, etc.

Timeline editing

The timeline is a map of your sequence. A narrow vertical bar—referred to as the locator bar, strip indicator, or playhead—bisects the timeline and shows you which frame you're parked on in your sequence. Dragging this bar is one way to move around the sequence or footage. To make edits and VFX and perform the myriad of actions necessary to build a sequence on a digital system, your editor presses keys, clicks on buttons, tools, or menus, makes *marks* (electronic in and out points), drags and drops clips or scenes around, and imports shots directly into the timeline.

DIRECTOR'S CUT

> The Director's right to prepare his or her Director's Cut is absolute. (7-508)
> You must supervise the editing of the First Cut following completion of the Editor's Assembly.
> You have the right to instruct the Editor and to make whatever changes you deem necessary in preparing the Director's Cut. (7-505).
> No one can interfere with or cut behind you during the period of the Director's Cut. (7-504)
> —Summary of Directors' Creative Rights Under the Directors Guild of America Basic Agreement of 2017

No matter how you felt after the screening of the First Cut—freaked out, elated, anxious, or all three—now is the time to shift into editing mode. You have seen what all the writing, planning, and shooting have produced, that is, you know what the show looks like and what shape it's in. Hopefully, you've had a good night's sleep or a week or two off or a breather of some kind. Now it's time to supervise your show's final form—its look, story, and sound—starting with the Director's Cut.

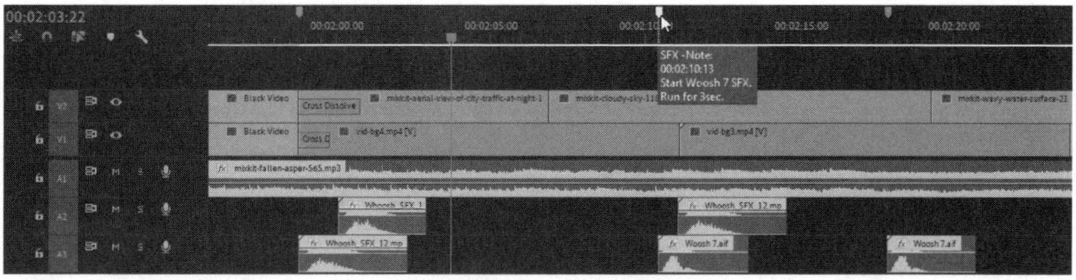

Some editors add *markers* a.k.a. *locators* and notes on the timeline where changes need to be made. These multi-colored, multi-purpose indicators make it easy to spot change points during re-cutting and hover the mouse to read the notes as shown here. *Photo courtesy of Jay Scherberth.*

To create the Director's Cut, the editor will follow the *change notes*—the changes you requested after screening the First Cut. Your editor will not only follow the notes but as a lot of editors like to say, they will listen to the spirit and the intent of what you said, in addition to your words. You may not know or be able to articulate exactly what you want. Maybe you just have a feeling that something isn't working or is off. An experienced editor will sense the problems and be able to intuit your reactions as you work along together. You may return to a troublesome area over several cuts or the entire course of re-cutting.

Normally, you will leave the editor to make the changes and return to screen them. Alternatively, you may work side by side in front of the digital system for part or for all of re-cutting. However it works on your particular project, the editing process will continue this way: Screen, give notes, editor makes changes; screen, notes, changes . . . until you bring the show to a final state and lock it. Here are more details of the journey from how re-cutting will proceed to what to do when problems or challenges arise to how to prepare for screenings and previews.

RE-CUTTING

> The hardest thing about editing and the most challenging, is, 'Why isn't this working,' and then, 'How do you fix it?' —**DEDE ALLEN**, A.C.E., *The Breakfast Club, Dog Day Afternoon, Bonnie and Clyde*

It's not uncommon to see more potential in the script, doc idea, or dailies than in the First Cut of the footage. Keep the faith: What you expected to see and the First Cut you screened are not where you'll finish. Your initial expectations will fade as you shape the final version of the show during re-cutting. This is the reality of filmmaking—where the sweat and magic of editing plays its role. You and the editor can transform the First Cut into a show that rises above its original intent and production footage. Let the work begin!

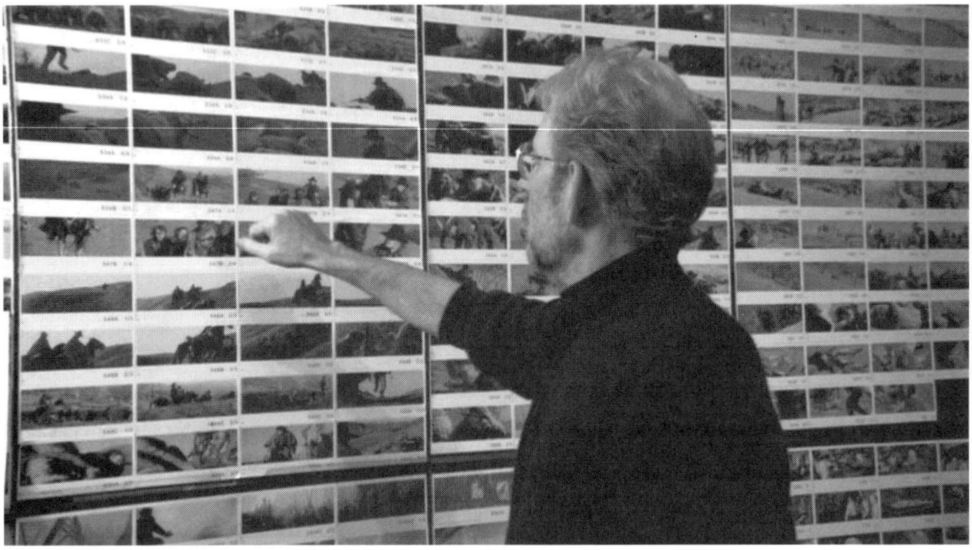

Walter Murch relies on print outs of key frames (pictured) to storyboard and edit scenes along with his system of cards of different shapes, sizes (indicating importance), and color (signifying emotion). *The Cutting Edge: The Magic of Movie Editing* (2004).

On non-scripted shows

In working through your list of changes, it's routine to re-comb transcripts, shot logs, and footage, including outtakes, for fresh ideas and improvements. You may write a new paper cut, play around with rearranging sections, and drop some sections entirely. You will start to consider VO (voiceover)—if, when, and where you need it. If you are using VO, you will re-write it continuously over the course of re-cutting.

On scripted shows

You will refer to the script to cross out or rearrange lines. Some ADR (automated dialogue replacement) lines may be called for, as well as pick-up or insert shots.

Cards and corkboard

Even in this "going green" age, many editors and directors still like to tack index cards with a description, a line, and/or a representative frame from each scene onto a corkboard or bulletin board. These cards on the wall constitute a postproduction storyboard and provide an overall flow of the show—a changeable map of its scenes, segments, and act breaks. As you re-cut and rethink the show—be it drama or doc—you can eliminate and move the cards around and see how the new order works.

Working together

> Editing *Sicko* was completely collaborative. Michael [Moore] is the type who lets the editors do the initial shaping of the film. Then he watches from the approach of an audience. That's how he shapes it. He gives a lot of freedom to the editors to put things together and write the film. —**DAN SWIETLIK**, editor, *Happy Valley, Sicko,* and *An Inconvenient Truth*

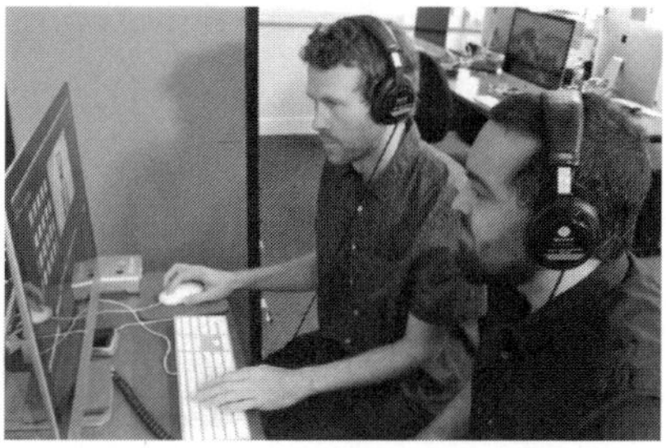

Editor and director at work re-cutting. *Photo courtesy of the Community Media Center County of Marin, CA.*

As editors work their way through the changes and the cuts, they check off each change they make or report back during your next screening as to why it wasn't possible to do the change. Usually, the reason is because the footage doesn't exist or the cut just didn't work. Many editors will show you the sub-par result; if there's trust, most directors will have faith that the change wasn't doable. Always remember, editors feel loyal to you and duty bound to serving all your ideas and requests. Regardless of if they agree or disagree with your notes, they will do everything to make them work.

As you work together, you should develop a partnership of trust and shared commitment to extracting the best from the footage and sculpting the most vibrant story. The editor is your accomplice, dedicated to putting the story together; making the cuts is just a part of that. Call on your editor for their insights, opinions, questions, and solutions. As the person most intimate with the footage, they will give feedback based not on ego or personal taste but steeped in the footage and driven by how best to tell the story. How can you help the editor? Realize that you're both on the same mission, communicate clearly, listen to them, and understand what their job entails. You are co-parenting the show to delivery together, a journey that can be stimulating and rewarding for both of you.

Experimenting

> Editing is the voice of the film, and also a deeply collaborative art . . . Out of all processes, I love editing the most. —**JAMES CAMERON**, director, *Avatar, Titanic, The Terminator, True Lies*

Because a DES allows your editor to create an infinite number of versions of scenes or of your entire show, you are free to experiment as much as you desire, and time permits. You may go down some unfruitful paths, but this is how your baby takes shape. You'll discover what works and what doesn't, which will pay off not only on your current project but also on future projects.

Don't get hung up on preconceived notions. Pay attention to how the show is unfolding before you: What plays? What calls for amplification? What needs to be dropped or requires a major shakeup or minor tinkering? Look for the heart of a scene. What makes it beat? Why is it important? Does another scene say almost the same thing? Can the scene be shortened or reduced to a line or a look? Less is more, as the old adage goes. This is a time to ping off one another, toss ideas out, test solutions. You may say "the scene works," while your editor plays Devil's Advocate.

Multiple versions and alts

It's common for editors to prepare *alts*—alternative versions of a scene—so you can view several possibilities. You may choose one version or another, combine versions, or find they lead you to a different place entirely.

Lifts

Often during re-cutting, you will cut out—lift—sections, scenes, or parts of scenes, which are called *lifts*. If you decide to put the lift back in, it's easy to pluck from a former version of the cut. Some editors consign lifts to a special lifts bin, a habit left over from editing on film, where a lift was a physical roll of spliced pieces of film left to hang in the Moviola trim bin. So, don't hesitate to cut out footage. You can always put it back in.

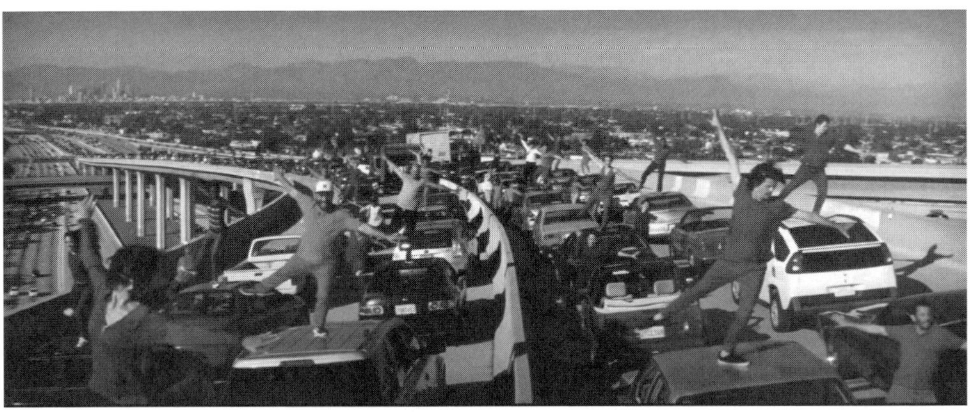

Director Damien Chazelle lifted this opening scene from *La La Land* (2016) until he restructured the musical and realized he needed to begin with a dance number that captured LA.

CHANGES, PROBLEMS, AND SOLUTIONS

> Great editors . . . understand, like a great diagnostician in medicine—this is the problem, this is how we can treat it, but you're going to have side effects. They'll see the whole picture.
> —**BO GOLDMAN**, screenwriter, *Scent of a Woman, The Rose, One Flew over the Cuckoo's Nest*

"We'll fix it in post." Now's the time you'll actually be accomplishing this hopeful adage. Each film is a new jigsaw puzzle for both you and the editor to fit together. No matter how practiced you each are, every show is unique and neither of you will have all the answers. Here are some common problems and ways you and your co-pilot can overcome them.

The story isn't working

You've dealt with story problems from the first draft of the script through production. Now you've got the picture and sound, and it's time to fill plot holes and solve the issues once and for all. Start by diagnosing what isn't coming together. Is it the beginning, middle, or ending? Is it a character? A performance? An interview? Does the story fall apart, lack believability, not make sense? Reshooting scene(s), shooting additional scene(s), or making some pick-ups could solve some or all of your problems but may not be feasible for budgetary or other reasons so we'll focus on editing solutions.

Missing shots

If you're lacking certain angles, say a close-up, the editor may be able to blow another shot up to create it on the digital system. They may also be able to stitch together two masters to make one usable shot. The ability of digital systems to blend shots (known as *flow cuts* or *morph cuts*) is also useful on documentaries for cutting from Part A to Part C of an interview and making it appear to be one seamless shot.

Story solutions

> As a loyal believer of the Auteur Theory, I first felt editing was but the logical consequence of the way in which one shoots. But what I learned is it is actually another writing.
> —**BERNARDO BERTOLUCCI**, director, *The Dreamers, The Last Emperor, Last Tango in Paris*

A First Cut contains and lays out everything. Now you must put yourself in the audience's seat and determine: What do they need to know with every shot and scene? No matter how beautifully shot or arduous to obtain, delete shots and scenes that repeat information or don't forward the action. You will usually not miss them, but if you do, the editor can always drop them back in with the next cut. It's not unusual for a scene to be dropped in and out or moved around repeatedly during re-cutting.

Are you tipping off something too early or too late? Try rearranging, reordering, or truncating scenes. You can also intercut scenes that were linear to strengthen the connections, contradictions, or contrasts between characters or doc subjects. If there's too much going on or your movie lags, look at dropping plotlines, scenes, characters, interviews, or subjects.

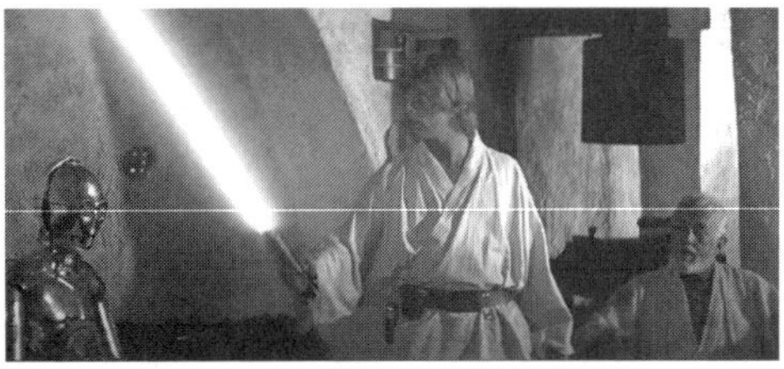

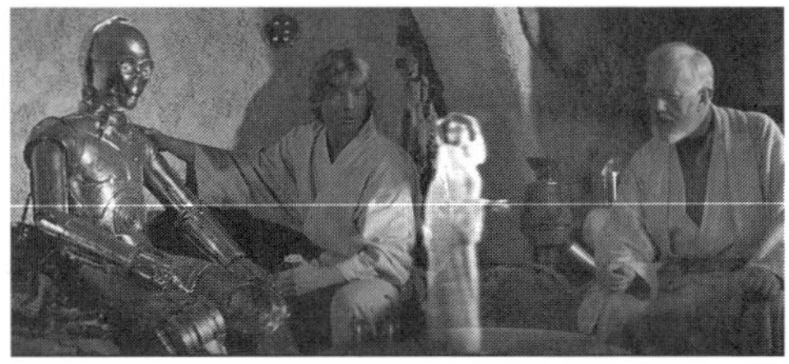

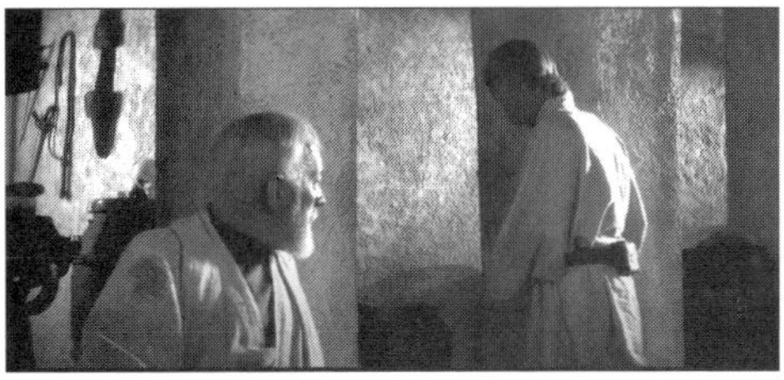

Star Wars (1977) was significantly restructured over many months of editing. In this scene, as these three edits illustrate, there are three main beats: 1) Luke learns his father was murdered for being a Jedi fighter and receives his light saber from Obi-Wan Kenobi. 2) Princess Leia appears with an urgent message. 3) Obi-Wan asks for Luke's help to rescue Leia but he refuses, asserting his aunt and uncle need him and he exits. As originally written and edited, the beats were 2-1-3, making Luke and Obi-wan seem callous for not reacting to her message right away and not propelling the story as the final version does.

If you're stuck, one way to analyze a scene is to say out loud what's happening in it, cut by cut:

Example:
1. She gets into her car.
2. He sees her through his windshield.
3. She drives off.
4. He pumps his fist.
5. He follows her.

You could then reorder the scene to shorten it, and tell it from his POV as follows:

4. He pumps his fist.
1 & 2. She gets into her car and drives off.
5. He follows her.

If your film is in decent shape, you'll do less radical surgery: You may add or eliminate some foreshadowing, shave scenes, delete lines, or trim shots. (More on trimming in the upcoming Fine Tuning section.) You may also need to open up certain sections, extend scenes, or expand shots to make things clear and let them breathe (give the audience a chance to catch their breaths).

When you're stuck

Take a break. Let your thoughts marinate—not stew—marinate! The British referred to editing film as *joining,* emphasizing the splicing, connective part, not the cutting part, like Americans. Think of that as you're reflecting upon your show: What thoughts, emotions, and plot are you joining as you edit shot after shot, scene after scene?

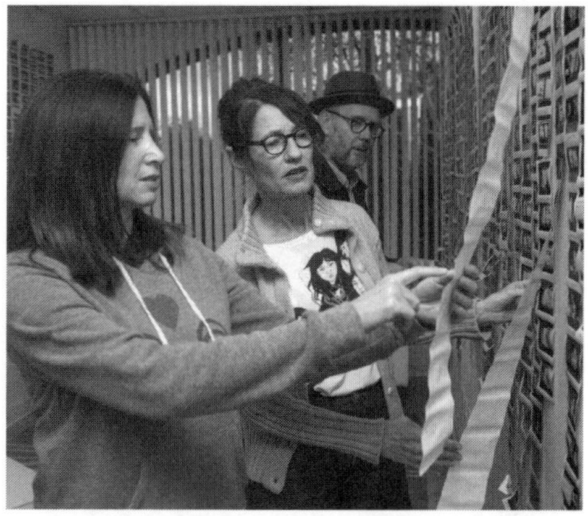

The editor and directors go back to the well and examine their key frame print outs on *The Battle of the Sexes* (2017). *Photo courtesy of Pamela Martin, Valerie Faris, and Jonathan Dayton.*

Don't attack the footage, listen to it. Let it speak and key you to the voice of your film. Re-watch dailies with fresh eyes. Dig into B-roll. It's not uncommon to find useable material from before you said "Action" or after you've said "Cut." Extreme situations sometimes call for starting over, cutting a scene, section, or an entire show from scratch. Listen to your editor-partner. Editors love coming up with show-saving solutions.

You can also bring in fresh eyes, by screening the cut for people you trust. Get their feedback but do not let them have a vote in or be a part of the editing process—you will be ceding your power. "Editing by committee" all too often infuses conflicting needs, notes, desires, and intents, and can impede progress and keeping to the schedule. Group supervision also puts your editor in an untenable position as it's nearly impossible to incorporate everyone's views. Resist letting this happen to your show.

Repercussions

Restructuring the story will impact pacing and often character and performance which we'll address next.

Character, performance, and interview issues

Begin by figuring out where the problem lies: Is it in the character or the performance, the interviewee or the interview? Know that all these problems have presented themselves on both major and minor shows to both seasoned and novice directors and editors.

Character

If you've determined the problem is in the character, what is lacking? Here are some questions to consider along with ideas for fixes:

Does the character have too much backstory?

- Be merciless: Eliminate all backstory that is unnecessary or bogs down the story.
- Reveal the backstory at a better, more story-forwarding moment.
- Trickle it in over the course of the film to deepen our understanding of the character and motivate the action.

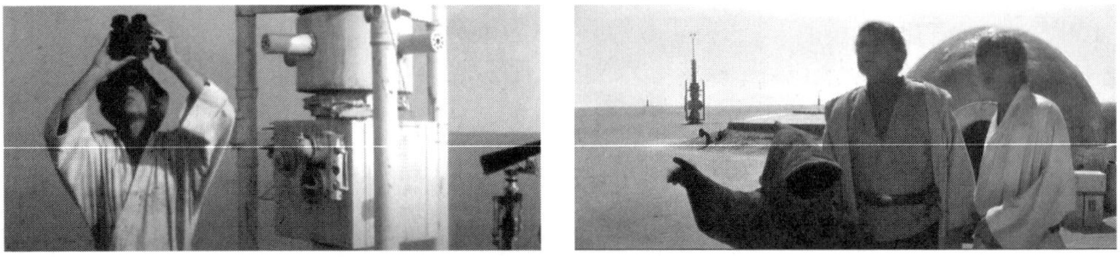

As originally edited, Luke Skywalker was introduced hanging out with his robot pals (unimportant characters) in the desert, interrupting the initial battle scene where Leia is captured. As re-edited, Luke's entrance is integrated with haggling for two droids (C-3PO and R2-D2), making all three characters and the action flow forward. *Star Wars: Episode IV- A New Hope* (1977).

Do we know too little about a character? Is the character poorly defined?
We need to see more of them to know them better and fathom their desires and motivations.

- Decide if the character is truly necessary and if they can be cut out or cut down. (If you do eliminate a character or strip down their appearances, inform the actor and give them their big scene(s) for their reel.)
- If the character is a keeper, beef up their reactions and others' reactions to them. Add wild lines for the character to speak off camera during actions scenes or while we're seeing other characters.

Do we understand why the character does and desires the things they do?
We must witness both their inner turmoil and outward reactions and motivations as they deal with the obstacles thrown at them.

- Add reaction shots—facial expressions and physical actions—so we know and understand them intimately.
- Dig into interstitial material: Their house or living situation, clothes, pet etc.: Their attitude toward their environment may reveal more about them.

Do the character arcs work?
Character arc is the evolution—for better or worse—of a character from their first appearance in the show until their last. Typically, the editor pulls lines and reactions from multiple takes to construct the character's arc, scene by scene, over the course of the show.

- Is each character's arc clear? Do they evolve too quickly or too slowly? If so, you need to rearrange scenes so that you are doling out information at just the right pace. Viewers must experience characters' growth or refusal to grow leading to their success, newfound wisdom, or downfall at a believable rate.

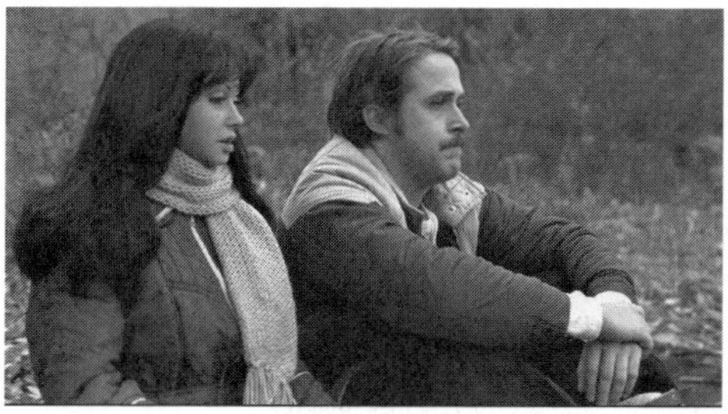

Even the doll has a character arc in *Lars and the Real Girl* (2007).

Are there too many characters?

They will put a drag on the pacing and the story.

- Remove redundant characters.
- Remove or significantly cut down characters and their plotlines who least impact the main character(s).

Is the character engaging? Are we drawn to them and their conflicts?

Hero, villain, sidekick or supporting character, we must care about them and what happens to them. Chris Innis and Robert Murawski, a married couple and co-editors on *The Hurt Locker* (2008) believe: "If audiences care about the characters, then they will be willing to submit to almost any film structure or rhythm."

- If the audience doesn't care, you've got a major problem which wasn't caught in the script. If you cannot fix this with the remedies in #1-4 then you will need to eliminate the character, minimize their appearances, or re-write and reshoot.

Performance

Good actors expose themselves emotionally and make us believe. Their willingness to be fearlessly vulnerable and show the negative and positive range of human feeling makes us laugh, cry, fume, etc. They listen and react as well as speak, making dialogue scenes compelling. They use their bodies in broad and subtle ways to create comedy and tragedy.

Editors work hard to bring out the best performance of every actor in every scene and create their character's persona and arc. Still, there will be issues which you two will identify and work on to overcome. Here's a list of problems you may encounter followed by solutions. The actor's performance:

- Lacks believability or truth, projects shallow emotion, or seems fake.
- Is boring, flat, predictable, wooden in body and voice, or otherwise emotionally deficient.
- Is over the top, hammy, or at odds with the essence of the character.
- Doesn't mesh with other actors; fails to respond or listen. Is out of sync with the character, period, place, or movie.

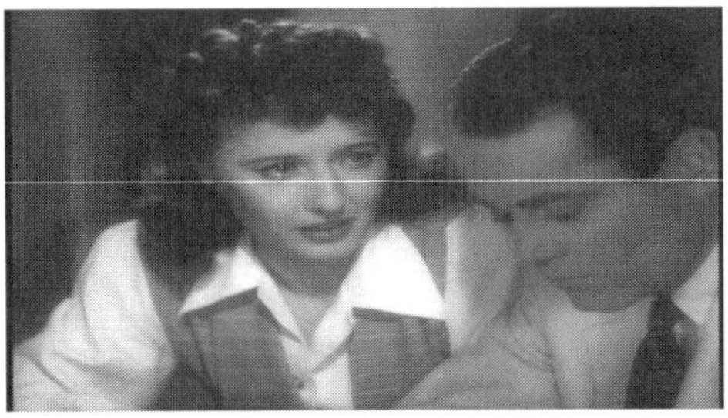

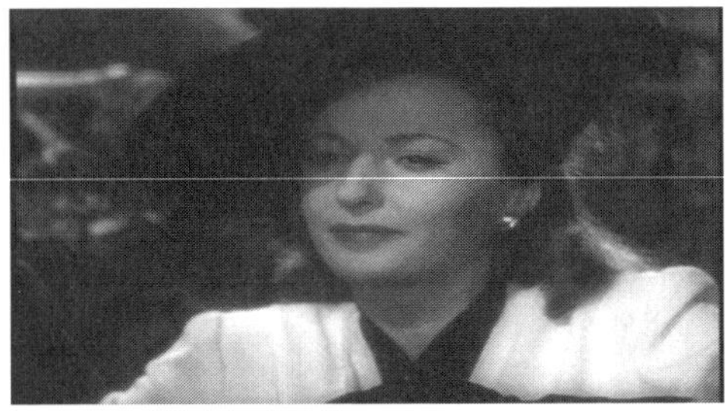

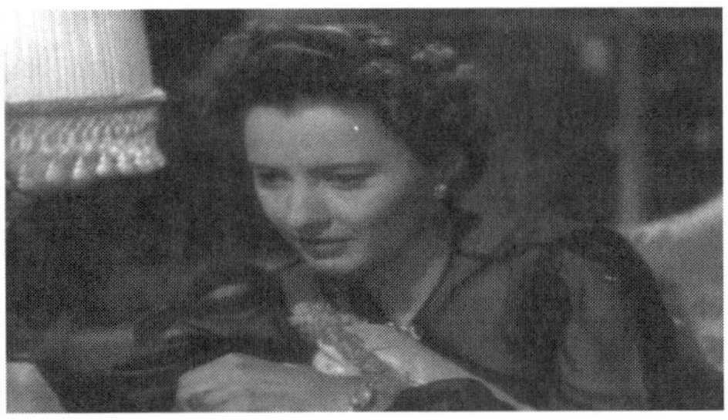

"The eyes are the window to the soul" is a truism never truer than on the screen. Outstanding actors' eyes nakedly project truth and the depths of the human soul. In *The Lady Eve* (1941), Barbara Stanwyck transmits: 1) Love and regret as a con who has fallen for her mark, Henry Fonda; 2) Satisfaction at plotting revenge upon his rejection and 3) Devastation when he rejects her again.

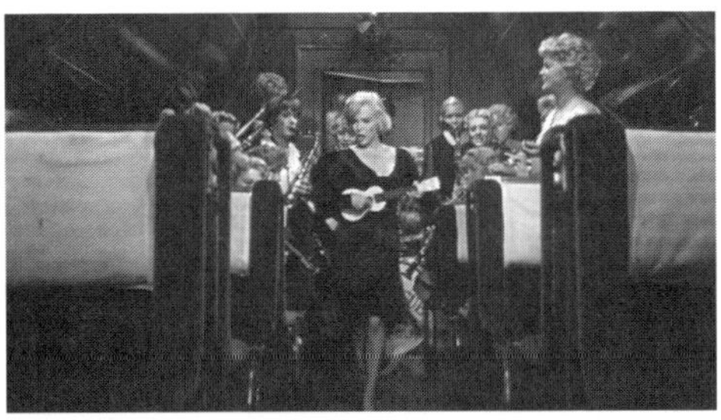

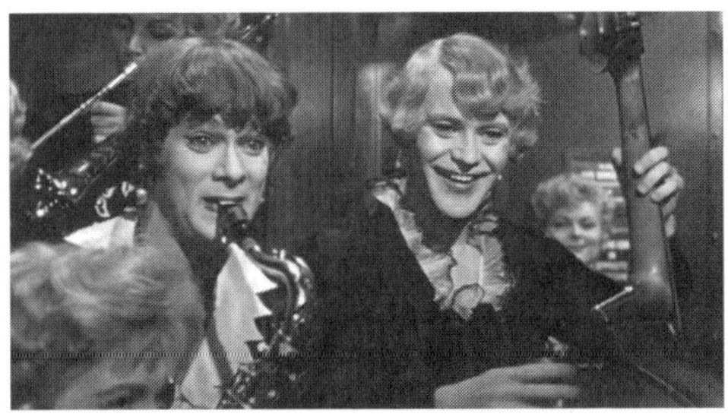

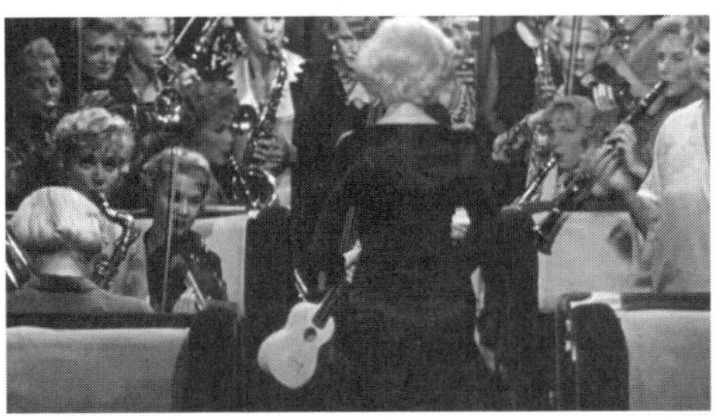

The sound editor on *Some Like it Hot* (1959) pieced Marilyn Monroe's ukulele number together syllable by syllable to make her appear to sing. Much of the song is played at a distance, on passengers on the train, or on her back.

If you cannot edit out the character, recast, or reshoot them, you can improve the performance in several ways. First, scrounge the outtakes and all the character's footage for better reactions and line readings. Second, shrink the performance by reducing the character's onscreen time and playing their lines on others. Third, put "words in the actor's mouth" by marrying the best audio take of a line, with its best video take. Lastly, plan on ADRing (rerecording after picture lock) lines to improve the performance.

Interviews and interviewees

On a documentary, you'll pull from different sections of interviews to stitch together speakers' words. As with fiction stories and characters, each major interviewee should have an arc: a beginning, middle, and conclusion (which may be narrated or revealed in text if the person dies). For example, let's say you're telling the story of a non-binary teen. Where do their family members, friends, teachers, religious leaders start in their awareness and views and where do they finish?

While the issues and fixes on documentaries are similar to those for actors' performances, these problems and editing solutions are specific to interviews:

Interviewee is not credible, dishonest.

- If you're relying on this person for credible information, dump the entire interview. If your aim is to debunk this person with other credible interviews, keep the interview.
- Credible or not, you must fairly and ethically edit and present every interviewee's words and beliefs.

Acceptable: Dissolves between sections of interviews and removing "ums," uhs," and insignificant pauses. *Morph cuts,* which allow you to seamlessly jump from one part of an interview and only work when shots are similar in framing, background, subject position, etc., are also okay.

Unacceptable: Creating *Frankenbytes* (editing words and sentences together to manufacture and inaccurately present what a subject is saying). While there is no Hippocratic oath of filmmaking, do not fabricate people's stories: You sell out the material, your interviewees, your profession, and yourself.

Interviewee rambles, is boring, or talks in a way that is hard to understand or follow.

By cutting the audio to forge a sensible, clear narrative, along with inserting cutaways and B-roll, your editor can ordinarily make an interview passable.

- If not, do you need this interview? Can you use another speaker to cover the topic? Can you get someone else or a narrator to discuss it?
- If the interviewee speaks low or is otherwise hard to understand, you can clarify their words with text or quote them in narration or text.

Poor audio.

This is the scourge of nonfiction, low budget interviews.

- Your editor can raise the volume, balance the sound, and remove background noise to ameliorate the problems.
- If a speaker's words are still difficult to decipher, you may need to add text or have a narrator quote them.

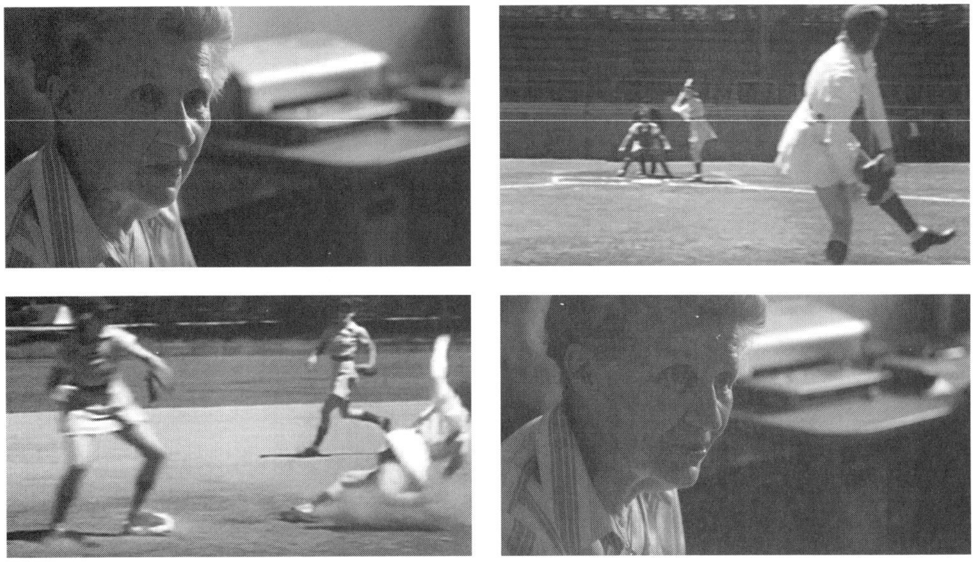

Cutaways can illustrate what the interviewee is saying, break up the flow of words on camera, or bridge audio gaps to help create a coherent narrative as these frames from the documentary *A Secret Love* (2020) demonstrate.

Rhythm and pacing are off

Is too much happening in your film, leaving viewers feeling assaulted, overwhelmed, lost, confused, or turned off? You may need to loosen things up by inserting a montage or extending cuts to add rests and pauses. Or does your picture drag, causing the audience to nap, be bored, or drop out? This calls for compressing things: shortening scenes and tightening dialogue, looks, lines.

Like the stone causing a proverbial ripple in the pond, commonly you will find that making changes, even if only a frame or two, affects every subsequent cut in a scene. Your editor will adjust the duration of the cuts and recalibrate the scene's timing. You two are altering the pacing, slowing it with added shots or frames, or goosing it by deleting shots or frames. You can also do this by slo-moing or speeding up shots, both video and audio.

Time

> The great thing about the movies is . . . you're giving people . . . tiny pieces of time . . . that they never forget. —JIMMY STEWART

The way you perceive time is reflected in the way you weave together your shot material during editing. Time is the fourth element you are playing with during editing in addition to picture, sound, and space. You and your editor will manipulate time by setting the duration of shots and scenes which will differ from the filmed timing. You can also finesse time by putting the audience inside a character's head. As film is considered

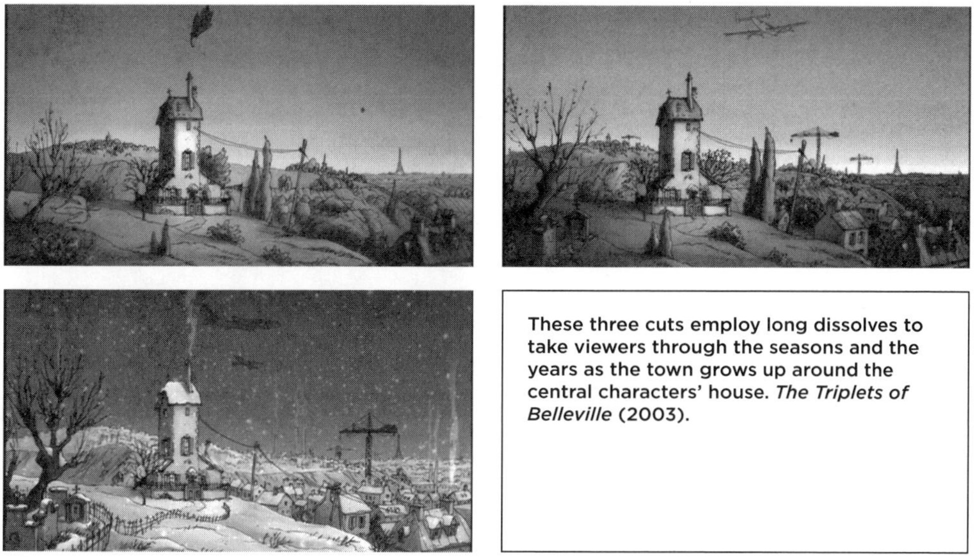

These three cuts employ long dissolves to take viewers through the seasons and the years as the town grows up around the central characters' house. *The Triplets of Belleville* (2003).

to be the art that most mimics the workings of the human mind, your audience will experience time subjectively from the character's point of view, darting from thought to feeling, knowledge to discovery, past to present in a matter of seconds or frames.

Flashbacks and flashforwards

These narrative conventions also play with time and you can use them to forward the drama.

Flashback

You can create a flashback to illuminate a character's feelings, thoughts, memories, or earlier life. You can also deploy a flashback to rerun an event and fix it in viewers' minds or make them see it anew. Flashbacks are often used—and overused—as exposition but you can also employ them to foreshadow the future, clarify plot points, or spin the story in a new direction. They can be quick—composed of a flash cut or two—or long and run the length of the movie. Lastly, they may contain other flashbacks and occur in non-chronological order. No matter how your flashback functions, it's vital that as it sends the story backwards in time, it drives your film forward.

Flashforward

Consider using a flashforward to presage upcoming events or disclose parts of the story that have not yet been told but may be dramatized later in greater detail. You can also insert a flashforward to reveal a character's hopes and fears for the future. Frequently flashforwards (like flashbacks) appear as dreams or nightmares.

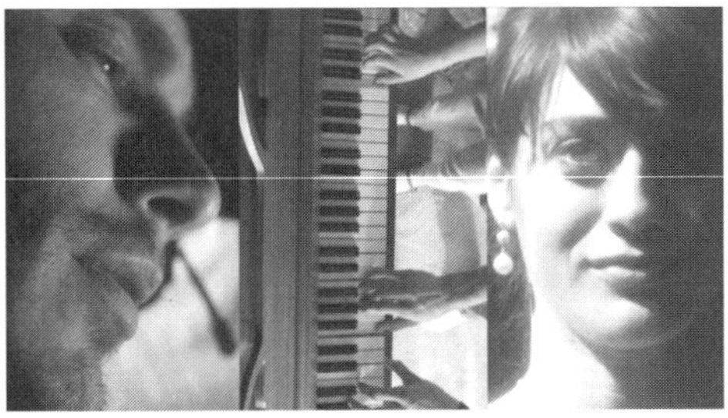

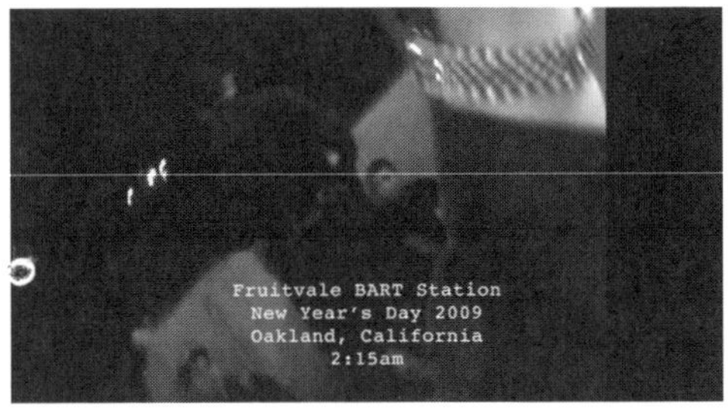

LEFT: In *127 Hours* (2010) after being pinned by a boulder in a crevice for five days, Aron Ralston (James Franco) hallucinates. In progressive split screen shots, he flashes back to playing piano with his sister. **RIGHT:** *Fruitvale Station* (2013) starts with a flashforward to the actual footage of the 2009 BART police killing of Oscar Grant. The movie then gives a fictionalized version of his last day, culminating in his murder.

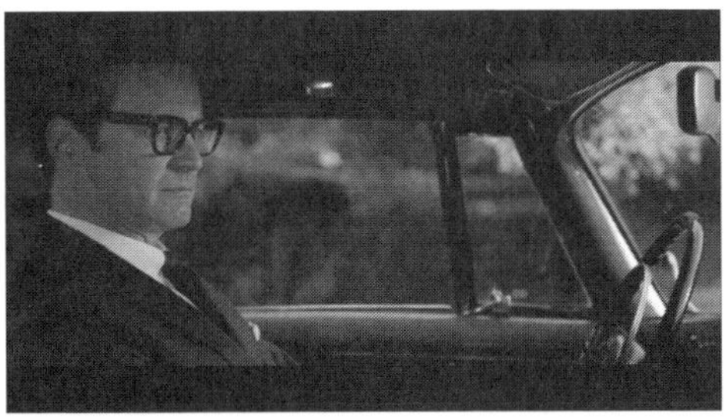

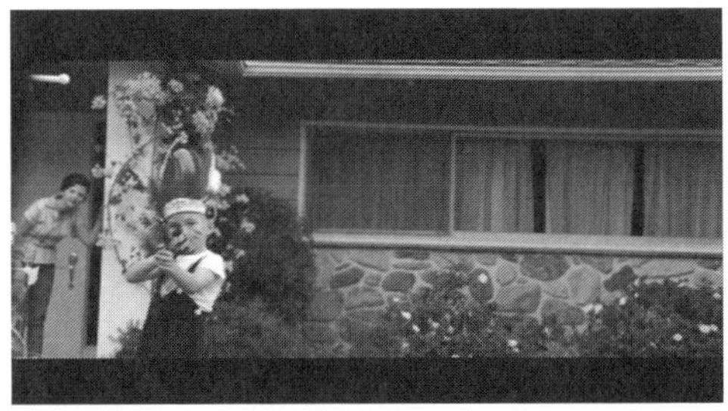

In *A Single Man* (2009) time is altered for George Falconer (Colin Firth), grieving in secret after the sudden death of his male partner. As George drives to work, slo-mos and reaction shots portray how he sees his neighbors going about their everyday activities in a world far removed from his.

Sound and music come to the rescue

> I really enjoy editing the most . . . It's the part I rely on most to save things, for better or for worse. —**GEORGE LUCAS**, director, *Star Wars, American Graffiti, THX 1138*

We'll cover the powers of sound and music in the next two chapters, but here we'll focus on how you can use them to solve story, character, and performance problems.

Play dialogue off screen.
When you've rearranged a scene or set of scenes, some or all of the on camera lines may not work. You can play these sync dialogue lines over other characters' reactions. You can also record wild lines to accomplish this and to cover missing or connecting information, help performance and character deficiencies, and streamline the action.

Add new narration or VO.
Narration and VO—planned, unplanned, or rewritten—have come to the rescue on more shows, both fiction and non, than viewers would ever suspect. You can use them to glue together disparate sections, supply plots on a comedy

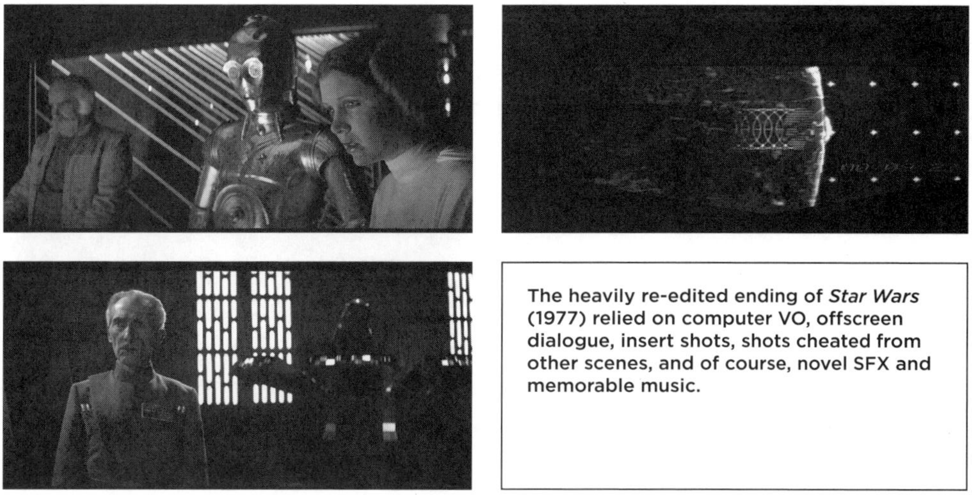

The heavily re-edited ending of *Star Wars* (1977) relied on computer VO, offscreen dialogue, insert shots, shots cheated from other scenes, and of course, novel SFX and memorable music.

consisting of running gags, and turn nonsensical shows into coherent, watchable, and even sometimes award-winning entertainment.

Dialogue and music.

You may want to drop out dialogue and express your story with images, SFX, and wild track. A silent scream can be more chilling than a voiced one. Music has long come to the rescue on many a film, zinging a lackluster section, aiding a transition, smoothing over a scene with an instrumental riff, and bringing a montage to life.

FINE TUNING: OVERLAPPING, TRIMMING, SLIPPING, AND SLIDING

> I've always been concerned when editors get awards and directors don't. It seems wrong to me, because without the material we can't do a thing. We are only interpreting what we're given . . . We repair other people's dreams. —**JIM CLARK**, *from his book The Dream Repairman*

Throughout re-cutting but especially as you near locking the picture and "getting it to time" (a required length), you will be massaging cuts and transitions between scenes by adding and subtracting frames to perfect your show's timing. The next sections cover the types of edits your editor will make to fine tune your show. It's useful to understand these, in order to know what is possible and to explain what you want. First a few definitions:

Straight cut: Cutting to a new picture and sound at the same time.

Overlap: Cutting to picture and sound at different times, so that one overlaps — extends beyond — the other.

Prelap. Starting the sound of the incoming shot before cutting to its picture.

Postlap. Continuing the sound of the outgoing shot after cutting to the picture of the incoming shot.

Overlapping

Overlapping enables you to show reactions to lines, strengthen performances, manipulate time, and control the pace. While it usually has the effect of tightening a scene—shortening time—overlapping can also expand time. Documentaries overlap narration or interviewee's words over pertinent images, shortening time. Regularly, comedies rely on the overlap to extend jokes and time. So do dramas, such as in courtroom scenes when the verdict is due, hospital scenes when a baby is arriving, and competitions that come down to the last second.

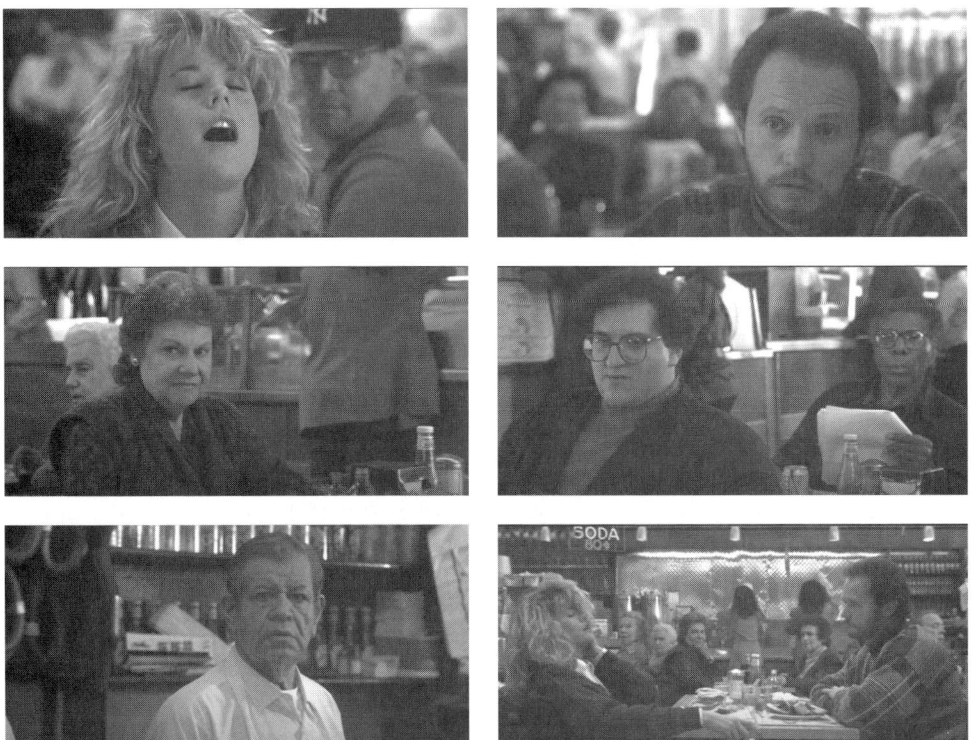

In this well-known Katz's Deli scene from *When Harry Met Sally* (1989), the editor extends Sally's (Meg Ryan's) dialogue sound and cuts around to Harry (Billy Crystal) and others to extend the laugh.

Trimming

Digital systems define trimming as adjusting an edit by shortening, extending, slipping, or sliding it. Editors trim by manipulating the sequence on the timeline, selecting an icon, menu, button, or tool or pressing a key on their keyboard. There are times,

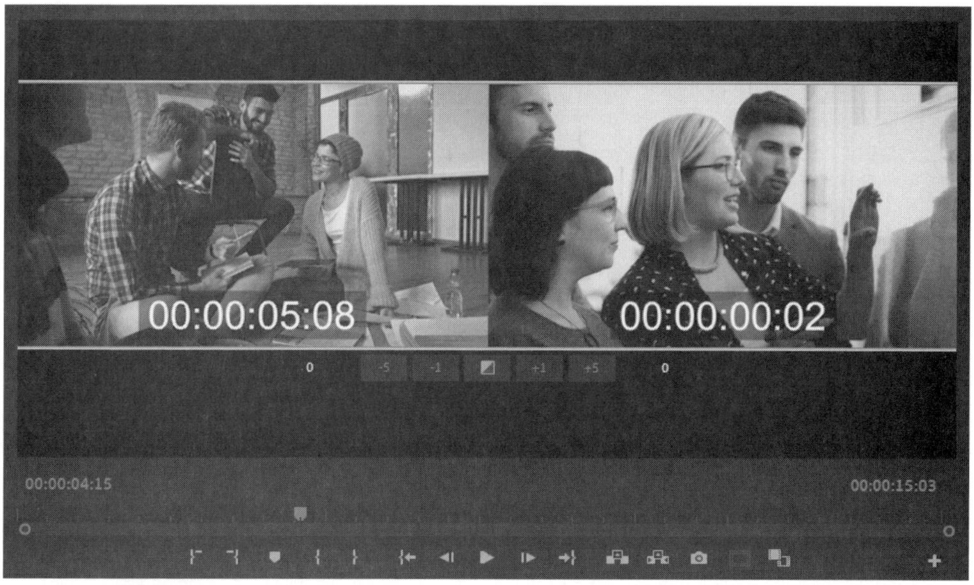

Trim view on Adobe Premiere. Notice that the source and record viewers have been replaced by two smaller viewers which display the A side of the edit on the left and the B side on the right. *Photo courtesy of Jay Scherberth.*

however, when you'll want to open up an edit and examine its frames closely. This calls for using a system's trim view. Trim view lets you work with the *A side* (the outgoing clip) and the *B side* (the incoming clip) of your edit either together or independently. Your editor can trim and preview until you're satisfied with the new edit, then exit trim view to see the normal, larger source and record monitors.

Trim view on Adobe Premiere. Notice that the source and record viewers have been replaced by two graphic viewers which display the A side of the edit on the left and the B side on the right.

Sync

Trimming even one frame changes the duration of your show and affects all other video and audio tracks on the timeline which must be adjusted so you don't go out of sync. Normally sync is paramount but there are times you'll want to throw things out of sync e.g., to portray discombobulation, discontinuity, mental breakdown, a nightmare, violence, alienation, etc.

Slip-sliding around

Slip and slide are two common ways to trim edits that do not change the duration of your show or the edit itself; a 2" clip will still be 2". Slipping an edit affects it internally by changing the head and tail frames. Sliding an edit changes it externally, so it occurs earlier or later in the sequence. The following examples will make this clear.

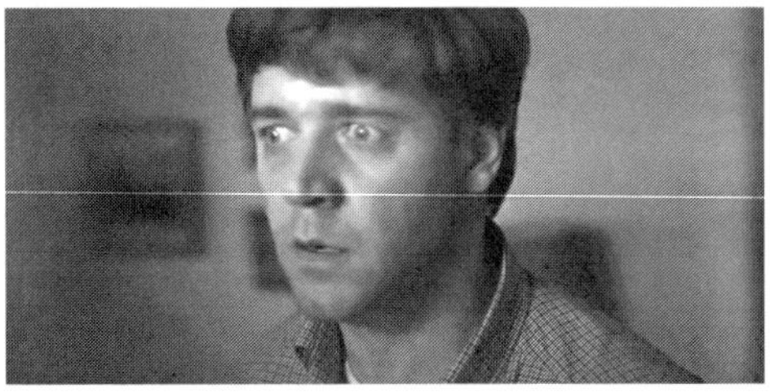 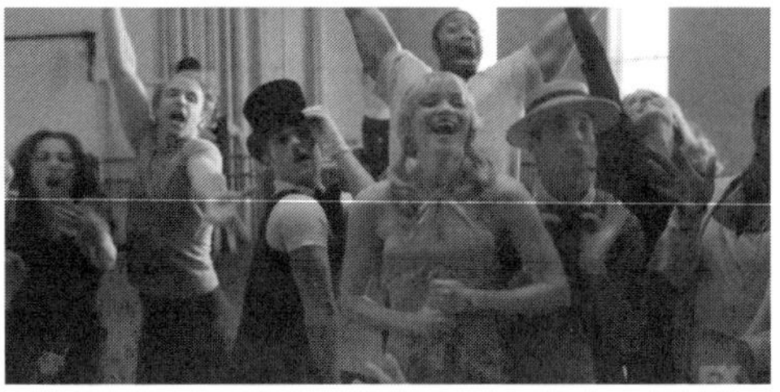

LEFT: In an out of sync sequence, mathematician John Nash (Russell Crowe) breaks down mentally, overwhelmed by voices and people from his past in *A Beautiful Mind* (2001). **RIGHT:** Slipping allows the dancers' raised hands to match the music in the mini-series *Fosse/Verdon* (2019).

Slipping video and audio
Problem: Your edit shows a monkey scampering up a tree and starting to swing into the foliage. You want to begin the edit with the swing and see the monkey fly from tree to tree.
Solution: Slip the head of the shot so that it starts when the monkey swings.

Slipping video only
Problem: The audio on the edit, a song, is fine. The picture edit, however, shows dancers dancing in a circle, raising their hands together, then circling again. You want the picture edit to end with their hands raised.
Solution: Slip video at the tail of the edit, so it ends earlier with the dancers' hands raised.

Slipping audio only
Problem: You want a song to start on a certain word; where it fades out isn't an issue.
Solution: Slip the song to the right word at the head. This keeps the music in the same place in relation to the video.

Sliding
When you slide an edit, you can see its position change graphically on the timeline. The preceding edit gets shorter if you slide an edit up (to the left in the timeline), while the following edit (to the right in the timeline) gets longer by the same number of frames. You can slide a video edit or a group of video edits up or down to reposition them against a bed of music or narration. Conversely, you can slide the music or narration into position.

Pulling up and pushing down

These are terms that have been around since film, and aid in describing what you want. When you slip, slide, or trim an edit so it starts sooner, you are pulling it up and this is reflected on the timeline. When you slip, slide, or trim an edit so it starts later, you are pushing it down the timeline. For instance, you routinely pull-up or push-down a video edit to hit a music beat or better match the dialogue or narration.

SCREENINGS AND PREVIEWS

You've deleted, reordered, intercut, and trimmed: The re-cutting is complete. You're satisfied that the show is ready for the vital screenings that will move it closer to picture lock, and the next phase of postproduction. First, a few preparations.

Preparing for screenings

You will accomplish as much picture and sound work as time and budget allow to make your show as presentable as possible.

Picture

Your editor can create titles and subtitles, drop in the latest VFX, slug for missing shots or scenes, do some temp color grading, and insert countdown leader.

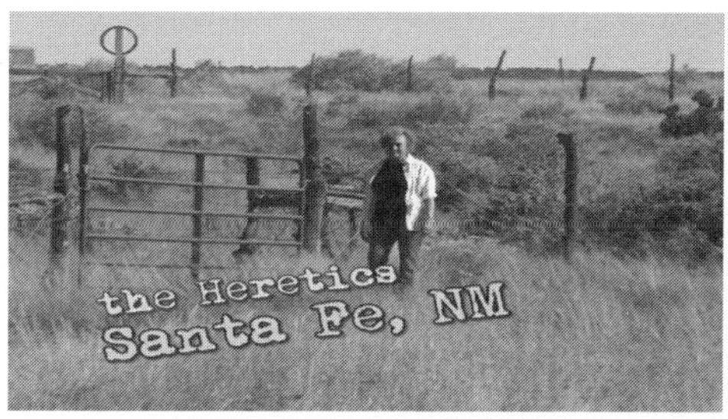

This shot would be a mysterious segue without its subtitle. *The Heretics* (2009).

Sound

You will likely add some temp music, narration, and crucial SFX.

Temp mix a.k.a. temp dub, slop mix, rough mix, or scratch mix

You may undertake a temp mix of music, dialogue, and sound effects for the purpose of previewing to a test audience, the network, or a potential buyer or distributor. If your production company can afford it, you'll engage sound editors and go to a mix stage.

Alternatively, your editor can create a temp mix right on the editing system. Since the audio tools on current digital

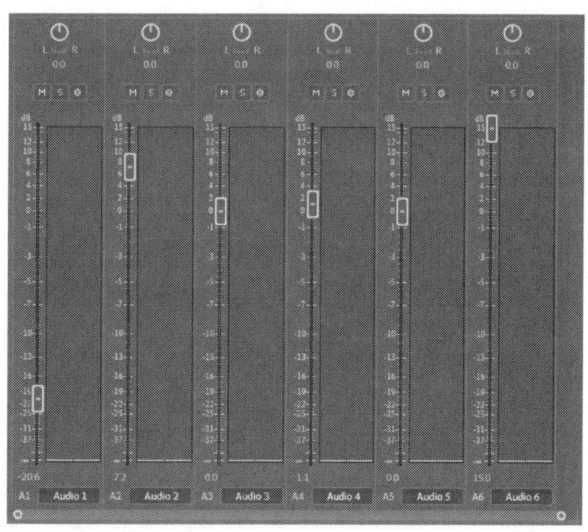

Audio tracks on Adobe Premiere Mix tool. *Photo courtesy of Jay Scherberth.*

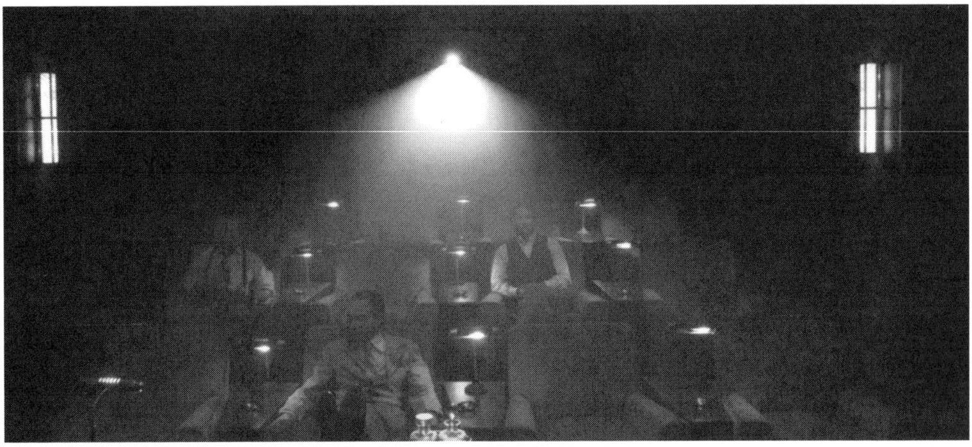

A screening room of yesteryear at a 1940s Tinseltown studio, from the mini-series *Hollywood* (2020).

systems are pretty slick, money is not always the issue as James Cameron makes clear: "A lot of filmmakers go to the [trouble of preparing] a true "temp mix," where you go on a dubbing stage for several days and have mixers and all that. We previewed *Titanic* all three times . . . with a mono track, mixed out of the Avid's four tracks. And it played fine."

Screening

You, your editor, and the assistant editor (for note taking) will attend the screening. The producer and you have been working together since the beginning of the picture. Ideally by this time you've established a good working relationship, and each believe in the film, so the producer is aware of the state of the show before arriving at the screening room. At the screening, you should both focus on the film and the producer should support you to complete it. If necessary, set expectations for any glaring issues (shots due, reshoots, etc.) and then let your show speak for itself.

After the screening and discussion with the producer, editorial will send a link to or make a copy of the cut for those wishing to review it as well as to anyone who couldn't make the screening. As your show progresses, editorial will also loop in everyone who needs to view cuts, but isn't part of the editing process: post supervisor, VFX personnel, composer, sound editors, trailer editor, promo folks, etc. And your screening audience may grow to include the client, studio execs, and others or there may be a series of small, targeted viewings to get sign-off from executives and others.

Preview

> You have the right to request a preview of the Director's Cut of a theatrical motion picture before a public audience or, at the Producer's choice, a private audience of no less than 100 persons (excluding relatives and employees). (7-505(e)) This preview cannot be conducted using the "Avid output" or other substandard processes. (7-705)
> —Summary of Directors' Creative Rights Under the Directors Guild of America Basic Agreement of 2017.

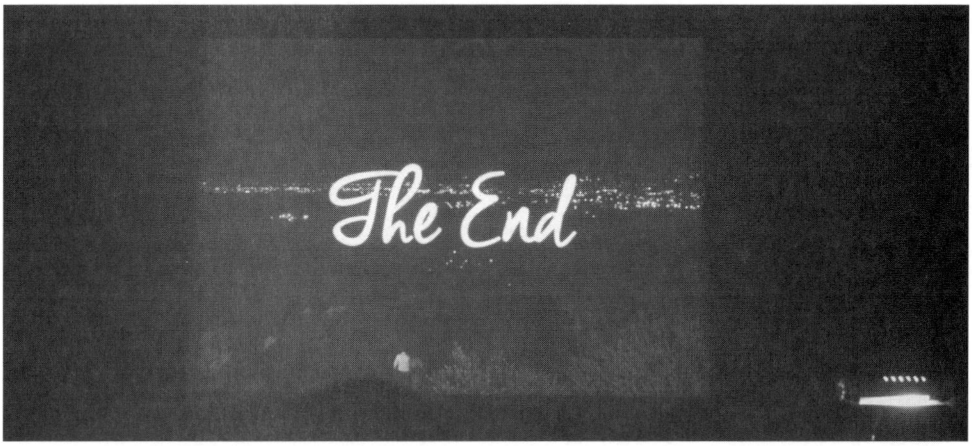

End of preview from *Hollywood* (2020).

A preview can be pricey, taking place at a theatre and gathering verbal and written responses from the audience or a small "focus group." Or a preview can be a matter of inviting friends and trusted cohorts over to sit on your couch and view your work-in-progress. Or it can be somewhere in between, occurring in a small studio or company screening room. Big, medium, or small, previews are a way to test your movie and your audience, and move you one step closer to lock.

LOCKING THE SHOW

As you sprint toward the final cut, hopefully the picture has reached a point where everyone is confident that it's the best it can be, and you will lock it. Locking a cut simply means that you're done editing—you won't be changing another frame. A delivery deadline—air date, exhibit date, or festival entry date—often clinches a lock. Once locked, a show must be approved by the exhibitor: For a TV show, this is the network; for a movie for theatrical release, it's the studio. Following approval, if you're working on a TV show, your editor will *bring it to time*—shave frames here and there to get it precisely to the last second to meet the network's required running time.

Unlocking the show

Ordinarily, once you lock a show, it remains locked. It's not uncommon however, for it to become unlocked and relocked when the studio, network, or life events demand last minute changes or a client, producer, or you make last minute fixes. Many filmmakers point out that with digital technology, nothing seems to ever be finished. As with other computer creations, the polishing and reworking carries on even after it has been released. George Lucas has re-edited several of the early *Star Wars* films. Web pieces are revised and re-uploaded daily. Some view this "never locked" state of affairs as a good

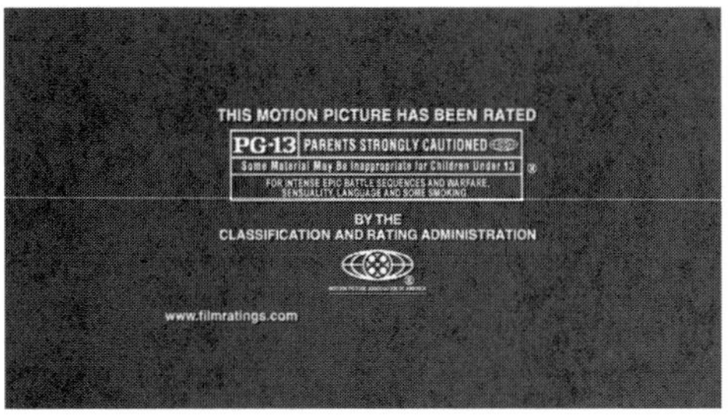

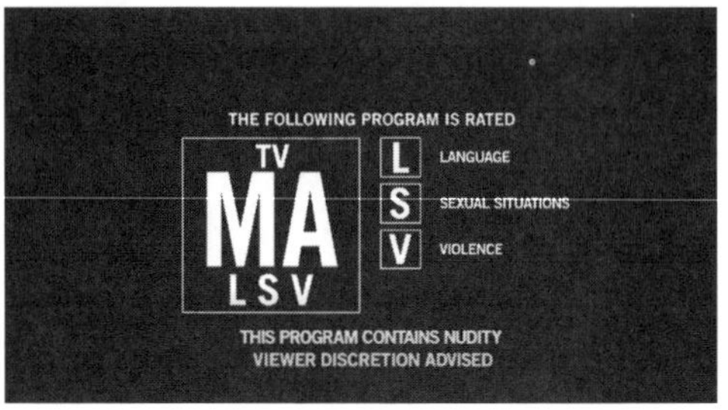

thing, since improvements and inspirations can be brought to bear for a much longer time period than film and tape ever allowed; others believe this makes for never ending projects that you don't ever really let go of.

Rating the show

Following studio or network approval, a ratings board will rate your show. This is voluntary. You do not have to get your show rated, especially if it's going straight to DVD. A movie is reviewed and designated G, PG, PG-13, R, or NC-17 by the Motion Picture Academy of Arts (MPAA). A TV show goes to the TV Parental Guidelines Monitoring Board, which bestows a TV-Y, TV-Y7, TV-Y7 FY, TV-G, TV-PG, TV-14, or TV-MA rating, and often, a sub-rating of D, L, S, or V for the last three categories, except for TV-MA for which the D sub rating is not applied. After your film goes to the ratings board, you will contest or make any requested changes.

LAST WORD

Once locked, the show moves into the two final phases of postproduction: sound editing and finishing, which is what the final three chapter are all about.

WHAT DIRECTORS SHOULD KNOW ABOUT HOW TO GET TO A LOCKED CUT

- ☐ A digital editing system is a tool that you and your editor harness to collaborate and create your vision.
- ☐ With the goal of locking the picture, the re-cutting process involves three repeating steps:
  1. Screening cuts with the editor (and others if you choose);
  2. Giving change notes to the editor;
  3. Editor making the changes.
- ☐ A First Cut contains and lays out everything. To re-edit, put yourself in the audience's seat and determine: What do they need to know with every shot and scene?
- ☐ The editor is your accomplice and the person most intimate with the footage. Call on your editor for their insights, opinions, questions, and solutions. Depend on them to give feedback based not on ego or personal taste but steeped in the footage and driven by how best to tell the story.
- ☐ You can ask your editor to prepare alternative versions of a scene so you can contemplate different possibilities.
- ☐ To solve problems, start by diagnosing if they are story problems, character or performance problems, or interview or interviewee problems.
- ☐ In addition to or in lieu of reshooting or picking up shots, editorial solutions for problems include dropping plot lines, scenes, characters, or interviews and rearranging, reordering, intercutting, dropping, or truncating scenes or interviews.
- ☐ Narration, wild lines, VO, and music can help fix character, performance, and story issues.
- ☐ Fine tuning—trimming, overlapping, slipping, and sliding edits—aids in tightening your tale or opening it up and letting it breathe.
- ☐ To prepare for screening your show, you can add titles and perform a temp sound mix on a mix stage or on the editor's digital editing system.
- ☐ Screenings and previews are avenues for audience input and executive approval and to advancing your film toward picture lock.
- ☐ Picture lock means that you've completed the editing phase and are ready to move on to sound editing and mixing and the final finishing postproduction phase.

8

CREATING SOUND AND MUSIC

After locking the picture, your next critical task will be to launch the sound and music phase of postproduction by spotting the show with the music composer and the sound designer. At the spotting session, you will run the film scene by scene, and express what you'd like to hear. To enable you to best articulate your desires, this chapter begins by immersing you in the world of sound and music and what they can do for your movie as well as their players, practices, and workflows. It then moves on to the sound acquiring and music composing phase, starting with the spotting session, and ending with the sound and music, cued and ready for editing and the mix. Whether your editor is performing all the sound and music work on their digital system, or you have an entire sound and music team supporting you, this chapter and the next guide you through the sound and music process, from acquisition through editing and the final mix.

WHAT SOUND CAN DO FOR YOUR FILM

> . . . the first thing I thought about was how the war did not sound like war. Having grown up watching Hollywood war movies, I expected a lot more sound and much bigger sound. It was not until I was hit that I realized what I was in was real. —**WWII VETERAN**, recollecting his first day of combat at Anzio

This soldier's reaction was replayed on September 11, 2001 when a New Yorker told a TV interviewer that when he saw the first plane hit, his immediate thought was that it was just like a movie. Increasingly, our dreams, fantasies, memories, the shows we watch, and our waking lives are intersecting to mix and meld reality, documentary, and drama. Sound, being the important sense and sense memory that it is, plays a dominant role in this.

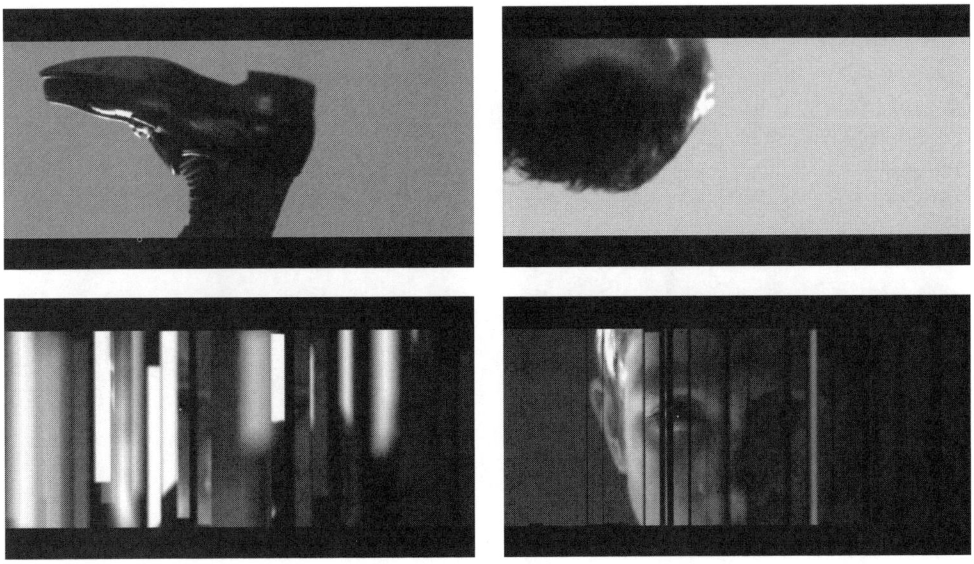

The aural world created in *Extremely Loud, Incredibly Close* (2011) captures what a boy with autism experiences. His father died in a WTC tower on 9/11, but he imagines (falsely) that he jumped to his death.

Whether your viewers will be venturing down a rabbit hole or inside a computer, to outer space or back to the past, sound plays a vital role in your placing them in that world, and making them accept the creatures—hobbits, robots, or humans—that inhabit it. And that role includes the sound of silence. Sound design invariably contains planned sections of silence or minimal sound. (No show is entirely silent as there is always ambient sound. If you drop out all sound, you risk hostile glares at the projection booth and channel surfing.) Silence, especially following a gripping scene or a cacophony of sounds, lets your audience take a breath and recover.

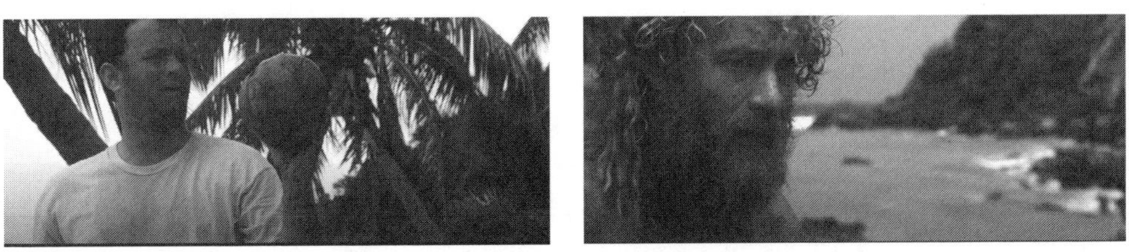

In *Cast Away* (2000), for the nearly 80 minutes that Chuck Noland (Tom Hanks) survives on an island, there is no music, only ambient sound and minor dialogue which succeeds in marooning the audience along with him.

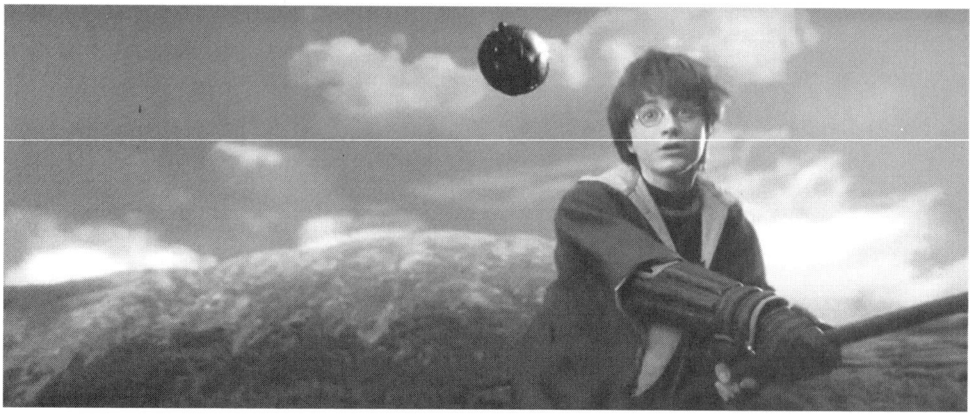

A Quidditch match sounds like any other after school sport . . . except for the Quaffle and the Golden Snitch. *Harry Potter and the Sorcerer's Stone* (2001).

Creating sound

> Sound may be the most powerful tool in the filmmaker's arsenal in terms of its ability to seduce. —**RANDY THOM**, C.A.S., sound designer and mixer, *Vivo, Cast Away, The Incredibles, Return of the Jedi*

We've all come to expect realistic, natural sound in movies. In truth, sound in films is anything but realistic or natural: A dozen sound editors and mixers have created and positioned the audio so that we—the audience—will accept it and the movie. We accept that Barcelona sounds like this, the "wild west" sounded like that, and Middle Earth sounds like it does due to the world of sound conceived by the sound designer, sound editors, and mixers. Sound lets us enjoy the ride, albeit through a twister, typhoon, or game of Quidditch. It enables us to believe in the movie; if the sound seems phony or unreal, we discount the film.

Well designed and mixed sound—meaning sound effects and dialogue—voices your visuals, adding dimension to the picture that your audience may not consciously perceive. Sound can set the pace for a scene, signal changes in time or place, heighten the action or diminish it, and smooth scene transitions. It can connect characters, images, locations, and ideas. Sound also helps define characters—both animated and human—by building their aural persona, so we can know what they're feeling and experiencing.

The buzz words today for sound are "organic," "real," and "natural." *The Hurt Locker*, which won the 2010 Academy Awards for sound editing and sound mixing, exemplifies this trend. A memorable scene of GIs on a night-search in Iraq depended entirely on the bed of sound the editors built. *Avatar*, a runner-up for sound Oscars that same year, embodies the other end of the sonic spectrum: Its audio palette paints an imaginary planet where the synthesized sounds are anything but real. What these two sound styles have in common, however, is crucial: They both aurally plant the audience in the movie's environment.

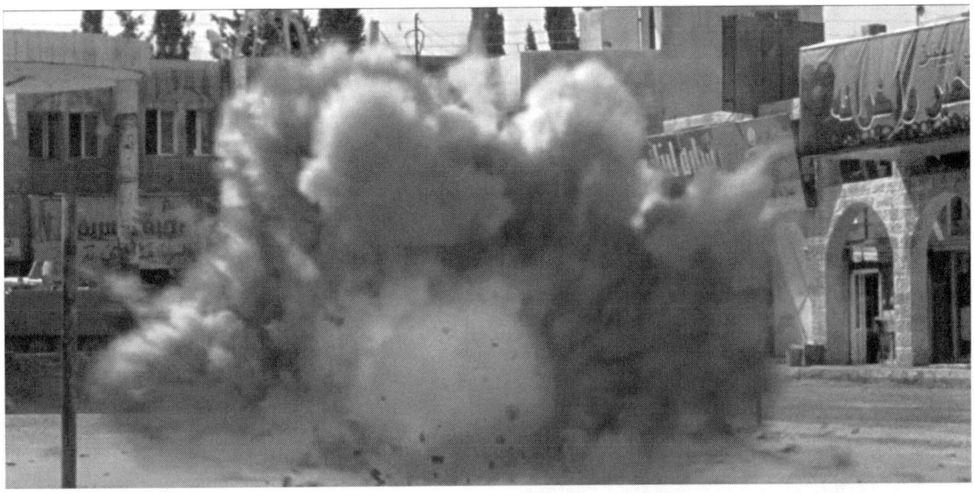

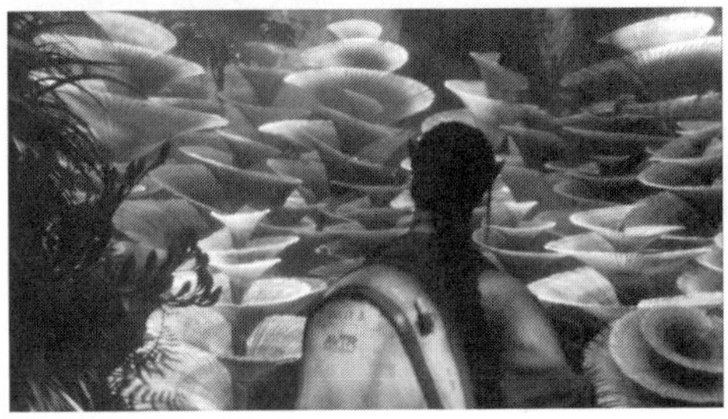

ABOVE: An army sergeant defuses bombs in Iraq in *The Hurt Locker* (2008). **RIGHT:** A former Marine looks for a valuable mineral on a distant moon in *Avatar* (2009).

Whether you create many layers of sound or minimal sound, sonics are pivotal to the audience's perception and reception of your show. They transport viewers away from the filming on the soundstage and into the characters' world. Sound sustains and is an integral part of a film's voice and vision. Bear this in mind when you design sound; every sound effect and piece of dialogue should strengthen its purpose. As with all phases of filmmaking, be open to experimenting, discovering, failing or succeeding, and always, to learning. Steve Boeddeker, sound designer and supervisor on *Alice in Wonderland 3D* advises, "Don't be afraid to make mistakes. Any time you want to do something new . . . you're going to make mistakes. The trick is to try the experiment and fail as early as possible in the project, and as inexpensively as possible."

Meet the sound department

In film lingo, the sound department and personnel are referred to as "Sound," the music department and its personnel as "Music," and the picture editor and department as "Picture." Here is a brief introduction to the Sound team. We'll add more details and players as we go along.

Sound designer a.k.a. supervising sound editor or sound supervisor. The sound designer has two main jobs: 1) To work with the script, locked show, and you to map out and envision the show's soundscape; 2) To lead a team of sound editors and mixers to design, record, edit, and mix the show. It is best to

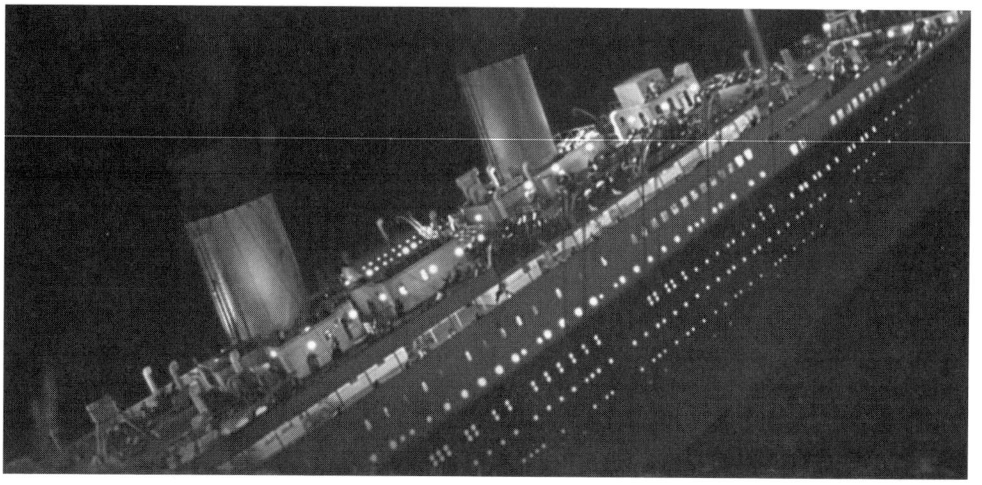

"I love the way the groans accompany the slowly sinking ship that make you feel as if . . . *Titanic* is a huge dying creature that's not giving up on life yet . . . That's really the function of a sound designer—to weed out what you don't want to hear and create an effect that plays for a specific moment on screen." Christopher Boyes, Sound Designer on *Titanic* (1997).

contract the sound designer during preproduction, so they can read the script, begin to formulate ideas, and contribute to the storytelling right from the start. This happens on major features, but on most shows, the sound designer and crew are hired when you lock the picture or a few weeks prior.

Sound effects editor. Sound effects editors are responsible for acquiring and placing all the sound effects in the show. They record the sound effects or obtain them from a SFX library (many online), edit them on their DAW (digital audio workstation), and shepherd them through the mix.

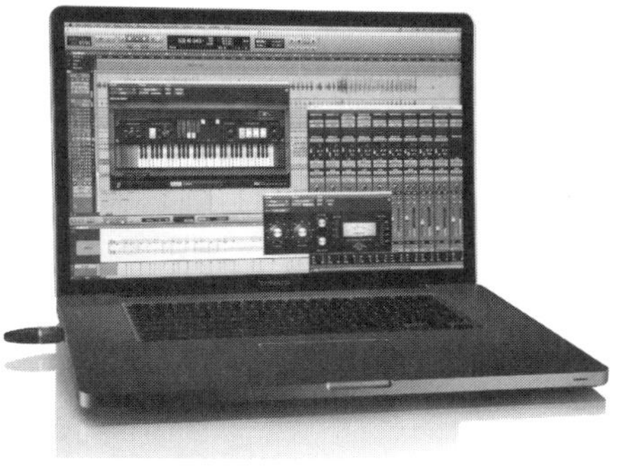

Pro Tools, a popular DAW. *Photo courtesy of Avid Technologies.*

Foley* editor. A *Foley effect* is a sound effect that is recorded in a recording studio in sync with specific actions on the screen such as footsteps in the snow or a dog panting. The Foley editor creates the Foley during a recording session, then returns to the cutting room to edit the Foley into the show.

* The technique gets its name from Jack Foley, a jack of all trades (location scout, actor, director, writer) who pioneered the audio recording technique in the 1930s with the advent of sound.

Dialogue editor. The dialogue editor labors to produce a pristine dialogue track, cleaning up the production track, adding wild lines, and smoothing everything out with room tone.

ADR editor. ADR (automated dialogue replacement) is the process by which a line of dialogue is recorded and re-spoken by an actor in sync with the picture to replace the original sync production line. The ADR editor is responsible for cutting in the recorded lines. On many shows the dialogue editor does this job.

WHAT MUSIC CAN DO FOR YOUR FILM

> The final anchoring point of the movie soundtrack is the music. Music provides an emotional bedrock for a film. —SKYWALKER SOUND LTD

Music strongly influences how the audience feels about your show's subject, characters, themes, and plot. Well thought-out music sets the appropriate tone for your picture, clueing viewers in as to what to expect: a comedy, romance, or a chance to rock and roll. Music, like sound, affects our hearts and senses and seals the movie in our memories e.g., John Williams' violin driven score in *Schindler's List* (1993) played by the incomparable Itzhak Perlman.

Music anticipates and foreshadows action, often warning that a villain is just around the corner, or as in M. Night Shyamalan's *The Village* (2004), hinting that this is no ordinary hamlet. It can also conjure a time or place. Scott Joplin's upbeat piano tunes in *The Sting* (1973) rooted the movie in the 1930s. The musical theme in *Somewhere in Time* (1980) sustained its time travel plot. Regularly, music accents key and not-so-key points: entrances, exits, scene transitions, and act outs.

Music can counter what's on screen to convey a larger truth. Composer Tôru Takemitsu delivered a renowned score (titled "Chaos") for writer-director-editor Akira Kurosawa's *Ran*. Here's what one scene in the script called for: "A terrible scroll of Hell is shown depicting the fall of the castle. There are no real sounds as the scroll unfolds

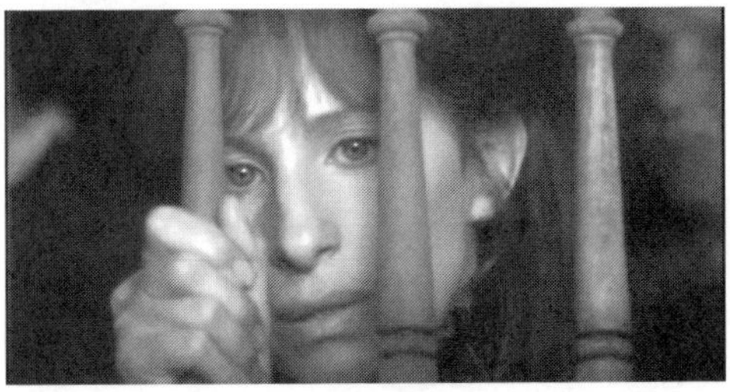

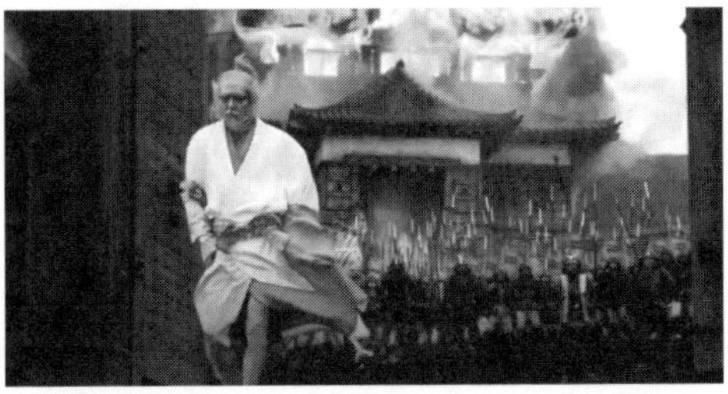

LEFT: Director and main character in *Yentl* (1983), Barbra Streisand expressed her character's hidden, rebellious thoughts in the song, "Where is it Written?" **RIGHT:** The destruction of the castle in Kurosawa's historic epic, *Ran* (1985).

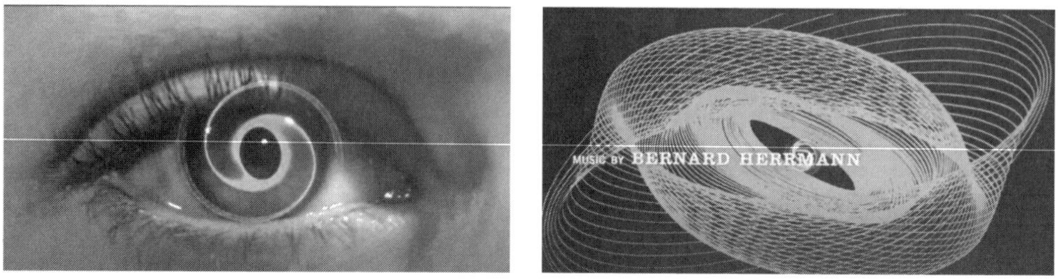

Hitchcock's *Vertigo* (1958) begins with shots of eyes; one eye spins out a whirling set of mandalas. Mirrored by Bernard Herrmann's tense, unbalanced carousel music, the mandalas set the tone for the film's spiraling mystery plot.

like a daytime nightmare. It is a scene of human evildoing . . . The music superimposed on these pictures is, like the Buddha's heart, measured in beats of profound anguish, the chanting of a melody full of sorrow that begins like sobbing, and rises gradually as it is repeated, like karmic cycles, then finally sounds like the wailing of countless Buddhas."

Music can let the audience know something before a character does—that good or bad news is on the other side of the door. It can also do the opposite—lull the audience—as the classical lilt in *Misery* (1990) does before the villain (Kathy Bates) delivers her first jolt of hobbling pain. Music often conveys characters' inner thoughts and emotions. Bernard Hermann's score for *Vertigo* heightened its characters' nightmares, dreams, and schemes right from his opening carousel music. Sometimes characters even have themes e.g., Lara's theme in *Doctor Zhivago* (1965) or the shark's theme in *Jaws* (1975).

Meet the music department

The music team consists of some or all of the following members:

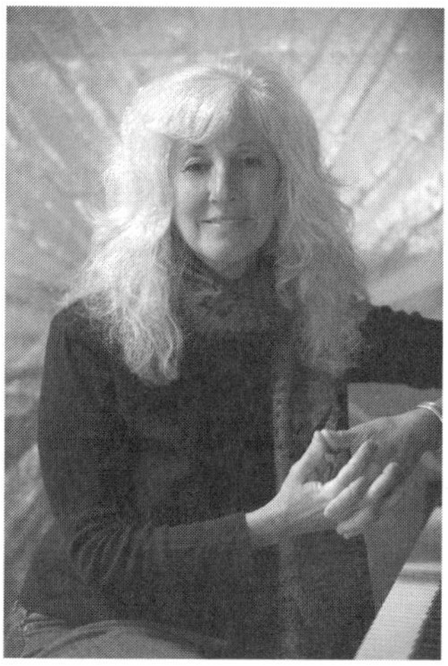

Composer. *Photo courtesy of Kim Bova.*

Composer. The composer writes long pieces of music, short pieces (stingers), and occasionally, songs for the show, ensuring that your desires are realized. A low budget show may not be able to afford a composer or may have the composer fill some of the jobs outlined below.

Songwriter. A show may hire a songwriter to compose a new song or may secure the rights to use an already composed song. Either way, you and the music supervisor will be heavily involved.

Music supervisor. The music supervisor functions like a producer, chaperoning the music from acquisition to delivery. More specifically, the supervisor secures song and music rights, oversees the budget, interfaces with the composer, and coordinates the music editing process with the music editor.

Music editor. The music editor edits the composer's and songwriter's work into the show and is responsible for creating the temp track, making the audio files and cue sheet for the mix, and representing the composer's wishes at the mix. The music editor also supplies the click track for dancers on the set and for the musicians during the scoring session.

TRANSLATING STORY INTO SOUND AND MUSIC

Like picture cuts, sound and music elements contribute to the story. Sound augments POV sequences, helps put the noir in noir, and is the backbone of many a dream and fantasy sequence. Sounds, words, and music can inform a character, prompting an action or reaction or revealing overt or underlying emotions.

Music and sound filmmakers strive to enhance and support the story with each piece of sound and music they place in the show. But it's not always a matter of "see a bird, hear a chirp effect." Sound can represent something or someone unseen—off screen—and comment on or deepen a scene. Yes! Routinely, sound and music bound from the backseat to drive the story. Think of the ways the off screen kaboom of a bomb

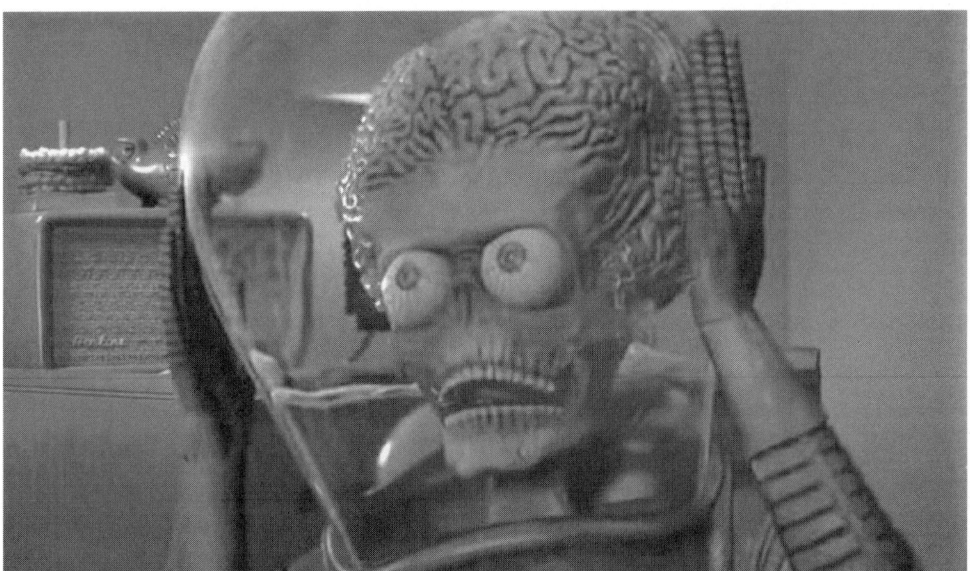

In the spoof, *Mars Attacks*, Earthlings are being decimated and their weapons have no effect on Martians, until the broadcast of a pop tune proves lethal.

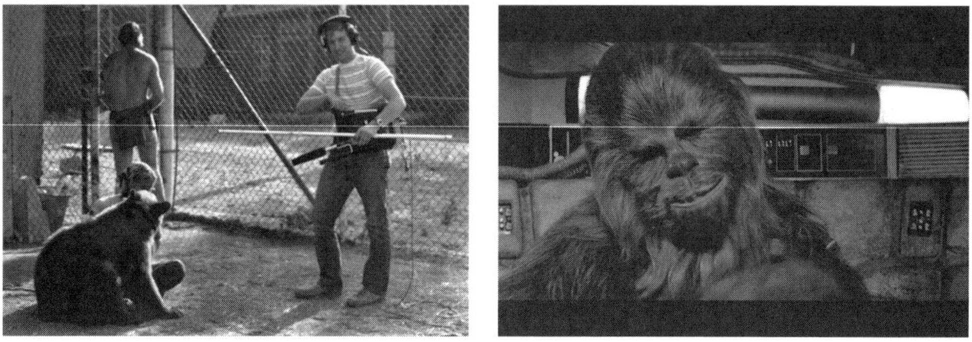

Sound designer Ben Burtt records a juvenile bear's sounds to voice the character of Chewbacca for *Star Wars* in *Making Waves: The Art of Cinematic Sound* (2019).

or swoosh of an advancing tsunami affects a town of people. Recall how Rick reacts to hearing "As Time Goes By" in *Casablanca* (1942) or the Martians respond to the radio blaring the "Indian Love Call" in *Mars Attacks* (1996).

Beats: Deciding where to Change Sound or Music

> As with picture editing, a soundtrack should evoke its own sense of logic, rhythm, and dynamic to help drive the forward motion of the image. —**TOM BULLOCK**, from his book *Sound Editing Nuts and Bolts*

Chapter 5 discussed how a picture editor often cuts in beats, meaning changes of action within a scene. Thinking in beats is also useful to sound and music designers in conceiving how a scene should sound, which sounds and music should be used, and where they should come in. A beat can call for a change in tempo, pitch, volume, or intensity of music or SFX. As you work with the Sound Designer and composer, the beats in each scene can help you decide where to bring in music and where to fade it out. Beats can also help you determine where to punch up a word or dial it down to a murmur, and when to plaster the picture with sound effects or restrict audio to a single, recurring effect or silence (ambience).

Beats of a familiar movie scene

To see how beats, sound, and silence work, let's study the cyclone scene in *The Wizard of Oz* (1939) where Dorothy is transported from black and white (B&W) Kansas to Technicolor Munchkinland. If you can, watch this two minute forty-five second scene. Notice how the sound effects work and how the music changes with the action. Witness the effect of silence as Dorothy gets her first glimpse of Munchkinland. The table below charts what happens with the sound and the music at each beat in the scene.

SCENE BEATS, SOUND, AND THE WIZARD OF OZ

<table>
<tr><th>Beat</th><th>Sound</th><th>Music</th></tr>
<tr><td>1. B&W film as D enters house and a chair crashes.</td><td>BG: cyclone/wind
FX: chair crash</td><td>None</td></tr>
<tr><td>2. D walks thru house to bedroom. D screams as a window knocks her out.</td><td>BG: cyclone/wind
DIAL: "Auntie Em"
FX: window crash
DIAL: "Oh!"</td><td>MX begins: Warning MX</td></tr>
<tr><td>3. D on bed, unconscious. Superimpose spinning house and cyclone.</td><td>BG: cyclone/wind</td><td>Unconscious MX (horns & other instruments)</td></tr>
<tr><td>4. Begin montage keyed thru window.</td><td>BG: cyclone/wind</td><td>Upbeat MX</td></tr>
<tr><td>5. D comes to and views the cyclone thru the window. Sees Miss Gulch on a bike, then on a broom. (End montage scene.)</td><td>BG: cyclone/wind
FX: animal sounds
DIAL: "We must be inside the cyclone."
DIAL: "Oh, Miss Gulch!"
DIAL: Scream</td><td>Upbeat MX
Munchkin theme
Miss Gulch/
Witch theme</td></tr>
<tr><td>6. House falls.</td><td>BG: cyclone/wind
DIAL: Witch cackles
DIAL: D screams</td><td>Active, big</td></tr>
<tr><td>7. House lands.</td><td>FX: crash</td><td>MX stops</td></tr>
<tr><td>8. D walks thru house and exits.</td><td colspan="2">Silence except for FX: door open</td></tr>
<tr><td>9. D opens door to COLOR film and Munchkinland.</td><td>BG: birds</td><td>"Somewhere over the Rainbow"</td></tr>
</table>

Key: D = Dorothy FX = Hard (specific) sound effect
MX = Music DIAL = Dialogue BG = Soft, background sound effect

THE SOUND AND MUSIC DESIGN PROCESS

> When I say sound, that's all of it, that's all the effects, all the detail work, and of course the score, because all of it needs to feel like it's one piece. It has to be able to be integrated and yet set itself apart at the same time, so it's a complicated proposition. —**KATHRYN BIGELOW**, director, *Zero Dark Thirty*, *The Weight of Water*, Academy Award for *The Hurt Locker*

The spotting session is the kick-off meeting for a show's sound and music design where you run the show scene by scene, stopping and starting to express the type of sound you're expecting. Spotting can take place online, in a screening room, on the picture editor's system, or on a DAW. On a low budget show, you may spot with the picture editor who will edit and mix the sound and music on their digital editing system. On a higher budget show, you will spot with the Sound and Music team, who may be seeing the show or discussing it with you for the first time. They will be coming up to speed, absorbing the show and your desires, bringing fresh eyes—and especially ears—to the spotting. Listen to their questions which will be general as to style and specific as to scenes and moments in scenes such as, "Do you want music here or to just let the moment play with natural sound?"

Usually, you spot sound and music separately, but you don't have to. Spotting both together is advantageous because everyone can share ideas and begin to develop a good working relationship. We'll cover them separately in order to discuss the different tasks of the sound designer and music composer.

The Sound Spotting Session

> Every movie has a sound style, just like it has a visual style . . . It's always about discovery and the most interesting stuff almost always happens when you're in the process of doing it, it doesn't come out of the so called grand vision. So, in a real sense, the spotting session is the very beginning of really figuring out the nuts and bolts of what the movie should sound like. —**RANDY THOM**, sound designer and editor, *The Revenant*, *The Incredibles*, *The Right Stuff*

You spot sound with the picture editor, the sound designer, and anyone else you deem necessary such as the sound editors (recommended) and the producer. The conversation is general as you explain what a scene, subject, or character should convey. And specific as you identify dialogue for ADR and specify SFX for certain places that you've identified. This is the time to put out your ideas, raise concerns, raise questions, and let the sound folks do the same e.g., "Do you prefer stylized sounds or organic sounds?" Together you want to formulate a clear idea of how the show will sound overall as well as in each scene.

Spotting notes

During the spotting session, all dialogue and SFX notes are written down, typed on a computer, or entered directly into a DAW. Some sound designers record the session

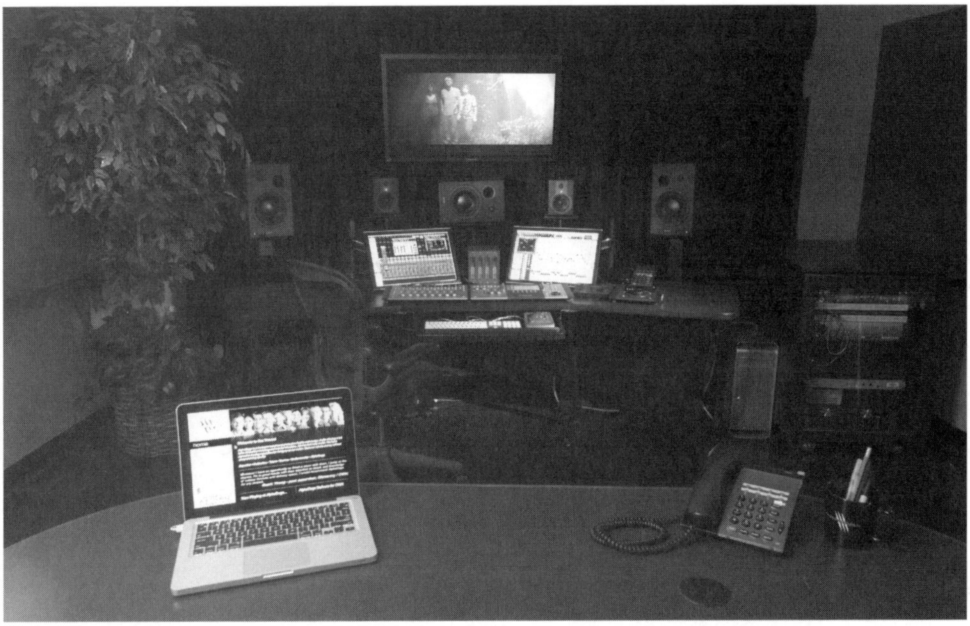

Audio suite in a post house where you may also spot sound or music. *Photo courtesy of AlphaDogs.*

as well as subsequent phone calls and reference them when they want to recall your intentions and instructions. Each note will be turned into a *sound cue,* consisting of a brief description of the sound (e.g., wind chime), its track number, and its start and end timecode.

Dialogue

Dialogue notes list dialogue that must be:

- Replaced by ADR.
- Added, such as new lines, wild lines, and walla*.
- Altered in some way, e.g., futzed to sound like it's coming through a phone.

SFX

> We must draw a distinction between those sound effects which are amusing only by virtue of their novelty (which soon wears off), and those that help one to understand the action, and which excite emotions which could not been roused by the sight of the pictures alone.
> —**RENÉ CLAIR,** French New Wave writer, from *Reflections on the Cinema*

Each sound effect will fall into one of three types and affect viewers in a certain way as the following table documents.

* Non-sync background conversation made up of indistinguishable words voiced by actors.

Types of SFX and Viewer Perception

Type	Description	Examples	Viewers . . .
Sync sounds a.k.a. hard sounds or diegetic sound	Sounds that sync with a specific action on screen.	Phone ring, dog bark, champagne cork pop, water splash, glass smash, toilet flush, keys in door, plane takes off, car tires screech.	Are conscious of hard sounds. Often react to sound, e.g., a gunshot before seeing the action.
Non-sync sounds a.k.a. asynchronous, non-diegetic, or soft sounds	Soft sounds that have a constant presence and do not sync to a specific action.	Ambience, wind, crickets chirping, a brook gurgling, rain, feet shuffling on a dance floor, traffic, windshield wipers.	Are only peripherally aware of soft sounds, since they usually play in the background.
Foley	SFX recorded in sync with specific actions on the screen, that can't be recorded on location or obtained from a sound library.	A kiss, clothes rustle, bubble gum popping, fight noises, body falls, creaky doors, alien hatching, monkey scratching.	Are conscious of Foley, though can't distinguish it from SFX.

Consider music

When spotting with Sound, it's important to let the crew know where music will appear. If you've already put temp music into the show, you'll have a good idea of the placement. When music covers a scene, it doesn't mean that the sound editor has no work to do. You may eliminate Foley but, at a minimum, you will add ambience. Also, since you may decide to drop the music during the mix, it's best to have the sound team design and edit sound for every scene. Better to overdesign sound and drop out a few cues than madly be adding and cutting in sounds while on the mix stage.

Sound must always aim to work hand in hand with Music (the music crew) to uphold the story and meet or exceed your intentions. Music editor Charles Martin Inouye (*Jumanji: The Next Level, Late Night,* and *The Jungle Book*) puts it this way, "Even if a composer has written music for it [the cue], don't fight the picture. If it's not serving the needs of the movie as much as maybe someone's bit of dialogue or some creaky windmill, there's cooperation and coordination between the sound effects and the music people that's very important."

The Music Spotting Session

> I record all my music with authentic instruments in a studio before we start editing, doing many, many versions. The music shapes the film as we edit so it has an organic relationship to the content. —**KEN BURNS**, producer/director, *The Central Park Five*, *Baseball*, *The West*

You spot music with the music supervisor, music editor and producer. The composer and songwriter may be present or, if hired earlier, may have already met with you and be off composing. You will discuss your ideas for the music's placement in the show, as well as its style and genre. You may think more visually or talk in dramatic or emotional terms when describing the music; the composer and music editor will translate these descriptions into music. Often monetary matters, namely music budget and rights, will crop up and play a role in the discussion.

During your session the music editor will make spotting notes detailing the location and duration of each music cue and how each cue should sound—melancholy, stealthy, frenzied, etc. The session's goals parallel those for spotting sound: To clarify the overall music design and vision, to set down the musical requirements including mood, purpose, and duration for each scene or sequence, and to develop rapport between you and the music team.

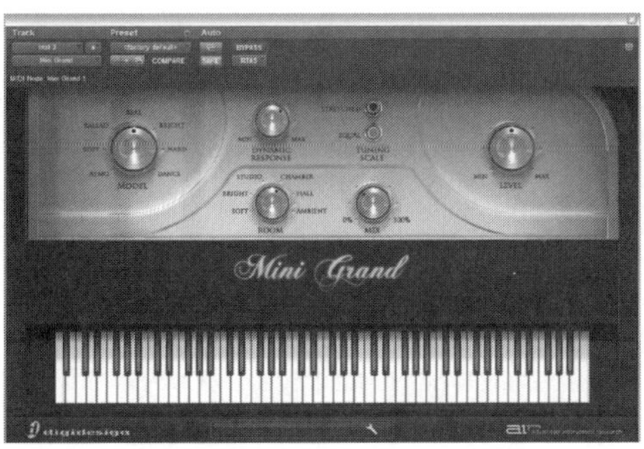

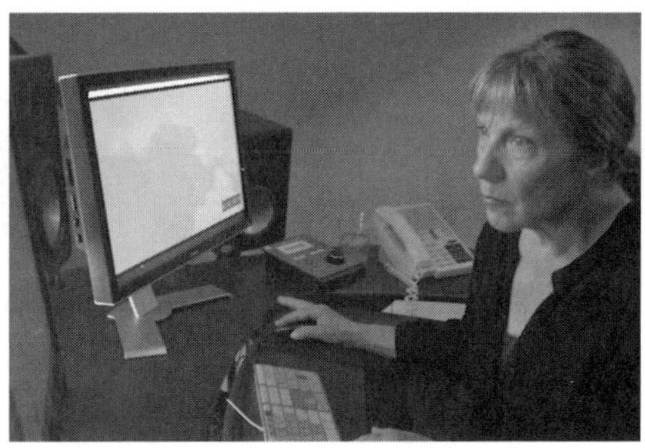

LEFT: Digidesign's mini grand composer. *Photo courtesy of Avid.* **RIGHT:** Cueing ADR from *Making Waves: The Art of Cinematic Sound* (2019).

AFTER SPOTTING: CUEING AND ACQUIRING SOUND AND MUSIC

Following the spotting session, sound and music editors cue a.k.a. *breakdown the show,* meaning they set the placement and duration of each piece of audio in their DAW. Then they go about acquiring the sound and music in preparation for editing it.

Cueing sound and music

The ADR editor cues ADR to be recorded on the ADR stage and the Foley editor the Foley for the Foley stage.

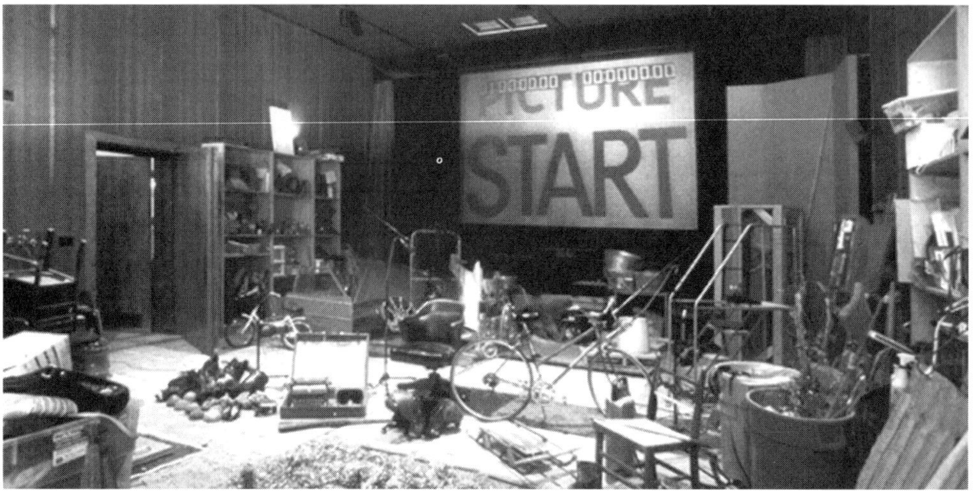

Foley stage a.k.a. Foley pit where Foley artist a.k.a. Foley walker or dancer, performs their magic. *Photo courtesy of Todd-AO/Ascent Media Creative Services.*

The music editor and assistant time each music cue, thereby turning the spotting notes into *timing sheets* a.k.a. *breakdown notes*. The timing sheets include dialogue lines so that music does not cover them along with the number assigned to each cue and a detailed description of what's happening on screen during the cue.

Acquiring sound

> Every time I hear a new sound, it gives me a new idea—it feeds my creative consciousness. As a result, I did a tremendous amount of field recording on *Titanic*—about 60 hours of raw field recording. We recorded all sorts of sounds: quadraphonic sounds of wind, tremendous amounts of recordings of water, in all sorts of environments—water treatment plants, hydro phonic recordings underneath ships, etc. We placed microphones in all sorts of strange places—into hulls of ships to get different types of sloppy water hits.
> —**CHRISTOPHER BOYES**, sound supervisor, *Avatar, Coco, Titanic*

Recording SFX

Sound designers get their kicks from creating, discovering, and manipulating sounds in inventive and memorable ways. They take the time to find and record the specific sound of a 1968 VW microbus, a Guatemalan tree frog, or the Garden State Parkway at rush hour. They ferret out these sounds from a variety of sources and mediums.

Sound libraries and production recordings

In addition to recording their own sounds, SFX editors also draw from online sound libraries. Many SFX editors have their own extensive sound libraries which they expand with each job. SFX editors also rely on the production recordings and the show's cut production tracks. They will dig into alternative takes and search through the *wild sound* a.k.a. *audio B-roll* that the on-set recordist made.

Foley

Ordinarily, it's difficult to distinguish Foley sounds from the natural audio recorded on the set during production. This is due to the talent of the Foley artist or editor, who re-enacts the scene to create these "natural sounds." The Foley artist works on a Foley stage, a purposeful junkyard which contains all sorts of surfaces: grass, gravel, sand, cement, etc. Foley artists originate realistic sounds from unexpected materials and props. For instance, crunching snow is Foleyed by walking on kosher salt coated with cornstarch.

Feature films and high budget TV shows use Foley, but normally it's out of range for TV, corporate videos, and other shows. To avoid Foley costs, record good location sound and hire a top-notch sound editing and mixing crew.

Typical Sound Workflow

Like picture, sound has workflows. Though no two projects will take the same course, here's a basic sound workflow.

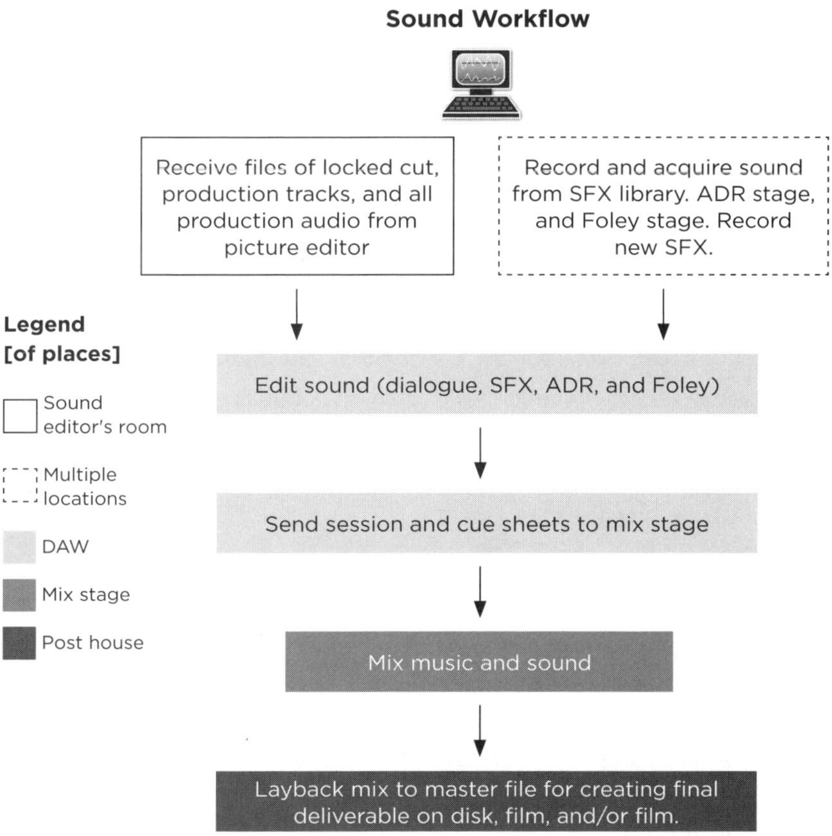

Acquiring Music

> What you can't do with a camera or dialogue, music has a way of taking care of. It gets at the deeper emotions that aren't always expressible on film. People who are skeptical about film music should be condemned to watch films without it. —**DAVID RAKSIN**, composer, *Laura, The Secret Life of Walter Mitty, The Bad and the Beautiful*

The music editor (or the picture editor, if your show can't afford a music editor) acquires music from a variety of sources and formats. This section describes these sources and spells out how to obtain the rights to use the music in your show.

Composed music

You can hire a composer to create a score and/or a songwriter to crank out a song or two. Or, if you have sufficient knowledge and instinct, you can create music yourself.

Composer and score

On low budget shows, the composer will create a score, record it on a synthesizer, and hand it over to the music editor. If your show is more flush, the composer will send the score to a recording session where a conductor will lead a group of musicians in making a recording.

Songwriter and song

> No one leaves the theatre whistling a two-shot. —**ANONYMOUS**

You may contract a songwriter to compose a new song, decide to use a previously written song, or record a new version of an already written song. Either way, you need to *clear* the song. *Clearing* the song entails paying and getting permission from both the songwriter who owns the *publisher rights* a.k.a. *sync rights* and the singer who recorded it who holds the *master rights*. Once the song is cleared, the publisher will grant you permission to sync the song to a picture image. If you want to use a tune from a band—especially an unknown band—you can probably negotiate a deal directly with its manager.

Music library

Many shows can't spring for a composer so your music editor will pull music from one of the many music libraries. The editor auditions tracks for every cue noted during spotting, and imports it into their DAW. You approve the music and the production company purchases the cues. Music libraries have copyrighted all the music, so there are no rights issues to deal with, but it's wise to scrutinize the contract for any hidden fees. You can get music free for certain venues, but normally you will license it for a specific time period and type of programming.

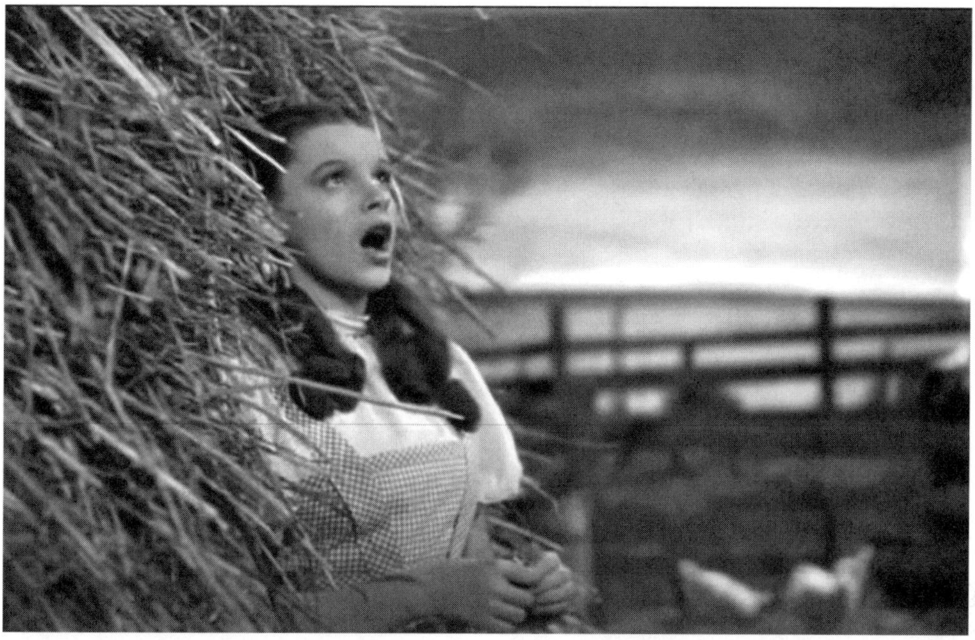

The studio wanted to remove "Somewhere over the Rainbow" from *The Wizard of Oz* (1939), believing it undignified for a character to sing in a barnyard, and that the song slowed down the film.

Music tracking

Even when a show has a composer, the composer frequently does not compose for the entire movie. For instance, a scene may be added or you may wish to purchase a previously written song. The composer then asks the music editor to *track* that part of the show. *Tracking* means that the editor adapts a song to fit the scene or rearranges music the composer has already composed. The music editor often *tracks the temp,* i.e., selects and edits the music for the temp mix. Some of this music may remain in the final mix but most of it will be replaced during the scoring session. A show that doesn't use any original music is referred to as *tracked.*

Source music

Source music is defined as music that has a clear, visual source on screen such as a radio, record player, or piano. Source music often plays in the background and is usually purchased, but can be composed.

Needle drop a.k.a. canned music

Needle drop is background music—often source music and a song—that requires a license fee. The term dates to the days of vinyl when each drop of the record player's needle required a separate fee.

Rights and licenses

You must clear each piece of music and all song lyrics that go into your film. *Free and clear* denotes music that does not have a copyright nor require a fee because it's considered public domain (unowned). For instance, all music composed during the classical period is public domain. However, if you use a public domain recording, you will have to pay the vocalist or orchestra who made the recording, as well as the recording company. If you play and record public domain music yourself or compose the music for your own film, you do not have to pay any fees. Temp music is also not subject to fees or rights searches, so anything goes!

Clearing music takes time. Hire a music coordinator to do the job and a lawyer if necessary. The coordinator will fill out a *music reporting cue sheet* a.k.a. a *publishing cue sheet* with the cue number, how the music was used, its title, composer, publisher, and performing rights organization, such as ASCAP,* BMI,** GMR,*** or SESAC**** and hand it over to the production company along with a disk or file of the music.

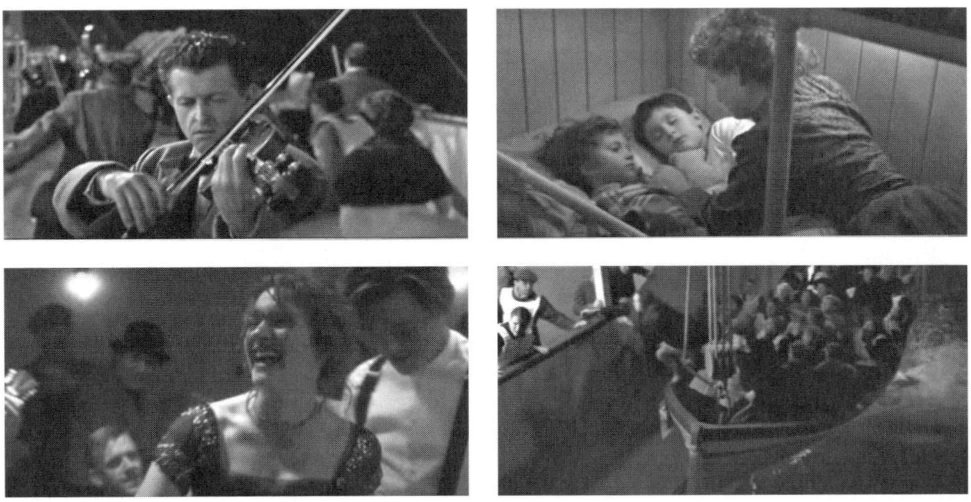

The source music of the violinist playing "Nearer My God to Thee" plucks at the heart strings in *Titanic* as the ship and its passengers live their last moments, and Rose and Jack are parted in a montage that also flashes back to the couple's short-lived happiness.

* American Society of Composers, Authors, and Publishers.
** Broadcast Music Incorporated.
*** Global Music Rights.
**** Society of European Stage Authors and Composers.

Typical Music Workflow

The workflow chart below illustrates the typical path music takes from its origin to the mix.

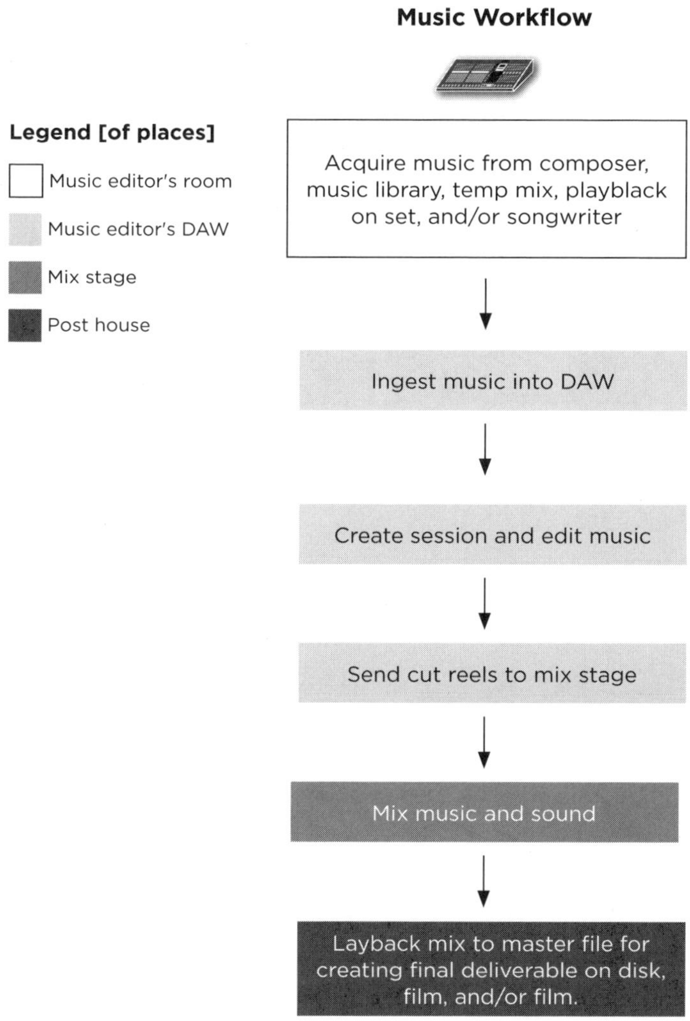

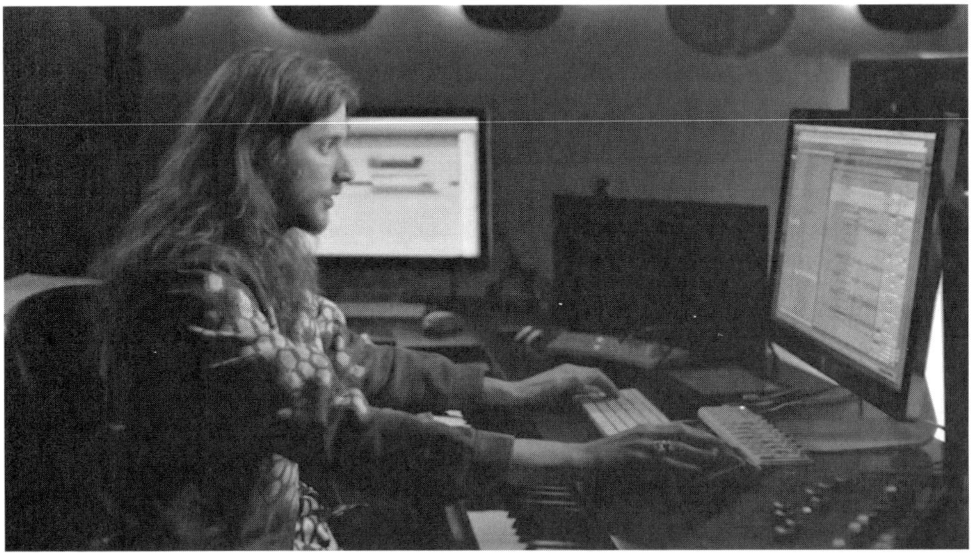

Composer. *Making Waves: The Art of Cinematic Sound* (2019).

The Composer and the Composing Process

> It's one thing to write a beautiful piece of music but it's another thing to have that beautiful piece of music be the right tone, and start at the right time, and be the right emotional variant that makes sense dramatically. —**JEFF TOYNE**, composer, *Filthy Rich, Damaged, District 9*

You or the producer hires the composer who begins work during preproduction (working off the script), or production (working off the script and dailies), or postproduction (working off cuts in progress). The timing of the composer's hiring depends on the size of the picture along with its budget and the scope of the music. The composer may create music for the temp mix. Before we continue with the composer's process, a few definitions are in order:

Synthesizer a.k.a. synth. A "band in a box," a synth is an electronic instrument that produces an endless variety of sounds and music that can imitate instruments or create new sounds. There are hard (hardware) synths that plug in to DAWs and soft (software) synths, that export the composer's MIDI file into the DAW.

MIDI. Musical instrument digital interface. Protocol for the types of control signals that one electronic musical device sends to another. In less technical terms, MIDI is a plug-in which enables a musician's computer to communicate with a host of devices, such as MIDI sound modules (samplers, synthesizers, etc.). A MIDI score is the representation of the music.

MIDI controller. Keyboard, drum kit, guitar, piano, or other electronic musical device that generates MIDI messages to adjust individual controls such as pan or gain, on devices in the MIDI network.

Sample. Take a part (sample) of a recorded instrument e.g., bass, voice, keyboard or strings or sound to use in recording a song or score.

Tempo. Speed at which a piece of music is performed. Measured in BPMs (beats per minute).

Creating the music

> I don't think it's about being a great composer or an amazing musician or anything like that. I'm none of those things. If you're able to feel, and if you're willing to allow yourself to really sit in front of the characters and feel what they're experiencing—and watch them and look into their faces and their hands and look around the picture—it will start to translate itself into music through you. —LISA GERRARD, composer, singer, and musician, *Undertow, Whale Rider, Gladiator*

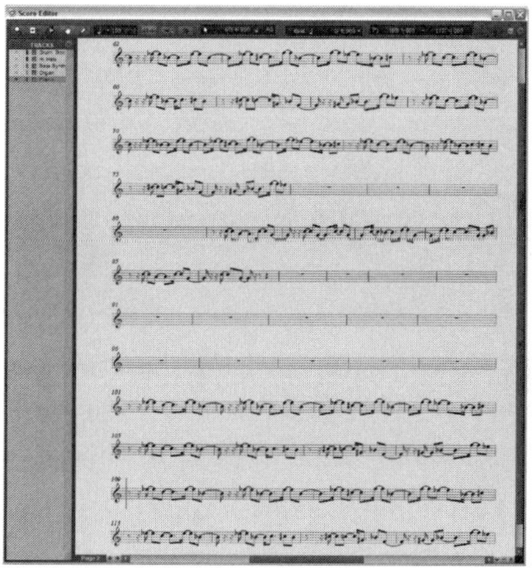

Score editor. *Photo courtesy of Avid.*

Some composers develop music using pen, pencil, and piano but most use synthesizers and a musical composition software e.g., Ableton or Pro Tools or notation software, for example, MuseScore or Sibelius. Working through the show cue by cue, the composer samples instruments on a synth to select their composition's instrumentation, playing the music back through the MIDI controller. The composer may add arpeggio, echo, or other effects and drop or add instruments along the way and will choose the pitch, tempo, accent, beat, key, and modulation.

Composing is an intense trial and error process: Every music cue—like every sound element and picture cut—should serve an emotional beat of the story. When ready, the composer will test the music by playing it back against the picture. Music spotting notes are like picture paper cuts: What works in theory may not meet the playback test.

The scoring session

Once the composer has completed the score, the music supervisor schedules the musicians for a scoring session. You may attend in person or remotely.

Streamers, punches, and click tracks

In preparation for the session, the music editor or assistant programs a *streamer*—a colored line—and a *punch*—a white or colored circle on the picture. Streamers and punches give the composer visual timing cues for when to start or stop the music, change tempo, or add an accent. Alternatively, the composer may request a *click track* which sounds warning clicks in advance of each music cue and sets the tempo for the musicians.

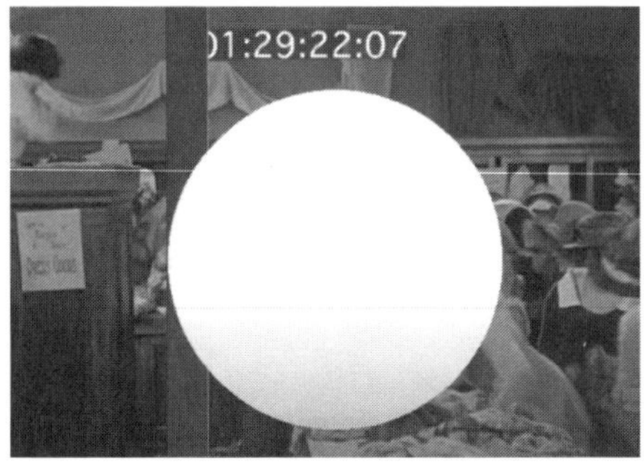

Punch (white circle) and streamer (solid vertical line on left behind punch) from *Punches and Streamers: The Making of a Film Score* (2014).

Scoring

The musicians come in cold and the assistant music editor hands them a *scoring cue list* with information on each cue: name, brief description of scene action, start and stop time code, duration, and tempo. The cue system is critical not only for ordering, editing and scoring music, but also for mixing music and filling out the licensing paperwork afterward. The sound recordist mikes and records each type of instrument—string, brass, woodwind, and percussion—onto a separate track for ease and flexibility during the mix.

To create the cue, the scene or section runs on a screen and/or monitors, the warning clicks sound, the streamer starts, the conductor conducts, and the recordist in the sound booth records the cue. Once the recording is complete, the take is played back. If it has problems such as wrong notes, coughs, chair scrapes, or is otherwise unacceptable to you, the composer, recording engineer, or music editor, it is rerecorded. You should feel free to give your feedback but keep these factors in mind: 1) Scoring sessions are expensive; 2) By now you have approved and are familiar with the music; 3) The composer is running the session; 4) You may drop cues on the mix stage.

If the take is acceptable, the music editor directs everyone to the next cue. Similar cues are recorded together rather than recording cues sequentially from the beginning of the picture to the end. Every take is timed by a digital counter. The timing of the recorded cue must match the original spotting timing as closely as possible in order to fit the picture. Both the recordist and the music assistant editor make timing notes and other notes on each acceptable take.

LAST WORD

Now that you're familiar with how sound and music are designed, created, and acquired, you're ready to move on to the mix stage and the next chapter to learn how sound effects, dialogue, and music are edited and mixed.

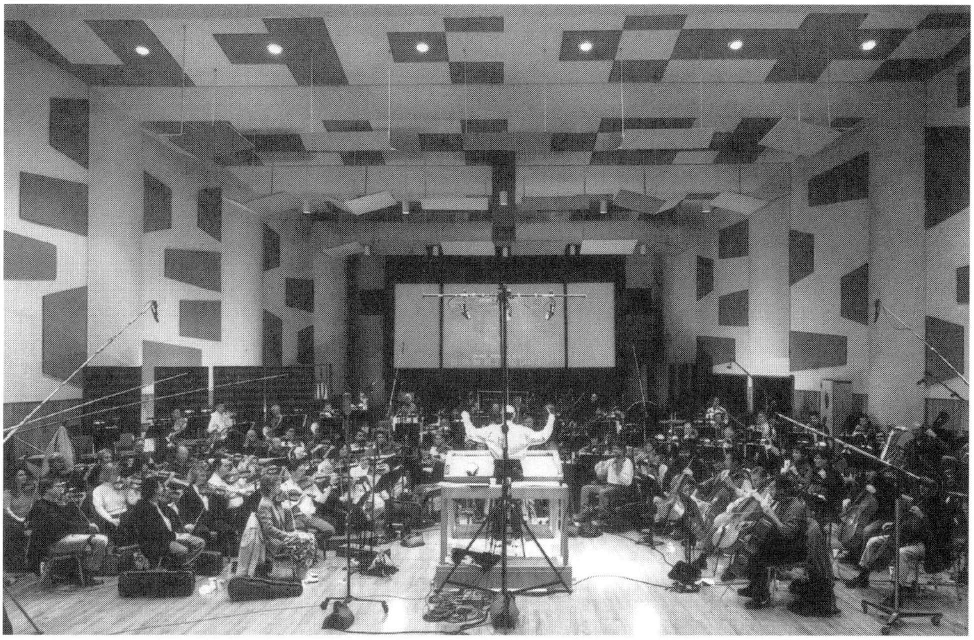

Scoring session. *Photo courtesy of Todd-AO/Ascent Media Creative Services.*

WHAT DIRECTORS SHOULD KNOW ABOUT CREATING SOUND AND MUSIC

- ☐ Sound is an integral part of your film's voice and vision. Every sound effect and piece of dialogue or music should strengthen its purpose.
- ☐ During the spotting session you run the show scene by scene, stopping to express your expectations, ideas, and questions and to listen to the questions and input of Sound and Music.
- ☐ The key sound players are the Sound Designer, the SFX editor, the Foley artist and editor, the Dialogue editor, and the ADR editor.
- ☐ Sound design creates SFX, Foley, and ADR along with moments of silence or minimal sound to place the right sound at the right place.
- ☐ The key music players are the composer, songwriter, music supervisor, and music editor.
- ☐ For each piece of sound or music, sound and music editors create a cue which consists of a brief description of the sound, its track number, its start and end timecode, and, for a music cue, its tempo.
- ☐ Clearing a song entails paying and getting permission from both the publisher and songwriter who own the rights.

9

EDITING AND MIXING SOUND AND MUSIC

You will be in charge of the sound mix. In order to realize the fullest potential of the sounds and music created for your show you'll want to know what goes into building the tracks and how work proceeds on the mix stage. This chapter demystifies the world and terms of editing tracks and mixing sound. You'll hear from editors about how they approach cutting SFX, dialogue, and music and be escorted to the mix stage where you'll be guided through the pre-mix and mix process, and the decisions you'll be making. Let's make tracks!

SOUND AND MUSIC EDITING

> Sound is 50% of the experience. —**GEORGE LUCAS**, director/producer, *Star Wars, Raiders of The Lost Ark, American Graffiti*

Sound and music are edited cue by cue, scene by scene, and, decreasingly, reel by reel (mainly on features bound for a film release). Editors and composers work in sessions on their DAWs (digital audio workstations). Akin to a project, a *session* can be a scene, reel, or an entire show, depending on how the editor sets it up. For each scene of picture there are multiple tracks of SFX, dialogue, and music. Why? Because many SFX, dialogue, and music cues occur near or at the same time. In order for the cues to be mixed efficiently, editors space them out over multiple tracks.

The handover from picture to sound and music

To get off to a good start, Picture communicates clearly with everyone about the current state of the show and provides Sound and Music with the files and audio tracks they need in the format they request, along with all the sound reports, the lined script, continuity list, and sound delivery requirements. If there was temp music and/or a temp mix, Picture also sends the temp's files or session.

During sound and music editing, your film may bounce from locked to unlocked (and only finally lock when time runs out and you have to hit the mix stage). The picture editor (or assistant) therefore regularly updates Music and Sound with a file of the changes called a *change list* or *change notes*. This assures the sound and music editors that they're editing and conforming to the latest version of the picture.

Manipulating sound

With the click of a mouse or press of a button on a DAW, editors manipulate audio, pitching it higher or lower, reversing it, reverbing, or EQing* it in many subtle and not so subtle ways. They can compress (shorten) or expand (lengthen) a sound's duration as well as repeat it, re-sample it, and copy it to another track. Importantly, editors *clean up tracks*, meaning they edit, equalize, level, and remove as much extraneous noise as possible. The *waveform tool* with its graphic plot of the amplitude—loud and soft spots of sounds—aids immensely in getting in between words or syllables and in pre-mixing effects.

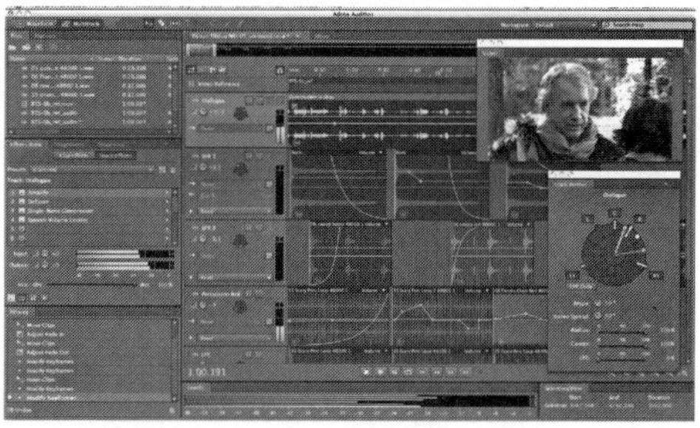

Pan, waveform, DeEsser (sibilance remover), and other tools on Adobe Audition. *Photo courtesy of Adobe.*

Sound Effects Editing

> See a sound; hear a sound. Every time you see some action on the screen, your mind expects to hear a complementary sound. The support of sound effects helps you "willingly suspend your disbelief," and become immersed in the movie experience. —SKYWALKER SOUND

The challenge of SFX editing: The sound of three dogs barking

Following spotting, the SFX editor or sound designer (routinely the same person) will be in contact with you and run ideas by you. The SFX editor, like the rest of sound and music editors, will give you choices on the mix stage by cutting alternative SFX for certain cues. The editor will audition each SFX cue against the picture to make sure it works. To work, the effect must do at least one, if not two or all three, of the following:

* Equalize (EQ): Adjust the volume level of individual frequencies of a sound in order to change its tone. For instance, dialogue is always EQ'd so that ADR lines match the production dialogue track.

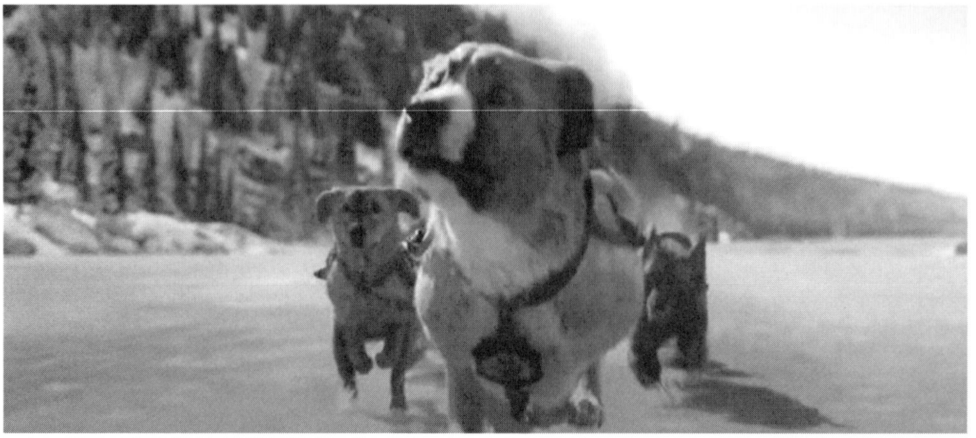

What does a CGI pack of dogs sound like? Watch *Call of the Wild* (2020) to find out.

1. Make the picture seem realistic or natural.
Example: The yipping yelp of a Chihuahua.

2. Trigger an emotion.
Example: The feeling of loneliness induced by a wolf howl.

3. Show something novel and imaginative.
Example: The sound of a lunar dog barking at the earth.

Cutting in Foley FX

The Foley editor starts by cueing the Foley on the DAW and sending the session to the Foley stage along with a Foley cue sheet of numbered cues containing their description, time code, and special instructions. To create the Foley, the Foley artist—properly positioned near a mic—performs the effect in sync to the picture playing on the screen while a recordist captures the sound.

Following the Foley session, the recordist sends the recorded cues to the Foley editor for fine tuning. The editor cleans up the Foley cues by making sure they're in perfect sync and removing extraneous noise. When finished, the editor sends the Foley session to the mix stage accompanied by the final Foley cue sheets.

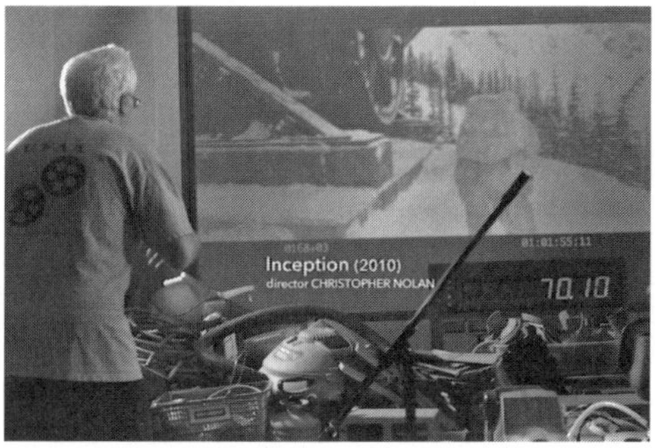

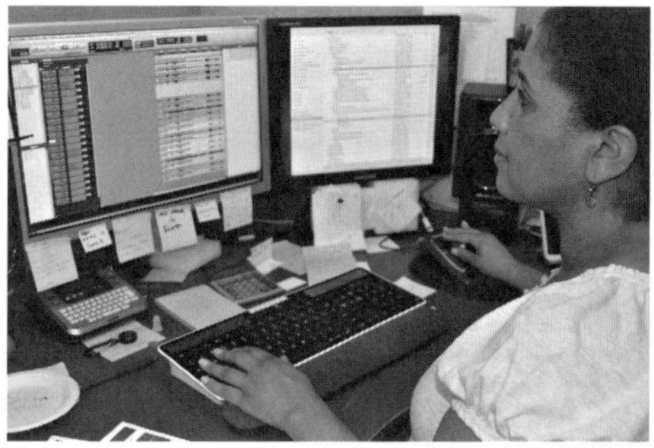

LEFT: A Foley artist walks footsteps on the Foley stage. *Making Waves: The Art of Cinematic Sound* (2019). **RIGHT:** Assistant Sound Editor prepares sound masters for the dub stage. *Photo courtesy of Sharon Smith Holley.*

Dialogue Editing

> Cooperation is important. We need each other. I respect the picture editor's cut and come to the table not just as an editor but as a filmmaker. I learn a movie's scenes and don't just think in reels, as some sound editors do. —**VICTORIA ROSE SAMPSON**, dialogue, ADR, and supervising sound editor *Scream 4, The Fighter, Sex and the City 1* and *2*

Dialogue editing is a critical part of sound editing that viewers aren't aware of ordinarily. But when they don't understand what an actor or narrator is saying or spy an out-of-sync line, they realize that dialogue work is lacking. It is meticulous work: The dialogue editor concentrates on every sentence, word, syllable, and utterance to ensure the dialogue, narration, and VO (voiceover) is clear and fits the show. This entails cleaning out undesirable sounds, then filling any audio gaps with ambience so the dialogue blends into the setting of each scene. When the dialogue cannot be fixed, the dialogue editor works with you and the ADR editor to identify dialogue that must be ADR'd.

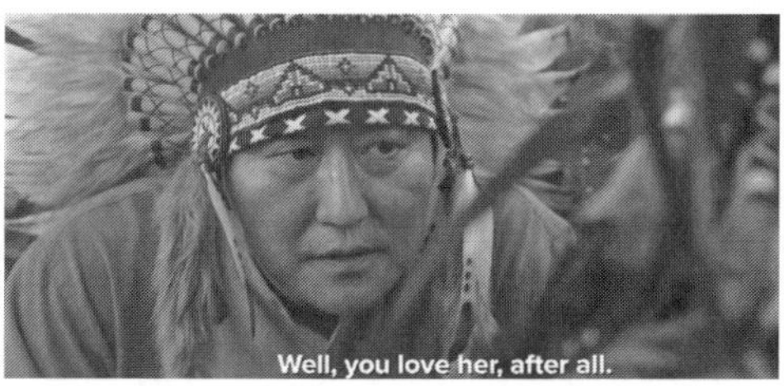

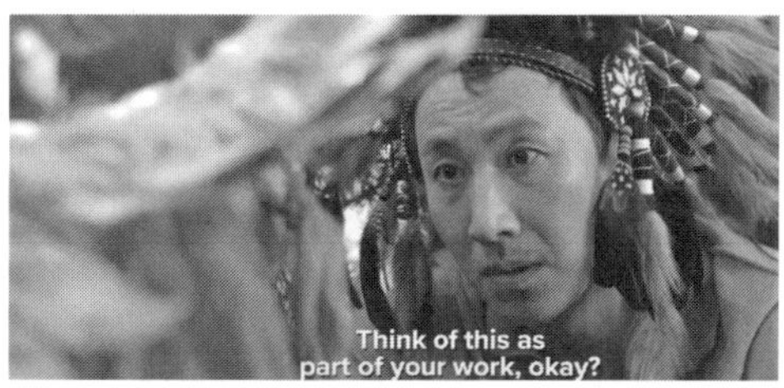

Short dialogue scene from *Parasite* (2019).

Splitting tracks

Production tracks—the dialogue tracks edited by the picture editor—cannot be delivered to the mixer. Why? Because the words are too close together for a mixer to get between them and properly mix the sound. The dialogue editor remedies this by splitting* (dividing) the tracks. Dialogue editors split tracks by camera set-ups, put-

* Splitting dialogue is sometimes referred to as checkerboarding dialogue, since each piece of dialogue is preceded and followed by sound fill and resembles a checkerboard when laid out on the timeline.

ting master takes on one track, two-shots on another, Darnella's close-up on a third, Floyd's close-up on a fourth, and so on. Why? Because each camera set-up requires a different microphone set-up. Part of any sound or music editor's job is to organize cues and tracks as efficiently as possible for the mixer. Cutting each mic set-up on a different track makes things easier for the mixer.

Reasons to split dialogue

> It's the ambience behind the words that we're editing. —VICTORIA ROSE SAMPSON

Editors split dialogue tracks to adjust and match levels between speakers and also to:

Match ambience between speakers
When two or more people are talking, there's usually a difference in the ambient sound between their two shots. For instance, if Ben and Jerry are talking, the editor would put Ben on one track, and Jerry on another. Then they would extend the ambience at the head and tail of each of their lines so that their backgrounds can be blended during the mix. This is the most important reason to split dialogue. Dialogue editors spend more time matching and manipulating ambience than on the words

Single out words or sentences for special treatment.
There are times when you will want to raise or lower the volume of a word or futz it, (filter it to sound like it's coming through a telephone line). Splitting it off to another track isolates it for futzing; indeed, it's called the *futz track.*

Dialogue problems and fixes

> I like solving a story problem with sound, for example by finding a take that helps you understand the film. —VICTORIA ROSE SAMPSON

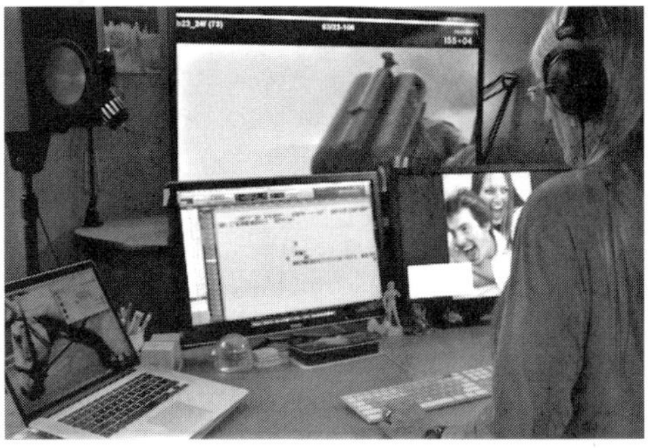

Cutting dialogue with headphones. *Making Waves: The Art of Cinematic Sound* (2019).

To hear the dialogue clearly and fix the problems, dialogue editors wear headphones. When they hear a click, pop, actor's lip smack, or other unwanted noise on the production or any other track, dialogue editors remove it and cover the sound hole with ambience. Occasionally a line of dialogue is distorted or all but destroyed due to technical or other reasons, and ADR is not practical. To fix the line, the dialogue editor pieces it together word by word, sometimes syllable by syllable, from several takes, so that it sounds acceptable and is in sync. An *upcut line* a.k.a. a *clipped line* is one that is cut off at the head or tail. Since the picture editor cuts without headphones, a syllable can get accidentally cut off. The dialogue editor finds the original sound take and adds back the upcut syllable.

Routinely, dialogue editors prepare additional takes or alternate versions of the same line. These *add* or *alt tracks*, referred to as the *X* and *Y tracks*, give you and the mixer choices. For example, when you get to the mix stage and decide to dump an ADR line, you may choose an alt line. Also, dialogue editors supply alt lines because while rooting around in the production takes, they discover a reading that is technically better or they think you might prefer. In either case, the editor mutes the alt tracks on the session but notes them on the cue sheet. This way, the mixer can unmute the tracks and play them back for you.*

Transitioning between sounds

There are three ways to transition from one sound to another: cut, dissolve, or soft cut. A cut is also called a *straight cut* or a *hard cut*. A sound dissolve, where one sound fades out, as another fades in, is referred to as a *crossfade*. A *soft cut* is a tiny dissolve—1 to 4 frames—between lines or sounds. Technically, a soft cut is a crossfade, but since it's only a few frames away from being a cut and has the effect of softening a cut, it's called a soft cut. Soft cuts are used ubiquitously by sound and dialogue editors to smooth dialogue.

ADR

The ADR editor notes the ADR lines during dialogue spotting. ADR is recorded in order to:

- Replace poor production track.
- Add any new lines that were written after the shoot.
- Change a performance (infrequently done).
- Re-voice a performance with a new actor (rarely done).
- Create walla or wild lines for groups of people or non-starring characters (see Loop Group on page 196).
- Replace the movie theatre version of a line e.g., swear words with the sanitized TV version.

* Sprocket of film history: Once upon a time, before *Star Wars* was fully conceived, George Lucas overheard a dialogue editor ask an assistant for R2-D2 (Reel 2 Dialogue 2); thus, a robot star was born.

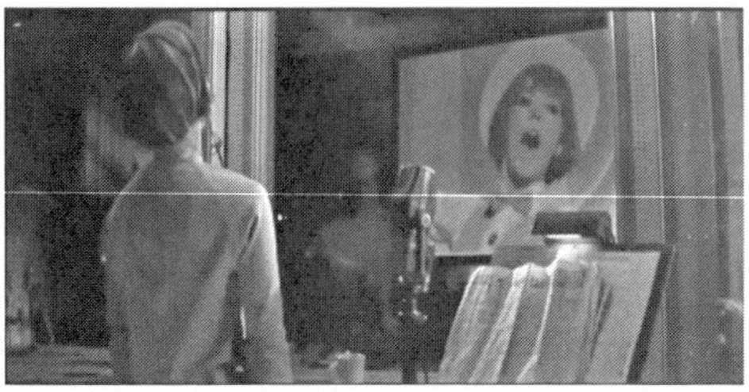

ADR shouldn't be this traumatic. Walled off in a glass booth, Natalie Wood's character, Daisy Clover, has a psychological breakdown while recording ADR in *Inside Daisy Clover* (1965).

Advantages and disadvantages of ADR

There are clear advantages and disadvantages to recording ADR. On the upside, you're not stuck with problems from the production shoot, you get clean audio, and the line and performance are exactly what you want—or close to it. The downsides are evident when the editor syncs ADR to picture: Some actors are super loopers, others are not. ADR editors cut parts of different takes together, massage words, syllables, and ambience to shoehorn in the ADR. They also pitch the ADR, remove recording glitches, and add EQ and reverb to make the ADR lines work. Despite these heroic efforts by actor and editor, it's nearly impossible to match a performance perfectly. Another disadvantage is that the ADR studio ambience never matches production ambience and requires skillful massaging to blend the dialogue seamlessly into the production track. Lastly, ADR ain't cheap.

Preparing for ADR

The editor prepares the ADR by cueing the ADR lines and making a session on the DAW for each character. The ADR editor then delivers the session to the ADR stage.

Recording ADR

> I usually have an idea of a performance in my head of what I'd like the actor to sound like, and I've always considered it my job to help them get there, especially if the director is not around at the time. There are reasons the actors are acting and I am not: I stink at acting! But I know how the mood of a scene should feel and the sound sweetens what is on the screen. I guess you could say I act it in my head. —**GWEN YATES WHITTLE**, ADR, dialogue, and sound supervising editor at Skywalker Sound on *Jurassic Park: Dominion, Mulan, Avatar, The Curious Case of Benjamin Button.*

ADR is recorded on an ADR stage, a small sound stage with a recording booth and screen. You will be present to work with the actor and approve takes along with the ADR editor, assistant, and possibly the picture editor and producer. The scene is programmed to start a few lines before the ADR line. Beeps and sometimes streamers are inserted to prompt the actor.

To lay down an ADR cue, the actor studies the line on the cue sheet. When ready, the actor dons headphones, stands at the mic on the stage, and watches the scene play

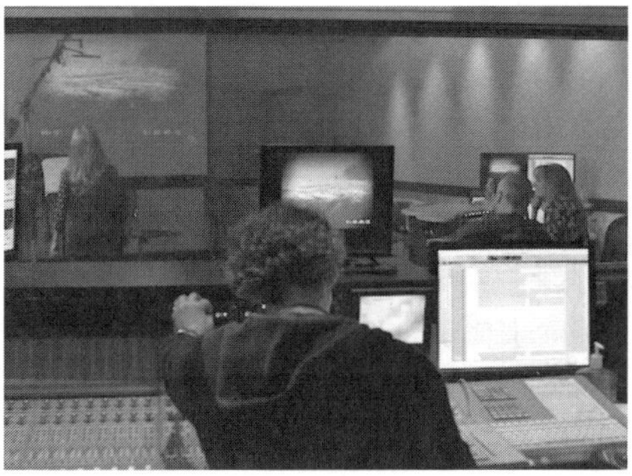

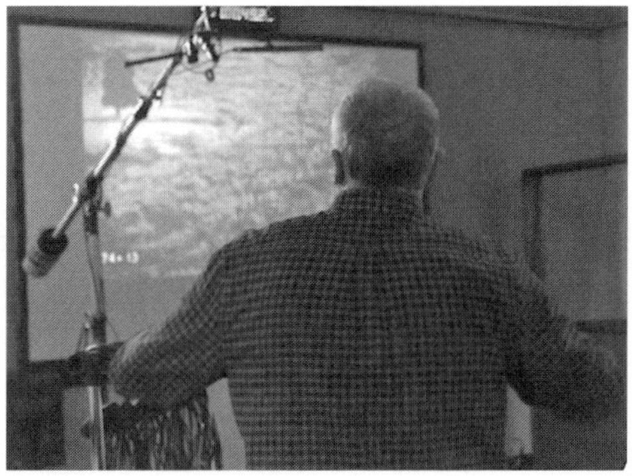

LEFT: Recording ADR: View of ADR stage from recordist's booth. *Making Waves: The Art of Cinematic Sound* (2019). **RIGHT:** An actor records ADR. *Making Waves: The Art of Cinematic Sound* (2019).

on the screen. As the scene nears the ADR line, the actor hears three beeps. Where the fourth beep would be, the actor speaks the line. It's important that the actor match sync as well as performance or your audience will notice the mismatch. Sitting in the recording booth, the ADR recordist monitors each take and makes notes on the ADR cue sheet about each take and which channel it was recorded to. The recordist saves the take to the editor's programmed ADR session in the DAW.

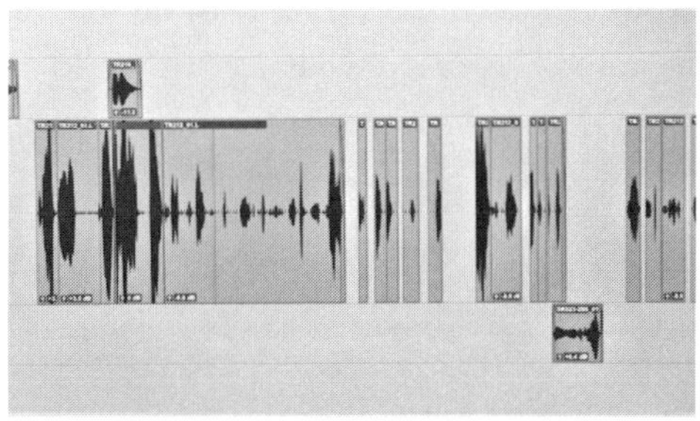

Top to bottom, three tracks of ADR with waveform laid out. *Making Waves: The Art of Cinematic Sound* (2019).

If the take is satisfactory, the actor moves on to the next cue. If not, the scene replays, and the actor redoes the line. On average, an actor can loop ten lines in an hour. Occasionally, two actors will loop a scene together but most of the time looping is a solo endeavor. In addition to ADR lines, you will record any added lines for the character.

ADR and looping: Why ADR is still called looping

Looping is the way dialogue used to be replaced. The looping editor fashioned three film loops of identical lengths—a picture loop, a guide loop (with the line to be replaced), and the record loop (for recording the replacement). The loops played in sync as the actor repeated the line, and it was recorded over and over until it fit right. This time-consuming process was made obsolete in the 1960s by the dubber, a film sound machine which could playback and hold more than one recording. It in turn was unseated by analog tape ADR in the 1970s which has given way to digital hard drives.

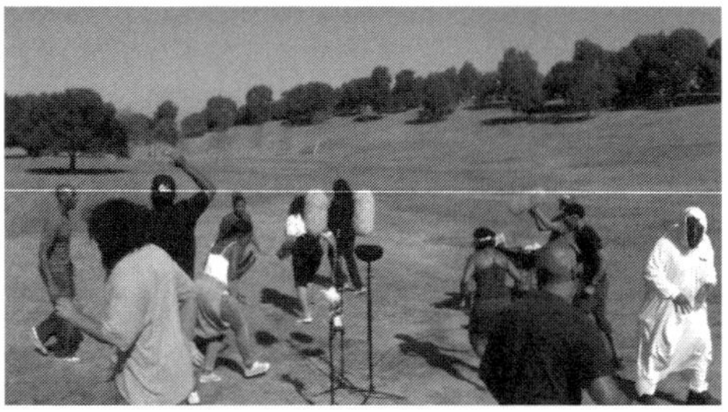

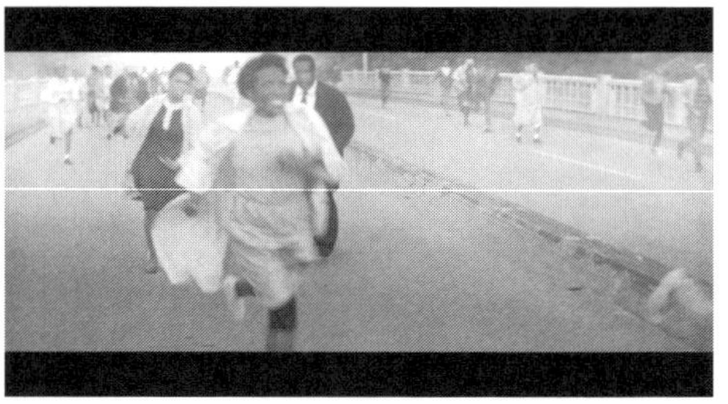

Loop Groups work outside on occasion to create more realistic sound. LEFT: This group runs and yells to voice the terror of people fleeing for their lives (RIGHT) across the Pettus bridge in *Selma (2014)*, from *Making Waves: The Art of Cinematic Sound* (2019).

The loop group a.k.a. loopers

When lines are needed to simulate a crowd, a *loop group*—a group of actors—shows up on the ADR stage. Working off the editor's cue sheets, loopers add two kinds of lines:

> **Walla.** Walla is non-sync background conversation made up of indistinguishable words. For example, you hear barroom walla when two characters converse in a bar or angry passenger walla when the airline agent announces a flight delay. Sometimes walla is scripted into the original scene as "audience walla, café walla, crowd walla," etc. During spotting, all walla to be recorded is noted. Walla can be created on location as well as by the loop group. The dialogue editor routinely increases the walla by duplicating it on two or more tracks.
>
> **Wild lines.** Loop groups also voice non-sync crowd lines you've asked for such as: "Lock them up" and "No justice, no peace." These lines are routinely placed on actors' backs (or at least with their mouths off camera) so there are no lip sync issues. The wild lines may also be created as off-screen lines to "punch up" the sound i.e., add energy and reality to the scene.

Music Editing

> Music editing is about tempo and feel, hitting the right spot in the right key to make completely different types of music, recorded in completely different locations, blend seamlessly together.
> —NICK CARR, music editor on *SpongeBob SquarePants, Modern Marvels, Power Rangers*

A good music editor possesses a knowledge of music and a willingness to experiment. The job also requires considerable collaborative ability as the music editor coordinates your requests as well as those of the composer, music supervisor, and picture and sound editors.

The music editor receives a *mixdown* of the scoring session, with all the instruments on their separate tracks mixed down (brought together and recorded) to fewer tracks. If the music was created on a synth, the composer will send a session or file with the music. The music editor imports the music tracks into their DAW and creates a session(s) of music for each reel. The music editor also imports non-scored music such as source music, head and tail credit music, and songs.

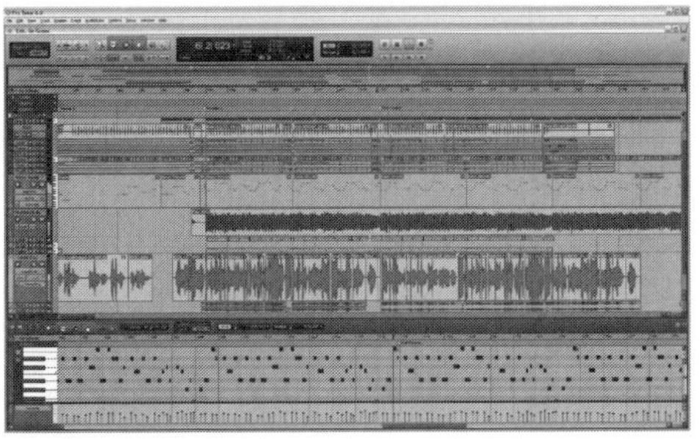

Music tracks laid out on Pro Tools. *Photo courtesy of Avid.*

Laying out tracks

Music editors *lay in* music, meaning they put in the music from first frame to last, to see how it works against cue time and picture. When the music *lays in*, it means that it's perfect and no adjustments are necessary. On a scored show or where the picture's been cut to music as is the case with a music playback number, the music should lay in nicely although some adjustments may be necessary.

On shows or areas of a show where the music has not been timed or scored, the music will not lay in, so the editor will make cuts in the music to fit it to the picture. This means chopping up Chopin or condensing Coltrane—repeating measures, slashing stanzas, and rearranging bars to shoehorn in the music. Sometimes the editor can camouflage the music edit under a sound effect or a bit of dialogue.

Once the music editor has laid in all the music and arranged the tracks, they send the session(s) to the mix stage.

Send in the Tracks: The Handover from Sound and Music to the Mixers

At last, you've locked the show for the final, final time and all the dialogue, sound effects, and music tracks are completely edited. Before sending their DAW sessions to the mix stage, sound and music editors make sure every reel and track is properly laid out, cued, and labeled according to the mixers' specifications.

Cue sheets

The DAW automatically generates *cue sheets* from the editor's cut tracks. Cue sheets show each track as a column from left to right. For the mix, the editor tapes the sheets together so the mixer can easily scan across a section and see which cue is coming up next. There are separate cue sheets for ADR, dialogue, effects, Foley, and music. If the mix is a stereo mix (the norm for TV shows, features, and many other shows), the editors pair the reels for the left/right (L/R) speakers and the mixer assigns them to two mix channels.

Many mixers rely solely on the sessions from the DAWs to locate cues and don't use cue sheets. Some mixers like them because they like to write notes on the sheets or because they lack a monitor to view the session's timeline of tracks and cues.

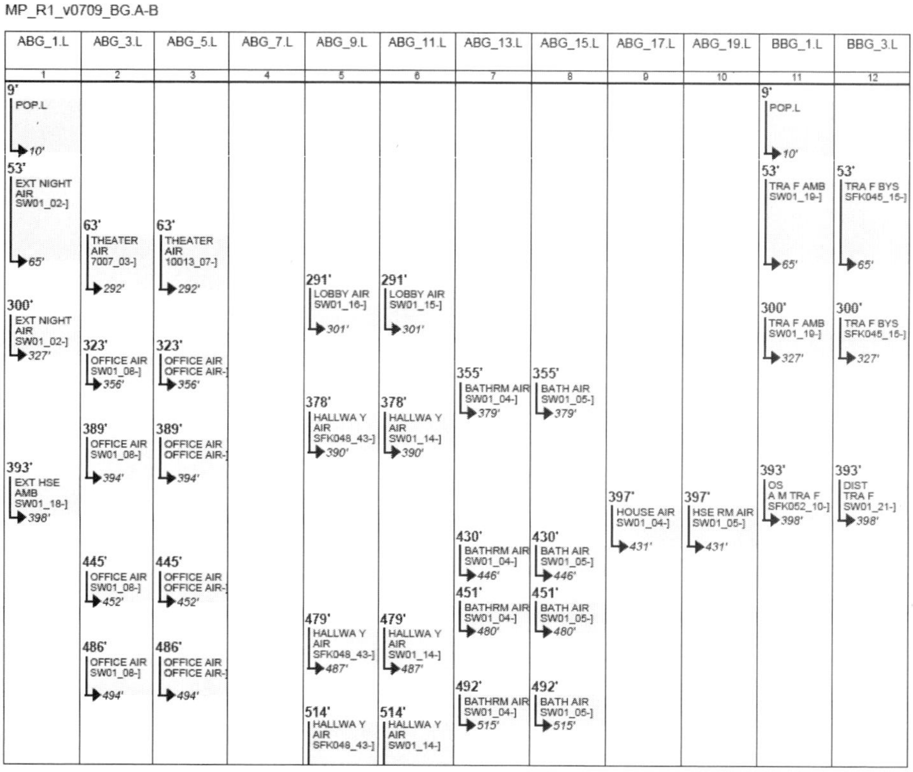

This SFX cue sheet is from a Pro Tools print out. It shows BG (background FX) and AMB (ambience) in L/R odd and even speaker pair assignments for a stereo mix with cue locations measured in film footages. *Image courtesy of Suhail Kafity.*

THE MIX

> A lot of the editing I do actually happens with the sound editors and the postproduction mixer. You can really change the feel of a scene by how you mix things." —JOHN SAYLES, writer/director/editor, *Eight Men Out, The Spiderwick Chronicles, Piranha*

The mix is a creative, technical, and time-consuming process. The goal of the mix is to rerecord the edited sounds—dialogue, effects, and music—and combine them so that they harmonize and can be heard in a way that supports the show's story and fulfills your intentions. The mix, a.k.a. the dub, can take from one day to several weeks, depending on the length, magnitude, and budget of your show; features often take a couple of months. A mix is expensive and advances like a herd of turtles at a common rate of one hour per show minute.

What arrives on the mix stage

You.

When you enter a mix stage—and you should attend a mix before doing your own—you may be overwhelmed: The room can be bigger than some movie theatres.

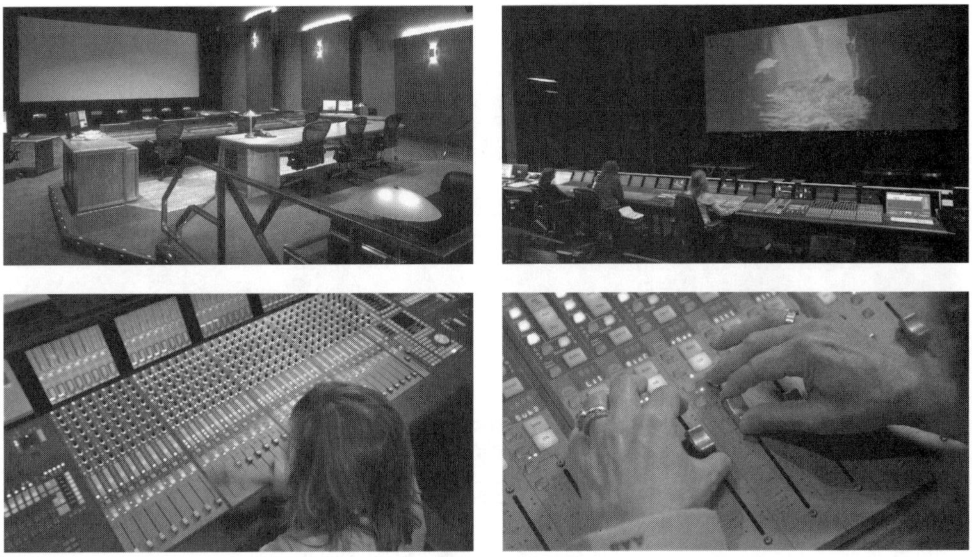

TOP LEFT: Hollywood mix stage with consoles for multiple mixers. *Photo courtesy of Todd-AO/Ascent Media Creative Services.* **TOP RIGHT:** Mixers, consoles, and picture on a Hollywood feature film. *Making Waves: The Art of Cinematic Sound.* **BOTTOM LEFT:** Mixer at her console with its columns of identical channel strips of controls for EQ, gain, muting, etc. *Making Waves: The Art of Cinematic Sound.* **BOTTOM RIGHT:** Mixer slides the faders which control the channel output level. *Making Waves: The Art of Cinematic Sound.*

Huge mix boards (consoles) with panels of lights and control knobs extend like a 3D landscape in front of a screen. At the back of the room is a long high table for you, the producer(s), client(s), and editors (picture, sound, and music), though typically not all are present at one time. Take a seat.

Observe. The show plays on the screen for a few seconds on up to a minute or two. The soundtrack comes to life then urrrh! The sounds die with a gurgle, the picture fades to black—the mix lurches to a halt. A few seconds later the picture and sound revive themselves and the process starts up again. Then staggers to a halt again. It's the stop and start nature of the process which will repeat until the mix is done. Once you've absorbed this rhythm and the visual pictures . . .

Listen. Become aware of all the sounds. At first there may be only dialogue and few effects, but then some music will come in. As the person in charge of the mix, you are creating the sonic environment for your show. You want to create *balance* i.e., make certain that all the audio elements blend and can be heard. Sound density does not equal story clarity; too many different sounds thrown together create a muddy soundtrack that does not speak clearly to your audience. You can change the balance from scene to scene—or even within a scene—according to the dictates of the story.

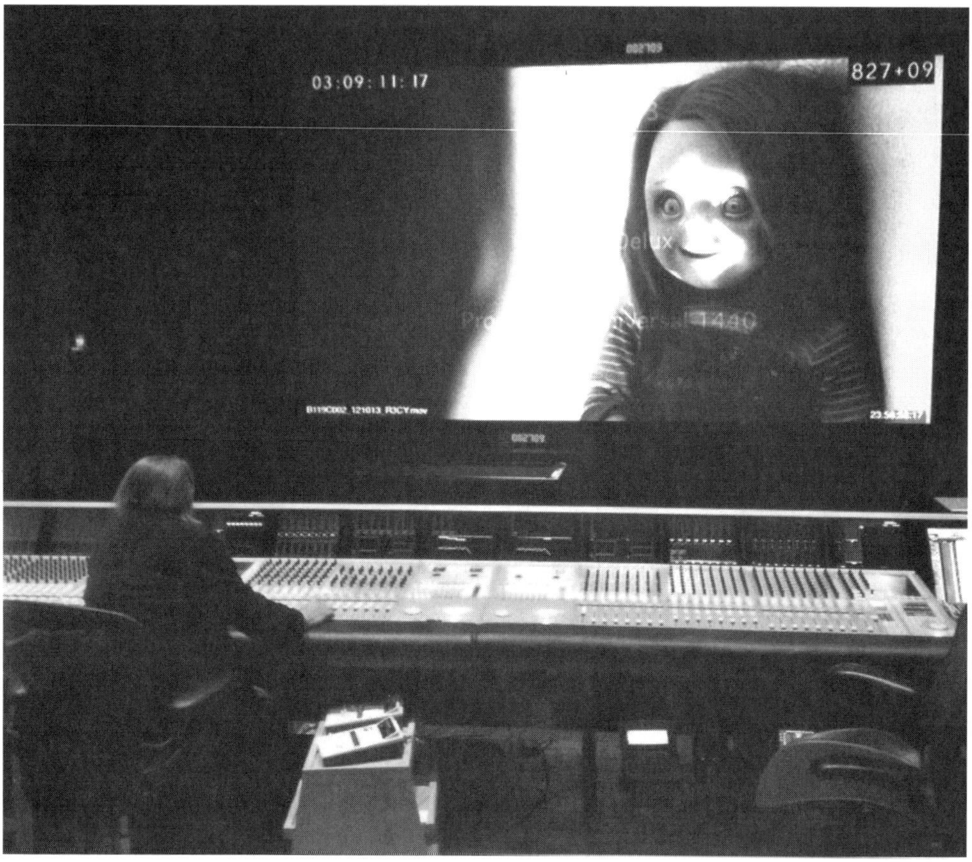

Mixing the *Curse of Chucky*. Notice the timecode in the upper left corner and corresponding film footage in the upper right. *Photo courtesy of Glenn T. Morgan.*

Focus on the mixers. Optimally, there are three mixers: a dialogue and ADR mixer, a SFX and Foley mixer, and a music mixer. If there are only two, the mixers double up; one handles dialogue and music and the other SFX, though they may trade Foley and music cues, depending on their placement. And there may be one mixer in charge of it all. The mixer(s) will bird dog the timeline on their monitor and/or the cue sheets spread out in front of them. Like other filmmakers, mixers are artists with expert technical skills, devoted to recording and delivering the sound you want to the contractual delivery specs. No matter how many shows they've mixed, each show is unique: They'll be listening to you and to the edited story to create the show's sonic palette and environment. To achieve this, you all will . . .

Tune in. Does each sound and music cue work to support the story? Is the audio too *hot* (loud)? Too *tubby* a.k.a. *basey* (low in frequency and overpowering)? Too *hissy* (high in frequency)? Or is the audio *clipping,* its signal distorted or overmodulated?

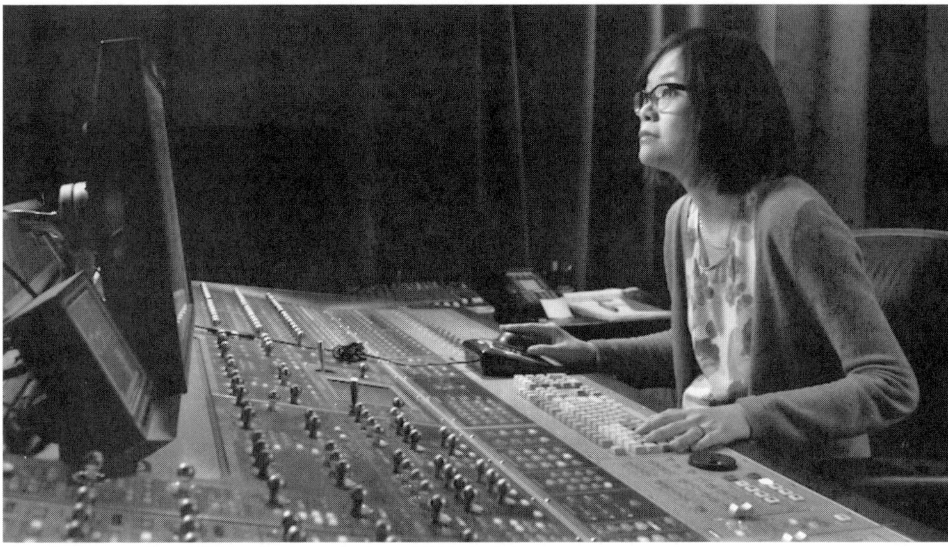

Mixer pre-mixes. *Making Waves: The Art of Cinematic Sound.*

And how's the *level* a.k.a. *gain* (volume level)?* As you absorb the lingo and land of the mix stage, you will be able to pinpoint issues and describe what you want. But don't worry how much or little you know, mixers—like the rest of Sound and Music—are there to guide you and are professional translators of your expressed desires into aural reality.

Perhaps you want the music to come in more gradually. The music editor tells the mixer there's an alternate cue with a longer (slower) start. The mixer spies the alternate on the timeline or cue sheet and switches to it. Again, the picture runs, the music comes in. You are happy, the mixers are happy. The picture runs on, advancing to a new area with new cues. Progress is made with each restart as you work through the picture, minutes, or seconds at a time.

The Pre-Mix

> The pre-mix is a very important part of the process . . . When I'm sound editing or sound designing, I'm not listening to all the other elements. It's only in the pre-mix that I start to combine all the elements together. —**CHRISTOPHER BOYES**, sound supervisor, *Avatar (1 & 2), Captain Marvel, Coco*

The *pre-mix,* a.k.a. the *pre-dub,* is a preliminary mix of certain sounds—BG effects and dialogue usually—performed ahead of the mix. In essence, a pre-dub is a mixdown of sounds in preparation for the mix. Feature films are most likely to pre-dub because

* Mixers constantly *ride the gain* to ensure a consistent audio level from show start to finish. If this weren't done, viewers would constantly be adjusting their TV sets. Tangentially, keeping dialogue levels equal—*leveling out* the dialogue—makes all the characters sound like they're talking to each other; one doesn't sound lower or farther away.

there are so many tracks that the mixers can't play them all at the same time. On other shows, the pre-dub is the initial stage of the mix and is sometimes called the *rough mix*. The main reasons to do a pre-dub are:

- To set levels and make primary technical decisions.
- To save time during the mix.
- To reserve the more important decisions for the final mix.

The sound supervisor and the picture editor, postproduction supervisor, and the producer may be present at least intermittently at the pre-dub. You absolutely want to be on hand for the mix; the pre-mix you may opt out of but why miss this opportunity to define your movie? The sound editors are definitely at the table, along with their DAWs, so if changes are needed they can make them on the spot. The pre-mix lays the foundation for the mix.

What is pre-dubbed

During the pre-dub, dialogue is mixed in dialogue groups and SFX in SFX groups. They are recorded to separate sessions so the mixers can readily reload them to make fixes or tweaks. The pre-mixers keep careful records of which sounds are put to which channels for easy locating during the mix. When a session or reel is complete, the sound editors update the cue sheets to reflect how cues were treated, e.g., dropped or moved.

Dialogue

All split dialogue tracks are rerecorded; alternate lines are not recorded, but their tracks are kept muted. ADR lines are pre-dubbed, and the original production track is held, in case you want to use it and ditch the ADR in the final mix.

Effects

SFX are pre-dubbed in various groups according to your film's demands. These groups include Foley, BGs, and specific FX for certain characters or entities e.g., the cell block, the creature of the bog, etc. Effects requiring major manipulation and decisions are left for the mix.

Music

Ordinarily, music is not pre-dubbed as it is pre-mixed by the composer and/or music editor and shows up at the final mix. However, on a musical or a music-dominated show, the music is pre-dubbed with the focus on levels and technical details. Instruments, songs sung on screen, and other important numbers are isolated so there is plenty of leeway for final decision making during the mix.

Pre-dub process

> It isn't enough for a sound to be merely loud, or high-fidelity, or digital. It needs to remind you of, or resonate with other sounds, places, feelings, in other times. —**RANDY THOM**, C.A.S., sound designer and mixer, *The Polar Express, Cast Away, The Right Stuff*

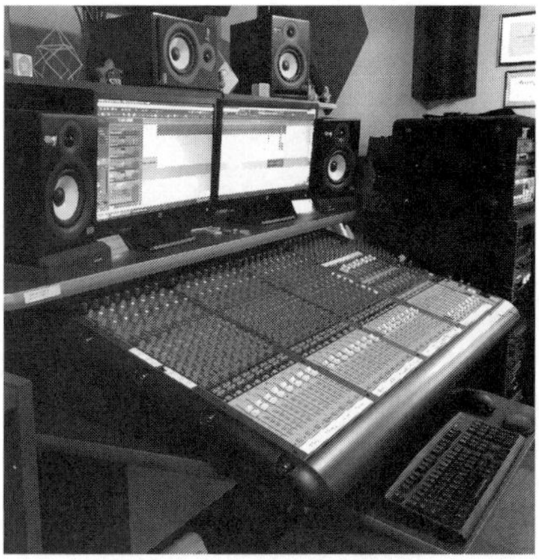

Solo mixer set up. *Photo courtesy of Lloyd Minthorne.*

The process of rerecording the audio is the same for the pre-dub and the mix. The show is mixed one reel or section at a time, though not necessarily in show order. As the picture advances and rewinds in sync with the audio being mixed, a counter runs at the bottom of the screen, counting in time code or 35mm feet and frames. The mixers hunker over their mixing boards, easing faders up and down and panning audio left or right to wrangle the sounds to fit your picture. Mixers also manipulate audio by adding echo, futz, and reverb and reducing noise with noise filters (denoisers) and hum filters. They can program a lot of these settings, which frees them up to finesse more demanding parts of the tracks.

The first time or two that the tracks play, the mixers audition them for levels, EQ, etc. They then mix the sound and save the recorded tracks to a session. When a section is complete, they play it back for everyone. Any changes you or others call for are made by *punching in**, re-mixing the area, and re-saving the session. Then the mixer plays back the section one last time. If you and everyone are satisfied, it's onward and forward to the next section of the show. Painstakingly, cue by cue, your show takes on a new life.

After the pre-dub

Once the pre-mix is complete, the mixers save the pre-mix sessions for the final mix, which may or may not use the same stage and the same crew.

The Mix

> I felt like I should be wearing a helmet doing the mix on *Saving Private Ryan*. The same effect a film that powerful has on an audience, it has on the people who work on it. We took a lot of breaks. You have to go out and have a candy bar, remind yourself that there's a candy machine just down the hallway, and that you're not really at Omaha Beach. —**GARY RYDSTROM**, C.A.S., sound designer and mixer on *Westside Story, Finding Nemo, Ad Astra, Jurassic Park*

The mix is the last creative chance to illuminate your film's story, characters, shadows,

* Isolating a section of a track to work on it and leaving the surrounding area alone.

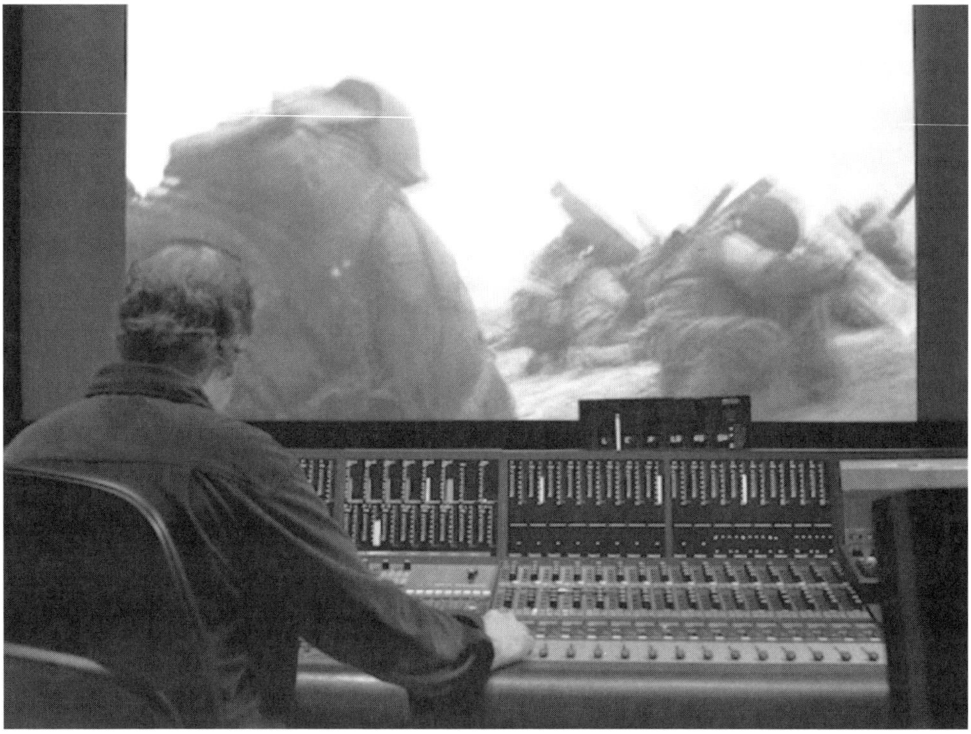

Gary Rydstrom mixes *Saving Private Ryan* (1998) which placed characters and the audience in Normandy on D-Day. *Making Waves: The Art of Cinematic Sound.*

and theme by sound. It should support and articulate the characters' thoughts and feelings and their connections to their world and to others. On nonfiction shows, the mix should clarify the story and subject and bolster the immersion of your audience. In addition to deciding what you want to emphasize and blend at a given moment on screen—FX, dialogue, or music—you want to notice where the sounds play on the screen and how they move. This way, the mixers can pan the audio with the action e.g., can bring alive the sounds your main character hears walking a city street at night. Keep your characters' perspectives in mind along with your audience's when mixing: You want to laser focus the audio so your soundtrack reflects what your characters are experiencing, and your audience can absorb.

Who's on stage

The players are the same as at the pre-dub: two or more mixers, the sound designer, the picture, sound, and music editors, you, the client, and producer. The mixers control the mix, taking direction from you and the sound designer. The mixers should have viewed the show if they didn't perform the pre-dub and be clued into the sound environment you'll be building.

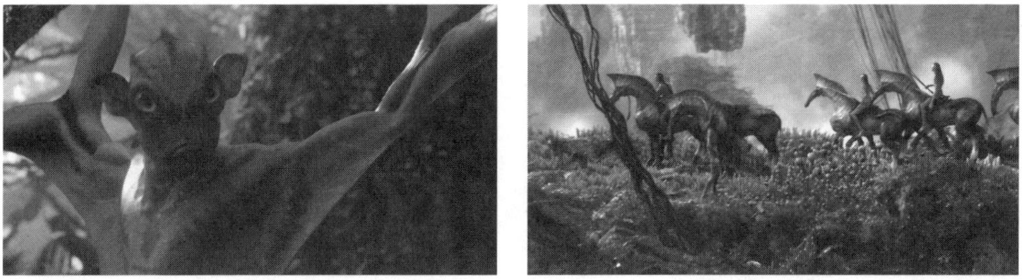

Creating the sonic world and creatures of the moon Pandora in *Avatar* (2009) was a highly creative challenge.

It's important that everyone be a collaborative team member and have the show's best interest at heart. Frequently, the mixer has previously worked with you and/or the sound supervisor, so a good working relationship is already established. Some directors and sound supervisors learn how to run the mixing boards and actively mix the show. James Cameron not only directed *Avatar* and *Titanic*, but also edited these blockbusters (along with two other picture editors) and co-mixed their sound.

Mix with an ear to the audience: Surround sound

> The trick in movie making, and certainly no less in mixing sound for movies, is to focus the attention of the audience. It's very misguided to think that every element has to be in play at all times, because then you just end up with visual and aural noise. —**RANDY THOM**, C.A.S., sound designer and mixer, *The Polar Express, Cast Away, The Right Stuff*

Just as the writing, shooting, and editing of a show are designed to tell the audience what they need to know when they need to know it, so is the sound. Throughout the mix be aware of what clues, what experience, and what information the sound and music must convey to your audience at each moment of the show. Does the audience need to hear the dialogue and what the DJ's playing is insignificant? During a storm scene, are the SFX and the experience of being there more important than the words? For the start of an "on the road" scene, is it better to hear a family express their hopes, fears, and dreams or to let music dominate and express foreboding?

Being attuned to your audience can also mean concentrating a lot on the surround sound. "That was really important: For the movie to always remind you where you are, that you're *in* the movie, that you're not watching a movie," stressed Paul Ottosson, sound designer and mixer on *The Hurt Locker,* which won Oscars for best sound editing and best sound mixing. Ottosson continued, "If all the sounds you created came from the front, they're assuming you're watching this movie, so by building the sound all the way around you, I'm putting you directly in the drama, its events, and where it's located."

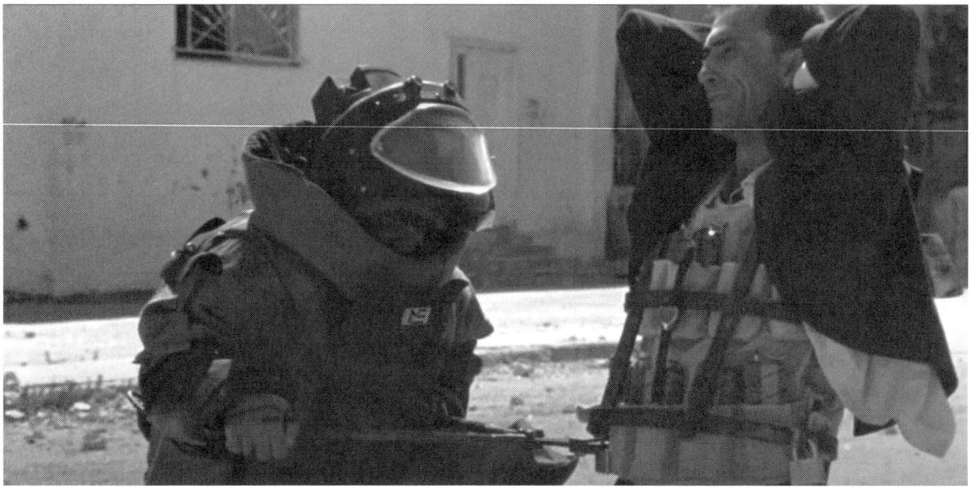

Frantic dialogue between U.S. soldiers and the fear-filled breath of the bomb-strapped Iraqi citizen put you inside this tense scene, where a sergeant attempts to defuse a bomb in *The Hurt Locker* (2008).

What happens during the mix

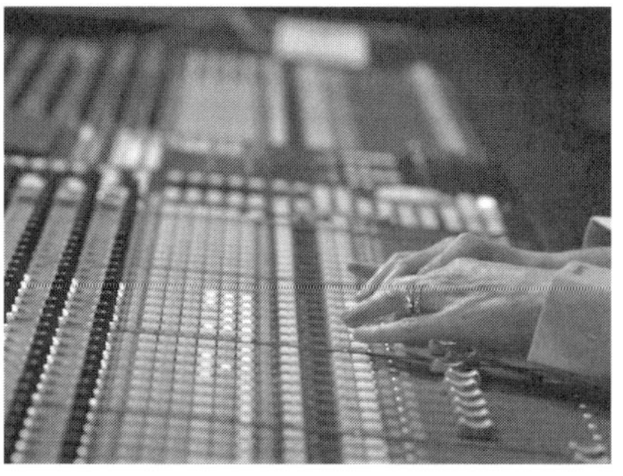

Mixer manipulates faders to create and adjust levels. *Making Waves: The Art of Cinematic Sound.*

As at the pre-dub, the show plays on the screen, the counter runs, and the mixers ride their boards, eyeing the music cue sheets and sound pre-dub layout sheets. This time around however, they mix the pre-dubbed dialogue and effects tracks together with the music and any dialogue and FX cues that were not mixed before. Again, it's a slow process of manipulating the levels and EQing; blending and balancing the sound to create the best soundtrack. The mixers will also assign tracks to LCRS (Left-Center-Right-Surround) speaker channels for home and movie theatre playback.

3D shows

> . . . once we were able to finally listen to the mix against the finished 3D picture it was still an amazing and exciting experience . . . you just go by what feels right and make sure that in the end, you believe it really happened. —**STEVE BOEDDEKER**, sound designer and supervisor on *Alice in Wonderland 3D, Black Panther, Se7en*

On 3D shows, mixers work to a 2D picture until the end, when the VFX are completed and the 3D version is finally available. However, due to 5:1 (and now 7:1) surround sound, sound designers and editors have operated on a 3D plain in essence for many years, moving characters and objects front, left, right, back, and around in the

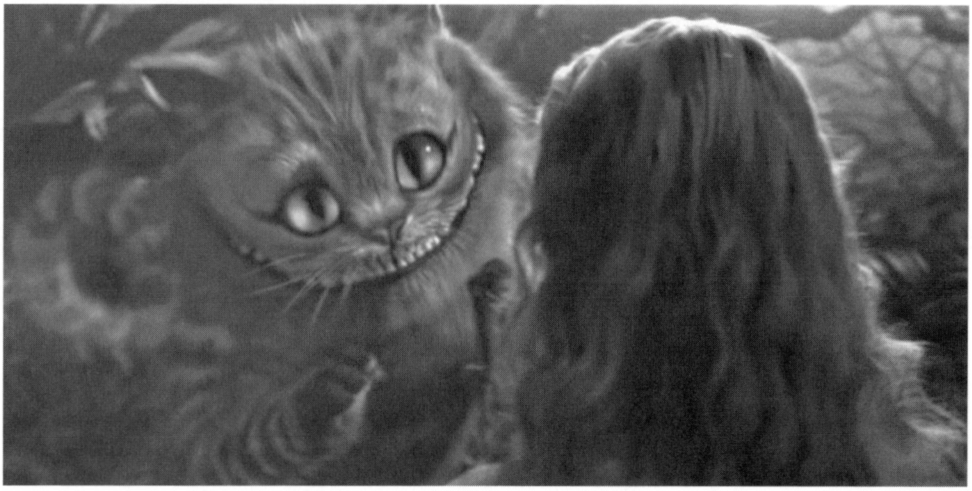

The Cheshire cat leaps in and grins in *Alice in Wonderland 3D* (2010).

soundtrack's acoustic space to match the actions on screen. Boeddeker reflects on mixing *Alice in Wonderland 3D,* "You can really get away with a lot of sound tricks in 3D . . . so as we all were making, editing, and mixing the sound effects, we tried to always keep in mind that things will be more extreme in 3D. The Cheshire cat won't just fly off, he will fly right over your head, and the Red Knights will seem to march right into the theater. So we tried to push the surrounds as much as possible, knowing it will be much more believable in 3D."

Hitting the finishing line with just the right amount of sound

> There's a law of diminishing returns in sound editing and mixing. If you start putting in too much stuff, then it doesn't sound good anymore, it just sounds like mush.
> —**GARY RYDSTROM**, C.A.S., sound designer and mixer on *Westside Story, Finding Nemo, Ad Astra, Jurassic Park*

On most shows, not all the sound and music cues will make it to the final mix. You'll consider: "Does the ADR work or should we drop certain cues and live with the production track?" "Do we really need music here?" "We need a music sting right here." You will drop some cues; others will be altered, advanced, or delayed. Your goal is to create a final mixed soundtrack that compliments and enhances the show at every frame. Once the mixers have mixed everything, the mix will be played against the final version of the picture for your final approval.

What the mix produces: The DME and stems

The result of the mix is that all the tracks are mixed down to three groups: dialogue, music, and effects. This three-group mixdown is called the *DME*. The individual, split off parts of the DME, are called *stems* or *splits*: There's a dialogue stem, a music stem, and an effects stem. The combined music and effects stems are referred to as the *M & E*. These are the four basic stems which, in addition to the full mix stem, form the standard minimum set of stems. DME stems are used for:

- Re-mixing: It's not uncommon for a section of a show to be re-mixed.
- Making mono stems from the original stereo mix.
- Creating the TV version of a feature film.
  - The show will be re-mixed at a later date with alternative ADR lines and production lines to cover words barred from TV.
- Creating *foreigns* (non-English versions of your show). The dialogue stem serves as a guide track for recording the new language and is muted in the mix. The M&E is re-mixed with the PFX* track and the dubbed foreign language.

Mixers create as many stems as your delivery requirements specify, such as an ADR stem, Foley prop stem, Foley footsteps stem, 5:1** or 7:1*** stem, and narration stem. They also *bounce* (group) similar tracks or stems into one file e.g., all the drumbeats. Finally, to prepare for the finishing process, the mix is saved as a session and transferred to a master file or tape. If your show is destined for a theatrical release, the mixers will create a printmaster which will be put to file or film for projection.

LAST WORD

Now that your sound is edited and mixed, it is time to marry it to picture and finish your show. This merging and finalizing are what the last chapter covers.

* The production effects track consists of sound effects that you recorded on location that are part of the production (dialogue) track e.g., footsteps, hand slaps, lip smacks etc.
** Surround sound with five channels: left, right, and center channels in the front and left and right surround channels. The "1" stands for the LFE (low frequency effects) channel.
*** 5:1 plus left and right rear channels.

WHAT DIRECTORS SHOULD KNOW ABOUT EDITING AND MIXING SOUND AND MUSIC

- ☐ Sound and music editors will be in contact with you and run ideas by you. They will give you choices for the mix stage, by cutting in *alts* (alternatives) for certain cues.
- ☐ The SFX editor auditions each SFX cue against the picture to determine it works to make the picture seem realistic or natural, trigger an emotion, and/or show something novel and imaginative.
- ☐ A Foley artist walks and records the Foley based on the cue sheet sent to the Foley stage by the Foley editor. After the Foley recording session, the editor cleans up the Foley cues, making certain they're in perfect sync and cutting out extraneous noise before sending the session to the Mix Stage.
- ☐ Dialogue editors ensure that every sentence, word, syllable, and utterance of dialogue, narration and VO is clear by cleaning out undesirable sounds, then filling any audio gaps with ambience so the words blend into the setting of each scene. They split tracks by camera set-up so the mixers can mix between different speakers' words and syllables with ease. This allows you to single out words or sentences for special treatment.
- ☐ The purpose of ADR is to replace poor production track, add newly scripted lines, change or re-voice a performance, create walla or wild lines, or substitute words for the TV version.
- ☐ Music editors lay in music from first frame to last to see how it works against cue time and picture.
- ☐ Because many cues occur near or at the same time, editors space them out over multiple tracks of SFX, dialogue, and music so they can be mixed efficiently.
- ☐ The mix is another creative chance to illuminate your film's story, characters, shadows, and theme by sound. You want to balance all the audio elements—dialogue, SFX, and music—so they blend and can be heard by your audience.
- ☐ Mixers are artists with expert technical skills devoted to recording and delivering the sound you want to your show's delivery specs.
- ☐ The pre-mix is a preliminary mix of certain sounds—BG effects and dialogue usually—performed ahead of the mix.
- ☐ The mix produces a group mixdown of dialogue, music, and effects—the DME—which the mixer breaks into stems that meet delivery requirements. A common stem is the M & E (music and effects). For the finishing process, the mix is kept as a session and transferred to a master file or tape or for film shows, a printmaster.

10 FINISH AND DELIVER

All of preproduction, shooting, and post has led to the steps you'll take now to finish and deliver your show. This phase may not be as demanding as being on the set, but it requires your full attention: You want to see your show to the finish line completed the way you intend.

The last phase of postproduction recreates your locked cut from the best quality source media available—file, film, disk, or tape—to create your final deliverable(s) on file, film, or disk. The process consists of dropping in the final VFX, making a master file or film negative, color grading, adding titles and credits, laying back the final audio mix, and outputting the deliverable(s). Your editor or the post house performs these finishing tasks. We'll go over both options starting with the common task of designing titles and credits. Once your show is out the door, you'll want to think about trailers and marketing and archiving, which will be our last topic.

TITLES AND CREDITS

> A main title in its best form is like a prologue to a movie. Ideally, it sets you up for the emotional content of the film and gets you excited about it. —**KYLE COOPER**, title designer for *Kong: Skull Island, Beauty and the Beast, Tron: Legacy, Ironman, Spider-Man 2*

Titles and credits—lettered graphics added to the head and tail of your film—display information and list those who worked on the show. Head credits and the show's title introduce the audience to your show and give you another opportunity to be creative. You may opt for a plain title sequence for budget reasons or due to taste as Christopher Nolan and Steven Spielberg do. Or you may shoot a title sequence or hire a title designer to fabricate one that provides a deeper or more scintillating experience for your viewers.

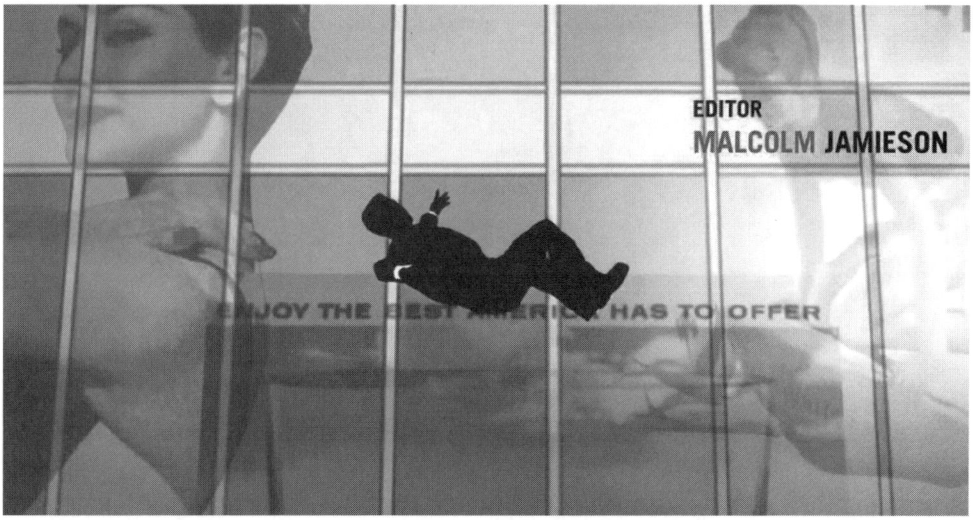

The falling man head credits of the series *Mad Men* (2007-15) evoke the world of advertising, the cool despair of the early 1960s, and the opening credits of Hitchcock's *North by Northwest* (1959).

This can apply to tail credits also. Whatever your choice, this section covers the decisions you'll need to make and provides examples that will illuminate possibilities.

Head credits

> Titles can do very much or very little, but really shine when they live within the story and reflect an important quality driven by your director. —**SUSAN BRADLEY,** title designer on *Frozen, Toy Story 3, Wall-E, Up, The Motorcycle Diaries, An Inconvenient Truth*

Ostensibly, main titles a.k.a. head titles, head credits, or opening credits provide the names of the principal actors and creators of your film. But since they are part of the initial image viewers see, they make a first impression and can do a lot more. A head credit sequence can clue your audience into your film's plot, location, time-period, style, characters, and, along with music, help establish its emotional tone or viewpoint.

A title sequence can stand on its own; paired with the perfect music, it can establish

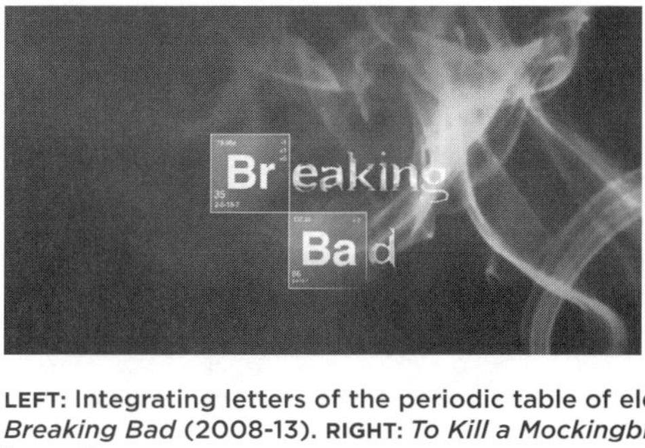

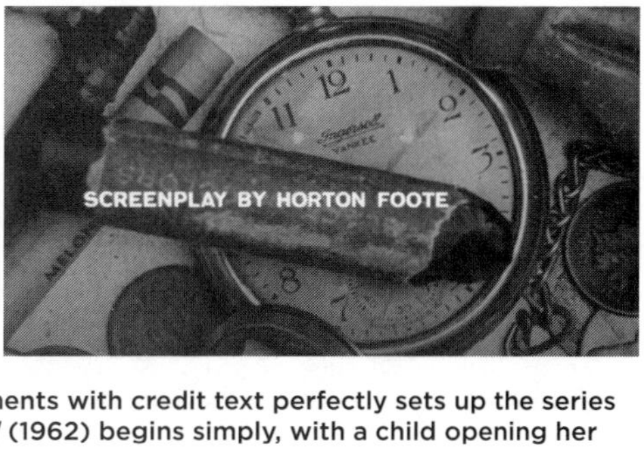

LEFT: Integrating letters of the periodic table of elements with credit text perfectly sets up the series *Breaking Bad* (2008-13). **RIGHT:** *To Kill a Mockingbird* (1962) begins simply, with a child opening her box of treasures.

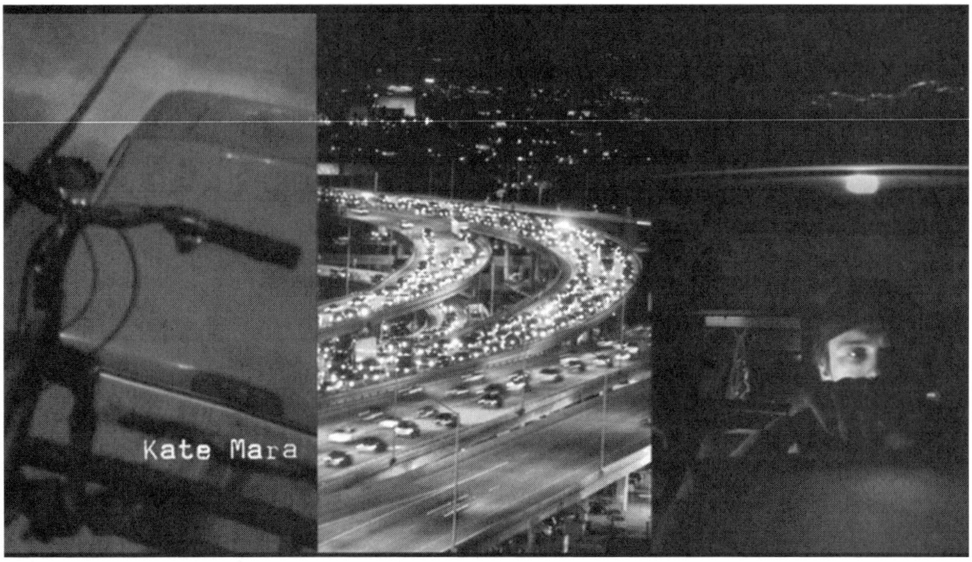

The split screen head credits of *127 Hours* (2010) introduces the film's risk-taking protagonist as he drives through the night to escape the city and set off on his fateful hike.

the mood for a show. The jaunty title sequence of *The Pink Panther* (1962) gave birth to a cartoon star with his own series. Thanks to the internet, we can now freely savor this memorable title sequence and others such as *Catch Me If You Can* (2002), *It's a Mad Mad Mad Mad World* (1963), and *Dr. No* (1962).

Conversely, many filmmakers don't want titles to stand apart from the movie but prefer them to blend in and be a part of the story's exposition.

Tail credits

Tail credits a.k.a. end credits or closing credits are usually more utilitarian than head credits, parading cast, crew, filming location(s), and acknowledgments. The crew gets little respect when networks routinely *squeeze and tease*—cram end credits to one side of the TV screen—to make room for promos.

Crawls and cards

Most closing credits crawl, rolling name after name with job title after job title, from the bottom of the screen to the top. Instead of crawling, credits can pop on and off the screen. In this situation each credit is referred to as a *card*. A show's top players are credited first and have a *single card,* meaning no one else is on their card. Their card may be up longer than others. The majority of the U.S. films run VIPs' end credits on cards as the action ends and freezes, then fade to black and roll the rest of the credits. But you can goose your end credits with added information or antics (bloopers are common) to extend the movie and give your audience a softer return to reality.

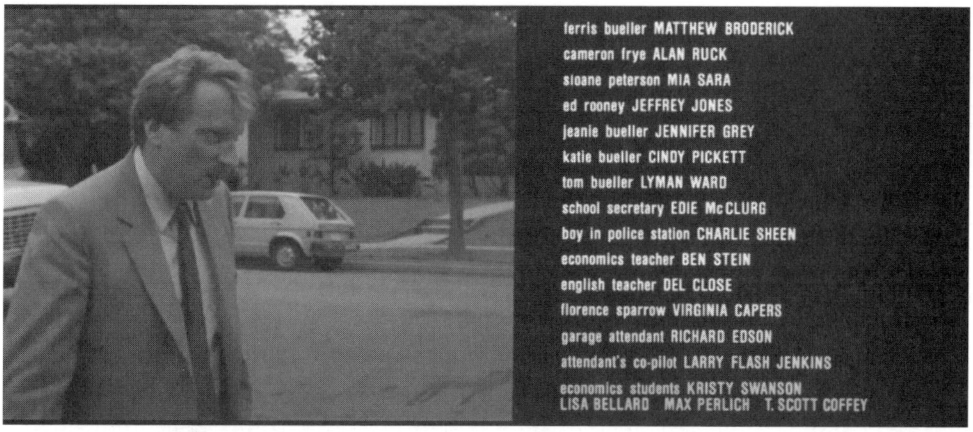

In *Ferris Bueller's Day Off* (1986), the tail credits hand Dean Rooney, Ferris' nemesis, a humiliating end.

Creating titles and credits

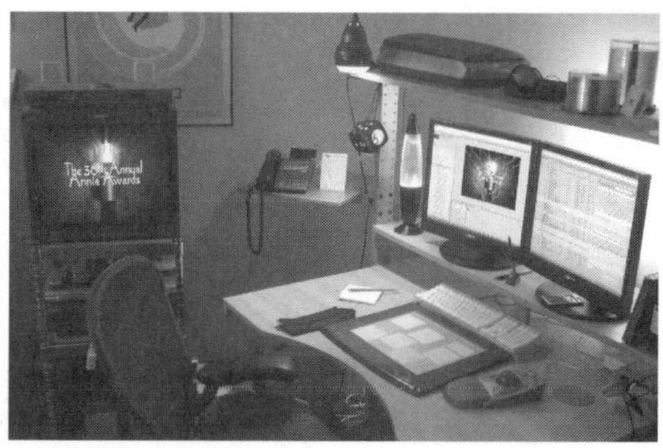

Post house suite with tablet for creating GFX (graphics). *Photo courtesy of AlphaDogs.*

The producer provides a list of the credits and is responsible for its accuracy i.e., job titles, spellings, credit order, and professional associations, like DGA or A.C.E. Typically your editor lays out head titles and credits temporarily on the digital system. You (or the producer if the show is a TV series) will have the final say on the look and placement of titles and credits. Next, depending on where you're finishing the show, the post house or the editor will lay out and be responsible for accurately duplicating the final list. You may be present during the lay out or wait until the credits are fully laid out before viewing and approving them.

Credit hierarchy

Hollywood has a hierarchy for who gets a front (head) credit and who gets a back (tail) credit. The director's credit is always the closest to the body of the show which makes it the last credit before the show starts. Editors (except for additional editors) always get a front credit; the assistant editor and the rest of the postproduction crew receive a back credit. (On television shows these credits and their placement vary from network to network.)

From time to time, everyone's credit appears at the back of the show. This is done when you decide to involve the viewer immediately in the film. With this scheme, the director gets the first credit after the show. Moving the credits to the back means

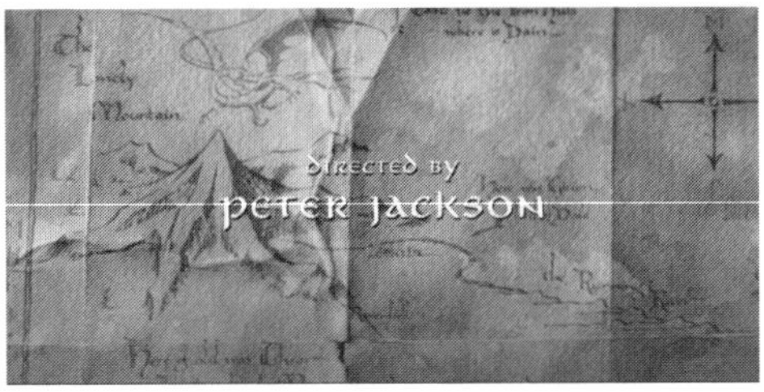

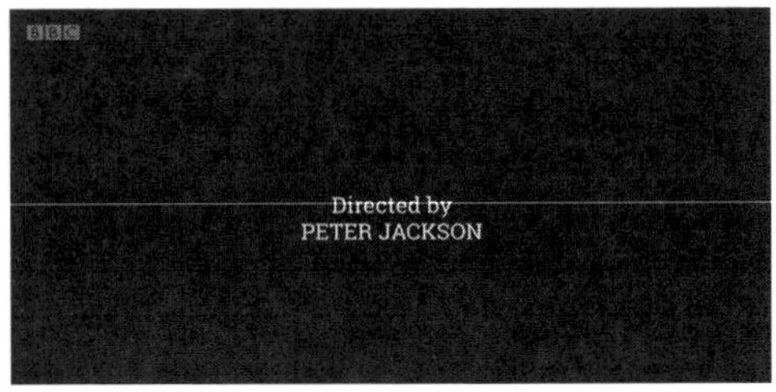

Director Peter Jackson pushed the credits to the end in both *The Hobbit: The Battle of the Five Armies* (2014) and *They Shall Not Grow Old* (2018).

that those who contractually have a head credit, (major actors, the writer(s), producers, DP, editor, sound designer, costume designer, etc.), have to "sign off"—sign a waiver—about the placement of their credit.

Backgrounds

You most commonly set titles against picture ($$$) or a colored background ($$) or think in black with white lettering as Woody Allen often has ($). *Clean titles* are those that are the easiest to read and don't bleed (appear to run into the background). In order to achieve the cleanest titles, bear in mind that:

- White lettering is the cleanest.
- Script takes longer to read as do fonts with curlicues or indistinct letters.
- Blue and red lettering are prone to bleeding and poor readability.
- Drop shadows can sometimes enhance readability.

Screen placement

When placing titles in a show, be aware of how they and the action in the frame appear on the screen: You don't want a critical action or part of a title cut off from the audience. Checking for cut off is particularly critical when you're finishing on multiple formats with different aspect ratios. Broadcasters require that credits and action appear within certain areas on the screen; they want to see their bug e.g., BBC, NBC. There are two ways to measure how the credits and action will be seen: Safe Title Area and Safe Action Area. Editing systems have graphic overlays which outline these areas (and others) on the frame like those shown above.

Safe title is the area in the center where it's safe to place a title or graphic so that it won't get cut off on the viewer's screen. With the 16:9 screen you can fill out 80% of the screen. Slightly larger than safe title, *safe action*, is where you should restrict the action so your audience can see all of it. You and your DP anticipated this during the shoot. If you forgot, the post house or editor can resize the frame or pan and scan the scene,

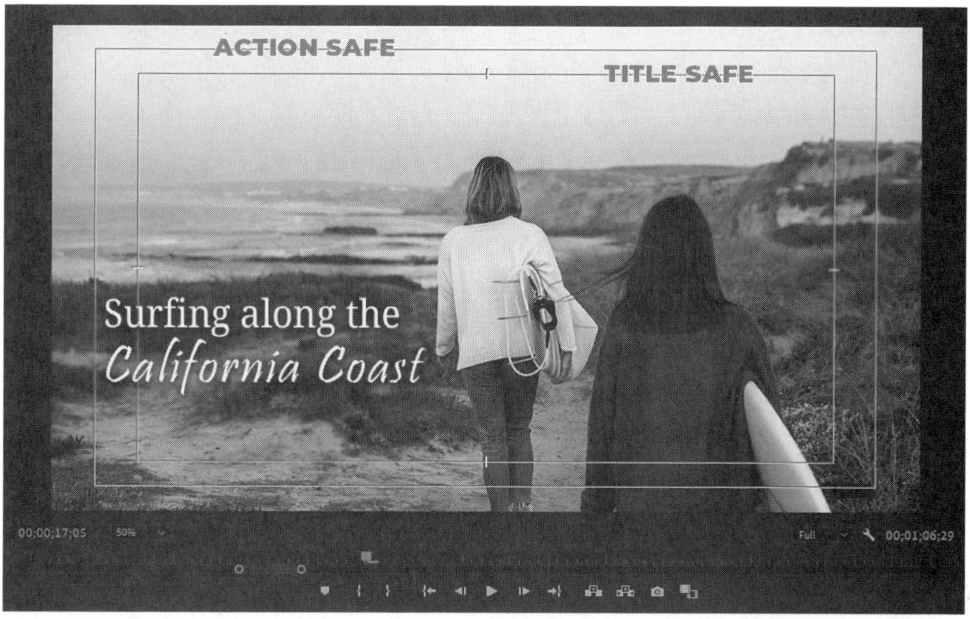

Title and action safe overlay lines on Adobe Premiere. Notice the overlay for title safe: The title is outside the safety zone; viewers will not see the first letters on each line. Action safe is your call: If you want to see more of the surfers, pick a frame later in the shot. *Photo courtesy of Jay Scherberth.*

so viewers can see the necessary action. If you ignore safe title and action areas, your credits and action may be cut off on iPhones and other devices as well as on YouTube and TV screens, particularly on older, 4:3 sets.

Timing credits

Your post supervisor will inform you of any timing requirements. You and your editor will time the head credits to be certain they fit against picture. TV credits typically fade up for a minimum of 15 frames, hold full up on screen for two seconds, and fade out for another 15 frames for a total of three seconds. This means you need a shot at least three seconds long to run underneath the credit as normally you don't want to change shots under a credit. You can adjust shots to cover credits by slipping, sliding, or slowing them down.

A long time ago in a galaxy far, far away . . . How long to keep subtitles up on the screen

Normally subtitle text is short: "Somewhere on the eastern front" or "Ten years later." Often the text consists of an interviewee's name and title e.g., "Speaker, Nancy Pelosi" or "Lorenzo, next door neighbor." To ensure they can be understood, leave a subtitle up long enough to be read three times at a moderate pace. For superior readability, editors habitually place subtitles on the lower third of the screen so they don't block any important action or body features; hence they are often referred to as "lower thirds."

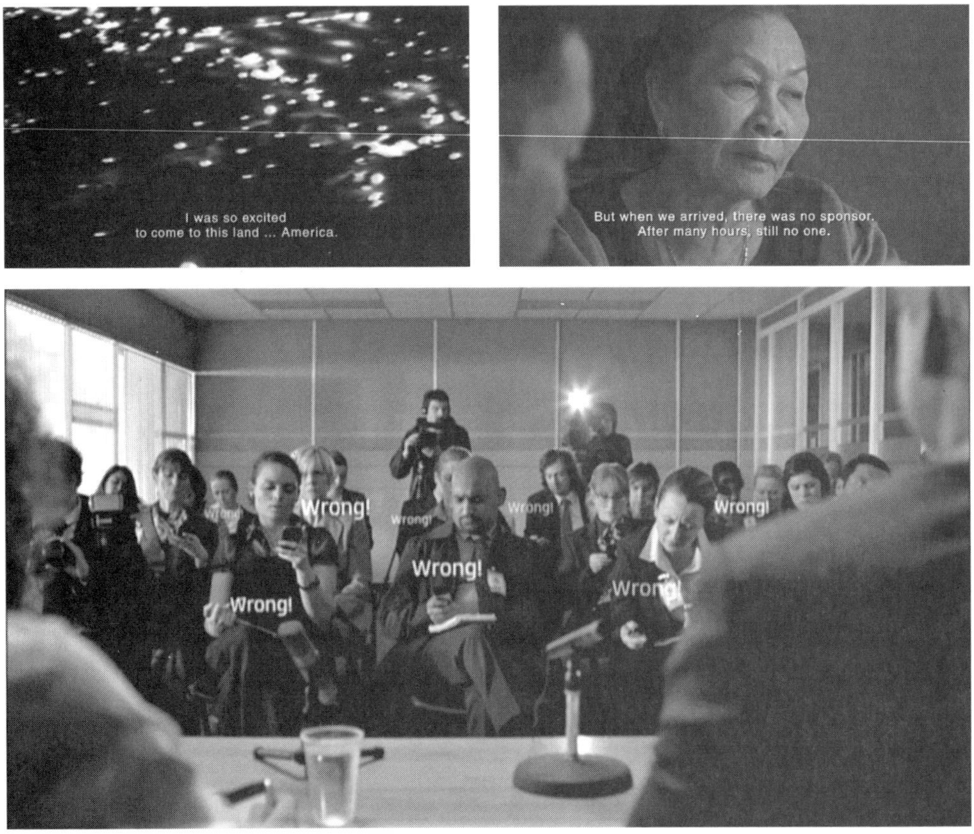

TOP: Subtitling rules also apply to captions as illustrated by these frames from *The Betrayal* (2008), an Oscar-nominated documentary about a Laotian family emigrating to the U.S. **BOTTOM:** Leave it to Sherlock Holmes to prove an exception to the lower third rule. *Sherlock: A Study in Pink* (2010).

Who designs the titles?

Titles and credits are designed and built at the post house, a title house, a design company, or a production studio. They can also be created by your editor.

Editor

Most digital systems incorporate a titling tool with a variety of fonts, colors, drop shadows, transparencies, sizes, and other choices such as 3D. Your editor can create credits that move vertically or horizontally or appear with a transition and/or keying effect. They can import credit files, text styles, and fonts from other programs, e.g., Adobe After Effects.

Post house

The post house adds the titles and credits for television and low budget shows after color grading and finalizing the show. If the show is finishing via digital intermediate (DI), titles are added during the DI process.

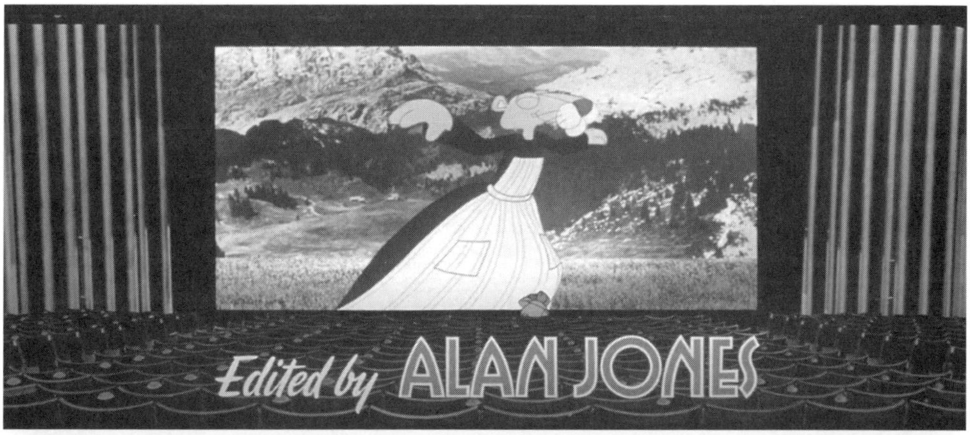

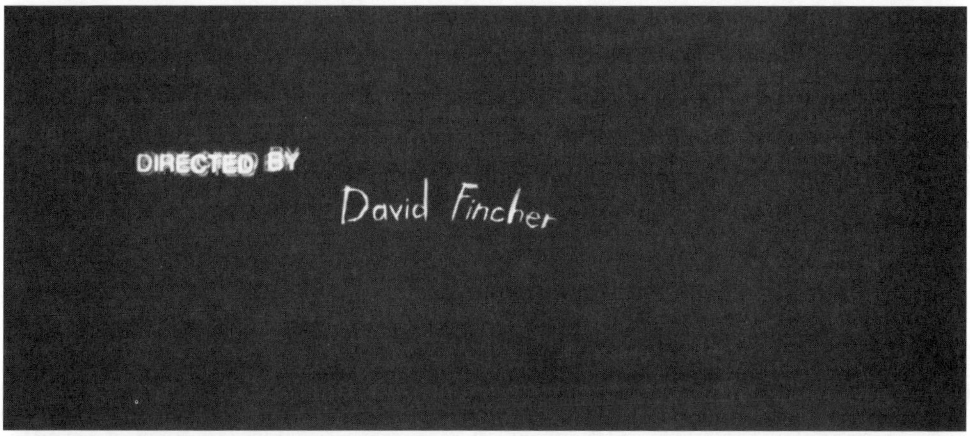

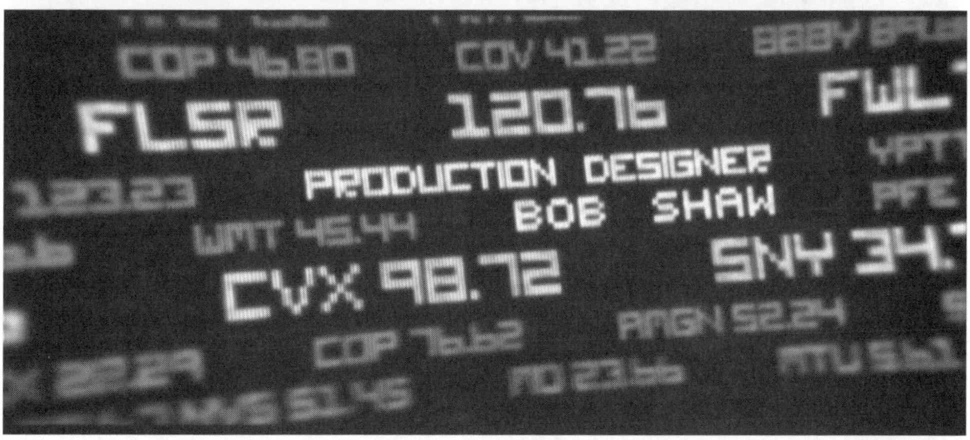

TOP: In *The Pink Panther Strikes Again* (1976), Richard Williams' title house spoofed major movies in the opening credits. **MIDDLE:** Evocative typography alone can inexpensively usher in your film as evidenced in director David Fincher's *Se7en* (1995). **BOTTOM:** *Too Big to Fail* (2011) cleverly embedded the opening titles in the horizontal movement of the Dow Jones digital ticker tape.

Title house
For decades, title houses have produced optical titles and titles sequences for film shows. Now they've added computer designed titles and other services such as pan and scan, film restoration, and Web site design. In fact, title houses, design companies, and post houses overlap services.

The designer at the title house creates the entire title sequence with input from you and help with footage from your editor. Alternatively, the editor cuts the background footage for the title sequence and the title house designs and marries the titles to it. Spectacular sequences designed at title houses include the James Bond series, Sergio Leone's films, and the *Pink Panther* flicks.

Design company
In the 1990s, digital technology brought down the cost of creating titles with new and fast compositing, motion graphics, and editing software. A boutique industry of design companies sprang up whose prominent designers created titles as well as commercials, GFX, effects, Web sites, and corporate content. These designers have advanced the art of making titles with *Up in the Air, Thank You for Smoking,* and *Kiss Kiss Bang Bang*. The graphic designer works with you to craft the title sequence.

Studio
Some studios, notably Disney and Pixar, control their pictures and brand by employing in-house design teams. These teams have produced some notable title sequences in *Toy Story 3, Ratatouille,* and *WALL-E.*

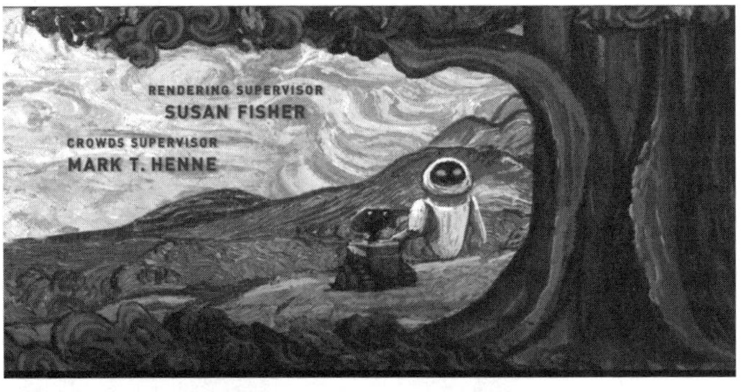

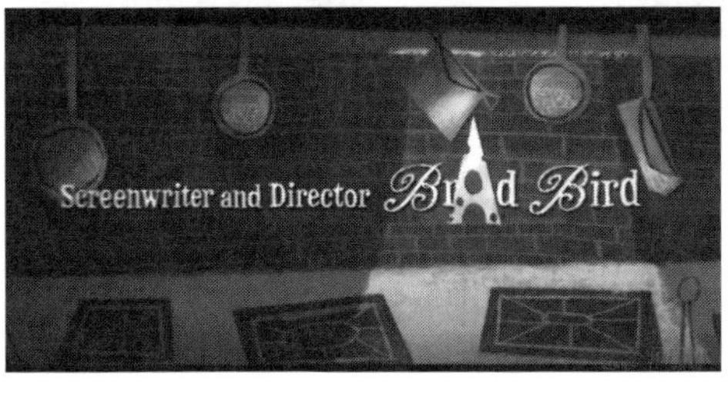

ABOVE: The garbage packed, uninhabited earth in *WALL-E* (2008) is given promise in the end credits in the form of an art history lesson as the land and people rebound. **LEFT:** The tail credits of *Ratatouille* (2007) keep the film cooking through the last frame.

CONFORMING

Before color grading can take place, the final locked cut with all the final graphics (GFX) and video effects (VFX) of your show needs to be conformed to the highest quality media—digital or film. This conforming operation is carried out by your editor (a straightforward process) or your post house (a lengthier process if a Digital Intermediary is being created).

Editor conforms show

Your editor will make a file of the Final Cut in one of two ways:

1. If your editor cut natively using the original, high quality, high-res files you shot, they will generate the file from the timeline.
2. If your editor cut using proxies (low quality, low-res files), they will relink the edited clips to the original high quality, hi-res files before creating the file.

Post house conforms show

On larger and higher budget shows and/or when the editor's commitment is to the next project or episode of a series, the post house does the final finishing: dropping in the final VFX, relinking to the native high-res files, color grading, adding titles and credits, laying back the final audio mix, and ensuring it meets broadcast and streaming specs or other delivery requirements. Overseen by the post supervisor, the post house may also shepherd the GFX and VFX to the finish line.

If film is involved as source material and/or final deliverable, the post house will create a *DI* (digital intermediate or intermediary). A DI—also commonly employed on digitally shot shows and in film restoration—corrals all source formats to generate a digital file of your locked cut for the final finishing processes. This file is used to produce your final deliverable(s) on film, disk, or file for projection, streaming or broadcast. As soon as the file is created, you and the DP will commence color grading the show which we'll discuss next. But first, it's helpful to understand how the DI process arrives at the images you'll be manipulating.

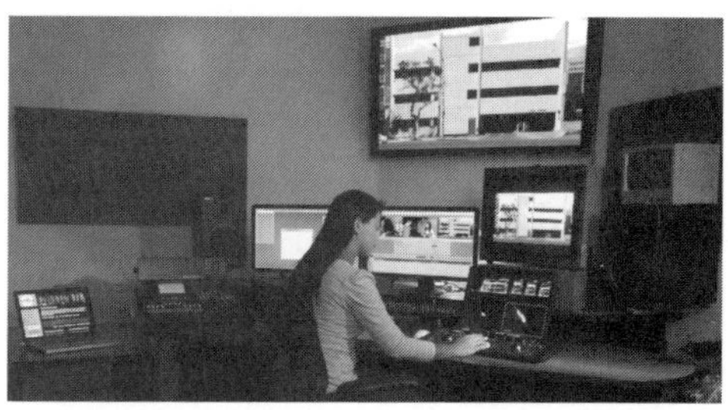

Finishing at a post house. *Photo courtesy of AlphaDogs.*

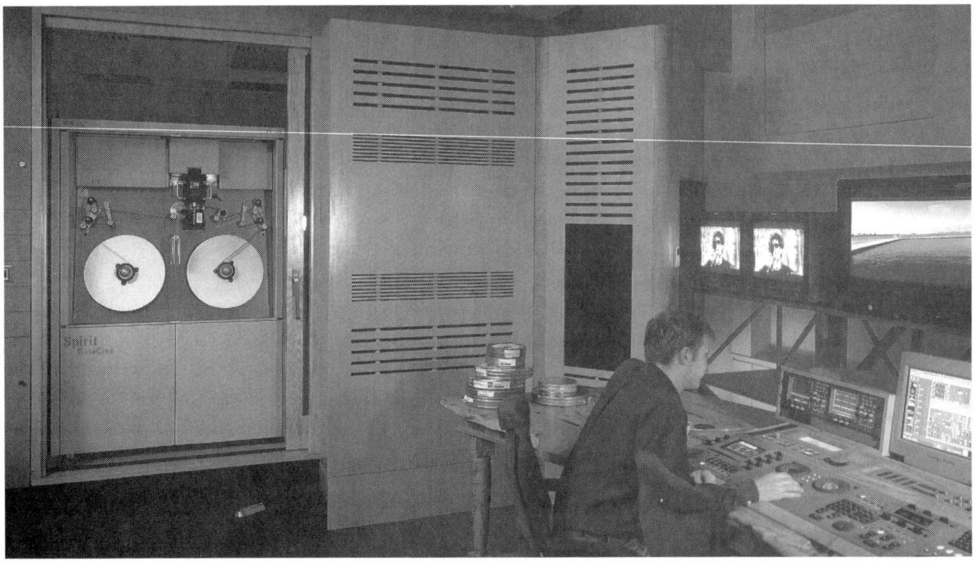

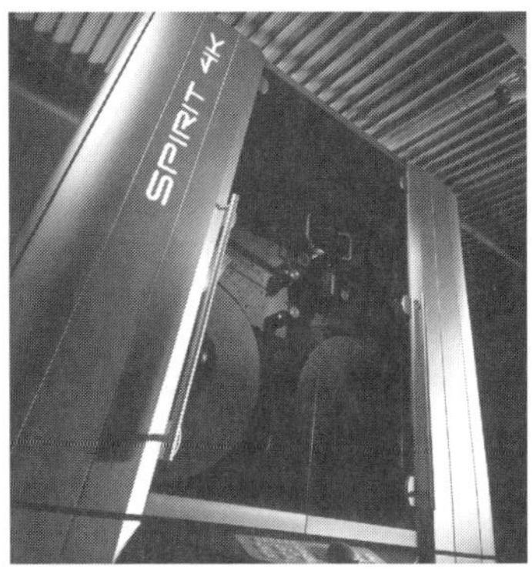

ABOVE: Sometimes referred to as the DI lab due to its multitasking abilities, the DI workstation interfaces with the scanner and other devices in the pipeline along with editing, color grading, compositing VFX, and creating the master file. *Photo courtesy of Digital Film Technology and the New Hat Post facility.* **RIGHT:** Spirit 4K DataCine film scanner. *Photo courtesy of Digital Film Technology and the New Hat Post facility.*

DI process

> The show is a blank canvas; the DI writes the picture. The process has brought about more collaboration between the DP and postproduction than ever before. Together we can create a look for every state of mind of a picture. More and more, we get the script and make our recommendations before the budget is set and the show begins to shoot. —**PETER WARE,** COO and Senior VP of Worldwide Production, Stargate Digital Films

The DI process begins with the commandeering of all the highest quality data files and media—file, film, and/or tape—for the images in the final locked cut. If the medium is film, the *OCN,* original camera negative, will be used. The DI process proceeds in four steps: transfer, conform, edit, and master as described and charted below.

Transfer

The post house transfers all media to digital data: uncompressed tapes are captured, digital files are imported, and the OCN as well as positive film are scanned via a film scanner or datacine machine. A 2K file contains the minimum amount of data necessary for color grading and other finishing work.

Conform

The DI editor imports files with your show's data into the DI workstation. The editor then conforms the media to the locked cut and creates a DPX (digital picture exchange) file commonly referred to by its resolution e.g., a 2K file, 4K file, etc.

Edit

> The DI is the most significant contribution that has happened to image making since I've been a cinematographer . . . You can do different timings and watch them, and you can flip through different versions of the timings, to see which way you want to go. —**ROGER DEAKINS**, ASC, Oscar winner for Best Achievement in Cinematography for the films *1917* and *Blade Runner 2049*. Also known for *Skyfall, Fargo, A Serious Man, Revolutionary Road*, and *O Brother, Where Art Thou*? which in 2000, was the first feature to use the DI process

In DI work, editing means image manipulation and the final finishing processes; the locked cut is not re-edited. This is the creative phase of the DI process where you and the DP sit with the colorist to grade (color time) the picture and achieve the precise look you desire. The WYSIWYG* principle applies, as with each evolving version you view your vision anew, exactly how the audience will see it. The colorist may create a *LUT* (look up table) with different color grades for each deliverable: e.g., HDTV, disk, film, airline version, etc.

This phase can also include titling, resizing frames, and finalizing opticals as well as panning, scanning, and stabilizing the images. In short, this phase combines the online process with the film lab process, perfecting the digital file for output to film, file, tape, or disk. Once you approve all the edits, the DI is complete.

Master

The completed DI is used to make the digital masters (DPX files) for all the different deliverables and then archived. There are three types of masters: film, disk, and file.

Film master

> We believe that digital cinema is not a product, but a process . . . a system that begins with the conversion of film images to high quality digital files that are color graded by the cinematographer. Once the look is locked, we ensure that it is faithfully presented to audiences. —**ROBERT J. MAYSON**, former General Manager and VP of Digital Motion Imaging Digital Systems, Eastman Kodak Company

The film master known as the *DCDM* (Digital Cinema Distribution Master) becomes a digital *AP* (answer print) for digital projection. The digital AP is turned into a *DCP* (digital cinema package) which consists of encrypted files. The DCP arrives at theaters via hard drive, satellite, or the internet.

* What you see is what you get.

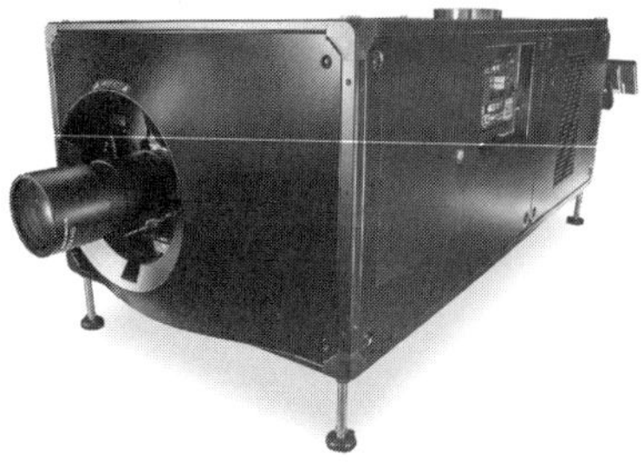

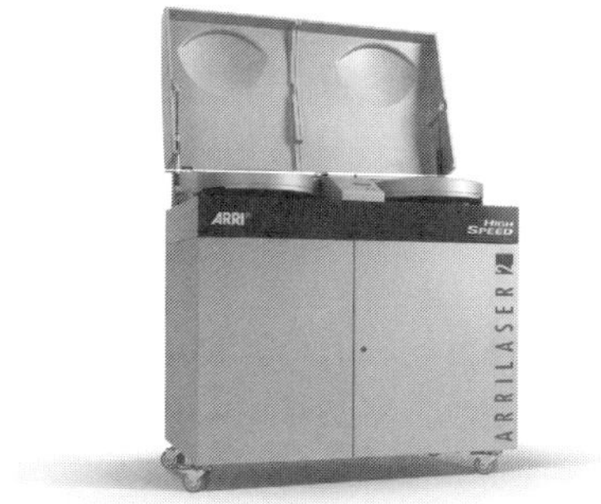

LEFT: Christie's top of the line digital projector projects 4K movies, 2D and 3D, with HFR (high frame rate) up to 120 fps. Digital theater projection is nearly universal—99% in U.S. and 97% for the rest of the world with ongoing conversion—while film projection carries on in museums, IMAX theatres, special events, and at the insistence of a few Hollywood directors with clout. *Photo courtesy of Christie.* **RIGHT:** Winner of an Academy Award of Merit in 2012, the *ARRILASER* film recorder receives the DI file and records its digital images onto film negative. *Photo courtesy of ARRILASER.*

For film print projection, a film recorder makes an internegative from the digital AP. The DI process eliminates the optical print and interpositive steps of the traditional photochemical lab finish and can produce 35mm, 70mm, and IMAX prints. The print-master is added to the AP and the audio is encoded. From the internegative, release prints are struck, distributed, and projected in the traditional way.

Disk and file master

A master file is created for making disks (one for DVD and one for Blu-ray) and the sound mix is added to it. Other master files are created for digital broadcast, trailers, and promo material, including high and low resolution requirements, such as print media and web content.

COLOR GRADING A.K.A. COLOR CORRECTING OR COLOR TIMING

> Color changes the story and how you feel about it. So, you want to make the color flow from shot to shot, and scene to scene. —**RICH MONTEZ**, colorist, Whipping Post Services

Color grading, a.k.a. color correcting, color matching, or color timing lets the images you shot say what you want in terms of color and lighting. Akin to the music in your film, color grading visually sets a mood, affecting viewers' emotions. You can correct color from shot to shot in each scene e.g., by making all the skin tones match. You can also create a color palette and establish a visual style and apply them to your show. With today's sophisticated mattes, masks, and key tools you can readily isolate areas within shots for different treatment.

Digital Intermediate Workflow

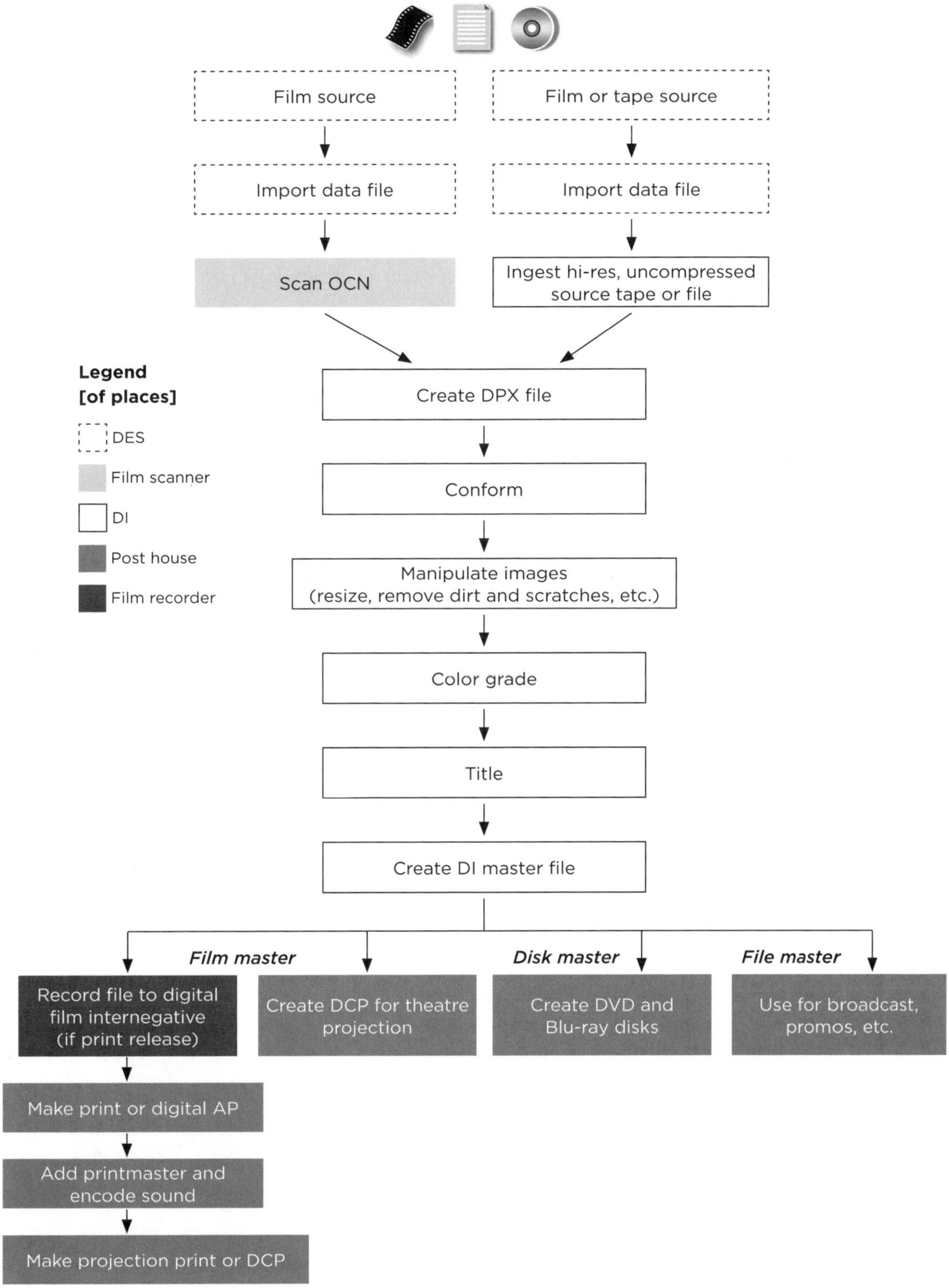

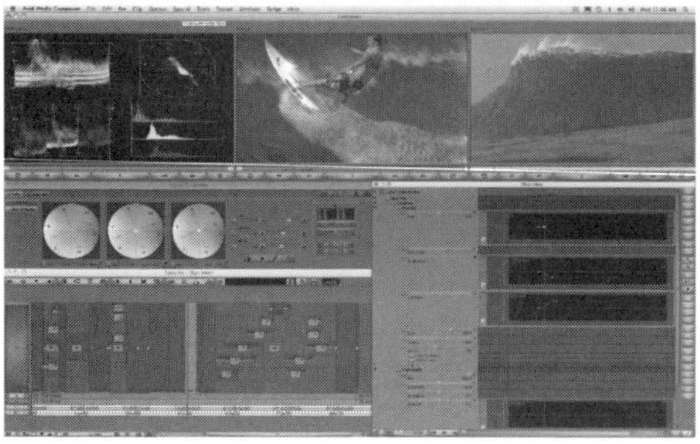

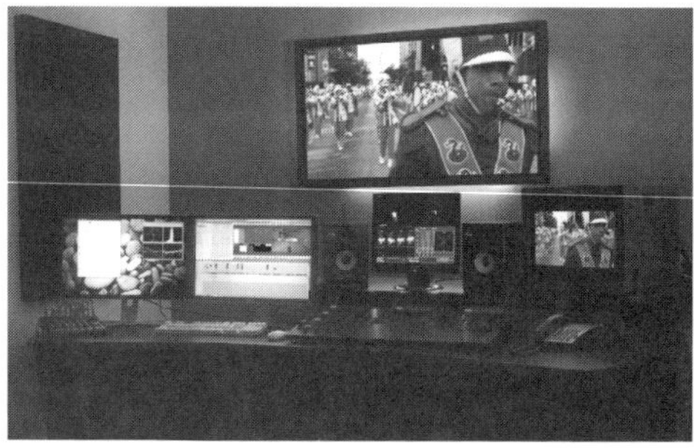

left: Avid color corrector. *Photo courtesy of Avid.* right: Color correction suite at post house. *Photo courtesy of AlphaDogs.*

Color grading is performed by your editor on their digital system or by a colorist sitting with your DP at a post house. You can be present to oversee the work or review scenes along the way until the grading is complete and you give your final approval*.

Editor color grades

Having relinked to the high-res native files, your editor works through the timeline of the Final Cut, keeping the color consistent from shot to shot within each scene. The color grading tools on digital editing systems allows editors to adjust skin tones, sharpen or diffuse light, saturate or desaturate images, and fine-tune color in a myriad of other ways.

Post house color grades

> You're creating the last version of your film, and it's so important to find a good colorist and a good facility that is willing to work with you, in order to finish the right way. —**RYAN PIERS WILLIAMS**, director, *X/Y* and *Dryland*

You start at the post house by spotting the show in its hi-res glory with the colorist and your DP who will be your collaborators for this phase.

Preliminary color grading

> The meat and potatoes of what a colorist does is to make stuff cut. —**RICH MONTEZ**

On some shows, chiefly TV series with established "looks" and locations, the colorist sets initial color values and performs preliminary color correction on dailies. This is done to maintain continuity during offline editing and cut down the time required for color grading following online. Shows that used a *DIT* (data image technician) will also need less grading and be aided by the *LUT* (look up table), a software chart containing the color value of each image.

* A major exception is episodic TV where the AP will be in charge of reviewing and approving color correction.

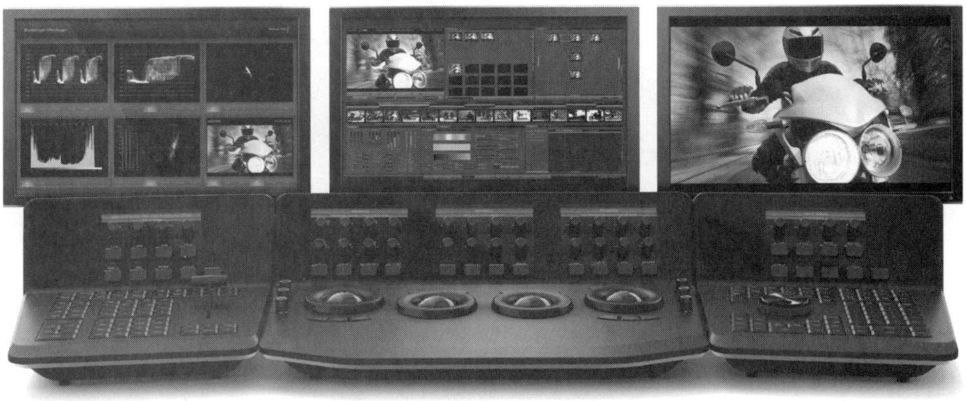

DaVinci Resolve, a popular color grading system. *Photo courtesy of Blackmagic Design.*

The process

Colorists correct image data that is encoded in three channels of a color space,* RGB (red, green, blue), being the model most frequently used. They fix white balance problems, lighting issues, and address black levels, *crushing the blacks*** if desired. They also grade with the viewing venue in mind, considering whether the lighting will be bright or dim. Colorists often start with a wide shot to establish the look, then match the rest of the scene's shots to it. For dialogue scenes, many begin by grading skin tones.

What you'll be working on

The specific parameters you'll be finessing in addition to those already mentioned include:

Chrominance (chroma). The color data of each shot, e.g., hue and saturation.

Hue. Amount of color in a video image or signal.

Saturation. The amount of color—intense to desaturated (colorless).

Color cast. Unnatural tint to a color due the white balance being off or mixed light sources.

Color gamut. Range of colors and brightness that a device displays and the colorist has to work within.

Luminance (luma). Noncolor portion of image that holds the brightness and contrast.

Dynamic range. Maintains the relationship between the black and white levels when you're correcting luminance.

Temperature. Warmth or coolness of a color.

---

* The organization of colors usually defined by the parameters of a physical device e.g., a monitor or a projector with the goal of portraying color uniformly across different devices.

** Removing all light from the darkest parts of an image to decrease detail in the shadows, increase the contrast, and effect a more eye-popping picture.

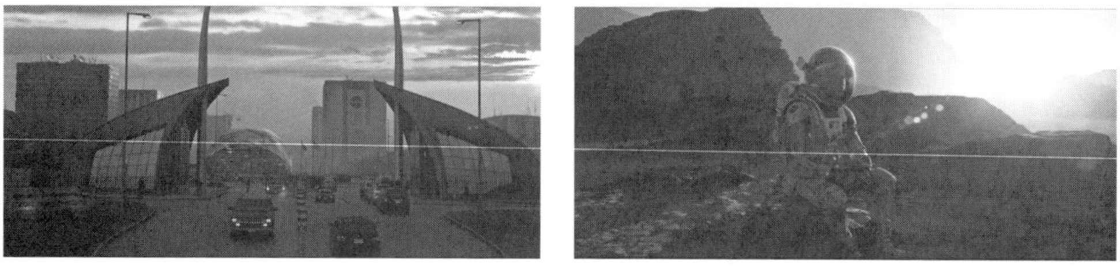

Vivid examples of color temperature are the gray Earth tones and red Mars tones in *The Martian* (2015).

What you can achieve

You can correct images to match other shots in a scene and to appear as you intended when you shot them. You can warm up scenes or cool them down and employ color filters—blue, red, yellow, sepia, etc.—to set a mood either subtly or blatantly. You can desaturate a scene over time or desaturate an isolated part of an image as part of a flashback, flashforward, or fantasy scene.

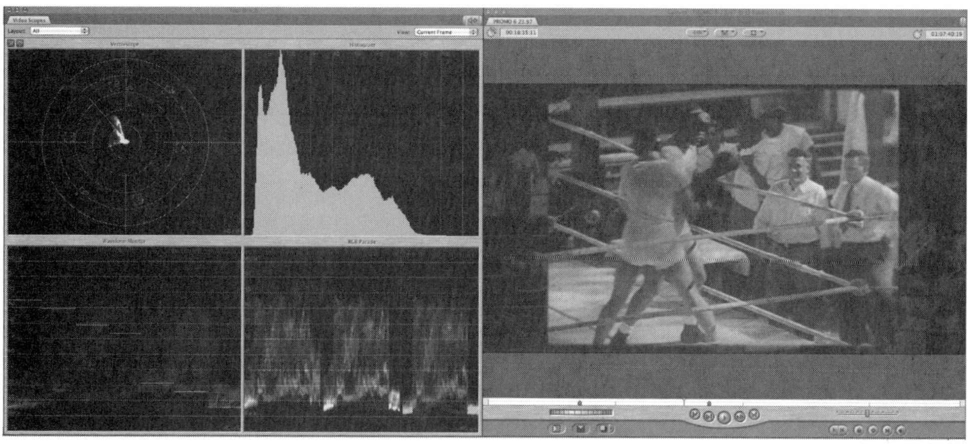

Color scopes on Final Cut Pro clockwise from top: vectorscope, histogram, RGB, and waveform.

Color scopes

You cannot rely entirely on your eyes to judge color. Nor can you rely on devices, as there is no uniformity from one screen to another. Knowing this, colorists trust in a number of digital software scopes for consistent, accurate readings of color and brightness levels, and for meeting broadcast signal standards. The primary scopes they rely on are the:

Waveform. Displays luminance values so you can see how light or dark your images are and work with their highlights and shadows.

RGB parade. A type of Waveform that displays the three colors—red, green, and blue—separately, side by side.

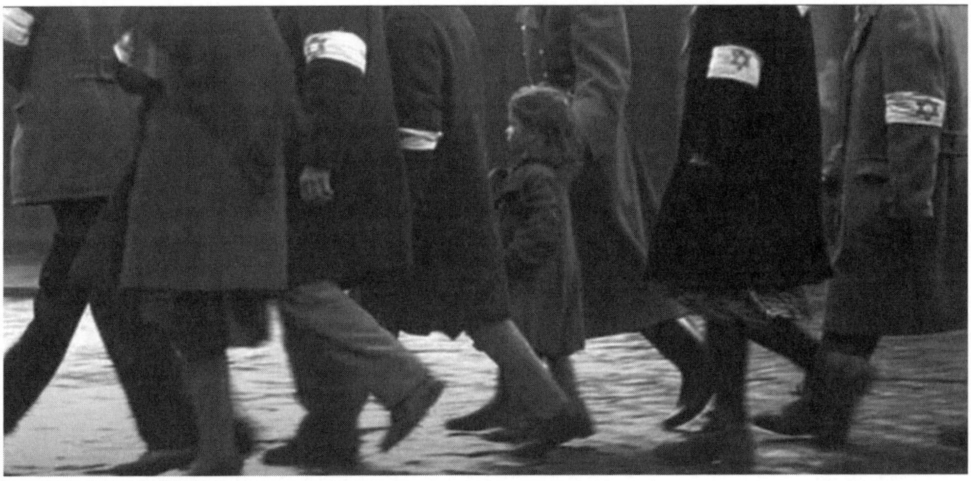

The color in *Schindler's List* (1993) ranges from one end of the gray scale to the other, except for the little girl in the blood red coat, who symbolizes the million murdered Jewish children.

Histogram. Another type of Waveform scope that shows distribution of bright and dark pixels in your image. Individual RGB histograms show the level of each color.

Vectorscope. Measures hue and saturation and is particularly useful for correcting skin tones.

Multiple deliverables

How do you color grade when you're delivering for the theater, DVD, and VOD? The best advice is not to grade for your main deliverable, and not to pick a happy medium for all, but to grade for each deliverable and create a LUT for each one. Your work deserves it.

What color grading produces

Color grading produces a new show master, the CTM (color timed master) a.k.a. CCM (color-corrected master). The CTM becomes the new edited master to which your titles will be added, and the final sound mix will be laid back.

FINAL STEPS: EXPORTING AND DELIVERING

After color grading, the titles and credits will be added to your show. Then the post house will *layback* (add) the sound mix to your CTM or your editor will output the mixed, color graded show from their digital editing system for distribution of your final deliverables.

Editor finishes show

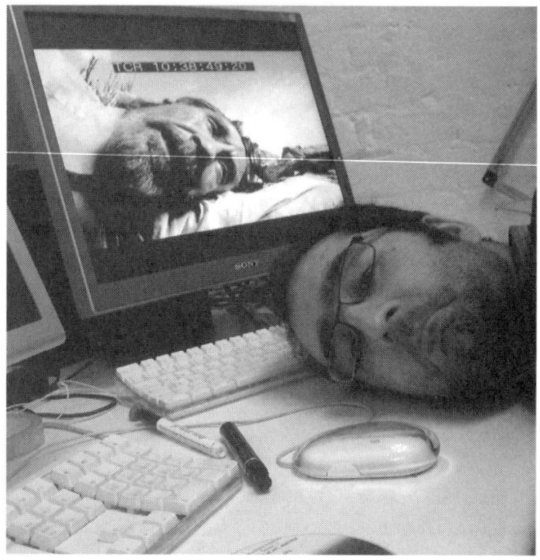

Editor finishes. *Photo courtesy of Sandip Mahal.*

Your editor will upload your show to the internet or company server or output it to disk to exhibit and distribute it. It's common to have multiple deliverables with different delivery requirements. You or your post supervisor need to keep on top of required formats. For instance, *IMF* (Interoperable Master Format), an emerging global format now required by Netflix, aims to cut down on the work by creating a standard package.

Post house finishes show

In addition to adding the sound mix to your CTM, the post house may *sweeten* (fine tune) the audio at your request or the producer's. Sweetening entails adding some final SFX or music or making other adjustments. On broadcast and other shows, the AP or post supervisor oversees most of these finishing processes while you and the editor move on to a new episode or project. You may review the show at various junctures, e.g., after sweetening or before it ships. Additionally, you may oversee the creation of the DVD of your movie if it includes extras such as an interview with you and others or dropped scenes and requires a graphic style.

Formatting the show

Your post house will make sure your show is formatted properly and meets delivery specs for broadcast, mobile devices, etc. Formatting encompasses putting in black for commercials to be dropped in at the network, adding closed captioning, and inserting bumpers and previews. Post house editors will also create a textless version of credits and titles for foreign versions and for creating disk and VOD menus as well as for marketing and publicity materials. They will also QC the show—check it for quality control—and be responsible for any problems.

Delivery

The AP or post supervisor oversees the uploading, shipping, and delivery of all elements required by broadcasters and exhibitors, as well as the dispatch of materials to the trailer, promo house, and marketing company.

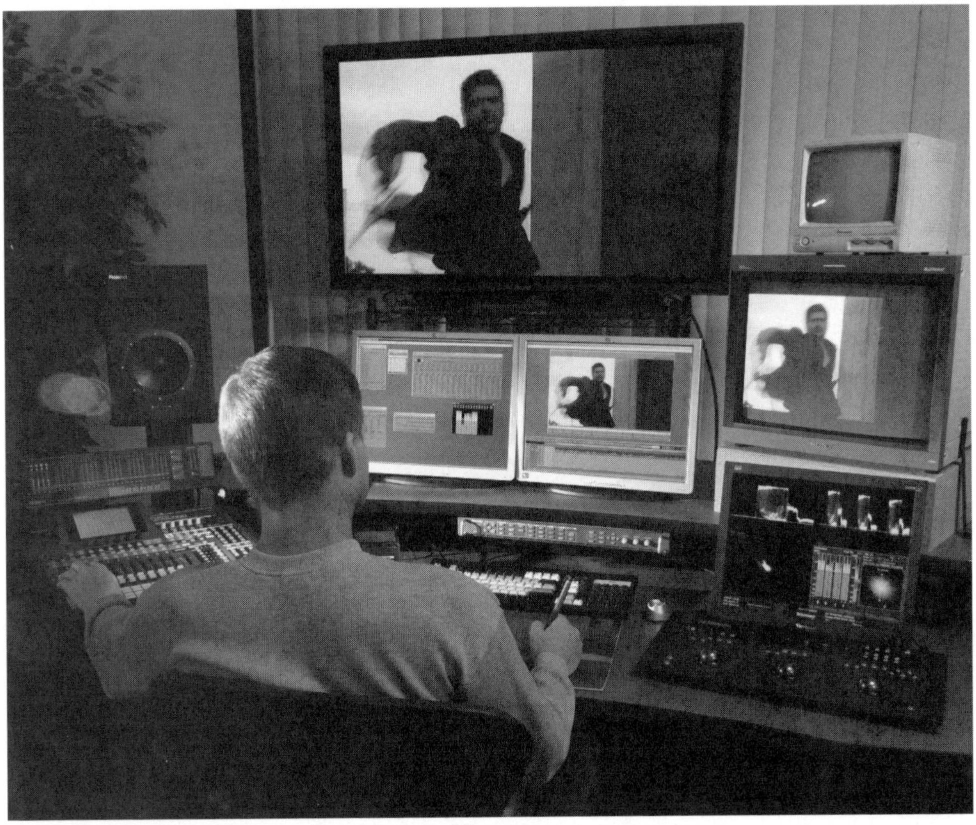

Finish at post house. *Photo courtesy of AlphaDogs*

TRAILERS

> They give away too much of the movie. They're better than the films. They only show the spectacular parts. All the best jokes are in the trailer. They lie. They're the best part of going to the movies. They're too loud. —**LISA KERNAN**, from her book *Coming Attractions: Reading Movie Trailers*

If you've written, directed, and financed your film, you may create your movie's trailer. Otherwise, unless it's written in your contract, more than likely you'll have no say as the distribution company typically creates the trailer. Hopefully, you'll at least be consulted, so a working knowledge of what goes into a trailer is helpful.

Challenge

The challenge of cutting trailers is to tell and sell the story of a story in 90 seconds or less. To pull off this micro mini-movie, it's best to divorce yourself from the order of your show's story and to disclose just enough to entice your audience.

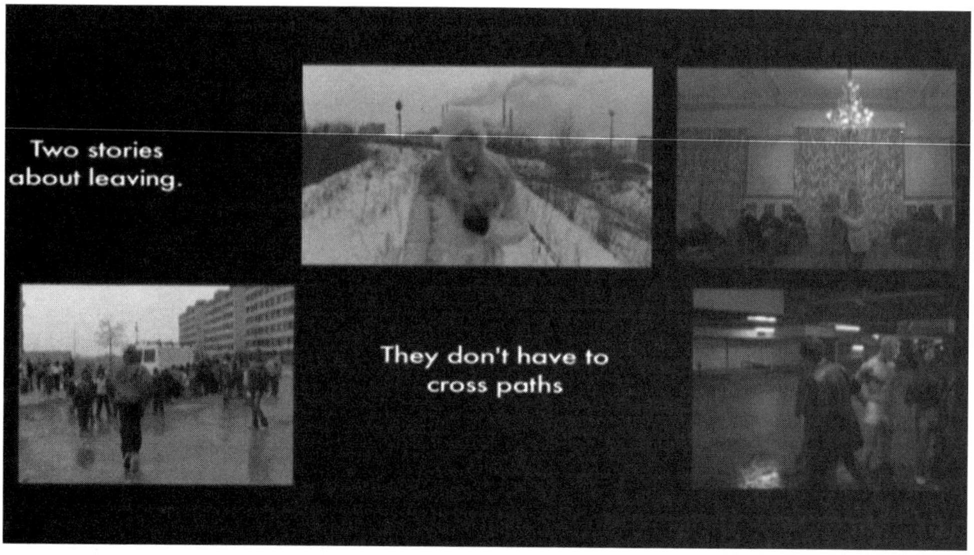

This unique trailer for the Austrian film *Import Export* (2007) consists of multiple matte shots and frames of text on a horizontal split screen that move—like filmstrips—in opposite directions (top strip to left, bottom strip to right).

Attitude

You may want nothing to do with the marketing side of things, including trailer making. You may have contradictory attitudes toward trailers. Moviegoers can use them to reject your movie and save themselves time and money. They can dismiss them as crass commercials and not worry about entering a theatre in the middle of them. On the other hand, IFC (the Independent Film Channel) believes, ". . . trailers provide a version of cinema that's essentially utopian, in which every film is perfect, if only for two and a half minutes." As such, trailers provide you with an avenue for creating a mini-film and letting people know why you think your movie is worth plunking down their hard-earned dollars.

Creation

The editor receives the edited scenes for the majority of the movie, and has a week or two to cut them to trailer length—two minutes or less usually. A knowledge of music and how to seamlessly join musical phrases is invaluable since fractions of different types of music are routinely used to pull the trailer together and highlight its action and scenes. Trailer editors use VO, wipes and other effects, and titles along with clips and shots from the movie in ways that reflect editing styles and current culture that can break through to new editing styles.

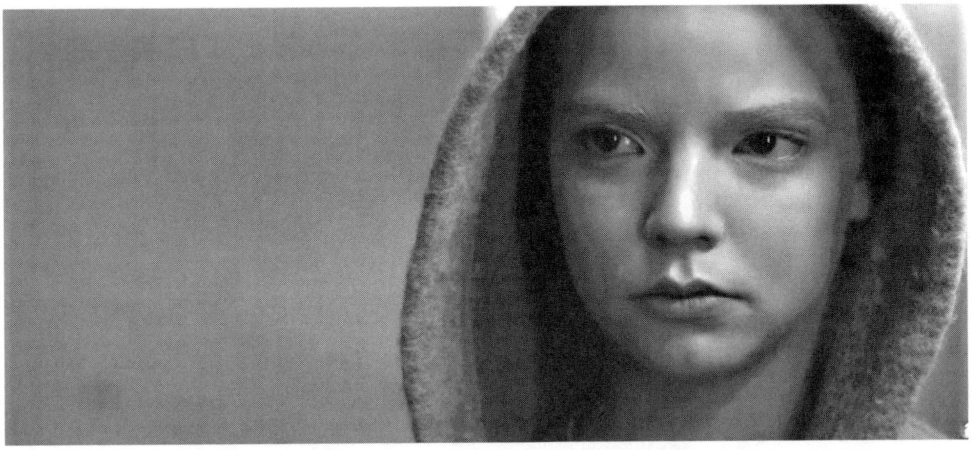

To create the trailer for its AI horror film *Morgan* (2016), 20th Century Fox tapped IBM to use AI. IBM researchers fed Watson, the AI software, 100 trailers and the entire movie along with recognition information. Watson selected 10 scenes for the editor to cut. Music was added and the trailer was finished in 24 hours, startling filmmakers, and researchers alike.

ARCHIVING

> I'm really terrified that once I die, all the work I've created will vanish with me.
>
> It's essential for every filmmaker to pay attention to preserving their work for future generations, as well as for future revenue options. —**INDIE FILMMAKERS' COMMENTS FROM AMPAS,** "The Digital Dilemma 2: Perspectives from Independent Filmmakers, Documentarians, and Nonprofit Audiovisual Archives."

Out of sight, out of mind: Where will the show you gave your life over to live after exhibition? You've been so occupied with getting the film made that its future life has been the last thing on your mind. This final section presents the current challenges and options for preserving your work for posterity and continued viewing.

AMPAS* studies

> The problems of "data extinction" are only growing, as more and more aspects of human activity move to the digital domain. —**AMPAS,** "The Digital Dilemma: Strategic Issues in Archiving and Accessing Digital Motion Picture Materials."

Films are being preserved at hundreds of archives, libraries, universities, studios, and TV stations across the U.S. In 2007, AMPAS probed the preservation of studio-made motion pictures and published "The Digital Dilemma," an 84-page paper. Four years later, the Academy put out "The Digital Dilemma 2," a 135-page report on independent filmmakers and archiving. So, what is the dilemma? Although film has been a trusted archival medium for decades and tape and digital files have been used for years, there is no standard, budget friendly solution that archivists view as guaranteeing future longevity of data or of devices to read the data.

* Academy of Motion Picture Arts and Sciences, bestower of the Academy Awards.

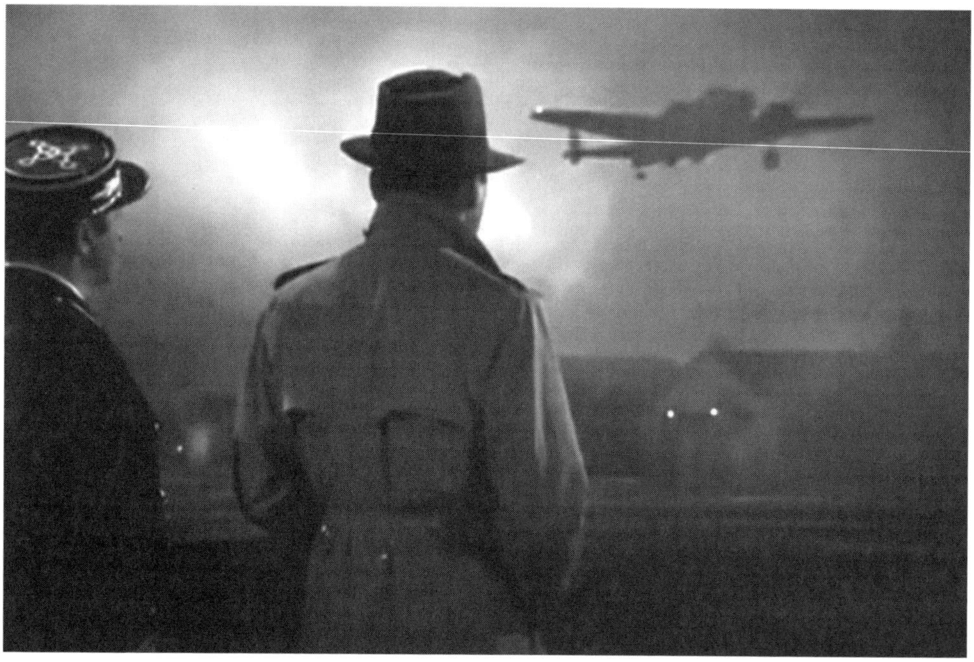

Digitally restored on its 70th birthday, *Casablanca* (1942) plays on via DVD and Blu-ray.

Digitally yours forever? Archival solutions

How are images and sounds being preserved? The four options are detailed below, followed by a summary table.

1) On film

The major studios are archiving the OCN (original camera negative) from shows shot photochemically on film as well as the internegative for shows shot digitally at 4K and above and scanned to film via the DI process. Vaulted like Sleeping Beauty in climate controlled rooms with passive deterioration detectors and established inspection protocols, these film elements can reputedly survive for a century.

For indies, this route is financially prohibitive.

2) Digitally

Cold storage isn't enough for the mass of digital data which includes files, hard disk drives, DVDs, and Blu-rays. Digital data demands active oversight on a continuing basis to ensure access to the data. To avoid digital decay, data management requires.

- Backing up the data to several drives in several locations;
- Routinely verifying the data to make sure it's pristine;

- Transcoding it to new formats and drives as they appear to have some staying power.

Film, and tape formats are being converted to digital data during the post process on a daily basis. Dealing with digital data presents a huge challenge due to its many potential failure points—computer, disk, hard drive, network, software, the actual media itself, etc.,—and its short cycle of technical obsolescence including file formats, drives, and data readers.

Expense and promise

In addition to longevity and reliability issues, another drawback to digital archiving is its price tag; storing a 4K print costs 1100% more than storing a film master. Engineers at work on this include those as Millenniata, Inc. which offers M-DISC, an optical storage solution the company claims will last almost 1,000 years.

The promise of digital archiving is immense in terms of accessibility and revenue. For years now we've witnessed the proliferation of DVDs and downloading of old and new movies and TV shows. Your work could be seen for several lifetimes past yours if digital archives become revenue generating enterprises. The paradox is that digital restoration is saving lost films, and archiving film negative is saving digitally shot shows.

3) On tape

If stored properly in a cool room, tape material is relatively simple to preserve and will last for decades, as long as the necessary recording and playback systems are retained. LTO (linear tape-open), a magnetic tape format, has been a standard, low-cost option for years. However, it has a hidden cost: You need to buy and make new tapes because LTO technology has been advancing in less than the certified 10-year LTO life span.

A more recent system, DOTS (Digital Optical Technology System), a.k.a. Digi Dots, writes digital files onto a metal alloy tape and can be stored at room temperature with no magnetic issues. On their website, inventor Group 47 promises that Digi Dots are "archival for no less than 100 years."

4) In the Cloud

Since you're probably already using the cloud for sharing and working on footage, the pros and cons of using it for archiving are summarized along with the other current solutions in the table below.

ARCHIVAL FORMATS

Format	Pros	Cons
Film (OCN) 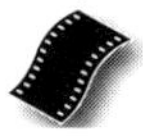	• Proven to last 100 years.	• $
Digital 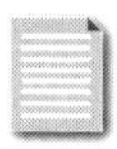	• Used to restore old films e.g., *Napoleon*. • Accessibility: Archival library potentially available to consumers for download.	• Rapid obsolescence of technology. • Failure of equipment. • $ for 4K and up scans. • Vulnerable to virus and hacking.
LTO tape 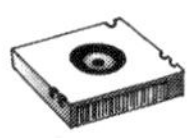	• Storage capability. • New formats promise longevity. • $	• Unproven. • Equipment obsolescence and durability.
Cloud 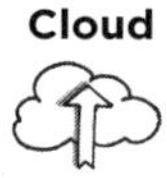	• Accessibility • $	• Data security. • Placing trust in a third party organization. • Retrieving large show with petabytes of images. • $ when retrieving frequently.

Conclusion

> The work we do becomes part of our collective history, even when it was not initially intended to be. —**AMPAS, "The Digital Dilemma 2"**

To preserve your work for future audiences and generations, store your show on the current, most durable format you can afford. Maintain and revisit the storage format and migrate to better solutions as they develop.

LAST WORD

Congratulations! Your show is on the air, up on the Web, headed toward home entertainment centers, or in theatres. Time to recuperate and look for the next job where the planning and shooting, editing, and delivering cycle begins anew.

WHAT DIRECTORS SHOULD KNOW ABOUT FINISHING AND DELIVERING

- ☐ Opening titles can clue your audience into your film's plot, location, time period, style, characters, and, along with music, help establish its emotional tone or viewpoint.
- ☐ A DI corrals all source formats to create a digital file of your locked cut for the final finishing processes that produce your final deliverable(s) on film, disk, or file for projection, streaming, or broadcast.
- ☐ Color grading allows your images to say what you want in terms of color and lighting and to visually set a mood, affect viewers' emotions, create a color palette, and establish a visual style.
- ☐ It's common to have multiple deliverables (mobile devices, the internet, VOD, etc.) with different delivery requirements. You or your AP, post supervisor, or post house must be aware of and meet all delivery specifications, and dispatch necessary materials to the trailer, promo house, and marketing companies.
- ☐ When you make a trailer, you create a mini-film—the story of a story. It requires divorcing yourself from the story order of your show and deft editing of expository, action, and dialogue scenes along with music. Avoid giving away too much of the plot.
- ☐ Archiving your show to the current, most durable format you can afford and migrating it to future technologies as they develop preserves your work for future audiences and revenues.

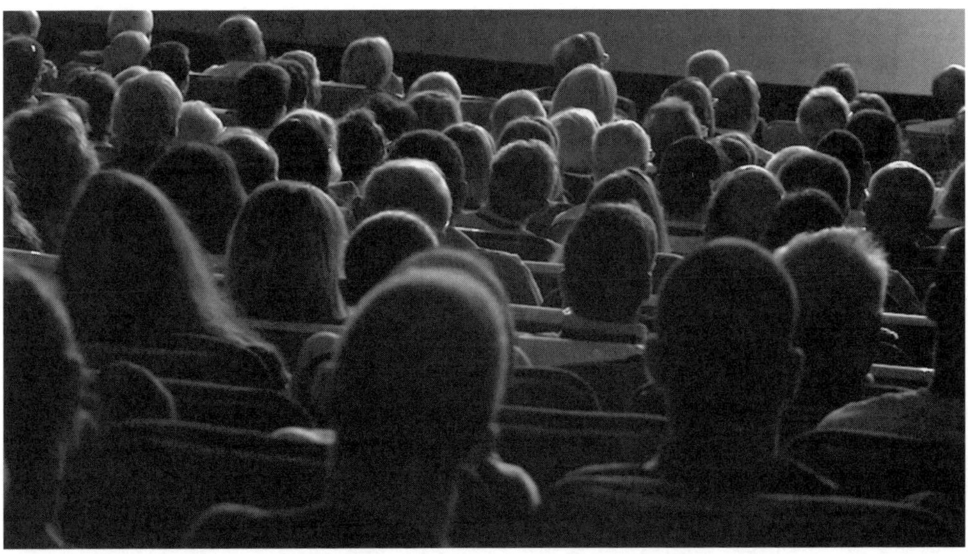

Reaching your audience from *Making Waves: The Art of Cinematic Sound* (2019)

AFTERWORD

With your newfound postproduction knowledge, you can now plan, shoot, and shape your show more astutely right from the beginning. I wish you many creative, collaborative journeys. A posse of editor-collaborators are ready to join you, so saddle up and ride off toward the cinemascape of tomorrow.

ACKNOWLEDGEMENTS

None of this would be possible without a posse of generous experts beside me. Unbridled thanks to:

Michael Wiese for proposing this book.

Jayne Weber for her illustrious drawings.

Jay Scherberth for countless screen shots, lunches, and an ongoing friendship ever since we met in a cutting room.

Steve McCord, Lori and Bruce Motyer, and Fawn Yacker for being savvy, supportive sounding boards.

Ally Acker of Reel Women: Pioneers of the Cinema, Professor James Forsher, Editors Guild board member Sharon Smith Holley, Director Jill Lessard of the Community Media Center of the County of Marin, and Victoria Rose Sampson for providing significant photo help.

Doreen Alexander Child for enthusiastically jumping on board and copy editing. Writers need editors too.

For puzzling out over 450 images along with the text of this book, praise and thanks to layout artist Debbie Berne.

Ken Lee for shepherding the book from the starting line to the finish line.

Sherry Green, for being there, book after book as only a spouse can be.

PERMISSIONS

All illustrations are by Jayne Weber. All charts are by the author. All quotes, unless spoken in the author's presence, are credited in the Bibliography.

The author is grateful to the following virtual friends as well as actual friends for their time and effort in providing or directing her toward photo material: Ally Acker of Reel Women: Pioneers of the Cinema, Sandra Adair, AlphaDogs, Marty Barkan, Lillian Benson, Kim Bova, Bart Brevé, Stephanie Brown, Dann Cahn Jr., Bruce Cannon, Jonathan Dayton, Leonard DeGraaf, Anedra Edwards, David Evans of the Magic Lantern Society, Valerie Faris, Nancy Frazen, Professor James Forsher, Ginny Hashii, Sharon Smith Holley, Suhail Kafity, Jill Lessard, Sandip Mahal, David Mallory, Pamela Martin, Lloyd Minthorne at Synoptic Productions, Steve Mirkovich, Glenn T. Morgan, Sue Odjakjian, Matt Orfalea, AnnaLee Pauls at the Special Collections of Princeton Library, Les Perkins, Justin Russell, Victoria Rose Sampson, Jay Scherberth, Chris Senchack, Omid Shamsapour, John Singletary, Joe Staton, Tom Turley, Luyen "Lu" Vu, Scott Ward, the Jack and Beverly Wilgus History of Photography Collection, and Jacques Zanetti.

The author acknowledges the copyright owners of the following motion pictures from which single frames have been used in this book for purposes of commentary, criticism, and scholarship under the Fair Use Doctrine.

127 Hours ©2010 20th Century Fox, All Rights Reserved.

2001: A Space Odyssey ©1968 MGM, All Rights Reserved.

20 Feet from Stardom ©2013 The Weinstein Company, All Rights Reserved.

Alice in Wonderland 3D ©2010 Walt Disney Productions, All Rights Reserved.

American Factory ©2019 Higher Ground Productions, All Rights Reserved.

Apocalypse Now ©1979 Zoetrope, All Rights Reserved.

A Beautiful Mind ©2001 Imagine Entertainment, All Rights Reserved.

A Secret Love ©2020 Blumhouse Productions, All Rights Reserved.

A Single Man ©2009 The Weinstein Company, All Rights Reserved.

Avatar ©2009 20th Century Fox, All Rights Reserved.

Babel ©2006 Paramount/Vantage, All Rights Reserved.

Bonnie and Clyde ©1967 Warner Bros, All Rights Reserved.

Bored to Death, "The Case of the Missing Screenplay" ©2009 HBO, Inc., All Rights Reserved.

Breaking Bad ©2008 High Bridge Entertainment, All Rights Reserved.

Breathless ©1960 Georges de Beauregard Productions, All Rights Reserved.

Carrie ©1976 Red Bank Films, All Rights Reserved.

Cars ©2006 Disney/Pixar, All Rights Reserved.

Casablanca ©1942 Warner Bros, All Rights Reserved.

Cast Away ©2000 20th Century Fox, All Rights Reserved.

Cave of Forgotten Dreams, ©2010 Creative Differences and History Films, All Rights Reserved.

Citizen Kane ©1941 RKO, All Rights Reserved.

Crash ©2004 Lions Gate Films, All Rights Reserved.

Crazy Rich Asians ©2018 Warner Bros, All Rights Reserved.

Extremely Loud, Incredibly Close ©2011 Scott Rudin Productions, All Rights Reserved.

Fahrenheit 911 ©2004 Lions Gate Films, All Rights Reserved.

Ferris Bueller's Day Off ©1986 Paramount Pictures, All Rights Reserved.

Fosse/Verdon ©2019 West Egg Studios, All Rights Reserved.

Fruitvale Station ©2013 Significant Films, All Rights Reserved.

Harry Potter and the Goblet of Fire ©2005 Warner Bros., All Rights Reserved.

Harry Potter and the Sorcerer's Stone ©2001 Warner Bros., All Rights Reserved.

Hero ©2004 Miramax, All Rights Reserved.

Hollywood Goes to War: The Army Air Forces 1st Motion Picture Unit ©1944 AAF, All Rights Reserved.

Hollywood ⊠Meg⊠ ©2020 Netflix, All Rights Reserved.

Import Export ©2007 Ulrich Seidi, All Rights Reserved.

Inside Daisy Clover ©1965 Warner Bros., All Rights Reserved.

Kill Bill: Vol. 2 ©2004 Miramax, All Rights Reserved.

Lady Bird ©2017 A24 and IAC Films, All Rights Reserved.

La La Land ©2016 Summit Entertainment, All Rights Reserved.

Lars and the Real Girl ©2007 MGM, All Rights Reserved.

Lawrence of Arabia ©1962 Horizon Pictures, All Rights Reserved.

Life is Beautiful ©1997 Miramax, All Rights Reserved.

Life of Pi ©2012 20th Century Fox, All Rights Reserved.

Love Actually ©2003 Universal Pictures, All Rights Reserved.

Mad Men ©2007-15 Lionsgate Television and AMC Original Productions, All Rights Reserved.

Making Waves: The Art of Cinematic Sound ©2019 Ain't Heard Nothin' Yet Corp., All Rights Reserved.

Mars Attacks! ©1996 Tim Burton Productions, Warner Bros., All Rights Reserved.

Midnight in Paris 2011 Sony Pictures Classics, All Rights Reserved.

Moonlight ©2016 Plan B Entertainment, All Rights Reserved.

Morgan ©2016 20th Century Fox, All Rights Reserved.

MTV ©1981 Viacom CBS, All Rights Reserved.

Nebraska ©2013 Blue Lake Media Fund, All Rights Reserved.

Olympia ©1938 Olympia-Film, All Rights Reserved.

Out of Africa ©1985 Universal Pictures, All Rights Reserved.

Pan's Labyrinth ©2006 Picturehouse/New Line Cinema, All Rights Reserved.

Paprika ©2006 Madhouse/Paprika Film Partners/Sony Pictures Entertainment, All Rights Reserved.

Parasite ©2019 Barunson E&A, All Rights Reserved.

Paterson ©2016 Amazon Studios and K5 International, All Rights Reserved.

Persepolis ©2007 Sony Pictures, All Rights Reserved.

Private Snafu—A Lecture on Camouflage ©1944 AAF, All Rights Reserved.

Punches and Streamers: The Making of a Film Score ©2014 Emerson College, All Rights Reserved.

Raging Bull ©1980 Chartoff-Winkler, All Rights Reserved.

Ran ©1985 Herald Ace, All Rights Reserved.

Ratatouille ©2007 Pixar and Walt Disney Pictures, All Rights Reserved.

Recorder: The Marion Stokes Project ©2019 Zeitgeist Films, All Rights Reserved.

Rocketman ©2019 Paramount Pictures, All Rights Reserved.

Roman Holiday ©1953 Paramount Pictures, All Rights Reserved.

Saving Private Ryan ©1998, DreamWorks, All Rights Reserved.

Schindler's List ©1993, Amblin Entertainment, All Rights Reserved.

Se7en ©1995, New Line Cinema, All Rights Reserved.

Selma ©2014 Pathé Productions Ltd., All Rights Reserved.

Sherlock, "A Study in Pink" ©2010 Hartswood Films, BBC Productions, & Masterpiece Theatre, All Rights Reserved.

Slumdog Millionaire ©2008 Fox Searchlight Pictures, All Rights Reserved.

Snowpiercer ©2013 The Weinstein Company, All Rights Reserved.

Some Like it Hot ©1959 United Artists, All Rights Reserved.

Star Wars ©1977 Lucasfilms Ltd, All Rights Reserved.

Steamboat Willie ©1928 Walt Disney Pictures©2004

Tangerine ©2015 Magnolia Pictures, All Rights Reserved.

The Aviator ©2004 Miramax, All Rights Reserved.

The Betrayal ©2008 The Cinema Guild, All Rights Reserved.

The Birds ©1963 Alfred J. Hitchcock Productions, All Rights Reserved.

The Bourne Ultimatum ©2007 Universal Pictures, All Rights Reserved.

The Call of the Wild ©2020 TSG Entertainment, All Rights Reserved.

The Civil War ©1990 Florentine Films, All Rights Reserved.

The Cutting Edge: The Magic of Movie Editing ©2004 Warner Bros., All Rights Reserved.

The Editor (movie poster) ©2014 Adam Brooks and Astron-6, All Rights Reserved.

The Jazz Singer ©1927 Warner Bros., All Rights Reserved.

The Heretics ©2009 No More Nice Girls Productions, All Rights Reserved.

The Hobbit: The Battle of the Five Armies ©2014 New Line Cinema, MGM, and WingNut Films, All Rights Reserved.

The Hurt Locker ©2008 Voltage Pictures, All Rights Reserved.

The Lady Eve ©1941 Paramount Pictures, All Rights Reserved.

The Last Black Man in San Francisco ©2019 Plan B Entertainment, All Rights Reserved.

The Man with a Movie Camera ©1929 VUKFU, All Rights Reserved.

The Martian ©2015 20th Century Fox, All Rights Reserved.

The Pawnbroker ©1964 The Landau Company, All Rights Reserved.

The Pink Panther Strikes Again ©1976 Amjo Productions, All Rights Reserved.

The Post ©2017 DreamWorks, All Rights Reserved.

The Social Network ©2010 Columbia Pictures, All Rights Reserved.

The Triplets of Belleville ©2003 Les Armateurs et al, All Rights Reserved.

The Wizard of Oz ©1939 MGM, All Rights Reserved.

The World Before Your Feet ©2018 Wheelhouse Creative, All Rights Reserved.

They Shall Not Grow Old ©2018 WingNut Films, All Rights Reserved.

Titanic ©1997 Paramount Pictures and 20th Century Fox, All Rights Reserved.

To Kill a Mockingbird ©1962 Universal Pictures, All Rights Reserved.

Too Big to Fail ©2011 Deuce Three Productions, All Rights Reserved.

Triumph of the Will ©1935 Transit Film GmbH, All Rights Reserved.

True Blood, "Everything is Broken" ©2011 HBO, All Rights Reserved.

United 93 ©2006 Universal Pictures, All Rights Reserved.

Vertigo ©1958 Paramount Pictures, All Rights Reserved.

WALL-E ©2008 Pixar and Walt Disney Pictures, All Rights Reserved.

Welcome to Chechnya: The Gay Purge ©2020 Public Square Films and BBC Storyville, All Rights Reserved.

When the Levees Broke: A Requiem in Four Acts ©2006-2007 HBO, All Rights Reserved.

When Harry Met Sally ©1989 Castle Rock Entertainment, All Rights Reserved.

Wonder Woman ©2017 Warner Bros., All Rights Reserved.

Woodstock ©1970 Warner Bros., All Rights Reserved.

Yentl ©1983 United Artists, All Rights Reserved.

GLOSSARY

180 degree rule. See **crossing the line.**

2-pop. A sync pop placed on the audio head leader aligned with the #2 picture frame, to serve as a sync reference during screenings, sound editing, and sound mixing. See also **sync pop.**

5.1. Sound configured with five channels: left, right, and center channels in the front and left and right surrounds. The "1" is for the LFE (low frequency effects) channel.

7.1. 5:1 plus left and right rear channels. See **5.1.**

A.C.E. American Cinema Editors. An honorary society of editors who are voted into membership based on their professional achievements, dedication to the education of others, and commitment to the craft of editing. A.C.E. always follows their name on screen. A.C.E. hosts its own editing awards ceremony after every year for which winners receive a Golden Eddie Award and runs an editing internship program.

Adobe Premiere Pro. Digital editing system manufactured by Adobe Systems.

ADR. Automated dialogue replacement. The process by which a line of dialogue is recorded and re-spoken by an actor in sync (hopefully) with the picture, to replace the original sync production line. Also referred to as looping or EPS (electronic post sync).

aliasing. An artifact that occurs while reproducing digital video or audio.

AMPAS. Academy of Motion Picture Arts and Sciences. "The Academy" hands out the annual Oscar Awards, holds screenings throughout the year to honor U.S. filmmakers, and generally promotes the recognition and preservation of motion pictures.

artifacts. Unwanted effects or distortions on a digital tape, file, or disk not found in the original (digital or analog) video or audio.

ASCAP. American Society of Composers, Authors, and Publishers. A prominent performing rights organization of which there are many. Composers and publishers affiliate with one of these organizations, which collect and pay out royalties when music they represent is exhibited in a movie theatre or aired on a television show.

aspect ratio. The width to height ratio of a frame of film or video linked to the size of the screen it will run on.

Avid. Professional digital editing system.

balance. During the mix, ensuring that all the elements—dialogue, SFX, and music—blend and can be heard.

banner. Useful, temporary graphic that functions as a placeholder (timed or untimed), until the final material can be dropped in e.g., stock shot missing, scene missing, insert commercial here, etc.

bars and tone. Video and audio references for setting up consistent video and audio levels.

black out. When a shot cuts to black.

BMI. Broadcast Music Incorporated. A prominent performing rights organization of which there are many, including ASCAP. See also **ASCAP.**

B side. Incoming shot or right side of the cut.

bumper. Five second re-cap of what just happened on a television show intended to hold the viewer's interest until after the commercial when the next segment airs.

C.A.S. Cinema Audio Society. Honorary professional organization of mixers which hosts an awards banquet and educational meetings throughout the year. C.A.S. follows a member's credit on screen.

canned music. See **source music.**

capture. Input footage from a digital tape into a digital editing system.

CCM. Color-corrected master. See also **CTM**.

CGI. Computer generated imagery. Digital effects created on computers, encompassing an ever-growing array of visual possibilities, both moving and static, animated and live action.

chroma. See **chrominance**.

chroma-key. A type of composite effect with a chroma background layer and a foreground layer which contains the image or subject. The background layer is keyed out and the subject, such as a weather forecaster, appears to be interacting with a second video layer, such as weather map. While any color can be used for the background, blue and green have proven to be the most keyable, so chroma-keying is often referred to as blue screen or green screen.

chrominance. The part of the color video signal that holds the color data. Video picture information contains two components: luminance (brightness and contrast) and chrominance (hue and saturation).

clip. Video: A shot ingested on a digital system. Audio: Distort or overmodulate an audio signal.

codec. Compressor/decompressor or encode/decode. A two-step process used in video editing, video conferencing and streaming media applications which 1) compresses huge multimedia files into smaller files so they can fit on a DVD, CD-ROM, or other media and then 2) decompresses them to their original file size, so they can be played back on a computer. Codecs can also encode and decode video signals.

color grading, a.k.a. color correcting or color timing. Changing or improving the color of a film, file, or tape image to be consistent with the desired look of the scene or project.

colorist. Telecine operator who syncs, transfers, and color grades film, file, or tape images.

composite. Create a shot by merging two or more separate images or shots.

conform. Reproduce the locked cut on the highest quality media.

continuity. Maintaining the physical relationships, performance, action, and narrative flow of the filmed scene from cut to cut (or during filming, from shot to shot).

continuity sheet. List of a show's scenes in editing order accompanied by a phrase or sentence describing what happens in each scene and its duration.

count down leader. See **Academy leader.**

coverage. Angles shot in addition to the master shot: close-ups, medium shots, over-the shoulder shots, etc.

cross-cutting. Editing two (or more) dependent lines of action together—characters, settings, or subjects—that interact directly and are aware of each other.

cross conversion. Transfer from one format of HD to another e.g., 720p to 1080i.

crossing the line. Ignoring the invisible line in every camera set up that bisects the scene horizontally at 180 degrees. Crossing the line results in two angles that when cut together appear to make people or objects jump out of position.

CTM. Color timed master. Master tape of color-corrected show created after online by the colorist.

cue. For each piece of sound or music, Sound and Music editors create a cue which consists of a brief description of the sound, its track number, and its start and end timecode.

cut negative. The original negative cut to match the locked film cut: From the cut negative, positive prints are made for movie theatres.

cut point. See **edit point**.

cut. (noun) 1) An edit 2) A series of edits 3) A completed edit or re-edit of a show. (verb) The joining together of two different shots or two parts of the same shot.

cutaway. (CA) Any shot that will be used to cut away from the main action in the master shot.

cutting on action. See action match.

DaVinci. A popular color grading and telecine machine.

dailies. Footage that arrives daily in the cutting room from the production crew normally shot the previous day.

DAW. Digital audio workstation. Computer used to record, edit, and mix sound and music.

DCP. Digital cinema package. The deliverable for digital projection.

deliverable. Materials contractually required by a distributor or network to exhibit a show such as a master tape, release print, sound elements, timing sheets, music cue sheets, and list of screen credits.

DI. See **digital intermediate.**

diegetic. Description for sounds that sync to an onscreen source e.g., a book slamming closed.

digital editing system. A computer used to edit digital audio and video input from files, film, or tape. Called by many names including digital system/editor/workstation, DES, or NLE.

digital intermediate a.k.a. digital intermediary or DI. Scanning process that brings together all source formats—film, file, and tape—to create a digital master of the locked cut for the final finishing processes, which will produce the show master on film, file, and/or tape.

digital. A digital signal that has limited variation within a small set of numerical variables. Digital formats record audio, video, and data as files composed of binary numbers (zeroes and ones) that can be read by a computer.

digitize. Input footage from an analog tape into a digital editing system.

dissolve. A transitional effect where the first/outgoing shot disappears as the second/incoming shot appears.

distribution. Phase of a project during which it's marketed and contracts are signed for exhibition in theatres or for home viewing on DVD, TV, etc. Distribution follows the postproduction phase of a project and precedes the exhibition phase.

DIT. Digital Imaging Technician. Data wrangler who works with the cinematographer during production to get the best digital images possible, by monitoring exposure and making certain camera settings such as codec and time code, creating LUTs, and ensuring that the shot images and their data are correctly transferred to the production drive, and more.

DME. Dialogue, Music and Effects. The three stems that form the mixdown of the final sound mix and are used to make the final soundtrack or Printmaster.

Dolby Atmos. Dolby Laboratories' immersive, 3D, object-based, audio surround system.

Dolby Digital. Dolby Lab's digital audio encoding technology that stores and transmits high-quality digital sound for digital formats e.g., computers, DBS, DTV, DVD, and video game consoles.

Dolby Surround. Dolby Lab's original audio surround system developed in 1977 to accompany *Star Wars,* which combines four channels LCRS onto two tracks—analog or digital—in an encoded signal for recording, projecting, and broadcasting. See also **LCRS.**

double system. Production method where audio and video are recorded on two different formats e.g., film and file and require syncing before they can be edited.

down res a.k.a. down rez or down convert. Convert from a higher resolution to a lower resolution, e.g., going from HD to SD or capturing footage in the digital editing system at a lower res than which it was shot.

DPX. Digital picture exchange. Standard file format used in DI and VFX work due to its ability to preserve the color data of scanned film negative and store the metadata associated with it.

DTS. Digital Theater System. Digital sound encoded on film, tape, and DVD and direct competition to Dolby Digital (DD). Since some theatres run DTS sound and some run DD, soundtracks are encoded with both digital tracks.

DTV. Digital broadcast TV.

dub. 1) Copy or rerecord audio and/or video. 2) The mix. See also **mix.**

duration. Length of a shot or edit on a digital or video editing system.

DV. Digital Video. Stores video, audio, and other information in digital form.

dynamics. Relationship between low and high volume on soundtracks, which if mixed correctly, will differentiate between soft and loud sounds, contain organic high points and low points and be uncompressed.

edit point. Frame that you mark and decide to edit in.

edit. (noun) A portion of a shot put into a show.

editorial. See **postproduction**.

editor's cut. See **First Cut**.

EFX. A sound effect or a special visual effect, depending on the context.

EOR. End of reel.

EPS. Electronic post sync. Another term for ADR. See also **ADR.**

EQ. Equalize. Adjust the volume level of individual frequencies of a sound in order to change its tone e.g., EQ'ing dialogue so that ADR lines match the production track.

equalize See **EQ.**

equalizer. An adjustable audio filter, measured in decibels (dB) that lowers or boosts frequency and alters amplitude.

essence media. Bits and bytes that represent the digital video and audio. Also called essence data.

essence. As opposed to metadata, the video, audio, graphics, animation, and text in a digitally edited piece.

export. Send a file out of a digital editing system.

extreme close-up. (ECU) A shot framed so tight that if it's on a person's face, you only see the eyes.

eyeline. A character's line of vision—the direction their eyes are looking.

fade in. A dissolve to a filmed shot from black, sometimes white, and once in a great while yellow, blue, or another color.

fade out. A dissolve from a filmed shot to black, sometimes white, and once in a great while yellow, blue, or another color.

FCC. Federal Communications Commission. Independent government agency that regulates interstate and international communications by radio, television, wire, satellite and cable in the US.

FCM. Frame Code Mode. Notation on a digital editing system's EDL that reports that the list is either DF (Drop Frame) or NDF (Non Drop Frame).

FCP. Final Cut Pro. See **Final Cut Pro.**

FFOA. First frame of action. First frame of a film or video after the leader, which is often black as the picture fades in. Same as FFOP.

FFOP. First frame of picture. Same as FFOA.

fill. Recycled movie film used to fill in the gaps and keep sync on sound reels where there is no sound or a portion has been removed temporarily. A film term that is also applied to digital editing where tracks and shots have electronic fill.

film lab. Facility that produces the final film reels that are projected in the theatres. The lab also creates the final special effects on film. Labs used to hum with the bustle of producing film dailies and the final prints for movie theatres. But the digital age has put this era in the past. Many film labs have teamed with postproduction facilities to stay alive.

film recorder. Machine that transfers digital images to exposed film, most often a color timed internegative. There two types of machines: the EBR and laser film recorder.

film scanner. Device that inputs OCN and outputs digital data which is used in the digital intermediate process or for digital VFX.

filter. A type of equalizing device that eliminates selected frequencies from a signal. For example, a high pass filter removes low frequencies, and allows high frequencies to pass. A low pass filter would do the reverse.

Final Cut Pro. A pro-sumer and professional digital editing system made by Apple, Inc.

First Cut., a.k.a. the editor's cut, is the First Cut put together of the show by the editor.

fix session. Post house session scheduled after the online to correct edits, add missing shots, and make dirt fixes.

flashback. Shot, sequence of shots, or scene which transports the story into the past.

flashforward. Shot, sequence of shots, or scene which transports the story into the future.

flatbed. Film editing machine where reels ran flat (horizontally).

flip. An effect where the frame is turned upside down vertically e.g., if you flop the shot of a person standing on their head, they will now stand on their feet.

flop a.k.a. mirror. Picture: An effect where the picture is turned horizontally 180 degrees, so that an object on the left side of the frame is now on the right. Sound: Turning the film track 180 degrees so it is silent when played.

Foley. Sound effects recorded in sync with specific actions on the screen. Foley is recorded by a Foley artist (a.k.a. Foley walker or Foley dancer), on a Foley stage as the picture runs on the screen.

fps. Frames per second. Rate at which frames move. Nominally film runs at 24 fps and tape at 30 fps in the U.S.

Frankenbite. Frankenstein + sound bite. New line pieced together from pieces of several lines and put in interviewee's mouth. Coined by reality TV editors, who struggle hard to tease out the veracity and continuity of the story from hours of footage.

free and clear. Music in the public domain that does not have a copyright nor require a fee. **freeze frame a.k.a. freeze or still frame.** Effect where the action holds (freezes) for as many frames as desired.

full shot. (FS) A shot framed to include the whole person, animal, or object being shot.

fully filled. Contractually required by foreign distributors, fully filled music and effects tracks are those which contain all the effects as originally mixed.

FX. Special effect. Also written F/X or referred to as VFX.

gag reel. Comic reel made of a show's outtakes and crew tomfoolery shown at the end-of the-season or wrap party. Sound effects, music, and narration are often added.

gain control. Audio pot that raises or lowers the record, mix, or playback signal strength.

gain. The increase or decrease in strength of an electrical signal measured in decibels or number-of-times of magnification. Mixers constantly "ride the gain" to ensure a consistent audio level from show start to finish.

garbage matte. A rough matte created when keying green screens to remove garbage (undesirable elements such as wires or models) or retain parts of images e.g., light spills that the green screen might wipe out.

grade. Color time a film or tape. See also **color correct** and **timing**.

gray scale. The 7-10 shades of gray, which form a test pattern that corresponds to the brightness range that a television system can reproduce. Used by cinematographers, film, and video technicians.

green screen. Special effect created by shooting a subject in front of a green (or blue) screen. Shot 1, a live action shot, is the background. Shot 2, the green screen shot, contains the subject (talent) and is the foreground. When the two shots are composited (merged), the green screen washes out, and the subject appears to react to what's happening in the background, e.g., a farmer reacting to a giant spider. See also **chroma-key**.

GVX. Graphics file.

handle. Extra frames at the head or tail of shot that allow for fades, dissolves and other effects.

hard effects. SFX created to match specific screen actions such as car bys, glass breaks, door closes, etc.

HD. High Definition, a.k.a. Hi def. High resolution television standard which uses 16:9 aspect ratio and is superior to SD (Standard Definition) due to employing more scan lines and one or two million pixels per frame, roughly five times more than SD. See also **SD**.

HDMI. High-definition multimedia interface. Compact interface that transmits uncompressed digital A & V data. HDMI also connects digital A/V sources such as DVD and Blu-ray disk players, PCs, etc., to compatible digital audio devices, computer monitors, video projectors, and digital televisions.

head. Start of shot, cut, tape, timeline, or reel.

head leader. Piece of film or a digital clip attached to the beginning of show for the purpose of maintaining sync between picture and sound. Head leader counts down from eight to two or 12 to 2 and is always followed by the FFOP.

head pop. A sync pop placed on the audio head leader aligned with the #2 picture frame to serve as a sync reference during screenings, sound editing, and sound mixing. Commonly called a 2-pop. See also **sync pop.**

hiss. Unwanted high frequency sounds attenuated through EQ'ing

hot. Loud. The VU meter is in the red.

hue. Color of a video image or signal.

Hz. Hertz. Standard unit for measuring frequency of a wave. One Hz equals one cycle per second (cps).

IATSE (IA). International Association of Theatre Stage Employees and Motion Picture Machine Operators. The umbrella union for picture and sound editors, cinematographers, and all below-the-line crafts. Within the IA, locals are divided by craft. The Editors' Guild is Local 700 and includes all picture and sound editors, assistants and apprentices as well as sound mixers and has taken in projectionists, story analysts, TDs, and videotape operators in recent years.

import. Copy a file into a digital editing system.

ingest a.k.a. input. Copy media along with data into a digital system.

in point. Starting edit point.

insert edit. In digital editing, a term for putting a clip into a sequence, so that the edits to the right of it get pushed down the timeline and time is added to the sequence for the amount of the clip's duration.

insert shot. Shot of some small but significant detail in a scene shot during postproduction on an insert stage or picked up on the set. Term used interchangeably with cutaway. Technically, an insert is filmed during the production phase.

inset. Effect where a reduced shot is placed on another shot, typically to highlight a detail of the main shot.

intercut. Taking two sequential scenes and cutting between them, so the scenes advance and complete together. Intercut scenes are either parallel action or cross-cut scenes.

invisible editing. Editing that is so smooth that viewers become engrossed in the movie and don't notice the individual cuts.

jump cut. A cut where objects or characters appear to jump because the shots are too similar. Technically, this is due to the camera angles of the two shots being less than 30 degrees apart.

KEM. Flatbed film editing machine.

key shot. See **matte shot**.

key. Cutting an electronic hole (think of a keyhole) in a picture, so another image or text can be seen. A key is a composite effect consisting of the background which contains the hole and the key element which fills the hole.

L cut. See **split edit.**

laser film recorder. Latest tape-to-film transfer finishing machine that works by scanning digital images onto negative film frames using three RGB lasers. Also referred to as a laser recorder or a laser printer.

lay in. Put in music or sound from first frame to last, to see how it fits against cue time and the picture. When the music lays in perfectly, no adjustments are necessary.

layback. Transfer of the completed sound mix onto the videotape show master.

laydown. (noun or verb) Record or transfer audio, black, picture, time code, etc., from one tape or medium to another tape or medium.

LCRS. Left-center-right-surround speaker channels in a movie theatre. During the pre-mix and mix, the mixers assign tracks to LCRS speaker channels.

level. Video: Brightness and contrast of the color. Audio: Amount of signal strength.

LFOA. Last frame of action. Last frame of picture or sound on a film reel which is the final frame to be included when measuring reel length. The LFOA is noted on mix sheets and in the notes for each reel sent to the negative cutter. Same as LFOP.

LFOP. Last frame of picture. See **LFOA**.

Lightworks. Professional digital editing system.

line cut. Tape of the switches from one camera angle to the other that a multiple cam director called out as the show was shot.

linear editing. Making or recording each edit sequentially from the beginning of the show to the end of the show.

lined script. Pages of script shot each day and marked by script supervisor with vertical lines indicating where each take starts and ends.

locked cut. The final edited version of the cut created by the editor in the cutting room.

long form. TV show that is feature length such as a variety show, MOW, or mini-series.

long shot. (LS) A shot framed long, that focuses on the action from a distance.

loop group. A group of professional actors who perform walla and wild lines to simulate members of a crowd and are recorded on an ADR stage. Also called loopers.

loop. Another word for ADR. To "loop" an actor means to replace their dialogue.

looper. A member of a loop group. See also **loop group.**

looping. ADR. See also **loop** and **ADR**.

LTO. Linear Tape-Open. Magnetic tape storage technology used for archiving since it can hold hundreds of GB on a single cartridge.

Luminance (luma). Non-color portion of a video image or signal that holds the black and white data (brightness and contrast).

LUT. Look up table. A software chart used on set and at the post house to maintain images' color values during shooting and finishing.

M & E. Music and Effects. The music and effects stems resulting from the final sound mix, which are used on the soundtrack of foreign (non-English version) movies.

M.P.S.E. Motion Picture Sound Editors is a professional organization of sound editors (like A.C.E.) that hosts the annual Golden Reel Awards to honor sound editors.

master shot. Shot that encompasses all the action in a scene from beginning to end. Although a master routinely starts framed close on a small object and can zoom and pan as needed to capture the action, it mostly stays wide to frame all the action.

match cut. A continuity cut where the majority of the elements are duplicated (matched) from the last frame of the first (outgoing) shot to the first frame of the second (incoming) shot. The elements to match are screen direction, eyeline, camera angle and framing, props, sound (wording, volume, or pacing), weather, wardrobe, hair, makeup, lighting, color, and action.

matte shot. Cutting a hole in a shot and placing (matting or keying) another shot in that hole.

media. A digital term for video and/or audio.

medium close-up. (MCU) Between a CU and an MS, an MCU is shot from the shoulders up, through the top of the person's head.

medium shot. (MS) A shot framed from the waist or chest up through the top of the person's head.

memory card. Re-recordable electronic flash memory data storage device used in cameras and editing systems as well as laptops, phones, MP3 players, and video game consoles for storing digital contents.

metadata. Summarized as the "data about data," metadata is the background information that identifies the condition, content, and other qualities of data. In film and video this means time code, blanking, frame rate, aspect ratio, sync, color burst information and descriptive data about clips, such the location of their media and effects layers.

MIDI controller. Keyboard, drum kit, guitar, piano, or other electronic musical device that generates MIDI messages to adjust individual controls like pan or gain on devices in the MIDI network.

MIDI. Musical instrument digital interface. Protocol for the types of control signals that one electronic musical device sends to another. In less technical terms, midi is a plug-in which enables a musician's computer to communicate with a host of devices such as MIDI sound modules (samplers, synthesizers, etc.) and to send and receive time code.

mise-en-scene. The design of the setting and all its elements—actors, props, costumes, etc.—and how they're positioned and move or are moved within a shot.

m**ismatch.** A cut in which continuity is lost due to a difference between elements such as action, eyeline, camera framing, camera position, prop, wardrobe, or makeup. See match cut: picture editing.

mix. Recording session where all the dialogue, ADR, sound effects, Foley, and music are blended together and recorded to make the final composited soundtrack.

mix. The blending of a show's sound and music to produce a final soundtrack.

mixdown. (noun or verb) Bringing together a number of recorded audio tracks by recording them onto fewer tracks en route to making the final mixed soundtrack.

mixer. Person or equipment that does the mixing.

mono sound. Where one track is recorded by a non-stereo mic and the same track is played to each speaker. As opposed to stereo sound.

montage. A succinct, self-contained sequence of images inserted to convey facts, feelings, or thoughts that usually functions as a transition in time or place.

morph. A special effect where one object or image transforms into another e.g., a man turns into a monster.

MOS. Without sound; no sound was recorded on the shot. Legend has it that the term originated from an early Hollywood director, a German immigrant, who would call for a shot "mit out sound."

Moviola. Upright film editing machine.

MOW. Movie of the Week. A feature-length show created for television.

MPAA. Motion Picture Academy of Arts. The board that rates a feature film, bestowing a G, PG, PG-13, R, NC-17, or X rating.

MPEG. Motion picture editors guild. See also **IATSE.**

MP3. MPEG-1 or MPEG-2 + Audio Layer 3. Digital audio encoding and storage format that uses lossy compression to transfer and playback MX and SFX on digital audio players.

native format. Uncompressed, high quality format footage was shot it at.

natural pause. Animation term. Three to four frames added to the dialogue track where a speaker would pause naturally, usually before and after every line and at spots the director calls for during a line.

needle drop a.k.a. canned music. Background music—often source and a song—that requires a license fee to use in a show. Term dates to the days of vinyl when each drop of the record player's needle required a separate fee. See **source music.**

NLE. Nonlinear Editing System. See also **Digital Editing System.**

nondiegetic. Description for asynchronous sounds that do not have a source and play in the background e.g., a river babbling.

nonlinear editing. Making or recording each edit in non-sequential order.

NTSC. National Television Standards Committee. U.S. videotape standard with 525 video scan lines which runs on a 60 hertz AC power cycle at 30 fps and has a frame size of 720 x 480. Also used in the rest of North America and central America as well as Japan and environs, South Korea, the Netherlands, and parts of South America.

OCN. Original Camera Negative.

one-liner. Script supervisor's sheet that contains a one-line summary of each take of dailies.

on the fly. Cutting between shots while they're being played without starting, stopping, or marking them first.

optical. A special effect made at an optical house on an optical printer from new film negative. Obsolete with digital VFX.

out point. Ending edit point.

output. Put out material --a show, sequence, or shot -- from a digital system to a tape. Outputting is also called printing or playing out (to tape).

over the shoulder. O/S or OTS. A shot from the waist or chest up that includes the shoulder of one character while focusing on the other character.

overhead. OH. Often filmed from a crane, an overhead shot looks down on the scene from above.

overlap. A cut where picture and sound cut in at different times so that one overlaps (extends beyond) the other.

package. A precut news story of timely human interest.

pan. 1) term: Shot where camera moves horizontally left to right or vice versa. 2) Sound term: The left-right position of a sound on a mixer or other sound device or piece of software. Panning directs the sound to the right, left, or center speaker channel.

paper cut. Outline that provides the initial plan of attack for editing a documentary or other non-scripted piece.

parallel action. Editing two (or more) independent lines of action together—characters, settings, or subjects—that do not interact directly and are unaware of each other.

persistence of vision. How the human eye takes in a series of still images and sees them as moving pictures.

pick-up master. A new master shot that is "picked up" (continued) from a slight bit before where an incomplete master left off.

picture editor. Editor who puts the show together initially.

pitching audio. How high or low the audio sounds. Pitch is the main way the audience distinguishes sounds.

pix. Picture.

pixel. Pix element. Smallest unit or sample of a digital image on a screen. It holds data such as black and white, color, and gray scale information.

playback. Running a recorded video or audio tape from a tape deck, camera, or other device. Commonly done for the purpose of reviewing material or recording it to another device. Raw or cut footage is frequently played back as a reference for actors or other performers so they can be photographed in sync with the action e.g., green screen, animation, music.

playback music. Music recorded for the sole purpose of being played (back) on the set on each musical take to help the actors maintain sync with the music while singing and/or dancing.

point-of-view shot (POV) A variation of a reverse shot, a POV shot corresponds exactly to where a character is looking; it is what they're seeing.

pop. See **sync pop**.

post lap. Continue the sound of the outgoing shot after cutting to the picture of the incoming shot, delaying its sound.

postproduction. Final creation phase of a show during which all editing and finishing work take place. Also referred to as editing, editorial, or post. Postproduction is followed by the distribution and exhibition phases of the movie.

postproduction house. Facility where the final cut of a show is reproduced in the digital format contractually required for airing on television or screening in theatres. Post houses also produce digital dailies and perform a myriad of other postproduction tasks. Frequently, they rent cutting rooms and screening rooms and provide free meals in an attempt to take care of their editing clients every need.

post visualization, a.k.a. postvis or postviz. On VFX driven shows as CGI and other VFX elements become available, the editor drops them into the edit for visualization, timing, and placement purposes. Similar to previz, except occurring during postproduction. See **previsualization**.

pot. Potentiometer. A resistor device controlled by a slider or knob used to change the EQ, gain, pitch, tone, pan, etc. during the mix.

POV See **Point-of-View shot**.

preditor. Producer/editor.

pre-dub. See **pre-mix.**

pre lap. Start the sound of the incoming shot before cutting to its picture.

premastering. Creating a disk image for a DVD; part of the authoring process.

pre-mix. Preliminary mix of certain sounds—background effects and dialogue usually—ahead of the mix. Also called the pre-dub or rough mix.

presence. See **ambience.**

previsualization, a.k.a. previs or previz. Determining camera moves, lighting etc. ahead of production. Often done on animation shows, heavy duty VFX shows, 3D shows, and those requiring playback or other preshot and/or cut scenes for use during the shoot.

production track. Original sync audio recorded at the time of filming.

Pro Tools. Popular sound editing and recording tool (DAW) manufactured by Avid Technologies, Inc. that runs on a Mac OS.

proxy. Low-res file that links to higher res file (2K, 4K, etc.) and contains all its data.

PSA. Public Service Announcement.

pull up. (noun or verb) Slip, slide, or trim an edit so that it starts sooner. Opposite of a push down.

punch in. Fix a particular section of a mixed track and leave the surrounding areas alone.

push down. (noun or verb) Slip, slide, or trim an edit so that it so that it starts later. Opposite of a pull up.

quad split a.k.a. q split. Locking four (or more) cameras on a screen (via software channel or hardware box) so that they play simultaneously and can be intercut easily, e.g., "on the fly." See also **on the fly**.

QuickTime. Apple's multimedia file format that's become a standard for the integration of full-motion video and digitized sound into application programs.

raking shot. A tight form of a two-shot, usually, (or other shot), that is filmed from the side and favors one character.

random access. Ability to locate any frame anywhere at any time on a digital system.

raw file. Common, uncompressed digital file format.

raw stock. Film or tape that has nothing shot or recorded on it.

real time effect. A video or audio effect on a digital system for which the creation time equals the time taken to select it and put it in a sequence. As opposed to rendered effect which takes time to make and for which new media is created.

re-master. Make a new master, usually in a different format or medium.

resolution. The clarity of an image on a screen based on different measurements according to format. Analog format measures resolution by the ratio of horizontal resolution lines to scan lines; digital uses pixels; and film goes by number of line pairs per millimeter.

reverse. 1. An angle shot from the exact opposite angle of the master shot action.

A cut to the opposite (reverse) angle. The cut can be from the *front* of a character to *behind* the character (or vice versa) or *from* a character (or characters) *to* the character (or characters) they're facing.

RGB. Red, green, blue. The three primary colors of light which can be mixed to produce all the other colors, and which are used in processing component and composite video or printing film. When generating video on a computer screen, RGB are displayed as separate analog or digital signals of red, green and blue dots. RGB are produced by the CRT which employs three electron guns to beam each color at the screen.

Rock 'n roll. Swiftly fix or finish a section of the mix and move on.

room tone. RT. Interior ambience. See also **ambience.**

rotoscope. Create animation imagery or mattes frame by frame via tracing or otherwise referencing live footage, to create new images or repair images.

rough cut. a.k.a. First Cut or editor's cut. The First Cut of show put together by the editor. In the past, the First Cut was considered rough because it lacked visual effects, music and sound effects, and additional dialogue tracks due to the limitations of the Moviola and KEM film editing machines. With digital editing equipment, an unlimited amount of sound and video tracks are available, and First Cuts are becoming more and more sophisticated, though lacking all the final ingredients of the final show. Editors have never considered their work "rough" as they have always worked hard to finesse character, story, action, and dialog. Many editors prefer the term "First Cut" or "editor's cut."

running time. The duration (length) of a scene, section, or an entire show.

safe action. The area where it is safe to extend the action so that it's visible on a television monitor.

safe title. The area where it is safe to place titles, so they do not get cut off on a television monitor.

sampling rate. Rate at which an audio signal is sampled (read) during recording.

saturation. Amount of color in a video image or signal.

scoring. Session where musicians play composer's score, cue by cue, while a tape of the show runs on a screen. The music is recorded and then edited into the show.

scratch track. Temporary VO track laid into a cut for editing and timing purposes that will be replaced with the voice of the hired narrator.

screen direction. The direction where a character or object enters or exits a shot.

script notes. Page opposite the lined script page that contains camera info and other notes.

scrub. Run sound back and forth to locate an exact right frame for marking or editing in.

SD. Standard definition. Television resolution that meets standards including a 4:3 aspect ratio but is lower quality than HD (High Definition) due to employing fewer scan lines and pixels per frame. See also **HD**.

seamless editing. See invisible editing.

sequence. Term used for a cut of an edited scene, show, or part of a show by many digital editing systems.

session. Created by the sound or music editor on a digital audio system, a session consists of the cut tracks and is where the editor works. A session can be a scene, reel, or an entire show depending on how the editor sets it up.

SFX. Sound effect(s). Also used to mean special effects. To avoid confusion, this book uses SFX for sound effects and VFX for special effects.

short form. TV show that is an hour or less such as a cartoon, comedy, or dramatic series, or a music video.

shot. Picture: Camera start to camera stop. Sound: Sound recorder start to stop.

skip frame. An effect where alternate frames are printed so the film looks speeded up or pixilated, e.g., printing every other frame or every third frame. Can be duplicated on digital systems.

slide. Change an edit's position in a cut by moving it up or down. Sliding an edit changes it externally, making it occur sooner or later in the cut, and causing the edits on either side of it to grow and shrink in duration by equal amounts. Sliding does not change the duration of the edit or the cut.

slip. Adjust an edit by changing where it starts and stops. Slipping changes the edit internally, but does not change its duration.

Slo-mo. Effect where the pace of the action is decreased from what occurred in reality in front of the camera. This retardation is accomplished during editing or, more traditionally, during filming by over cranking—running the film through the camera at a faster rate than it will be played back. Opposite of speed up.

slug. Inserting black fill in the timeline where a shot is missing.

smart slate. Electronic clap stick that generates time code which is jam synced to the audio recorder. It displays time code on a red LED and greatly speeds up syncing.

smash cut. Variation on a short cut. An unexpected, lightning-quick cut designed to deliberately jar the audience by zapping the action from one place/object/person/image to another.

soft cut. Short dissolve of one to four frames.

soft effects. Non-sync SFX that don't need to match on screen action, e.g., background sounds like water lapping, scene ambience, birds chirping, etc.

sound editor. Editor who labors to perfect the show's sound.

sound fill. See **fill**.

source music. Music that has a clear, visual source onscreen such as a radio, album, or piano. Source music often plays in the background and is usually purchased but can be composed.

special effects house. Facility where effects are created and finalized.

speed up. Effect where the pace of the action is increased from what occurred in reality in front of the camera. This acceleration is accomplished during editing or, more traditionally, during filming by undercranking—running the film through the camera at a slower rate than it will be played back. Opposite of slo-mo.

split edit. A video editing term for overlap. In a split edit the audio and video edit do not start at the same time; either video or audio is delayed. Also called an L cut or a delayed edit.

split screen. Dividing the screen into two or more parts with different shots in each division.

spotting session. Meeting where the director views the completed show with the Sound Designer and Music Composer (in separate sessions) to map out the sound and music work to be done on the show

stem a.k.a. split tracks or splits. Individual parts of the final mix: there's a dialogue stem, a music stem, and a sound effects stem. See also **DME.**

stereo sound. Identical tracks that are separated and played to different speaker channels, usually left and right. LCRS is a sophisticated form of stereo audio and is the standard. Created by recording two tracks at the same time with a stereo mic. As opposed to mono sound.

still frame. See freeze frame.

stinger. A short music cue.

stock shot. Shot used to establish a location that is independent of the show and can be used on other episodes or shows. Stock houses provide stock shots, or they can be obtained during the shoot. Examples: the Walton's barn, the NYPD Blue police station, the Indy 500 racetrack.

straight cut. When picture and sound are cut at the same frame as opposed to an overlap where picture and sound are cut at different times.

streamer. A diagonal line put on a tape or film to cue music for an orchestra at a scoring session or to cue a line for an actor in an ADR session.

subliminal cut. A cut consisting of a few frames which zip by so fast that the viewer is only subliminally (subconsciously) aware of them.

superimposition. A "super" is an effect where two shots (or more) are held on top of each other full screen.

sweetening. Adding extra audio elements to an effect to make it work.

switcher. Machine used in broadcast, live tapings, and postproduction that allows the operator to select video and audio sources and make transitional effects between them.

synchronize (sync). Align recorded picture and sound so they play together as originally shot and can be edited.

sync pop. A 1000 Hz beep tone placed on the audio head and tail leader to keep sync during screenings, sound editing, and sound mixing.

synthesizer a.k.a. synth. An electronic instrument that produces an endless variety of sounds and music that may imitate instruments or create new sounds. There are hard (hardware) synths that plug in to DAWs and soft (software) synths that export the composer's MIDI file into the DAW.

tail leader. Piece of film or tape or a digital clip attached to the end of a show for the purpose of maintaining sync between picture and sound. Tail leader runs for a few seconds after LFOP. See also **tail pop.**

tail pop. A sync pop that appears on the audio track two seconds into the tail leader, often corresponding to a flash frame (on film) or a frame with the word "End" printed on it. See also **sync pop.**

take. A shot that starts (or ends) with a camera slate (clapstick).

tapeless workflow a.k.a. file-based workflow. Filmmaking process where dailies are imported from a video camera that shot on card, disk, file, or film, edited on a digital system, and exported as a file.

telecine. Transfer of film-to-tape.

temp dub. A temp mix.

textless. A background bed of shots—the credit material—without the credits, used to redo credits or to make foreign or other versions of the show.

time code. Code based on clock time which is recorded on each frame of a video or audio tape.

timeline. Graphic representation of a cut on a digital editing system. A horizontal bar graph of a cut which reads left to right, starting with the first edit and ending with the last.

timer. Film lab person who times a film print.

timing. Setting the red, yellow, and blue printer lights and adjusting the degree of lightness or darkness on each shot or reel. Also used referred to as grading. During the digital intermediate process, grading, timing, and color correcting are used interchangeably to mean the same thing.

tracking. When the music editor is responsible for finding, arranging, and editing the music in a scene or a show. Frequently a temp dub is tracked or any show or project that cannot afford original music.

transcode. Convert from one digital format to another.

transfer. Recording picture or sound from one medium or format to another for viewing or editing.

transition effect. Effect, such as a dissolve or wipe, which moves the action from one cut to another.

trim. Shortening a scene by removing footage.

TRT. Total running time of a reel or show.

tubby. Overpowering, low frequency sounds attenuated through EQ'ing.

two-shot. A shot with two characters' faces that is usually framed medium.

upcut. Cut off a line at the head or tail, so that part of it is missing.

up res a.k.a. up rez or up convert. Convert from a lower resolution to a higher resolution.

VFX. Visual Effects. Digital effects created or completed during postproduction such as blue screen, composites, key frames, etc.

VU. Volume unit for both analog and digital signals.

VU meter. Calibrates audio to ensure consistent levels are throughout a show by displaying the dB (decibel) level of the audio during mixing or recording.

walla. Non sync background conversation made up of indistinguishable words voiced by actors.

white out. Effect where a shot cuts or dissolves to white. Often involves organic elements such as a light, a camera flashbulb, or steam.

wide shot. (WS) A shot framed wide that encompasses much, if not all, of the action.

wild line. Non-sync, sound only, line of dialogue recorded from an actor.

wild sound. See **wild track**.

wild track. WT. Sound effect that is recorded non sync. i.e., without picture.

wipe. A transitional effect where the incoming shot replaces the outgoing shot by appearing to wipe (erase) it from the screen.

worldizing. Aligning audio elements—usually ADR or Foley—to match a character's environment by placing them in a live room "world" to make them sound more real.

work track. Sound reel that the sound editor works with. A dupe of the production track, it's also referred to as the 1:1 (one to one) or guide track.

WT. See **wild track**.

WYSIWYG. What You See Is What You Get. Pronounced "Wizzy Wig," this expression is used to describe a myriad of works-in-progress. It's applicable to color correcting, the creation of titles or effects, and to any situation where a draft allows you see what the final product will look like.

YUV a.k.a. YIQ and Y'CBCR. Three-channel color space that encodes luma and chroma data and is the NTSC standard for broadcasting all tapes and files.

BIBLIOGRAPHY

Abele, Robert, "Shot To Remember: Dance Of Death," Winter 2009, *DGA Quarterly.*

Acker, Ally. *Reel Women: Pioneers of the Cinema: The First Hundred Years V. I.* Roselyn Heights, NY. Reel Women Media Publishing, 2012.

Almo, Laura, "Why is it Called 'Foley' Anyway?" February 1, 2016, *Cine Montage.*

AMPAS Science and Technology Council and Library of Congress NDIIPP, "The Digital Dilemma: Strategic Issues in Archiving and Accessing Digital Motion Picture Materials," 2007.

AMPAS Science and Technology Council and Library of Congress NDIIPP, "The Digital Dilemma 2: Perspectives from Independent Filmmakers, Documentarians, and Nonprofit Audiovisual Archives," 2011.

Azéma, Marc and Florent Rivère, "Animation in Palaeolithic Art: A Pre-echo of Cinema,"

Vol. 86, No. 332, June 2012, *Antiquity.*

Bailey, John, "The Life and Death of 9413: A Hollywood Extra," October 21, 2012, *American Cinematographer.*

Beauchamp, Cari, "The Real Women of Early Hollywood," The First Picture Show, September 1999, *Mark Taper Forum Performing Arts Magazine.*

Be afraid. Be very afraid: IBM's Watson makes AI trailer about 'Morgan' AI movie

Boyle, Alan, "Be afraid. Be very afraid: IBM's Watson makes AI trailer about 'Morgan' AI movie," August 31, 2016, *GeekWire.*

Breyer, Christopher, "There's no Business like Film Business," The First Picture Show, September 1999, *Mark Taper Forum Performing Arts Magazine.*

Brody, Richard, "The Worst Thing About "Birth of a Nation" Is How Good It Is," February 1, 2013, *The New Yorker.*

Buck, John. *Timeline: A History of Editing Analog 1-2* book series. Melbourne, Australia: Tablo Publishing, 2018.

Buck, John. *Timeline: A History of Editing Analog 3-6* book series. Melbourne, Australia: Tablo Publishing, 2019.

Bullock, Tom (Film Guy). *Film Editing Nutz and Boltz, Sound Editing Nutz and Boltz* (one volume), Emeryville, CA: Metro International, Inc., 1994.

Castañeda, Rick, "Attention, Filmmakers: Top Indie Directors on Why Color Correction Matters," April 17, 2015, *IndieWire.*

Catoline, A.J. "'When two people agree in a room': Guillermo del Toro on the Collaboration of Director and Editor," February 8, 2019, *CineMontage.*

Chandler, Gael. *Cut by Cut, 2nd Edition: How to Edit Your Film or Video.* Studio City, CA. Michael Wiese Productions, 2012.

Chandler, Gael. *Film Editing: Great Cuts Every Filmmaker and Movie Lover Should Know.* Studio City, CA. Michael Wiese Productions, 2009.

Clark, Jim and Myers, John H. *The Dream Repairman: Adventures in Film Editing,* Crockett, TX: LandMarc Press, 2010.

CPN Admin, "Editing *The Social Network* in Final Cut Pro with Angus Wall and Kirk Baxter," February 15, 2012, *Creative Planet Network.*

Cutting, James, DeLong, Jordan, and Nothelfer, Christine, "Attention and the Evolution of Hollywood Film," February 5, 2010, *Psychological Science Online.*

Dancyger, Ken. *The Technique of Film and Video Editing, History, Theory, and Practice, Fifth Edition.* Boston, MA: Focal Press, 2011.

Dargis, Manohla, "Overlooked No More: Alice Guy Blaché, the World's First Female Filmmaker," September 9, 2019, *New York Times.*

Dawson, Ron, "How to Match a Film Look with Basic Color Correction Tools," May 30, 2017, *frame.io.*

DiCesare, Ron, "A Look at the History of Audio Post Production," October 23, 2013, *postPerspective.*

Dirks, Tim, "The Great Train Robbery," undated, *filmsite.org*

Dmytryk, Edward. *On Film Editing, An Introduction to the Art of Film Construction.* Boston, MA: Focal Press, 1990.

Eagan, Daniel, "A Trip to the Moon as You've Never Seen it Before," September 2, 2011, *Smithsonian Magazine Online.*

Ebert, Roger, "Breathless," July 20, 2003, *RogerEbert.com.*

Ebert, Roger, "Woodstock," May 22, 2005, *RogerEbert.com.*

Ebert, Roger, "Martin Scorsese & Co. Reassemble Woodstock," February 15, 1970, *RogerEbert.com.*

Friedrich, Sue, "Edited By: Women Film Editors," *womenfilmeditors.princeton.edu/*

Frost, Jacqueline B. *Cinematography for Directors, Edition 2,* Studio City, CA: Michael Wiese Productions, 2020.

Gleiberman, Owen, "Bonnie and Clyde' at 50: A Revolutionary Film That Now Looks Like the Last Work of Hollywood Classicism," August 13, 2017, *Variety.*

Grant, August E., and Meadows, Jennifer H. *Communication Technology Update and Fundamentals 17th Edition,* NY, NY: Routledge, 2020.

Heimann, Uithol, Calbi, Umiltà, Guerra, and Gallese, "Cuts in Action": A High-Density EEG Study Investigating the Neural Correlates of Different Editing Techniques in Film," *Cognitive Science,* 2017.

Hellerman, Jason, "What is B-Roll and How Can You Make Yours Cinematic?" January 15, 2020, *nofilmschool.com.*

Hirsch, Paul. *A Long Time Ago in a Cutting Room Far, Far Away . . . ,* Chicago, IL: Chicago Review Press, 2019.

Holt, Jillian, *The 'Art of Editing': Creative Practice and Pedagogy,* submission for degree of Doctorate of Philosophy, Swinburne University of Technology, 2015.

Hullfish, Steve. *Art of the Cut: Conversations with Film and TV Editors,* Boston: MA. Focal Press, 2017.

Hutchinson, Sean, "17 Facts about Apocalypse Now on its 40th Anniversary," August 15, 2019, *Mental Floss.*

IMAGO: The Federation of European Cinematographers. *Making Pictures: A Century of European Cinematography.* NY, NY: Abrams, 2003.

Jordan, Larry, "Making the Best of a Bad Transition: Flow vs. Morph Cut," June 4, 2017, *Larry Jordan EditSmarter.*

Kaufman, Debra, "Video Spawned the Editing Star: What Hath MTV Wrought?" Vol. 27, No. 3, May-June 2006, *Editors Guild Magazine.*

Kernan, Lisa. *Coming Attractions: Reading American Movie Trailers,* Austin: TX. University of Texas Press, 2004.

Koppl, Rudy, "The Hurt Locker: Blurring the Lines between Sound and Score," 2009, Music from the Movies Media, *The Beek Blog, musicfromthemovies.com.*

Kunkes, Michael, Jan/Feb 2010: Vol 31, No. 1, "Dream Capturers: James Cameron's Brave New World of Filmmaking" and "Editing on Another Planet: John Refoua and Stephen Rivkin," *Editors Guild Magazine.*

LoBrutto, Vincent. *Selected Takes, Film Editors on Editing.* Westport, CT: Greenwood Publishing Group, Incorporated, 1991.

LoBrutto, Vincent. *Sound-On-Film, Interviews with Creators of Film Sound.* Westport, CT: Greenwood Publishing Group, Incorporated, 1995.

Magliano, Joseph P. and Zacks, Jeffrey M., "The Impact of Continuity Editing in Narrative Film on Event Segmentation," 2011, *Cognitive Science.*

Mateer, John, "The Evolution of Film Editing and its Implications to the Parsing and Summarization of Motion Pictures," *The Visual Systems Lab,* 2005-6, University of York.

May, Julia "The Art of Film Title Design Throughout Cinema History," Oct. 4th, 2010, *Smashing Magazine.*

McLane, Betsy A., "Who Were the True Auteurs in Post-Production? Ask the Monitor Man," June 7, 2019, *CineMontage.*

McMahan, Alison, "Alice Guy Blaché," Oct 16, 2013, *Women Film Pioneers Project.*

Millar, Gavin and Karel Reisz. *Technique of Film Editing, Second Edition.* Boston, MA: Focal Press, 1995.

Mitchell, Elvis, "Cut and Run: Where MTV Editing Got Its Chops," July 1, 2006, *CineMontage.*

Motion Picture Editor's Guild, "What Directors and Others Say About Editors," *Vol. 1, No. 1*—June 1997, *The Motion Picture Editors Guild Special Issue Newsletter.*

Meuel, David. *Women Film Editors: Unseen Artists of American Cinema,* Jefferson, NC. McFarland & Company, Inc., 2016.

Mott, Robert L. *Sound Effect: Radio, TV, and Film,* Boston: MA. Focal Press, 1990.

Murch, Walter, "A Digital Cinema of the Mind? Could Be," May 2, 1999, *New York Times.*

Murch, Walter. *In the Blink of An Eye, A Perspective on Film Editing, Second Edition,* LA, CA: Silman-James Press, 2001.

Murch, Walter, "Stretching Sound to Help the Mind See," October 1, 2000, *New York Times.*

Nicholson, Ben, "Five Wonderful Effects in Man with a Movie Camera . . . and how they're still inspiring filmmakers today," bfi.org.uk, January 17, 2017.

Oldham, Gabriella. *First Cut, Conversations with Film Editors,* Berkeley, CA: University of California Press, 1992.

Puchkoff, Carrie, "Still Loving Lucy," November 1, 2009, CineMontage.

Rosenblum, Ralph and Robert Karen. *When the Shooting Stops . . .the Cutting Begins,* 1979, reprinted 1989, NY, NY: Da Capo Press, 1989.

Saffari, Hilda, "The Most Iconic Title Sequences of All Time and Why They Work," June 4, 2018, *Frame.io*

Stamp, Shelley, "Lois Weber," Women Film Pioneers Project, Oct 16, 2013.

Serrurier, Mark, "The Origins of the Moviola," July 1966, *Journal of SMPTE Volume 75.*

Sklar, Robert. *Film: An International History of the Medium,* NY: NY. Harry N. Abrams, Inc., 1993.

Scorsese, Martin, from the foreword to *Woodstock: Three Days That Rocked the World,* edited by Mike Evans and Paul Kingsbury, NY, NY: Sterling Publishing Company, Inc. 2009.

Thom, Randy, "On Getting the Most Out of Spotting Sessions," interviewed by Teresa Morrow and Timothy Muirhead, March 31, 2020, *Tonebenderspodcast.com.*

Thom, Randy, "Designing a Movie for Sound," 1999 & 1998. *www.filmsound.org*

Thom, Randy, "More Confessions of A Sound Designer (A Sound Fails In The Forest Where Nobody Hears It)," 1995, *filmsound.org.*

Thompson, Roy. *Grammar of the Edit,* Boston: MA. Focal Press, 1993.

Tomlinson, Holman. *Sound for Film and Television,* Boston: MA. Focal Press, 2001.

Tucker, Jack. *Twilight of the Gods,* San Diego, CA: Cognella Academic Publishing, 2014.

Truffaut, Francois. *Hitchcock,* NY, NY: Simon and Schuster, 1966.

Welch, David and Scoma, Joey, "How Star Wars was Saved in the Edit," December 7, 2017.

youtube.com/rjfilmschool.

Weitzman, Elizabeth, "A Century Late, a Giant of Early Cinema Gets Her Closeup," April 26, 2019, *New York Times.*

Whalley, Zita, "How 'Man with a Movie Camera' Changed Documentary Filmmaking," April 12, 2018, *theculturetrip.com.*

Winter, Jessica, "The Lost Art of Editing," August 13, 2006, *The Boston Globe.*

Woodhall, Woody. *Audio Production and Postproduction,* Sudbury, MA: Jones & Bartlett Learning, 2010.

FILMOGRAPHY

Director/editor(s) (sometimes the same), release year.

127 Hours, Danny Boyle/Jon Harris, 2010.

2001: A Space Odyssey, Stanley Kubrick/Ray Lovejoy, 1968.

20 Feet from Stardom, Morgan Neville/Doug Blush, Kevin Klauber, Jason Zeldes, 2013.

A Beautiful Mind, Ron Howard/Daniel P. Hanley, Mike Hill, 2001.

A Fool and His Money, Alice Guy Blaché, 1912.

A Kiss in the Tunnel, AG Smith, 1899.

A Secret Love, Chris Bolan/Bernadine Colish, 2020.

A Single Man, Tom Ford/Joan Sobel, 2009.

A Trip to the Moon, Georges Méliès, 1906.

A Triumph of the Will, Leni Riefenstahl, 1935.

Alice in Wonderland 3D, Tim Burton/Chris Lebenzon, 2010.

American Factory Steven Bognar, Julia Reichert/Lindsay Utz, 2019.

Apocalypse Now, Francis Ford Coppola/Lisa Fruchtman, Gerald B. Greenberg, Walter Murch, 1979.

Avatar, James Cameron/Stephen Rivkin, John Refua, James Cameron, 2009.

Babel, Alejandro González Iñárritu/ Douglas Crise, Steve Mirrrone, 2006.

Birth of a Nation, DW Griffith/DW Griffith, Joseph Henabery, James Smith, Rose Smith, Raoul Walsh, 1915.

Bonnie and Clyde, Arthur Penn/Dede Allen, 1967.

Bored to Death "The Case of the Missing Screenplay," Michael Lehmann/Ken Eluto, 2009.

Breaking Bad, Vince Gilligan (EP), 2008-13.

Breathless, Jean-Luc Godard/Cécile Decugis, 1960.

Carrie, Brian de Palma/Paul Hirsch, 1976.

Cars, John Lasseter/Ken Schretzmann, 2006.

Casablanca, Michael Curtiz/Owen Marks, 1942.

Cast Away, Robert Zemeckis/Arthur Schmidt, 2000.

Cat Boxing, Laurie Dickson, 1894.

Cave of Forgotten Dreams, Werner Herzog/Joe Bini, Maya Hawke, 2011.

Citizen Kane, Orson Welles/Robert Wise, 1941.

Crash, Paul Haggis/Hughes Winborne, 2006.

Crazy Rich Asians, John M. Chu/Myron Kerstein, 2018.

Extremely Loud, Incredibly Close Stephen Daldry/Claire Simpson, 2011.

Fahrenheit 9/11, Michael Moore/Kurt Engfehr, Woody Richman, Christopher Seward, 2006.

Ferris Bueller's Day Off, John Hughes/Paul Hirsch, 1986.

Fosse/Verdon, Thomas Kail/Tim Streeto, Kate Sanford, 2019.

Fruitvale Station Ryan Coogler/Claudia Castello, Michael P. Shauver, 2012.

Grandma's Reading Glass, AG Smith, 1900.

Harry Potter and the Goblet of Fire, Mike Newell/Mick Audsley, 2005.

Harry Potter and the Sorcerer's Stone, Christopher Columbus/Richard Francis-Bruce, 2001.

Hero, Stanley J. Orzel/Zhai Ru, Angie Lam, 2004.

Hollywood "Meg" Janet Mock/Andrew Groves, 2020.

Inside Daisy Clover, Robert Mulligan/Aaron Stell, 1965.

Kill Bill 2, Quentin Tarantino/Sally Menke, 2004.

Lady Bird, Greta Gerwig/Nick Houy, 2017.

La La Land, Damien Chazelle/Tom Cross, 2016.

Lars and the Real Girl, Craig Gillespie/Tatiana S. Riegel, 2007.

Lawrence of Arabia, David Lean/Anne V. Coates, 1962.

Life is Beautiful, Roberto Benigni/Simona Paggi, 1997.

Life of Pi, Ang Lee/Tim Squyres, 2012.

Love Actually, Richard Curtis/Nick Moore, 2004.

Mad Men Matthew Weiner (EP), 2007-15.

Making Waves: The Art of Cinematic Sound, Midge Costin/David J. Turner, 2019.

Mars Attacks! Tim Burton/Chris Lebenzon, 1996.

Midnight in Paris, Woody Allen/Alisa Lepselter, 2011.

Moonlight, Barry Jenkins/Joi McMillon, Nat Sanders, 2016.

Nebraska, Alexander Payne/Kevin Tent, 2013.

Morgan, Luke Scott/Laura Jennings, 2016.

Olympia, Olympia-Film, Leni Riefenstahl, 1938.

Out of Africa, Sydney Pollack/Fredric Steinkamp, William Steinkamp, Pembroke J. Herring, Sheldon Kahn, 1985.

Pan's Labyrinth, Guillermo del Toro/Bernat Vilaplana, 2006.

Paprika, Satoshi Kon/Takeshi Seyama, 2006.

Parasite, Bong Joon-ho/Yang Jin-mo, 2019.

Paterson, Jim Jarmusch/Affonso Gonçalves, 2016.

Persepolis, Vincent Paronnaud and Marjane Satrapi/Stéphane Roche, 2007.

Punches and Streamers: The Making of a Film Score, Marc Fields/Tahirah Foy, 2014.

Raging Bull, Martin Scorsese/Thelma Schoonmaker, 1980.

Ran, Akira Kurosawa, 1985.

Ratatouille, Brad Bird/Darren T. Holmes, Stan Webb, 2007.

Recorder: The Marion Stokes Project, Matt Wolf/Keiko Deguchi, 2019.

Rocketman, Dexter Fletcher/Chris Dickens, 2019.

Roman Holiday, William Wyler/Robert Swink, 1953.

Saving Private Ryan, Steven Spielberg/Michael Kahn, 1998.

Schindler's List, Steven Spielberg/Michael Kahn, 1993.

Se7en, David Fincher/Richard Francis-Bruce, 1995.

Selma, Ava DuVernay/Spencer Averick, 2004.

Sherlock: A Study in Pink, Paul McGuigan/Mali Evans, Charlie Phillips, 2010.

Slumdog Millionaire, Danny Boyle/Chris Dickens, 2008.

Snowpiercer Bong Joon-ho/Steve M. Choe, Changju Kim, 2013.

Some Like it Hot, Billy Wilder/Arthur P. Schmidt,1959.

Star Wars, George Lucas/Paul Hirsch, Marcia Lucas, Richard Chew, 1977.

Steamboat Willie, Walt Disney and Ub Iwerks/editor unknown, 1928.

Tangerine, Sean Baker, 2015.

The Aviator, Martin Scorsese/Thelma Schoonmaker, 2004.

The Battleship Potemkin, Sergei Eisenstein, 1925.

The Betrayal, Ellen Kuras and Thavisouk Phrasavath/Thavisouk Phrasavath, 2008.

The Birds, Alfred Hitchcock/George Tomasini, 1963.

The Bourne Ultimatum, Paul Greengrass/Christopher Rouse, 2007.

The Call of the Wild, Chris Sanders/William Hoy, David Heinz, 2020.

The Civil War, Ken Burns/Paul Barnes, 1990.

The Consequences of Feminism, Alice Guy Blaché, 1906.

The Cutting Edge: The Magic of Movie Editing, Wendy Apple/Daniel Loewenthal, Tim Tobin, 2004.

The Great Train Robbery, Edwin S. Porter, 1903.

The Heretics, Joan Braverman/Scott Hancock, Kathy Schermerhorn, 2009.

The Hobbit: The Battle of the Five Armies, Peter Jackson/Jabez Olssen, 2014.

The Hurt Locker, Kathryn Bigelow/Chris Innis, Bob Murawski, 2009.

The Jazz Singer, Alan Crosland/Harold McCord, 1927.

The Lady Eve, Preston Sturges/Stuart Gilmore, 1941.

The Last Black Man in San Francisco, Joe Talbot/David Marks, 2019.

The Life and Death of 9413 a Hollywood Extra, Robert Florey/Slavko Vorkapich, 1928.

The Man with a Movie Camera, Dziga Vertov/Elizaveta Svilova, 1929.

The Martian, Ridley Scott/Pietro Scalia, 2015.

The Pawnbroker, Sidney Lumet/Ralph Rosenblum, 1964.

The Pink Panther Strikes Again, Blake Edwards/Alan Jones, 1976.

The Post, Stephen Spielberg/Michael Kahn, 2017.

The Social Network, David Fincher/Kirk Baxter, Angus Wall, 2008.

The Triplets of Belleville, Sylvain Chaumet/Dominique Brune, Chantal Colibert Brunner, Dominique Lefever, 2003.

The Wizard of Oz, Victor Fleming, King Vidor (uncredited)/Blanche Sewell, 1939.

The World Before Your Feet, Jeremy Workman, 2018.

They Shall Not Grow Old, Peter Jackson/Jabez Olssen, 2018.

Titanic, James Cameron/Conrad Buff, Richard A. Harris, James Cameron, 1997.

To Kill a Mockingbird, Richard Mulligan/Aaron Stell, 1962.

Too Big to Fail, Curtis Hanson/Barbara Tolliver, Plummy Tucker, 2011.

Train Arrives in Ciotat, Lumière Brothers, 1895.

True Blood "Everything is Broken," Scott Winant/Louise Innes, 2011.

United 93, Paul Greengrass/Clare Douglas, Richard Simpson, Christopher Rouse, 2006.

Vertigo, Alfred Hitchcock/George Tomasini, 1958.

WALL-E, Andrew Stanton/Stephen Schaffer, 2008.

Welcome to Chechnya: The Gay Purge, David France/Tyler H. Walk, 2020.

When Harry Met Sally, Rob Reiner/Robert Leighton, 1989.

When the Levees Broke: A Requiem in Four Acts, Spike Lee/Sam Pollard, Geeta Gandbhir, Nancy Novack, 2007.

Yentl, Barbra Streisand/Terry Rawlings, 1983.

INDEX

ABOUT THE AUTHOR

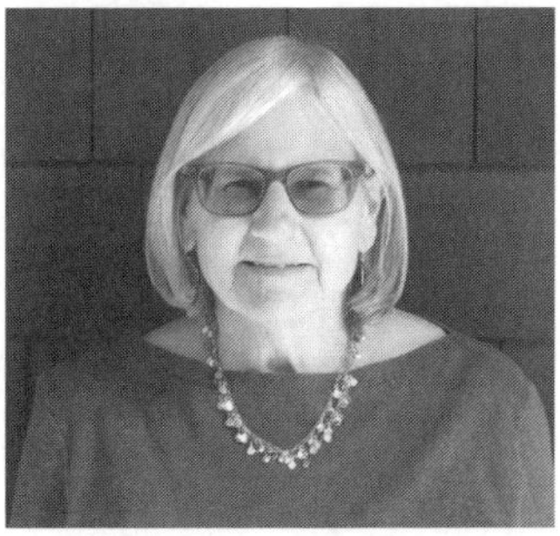

"It all started in a small drive-in theatre in Santa Rosa, California," to paraphrase Ted Baxter from *The Mary Tyler Moore Show*. The author got a job as a cashier at Starvue Motor Movies and became interested in the projection booth. There she learned base and emulsion, cement and tape splicing, and other 35mm basics. Eventually her union brothers and the town's theatre managers were persuaded to let her in the booth and the union. This meant she got to run *Rocky, Star Wars,* and *Saturday Night Fever* for months and take location assignments doing grip, electrical, and craft service work. Much film through projector and two BAs later, she headed for Hollywood and began slipping through studio gates.

Her first job was as an assistant at a sound studio where she transferred 500 tiger growls from ¼" to 35mm on her first day. It was a good place to meet editors and led to her first assistant editor job on the TV show *That's Incredible!* From there it was a whirlwind of jobs and trips to the unemployment office.

Chandler spent over three decades in Los Angeles editing comedies, dramas, documentaries, features, corporate videos, and promos. She cut on every medium: film, tape, and digital, and trained hundreds of professionals, professors, independent filmmakers, and students to operate digital editing equipment. Chandler worked on *The New Leave It to Beaver,* the first show to edit on Ediflex, a groundbreaking nonlinear editing system, and was nominated two years in a row for a Cable ACE award for Best Editing of a comedy series. She also taught classes on editing history, theory, and practice to college students.

Chandler wrote two editions of *Cut by Cut: Editing Your Film or Video* (2004 and 2012), and *Film Editing: Great Cuts Every Filmmaker and Movie Lover Must Know* (2009). In 2010 she retired to northern California and wrote *Chronicles of Old San Francisco: Exploring the Historic City by the Bay* (2014) and co-founded PictureYourBook to produce book trailers and enhanced eBooks. She continues to be an aspiring playwright and screenplay writer, and lectures periodically at a local media center.

The connecting thread in her work as a writer, editor, and teacher is the joy of creating and distilling material for an audience be it readers, learners, or video viewers. She hopes her work has meaning for you. The author may be reached at gnovato1@comcast.net

CUT BY CUT

EDITING YOUR FILM OR VIDEO (2ND EDITION)

GAEL CHANDLER

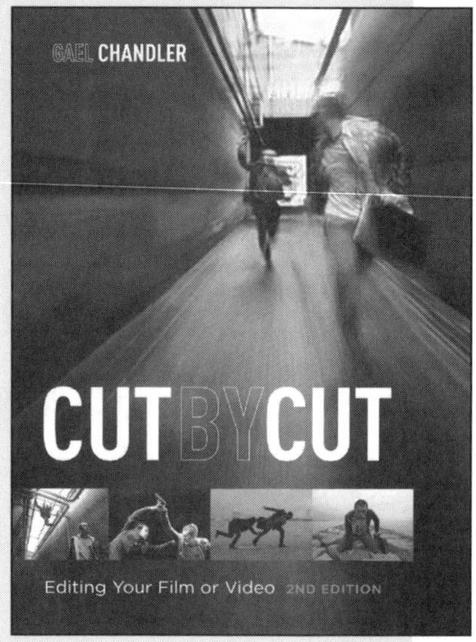

Although great films begin with great scripts, crews, and actors, it's good editing that takes a film the rest of the way.

COMPLETELY REVISED AND UPDATED FOR THE DIGITAL ERA, this second edition of one of film editing's best-selling books teaches readers how to organize and edit footage and see their project to completion. It's both a comprehensive guidebook and a friendly, dependable companion for anyone taking the editor's path or wishing to better understand it.

Learn how the skilled editor turns raw footage into polished art for film, television or web. With practical project guidelines and advice on organizing digital and film cutting rooms, *How to Edit Your Film or Video* de-mystifies action, montage, dialogue editing, SFX and explains sound/music editing and mixing.

With over 25 information-packed tables and forms, this guide includes an up-to-date glossary, an editor's resource guide and a section on how to land that elusive editing job.

"Chandler demystifies editing technology and reveals the creative work flows and story-telling secrets of professional editors. I highly recommend the book for aspiring editors, assistants, and anyone who is interested in how motion pictures are made."

Mark Goldblatt, A.C.E., *Rise of the Planet of the Apes, Armageddon*

"An essential guide for aspiring and professional editors and should be required reading for anyone who really wants to direct. Chandler gives us a bird's-eye view of what it takes to create our invisible art while proving that we are not invisible artists."

Briana London, A.C.E., *Army Wives, Grey's Anatomy*, and A.C.E. Eddie winner

"What most impresses me about this invaluable text is the way the author embraces new technology and wrestles it down to the very basic concept of storytelling... This book demystifies the editing process while encouraging each editor to find his or her own unique and individual method."

Michael Ruscio, A.C.E., director and editor, *True Blood*, HBO

GAEL CHANDLER, based in Los Angeles, was nominated twice for a Cable Emmy for comedy editing and has trained hundreds of professionals on digital editing systems and students on editing systems, practices and theory.She has edited comedies, dramas, documentaries, features, corporate videos, and promos, and cut on every type of medium: film, tape, and digital. Nominated twice for a Cable ACE award for editing a comedy series. Additionally she has taught editing practices and history at Loyola Marymount University and California State Universities at Long Beach, Los Angeles, and Northridge, and has trained hundreds of professionals, independent filmmakers, professors, and students to operate digital editing equipment.

$30.00 · 504 PAGES · ISBN: 9781615930906

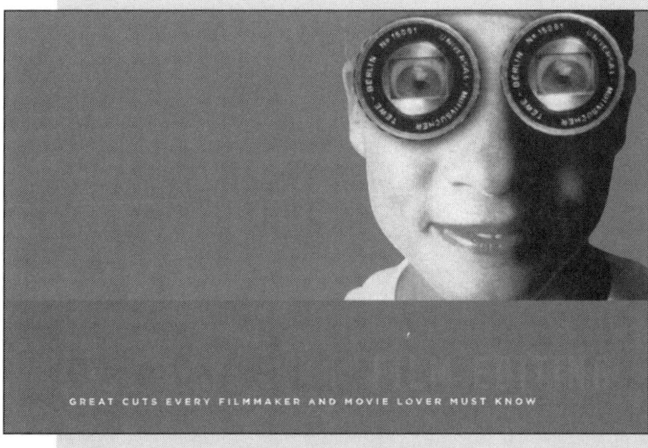

FILM EDITING

GREAT CUTS EVERY FILMMAKER AND MOVIE LOVER MUST KNOW

GAEL CHANDLER

Film Editing: Great Cuts Every Filmmaker and Movie Lover Must Know makes the invisible art of editing visible by using nearly 600 frames from popular, recent films. The frames, accompanied by brisk descriptions, make it perfectly suited for quick study readers who like to 'gaze' rather than 'graze' and don't want to read a book. Written by an editor and the author of *Cut by Cut: Editing Your Film or Video*, it shows how editors can make or break a movie.

This one-of-a-kind book is your 'must have' cheat sheet to learning to make great cuts. Great for filmmakers, students or anyone who wants to see how the editor makes us believe. YouTubers, prepare yourselves to add juice to your creations.

"*Those of us in the movie business often say that if we notice something, that means we didn't do a good job. Our job as filmmakers, is to do what we do as seamlessly as possible. Gael Chandler takes a microscope to those seams to show the subtleties and techniques used by seasoned professionals, using words and pictures that an average movie-goer or up-and-coming filmmaker can appreciate and experiment with. This dissection, together with quotes of working directors and editors, make* Film Editing *a practical and aesthetic addition to any film buff, film student, or filmmaker's arsenal.*"

– Victoria Rose Sampson, writer, director, film and sound editor; MPSE Award for Best Sound Editing: *Pirates of the Caribbean: Curse of the Black Pearl*, *Speed*, *Romancing the Stone*, *The River;* Grand prize winner for writing and directing, Harley-Davidson commercial contest short film, *Her Need for Speed*

"*A comprehensive and easy-to-read description of the techniques editors use to seamlessly tell stories. The use of film frames clearly illustrates the editing concepts. A must-read for any film student, or anyone just interested in the art of editing.*"

– Nancy Morrison, A.C.E., editor, *Desperate Housewives*, *Starter Wife*, *Malcolm in the Middle*

GAEL CHANDLER has edited comedies, dramas, documentaries, features, corporate videos, and promos and cut on every type of medium: film, tape, and digital. Nominated twice for a Cable ACE award for editing a comedy series, she is a member of the Editors Peer Group of the Television Academy of Arts and Sciences and annually judges the Emmy and College TV awards.

$34.95 · 208 PAGES · ORDER NUMBER 129RLS · ISBN: 9781932907629

CINEMATOGRAPHY FOR DIRECTORS

A GUIDE FOR CREATIVE COLLABORATION 2ND ED.

JACQUELINE B. FROST

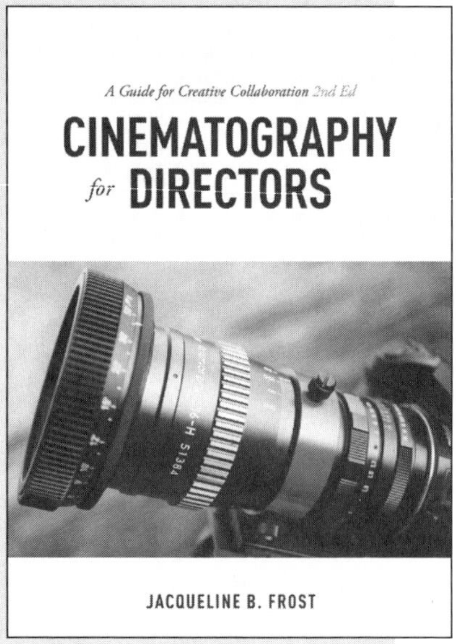

The essential handbook for directors and aspiring filmmakers who want to get the best visuals for their films while establishing a collaborative relationship with their cinematographer.

Through balancing interviews with working ASC cinematographers and the technical, aesthetic, and historical side of cinematography, this book guides directors toward a more powerful collaboration with their closest ally, the cinematographer. Topics include selecting a cinematographer, discussing the script with the cinematographer, choosing the appropriate visual style for the film, color palette, various film and HD formats, and postproduction processes including the digital intermediate.

"I urge all aspiring filmmakers to read Cinematography for Directors. *Frost has the ability to put the director at ease by bringing clarity to the notoriously elusive relationship between the filmmaker and thecinematographer... The numerous thrilling interviews she conducts create an empowering message: that the dynamic between the director and their cinematographer can be a relationship of understanding, ease, humor, passion and, above all, true collaboration."*

Bryce Dallas Howard, Actress (*Terminator Salvation*, *Spider-Man 3*, *As You Like It*, *Lady in the Water*, *The Village*), Writer, Producer, Director

"Far too few books about the filmmaking process address the complex, challenging, and intensely collaborative relationship that exists between the director and the cinematographer. Drawing on her vast experience as a working cinematographer and as a film school professor, Frost deftly combines her clear appreciation of the profession of cinematography with a pragmatic guide for how to accomplish these often startling and culturally-significant moments of visual artistry."

Denise Mann, Head, UCLA Producers Program; Associate Professor, Department of Film, TV, Digital Media, University of California, Los Angeles

JACQUELINE B. FROST has been teaching film and video production and film history for twenty years at various universities including Miami, Penn State University, and the University of Oklahoma.She currently teaches cinematography and advanced film production at California State University, Fullerton where she is an Associate Professor. She regularly teaches a course through UCLA Extension entitled, *Cinematography for Directors*, on which the book is based. in addition to teaching, Jacqueline has been the cinematographer on numerous short films, independent feature films, and documentaries that have been screened in film festivals.

$26.96 · 292 PAGES · ORDER NUMBER 127RLS · ISBN: 9781615932740

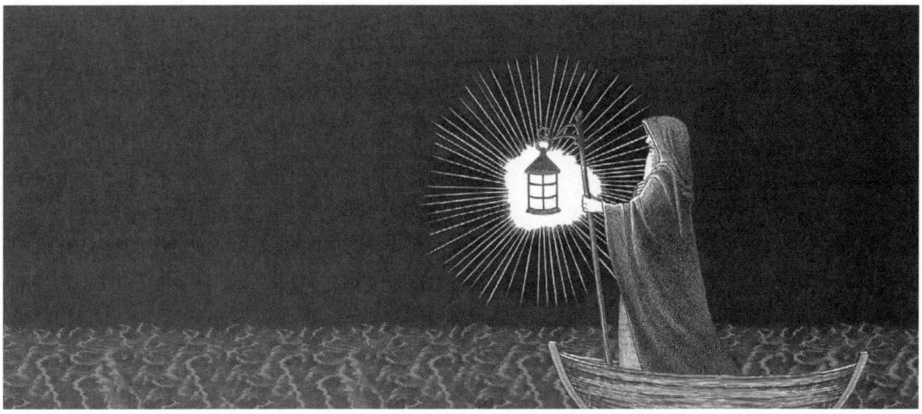

© Michele Montez

MICHAEL WIESE PRODUCTIONS

In a dark time, a light bringer came along, leading the curious and the frustrated to clarity and empowerment. It took the well-guarded secrets out of the hands of the few and made them available to all. It spread a spirit of openness and creative freedom, and built a storehouse of knowledge dedicated to the betterment of the arts.

The essence of Michael Wiese Productions (MWP) is empowering people who have the burning desire to express themselves creatively. We help them realize their dreams by putting the tools in their hands. We demystify the sometimes secretive worlds of screenwriting, directing, acting, producing, film financing, and other media crafts.

By doing so, we hope to bring forth a realization of 'conscious media,' which we define as being positively charged, emphasizing hope, and affirming positive values like trust, cooperation, self-empowerment, freedom, and love. Grounded in the deep roots of myth, it aims to be healing both for those who make the art and those who encounter it. It hopes to be transformative for people, opening doors to new possibilities and pulling back veils to reveal hidden worlds.

MWP has built a storehouse of knowledge unequaled in the world, for no other publisher has so many titles on the media arts. Please visit www.mwp.com, where you will find many free resources and a 25% discount on our books. Sign up and become part of the wider creative community!

Michael Wiese, Co-Publisher
Geraldine Overton, Co-Publisher

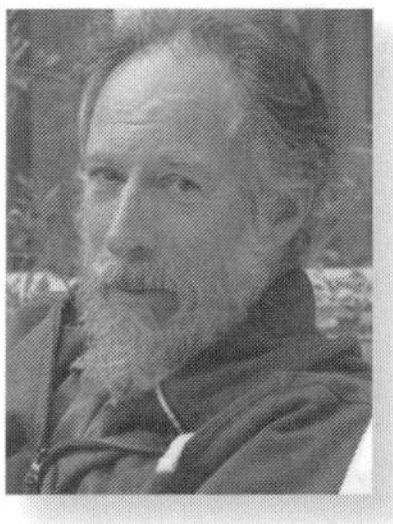

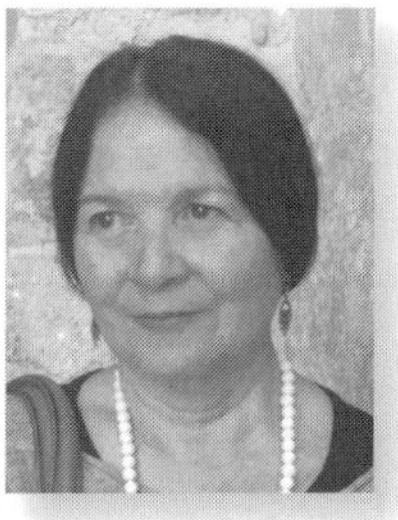